PROPERTY

Fifth Edition

By

Julian Conrad Juergensmeyer
Professor and Ben F. Johnson Jr. Chair in Law
Georgia State University

Carol Necole Brown
Professor of Law
The University of North Carolina at Chapel Hill

A Thomson Reuters business

Mat #40603824

Sum and Substance Quick Review of Property is a publication of Thomson Reuters

© 2000 WEST GROUP
© 2003 West, a Thomson business
2011 © Thomson Reuters

    610 Opperman Drive
    St. Paul, MN 55123
    1–800–313–9378

Printed in the United States of America

ISBN: 978–0–314–18095–7

TABLE OF CONTENTS

TABLE OF CONTENTS

TABLE OF CONTENTS

TABLE OF CONTENTS

TABLE OF CONTENTS

TABLE OF CONTENTS

TABLE OF CONTENTS

TABLE OF CONTENTS

TABLE OF CONTENTS

TABLE OF CONTENTS

TABLE OF CONTENTS

QUICK REVIEW OF PROPERTY	BERNHARDT American Casebook Series	BRUCE & ELY 6th Ed.	CASNER, LEACH, FRENCH, KORNGOLD, VANDERVELDE 5th Ed.	CRIBBET, FINDLEY, SMITH & DZIENKOWSKI 9th Ed.	DUKEMINIER, KRIER, ALEXANDER & SCHILL 7th Ed.	HILTON, CALLIES, HANDLER & FRANZESE 3rd Ed.	RABIN, KWALL, KWALL & ARNOLD 6th Ed.	SINGER 4th Ed.	JOHNSON, SALSICH, SHAFTER, BRAUNSTEIN & WEINBERGER 3rd Ed.	KURTZ & HOVENKAMP 5th Ed.	NELSON, STOEBUCK & WHITMAN 3rd Ed.	FREYERMUTH, ORGAN & NOBLE-ALLGIRE 3rd Ed.
IV. THE LAW OF PERSONAL PROPERTY [CHATTELS] §§3-1 - 3-100	1-30	143-211	34-114; 191-284	63-78; 101-168; 193 235	18-96; 151-181	3-15;32-73		32-63; 75-97; 101 102; 1087- 1171	1-22; 38-70	8-70; 86-163	31-90	56-156; 205-236
V. FRAGMENTATION OF OWNERSHIP; THE DEVELOPMENT OF TENURE §§4-1 - 4-18	76-77	212-215	299-318	238-250	183-190	407-409		493-505	115-118	251-265	245-249	237-240
VI. ESTATES IN LAND [FREEHOLD] §§5-1 - 5-95	77 78	215 227	319 361	251 306	191 252	410 419	179 200; 239-276	505 526	118 141; 147-152	268 298	250 272	240 290
VII. FUTURE INTERESTS §§6-1 - 6-218	78-104	228-242	361-401	307-370	253-317	419-437; 551-566	179-256	505-567	141-147; 152-196	294-355	273-338	290-333s
VIII. CONCURRENT RENT ESTATES AND MULTIPLE OWNERSHIP §§7-1 - 7-62	104-184	242-288	553-623	371-448	319-418	381-407	277-343	569-635	197-279	356-469	339-427	3334-392
IX. LANDLORD AND TENANT [NONFREEHOLD ESTATES] §§8-1 - 8-159	185-343	21-141	403-551	449-558	419-515	445-500; 675-703	39-178	639-742	280-447	470-622	428-627	393-519
X. EASEMENTS, PROFITS, AND LICENSES §§9-1 - 9-112	344-374; 398-416; 432-517	294-359	889-954	559-617	763-847	501-547; 567-577	345-460	317-365	711-774	623-686; 726-728	770-870	520-582
XI. COVENANTS RUNNING WITH THE LAND EQUITABLE SERVITUDES §§10-1 -10-102	374-398; 416-522	359-410	889-893; 954-1063	617-672	847-924	578-671	461-562	365-490	774-848	686-757	628-769	582-665

QUICK REVIEW OF PROPERTY	BERNHARDT American Casebook Series	BRUCE & ELY 6th Ed.	CASNER, LEACH, FRENCH, KORNGOLD, VANDERVELDE 5th Ed.	CRIBBET, FINDLEY, SMITH & DZIENKOWSKI 9th Ed.	DUKEMINIER, KRIER, ALEXANDER & SCHILL 7th Ed.	NELSON, CALLIES, MANDELKER & FRANZESE 3rd Ed.	RABIN, KWALL, KWALL & ARNOLD 6th Ed.	SINGER 4th Ed.	JOHNSON, SALSICH, SHAFTER, BRAUNSTEIN & WEINBERGER 3rd Ed.	KURTZ & HOVENKAMP 5th Ed.	NELSON, STOEBUCK & WHITMAN 3rd Ed.	FREYERMUTH, ORGAN & NOBLE-ALLGIRE 3rd Ed.
XII. ADVERSE POSSESSION §§11-1 - 11-67	30-63	496-518	125-190	153-193	116-164	221-237	859-903	179-226	71-98	191-250; 735-742	90-142	162-204
XIII. LAND SALES CONTRACTS §§12-1 - 12-27	751-857; 909-941	427-459	680-714; 734-744	915-1068	541-584	305-334	995-1046	748-779	477-489; 591-601	1078-1080; 1096-1150	872-995	671-715
XIV. DEEDS §§13-1 - 13-116	835-908	538-563;	714-733	1069-1128	585-615	335-357; 370-374	905-972; 1081-1101	779-783	490-510; 517-523	1151-1191	996-1140	715-725; 766-778
XV. RECORDING ACTS §§14-1 - 14-84	857-909	463-495; 519-537	744-784	1129-1188	645-727	357-370	1103-1141	783-799	523-530	1205-1229	1070-1108	725-757
XVI. RIGHT USE AND ENJOYMENT OF PROPERTY §§15-1 - 15-21	500-522	625-636	841-888	673-750	729-761	102-114	563-590	227-316	848-879	758-805	143-229	822-840
XVII. PUBLIC LAND USE CONTROL §§16-1 - 16-83	523-702	678-816	1065-1324	751-914	925-1195	75-102; 133-204; 243-302; 705-819	591-824	911-1067	887-1036	806-1019	1142-1344	841-970

CHAPTER I

INTRODUCTION

About the Authors—

Professor Julian Conrad Juergensmeyer holds the Ben F. Johnson, Jr. Chair in Law at Georgia State University and is an adjunct professor of planning at the Georgia Institute of Technology. He is also Professor of Law Emeritus at the University of Florida, where he taught property law for 30 years. Professor Juergensmeyer earned his undergraduate (summa cum laude) and J.D. (with honors and Order of the Coif) from Duke University. Professor Juergensmeyer is the author of nearly 100 books and articles on Property Law, Land Use Planning and Control Law, Environmental Law, Growth Management Law and Agricultural Law. He has also taught law at Duke, Tulane, Hastings, Indiana, and Louisiana State.

Carol Necole Brown is a professor of law at the University of North Carolina at Chapel Hill, where she teaches Property Law, Land Use Planning and Control Law, Mortgage Law, Real Estate Finance, and Real Estate Transactions. Professor Brown earned her undergraduate (cum laude), J.D., and LL.M from Duke University. Professor Brown is the author of many articles and lectures on the Sum & Substance audio tapes on Property. She is a past chair of the Property Section of the American Association of Law Schools, chair of the Real Estate Transactions Section of the American Association of Law Schools, and is a member of the American College of Real Estate Lawyers. Professor Brown would like to thank her research assistant, Katherine Blass Asaro, for her invaluable assistance.

From the Authors—

CAVEATS ABOUT THE STUDY OF PROPERTY LAW

1. THINK MEDIEVAL:

Our common law system began in 1066 with the development of property law concepts following William the Conqueror's victory at the Battle of Hastings. [Remember from your art history course seeing it depicted in the Bayeux Tapestries?] Not only did property law begin that long ago but many of the concepts you will study in this course have changed little since then. One of our more recent changes dates back to 1536, the Statute of Uses! See Chapter VI (Future Interests).

1

The moral of all of this is that a page of history often gives more understanding than a volume of logic, so if you have trouble grasping the reason for or logic of some of the rules, it may be that it isn't something wrong with you—it is that the rule is illogical and a result not of reasoning that escapes you, but the product of an historical accident. Caveat: The idea just expressed reveals the authors' adherence to the "Accidental School" of Jurisprudence which receives very little respect in Jurisprudence courses.

2. DO NOT EXPECT TO FIND REAL PROPERTY PRINCIPLES EXPRESSED IN PLAIN, SIMPLE, MODERN ENGLISH.

Old Norman French was the original language of property law. One of the early "reforms" was to throw in some Latin. Some of the key terms we continue to use in the twenty-first century are still corruptions (misspellings and mispronunciations) of the old French. Instead of being intimidated by those weird words, make a game out of identifying and "understanding" the old terminology. It makes great cocktail party conversation. Also, don't be surprised by what today seems like the constant use of two synonyms for each idea. For a long time there was an attempt (commendable, don't you think?) to use a Norman and a Saxon word for each important item so as to be understandable by both groups of the King's subjects.

3. PREPARE TO FIND BOTH OVERLAP AND CONFLICT WITH CONTRACTS PRINCIPLES IN SOME AREAS OF PROPERTY LAW.

Most students study real property law and contracts law during the same semester(s). The relationship between these two key areas of our common law system has always been close and controversial. Today, the conflict is "heating up" and the landlord-tenant and land sales contracts areas of property law are undergoing a revolution aimed at replacing many of the traditional property rules applicable in those areas with modern contracts rules and principles. Do not be surprised to discover the law in these two areas of the course in a great state of flux.

4. DO NOT BE AFRAID TO MEMORIZE SOME RULES AND GIVE SOME YES OR NO ANSWERS.

Some first year law students get the idea that law can be memorized and that there is always a right and wrong answer. They are wrong. Other first year law students get the idea that in law school there is never a right or wrong answer and that no material can/should be memorized. They also are wrong at least about property law. Many of the estates and future interests' rules can and should be memorized and there are right and wrong answers to questions about them.

5. PROPERTY LAW IS NOT JUST A COLLECTION OF OUTDATED AND IRRELEVANT RULES.

Yes, there are some silly and tedious parts of the property course. But there are also some fascinating examples of intense human conflict behind some seemingly mundane rules and principles. Do not miss the opportunity that the study of real property law offers to see how our common law system developed and how the ever changing concepts of the proper role of private ownership have been dealt with by many generations of lawyers before you.

CHAPTER II

AN OVERVIEW OF THE STUDY OF PROPERTY LAW

A. IMPORTANCE OF HISTORY. [§ 2–1]

History is very important in studying real property law. A page of history is worth a volume of logic. Many property rules and concepts are understandable, if at all, only by examining their historical context. Many of our concepts and terms are seven hundred, eight hundred, or even nine hundred years old and may have been easy to comprehend at the time they were developed but are often elusive for the modern mind untrained in the intricacies of English constitutional, political, social, and religious history. Professors and casebooks vary considerably in regard to how much history they cover, but the ambitious student will find supplementation of her knowledge of early English history rewarding when it comes to understanding property law.

Of course not all of our current property law can be traced back to the early common law, and many of the old common law doctrines have been changed or even abolished by recently enacted statutes. The important thing for the student to realize is that in spite of the modern changes by statute or judicial decision, there has never been a comprehensive revision of the basic concepts of property law in our American common law system, so that the "old" law applies unless there is a specific change in the jurisdiction in question. Many of these changes will be emphasized throughout your property course(s). The property law of some states has been changed much more than that of others. In fact, it is hard to find a common law real property concept that does not still exist in some jurisdiction.

The important point to note is that the rules of property law, much more so than the areas of law studied in other first year courses, are still grounded in the old common law. It is perhaps because of this that the Restatement of Property is controversial (some say it changes too much and others that it changes too little) and not nearly as important as the Restatement of Torts or Restatement of Contracts. (The Restatement of Property, like the other Restatements, is published by the American Law Institute, a respected group of law professors, judges, and practicing lawyers. Its purpose is to explicate the law of property as expounded by enlightened courts.) Courts are more likely to be concerned with old treatises and judicial interpretations

5

of common law property concepts than with modern attempts to restate or reform this body of law.

Having just emphasized the importance of history, the student should be forewarned that property law is beginning to change more rapidly. (Some would say "finally.") These changes are emphasized throughout this **Quick Review** and, as discussed in § 2–5, below, these changes are favorite exam topics.

B. VARIETY OF SUBJECTS INCLUDED IN PROPERTY COURSES. [§ 2–2]

The subject, Property, contains several distinct areas of law. In many law schools, Property is broken into two courses:

1. Property I which generally includes coverage of some personal property concepts, the historical development of ownership concepts, freehold estates, future interests, concurrent estates, and marital property interests; and

2. Property II which generally includes land transactions (i.e., land sales contracts, recording acts, and other title assurance concepts).

Landlord and tenant law (the law of leases) can be found in either Property I or II and sometimes in a separate course devoted exclusively to that subject. Servitudes (easements, real covenants, and equitable servitudes) and adverse possession are also likely to be found in either course. Public regulation of the use of land and land use regulation through nuisance principles are generally covered, if at all in the basic property course, in Property II. Water rights, fixtures, and lateral and subjacent support are now infrequently covered at all but may be slipped into either course.

It is becoming increasingly popular in law schools to consolidate property into a single course which is generally given fewer credit hours than the split courses combined. As a result there is an increasing tendency to leave out some traditionally covered areas. Whether you take a split or consolidated course be certain you understand which topics you are to be responsible for on the examination.

Because there is no generally agreed upon list of topics to be covered in the basic property course(s), this **Quick Review** may not follow the exact coverage or order of coverage of the exact course you are taking. It is important therefore to notice the organization and order of topics in this **Quick Review**. The goal of the authors has been to cover all major and most minor real property topics that are treated in "traditional" and "modernized" courses. However, since there is no unanimously agreed upon order of coverage for either type of course some students will find it necessary to "skip around" when using this **Quick Review**. The Casebook Table will assist you in doing this.

C. CHECKLIST OF PROPERTY TOPICS. [§ 2–3]

Check carefully the syllabus (assignment sheet) given to you by your professor and the table of contents of your casebook to ascertain exactly which topics you are to be held responsible for on the final examination. Use the table of contents at the beginning of **Quick Review** as a checklist of topics of potential coverage. Use the casebook table to identify the **Quick Review** material which corresponds to your casebook assignments.

D. DISTINGUISH BETWEEN REAL PROPERTY AND PERSONAL PROPERTY. [§ 2–4]

In our common law system the rules and concepts relating to the ownership and use of land (Real Property) developed very differently from those relating to the use and ownership of "things other than land" (Personal Property or Chattels). Until relatively recently, this difference was reflected in the course offerings of many law schools by the existence of a separate course concerning Personal Property or Chattels. Today, many property professors and casebooks include some coverage of personal property even when the course and/or the casebook are titled Real Property. Thanks to recent reforms, the more difficult issues regarding personal property tend to be covered in contracts and commercial transactions courses. Be attentive to your professor's coverage in the basic property course in this regard. The portions of personal property law most likely to be covered in property courses are generally treated as introductory material so they are placed at the beginning of the **Quick Review** (Chapter III).

E. TYPES OF EXAM QUESTIONS. [§ 2–5]

Most exam questions fall into one of two categories:

1. Questions designed to test your ability to apply the traditional rules. Very frequently the questions designed to test your knowledge of estates and future interest rules, recording act priorities and chain of title problems, and basic easement rules are objective in format since there are right and wrong answers. Numerous examples may be found in the Practice Multiple Choice Questions and Answers section of this **Quick Review**. Essay questions covering these subjects may be found in the Practice Essay Question and Answers section.

2. Questions designed to test your ability to analyze and discuss the issues raised by the conflict between the traditional property law and the new contracts oriented property approaches. Landlord and tenant law and land sales contracts—especially in regard to warranties—are the favorite subject matter for these questions. Sample essay questions and answers are found in the Practice Essay Questions and Answers.

F. IDENTIFY THE TIME FRAME OF YOUR EXAM QUESTION. [§ 2–6]

It is especially important when taking an objective exam to understand when the real property interests you are to identify and analyze are created. For example, if the creation of a future interest is involved it is very important to know whether you are answering a question concerning an interest created before or after the enactment of the Statute of Uses (1536). Property professors sometimes use phrases such as "early common law" or "late common law" but such labels have no universally accepted meaning. Be sure to pin your professor down before the exam on how she will indicate the time frame of the questions.

G. ADJUST YOUR STUDY APPROACH AS YOU CHANGE TOPICS. [§ 2–7]

Remember that the various segments of property law require very different approaches. For example, mastering estates and future interests requires memorizing rules and examples. Comparing the old law of leases to the new requires deep socio-economic policy analysis. Understanding land transactions is facilitated by practical work. Adjust your study approach as you change topics.

H. TERMINOLOGY FOR TRANSFERS OF INTERESTS IN PROPERTY. [§ 2–8]

Most property disputes, and therefore cases, and exam questions involve a transfer or attempted transfer of an interest in property. The terminology used to describe the transfer is potentially confusing because of the use of synonyms and because concepts from decedents estates law (usually covered in another course called Wills, Decedents Estates, etc.) are frequently used. The short glossary of terms which follows should help the student avoid confusion in regard to how the property interest was (or was intended to be) created. Note that the words are defined only in this context.

1. **Administrator**. An individual or institution (such as a bank or trust company) designated by a court with probate jurisdiction to "manage" and distribute the property of a deceased person who did not have a valid Will.

2. **Alienate**. To make an *inter vivos* transfer of an interest in real property.

3. **Bequeath**. To transfer personal property by Will.

4. **Bequest**. The term given to personal property transferred by a Will.

5. **Collateral Heirs.** Blood relatives of a deceased person who are neither descendants nor ancestors, e.g. siblings, cousins, aunts, uncles.

6. **Convey**. Technically the verb form of conveyance but sometimes used generically to refer to any transfer of a real property interest.

7. **Conveyance**. The act or document (also called deed) by which a real property interest is transferred *inter vivosly*.

8.   Demise. An old word for a leasehold interest or its transfer.

9.   Devise. The transfer of a real property interest pursuant to a valid Will.

10.   Executor. An individual or institution (such as a bank or trust company) designated by a testator or a court with probate jurisdiction to "manage" the property of a deceased person who left a valid Will. Note that in some jurisdictions today "Administrator" and "Executor" are used interchangeably.

11.   Grant. Technically the term which covers the transfer of nonpossessory interests in land (such as easements) but often used generically as the equivalent of "transfer" to refer to any *inter vivos* transfer of a real property interest.

12.   Heirs. Those persons who survive a deceased person and who are entitled to inherit real property pursuant to a jurisdiction's rules regarding intestate (without a will) succession. Remember, no living person has heirs. Also remember that at common law—unlike today—spouses were not heirs.

13.   Inherit (inheritance). The verb and noun which refer to the receipt of any property interest as a result of the death of the person previously the owner of the interest.

14.   *Inter vivos*. Literally "between the living." It is used to refer to all transfers of property which are not through inheritance. Sometimes called "non-testamentary" transfers.

15.   Intestate. Without a Will (i.e., if a person dies "intestate," she dies without leaving a valid Will).

16.   Intestate succession. Receipt of property from a decedent who died without a Will.

17.   Issue. Descendants.

18.   Per Capita. A deceased person's issue usually inherit on a per stirpes basis but if not then per capita which means all descendants receive an equal share whether they are members of the first generation of descendants (children) or later generations (grandchildren, great grandchildren).

19.   Per Stirpes. When issue inherit, their share is usually determined on a per stirpes basis which means that the basic division of shares is based on the number of people in the first generation of issue—usually children. Thus, if the deceased had 3 children and one has died leaving five children (grandchildren of the deceased), those five grandchildren share their parent's one third.

20. Personal Representative. The title given in many states to executors and administrators.

21. Testate. With a Will (i.e., if a person dies "testate," he died leaving a valid Will).

22. Testamentary. Pursuant to a Will. Wills are sometimes called Testaments or Last Will and Testament.

23. Testamentary succession. Transfer of property pursuant to a Will.

CHAPTER III

THE LAW OF PERSONAL PROPERTY

A. PERSONAL PROPERTY IN THE LAW SCHOOL CURRICULUM. [§ 3–1]

Not long ago, most law schools had two separate courses called "Personal Property Law" or "Chattels" and "Real Property Law." It became popular to merge these courses and rename the unified course, "Property." Over time, less and less of the property course is focused on personal property rules and principles. Some courses omit personal property altogether or merely use minimal personal property concepts and cases (e.g., cases concerning chasing wild animals or finding jewels) as a way of introducing the concepts of ownership and possession. Check carefully the coverage of your property course to ascertain the extent to which you are responsible for personal property law.

B. SUBJECT MATTER OF PERSONAL PROPERTY. [§ 3–2]

The subject matter of personal property courses is now most regularly covered within other substantive law school courses. Thus, for example, the most common method of transferring the ownership of personal property is the sale. The law relating to sales is covered in contracts and commercial law courses. Personal property law today is a collection of miscellany, covering only those elements of personal property law not covered elsewhere. The coverage which follows in this **Quick Review** concentrates on those personal property topics generally used as introductions to the study of property law.

C. PERSONAL PROPERTY TERMINOLOGY AND CONCEPTS. [§ 3–3]

Although the terminology of personal property is much more straightforward than that of real property, several terms and concepts merit discussion.

1. Personal Property. [§ 3–4]

In a broad sense, personal property is all property not classified as real property, (i.e., land and most, but not all, interests in land). Personal property can be tangible (e.g., a car, books, furniture) or intangible (e.g., stocks, bonds, bank accounts, copyrights). Tangible personal property can be classified as consumable—that which is "used-up" or worn out by normal use (e.g., strawberries, perfume) or non-consumable (e.g., a painting, a yacht). Personal property is fungible if, by nature or agreement, one unit is considered the equivalent of any other unit (e.g., kernels of corn).

2. Chattels. [§ 3–5]

Chattels is the old common law word for personal property. Today, it is used interchangeably with personal property. It probably came from the Latin word for cattle and livestock, which at one time were a major item of personal property. Personal property or chattels are also sometimes referred to as "movables" to distinguish them from land and most interests in land, which are referred to as "immoveables." "Goods" is another term commonly used to refer to tangible items of personal property.

3. Ownership and Possession. [§ 3–6]

Two fundamental concepts are basic to personal property law. These are ownership and possession.

a. Ownership Is Maximum Rights and Interests. [§ 3–7]

An individual is regarded as the absolute owner of personal property when he has the maximum bundle of rights and interests that the law recognizes with respect to a particular object. Ownership of property has been defined as the right to possess, use, and dispose of it. (See Case Squib: *Loretto v. Teleprompter*.)

(1) Owner Has Right to Possession. [§ 3–8]

An owner normally has possession or the right to possession, which means he can exclude others from use or enjoyment, and he also has the right of *inter vivos* and testamentary transfer. From a practical viewpoint, an owner is one who holds subject to no superior right to possession in another.

(2) Owner May Transfer Rights. [§ 3–9]

One of the attributes of ownership is the ability to transfer some or all of the owner's rights to another.

b. Possession: A Physical Relation and Intention to Control. [§ 3–10]

Possession is one of the most elusive concepts in the law. There are two elements to the legal concept of possession: (a) a physical relation to the object possessed, and (b) an intention to control the object. (See Case Squib: *Pierson v. Post.*) Physically, a possessor has actual power over the thing, the ability to control it, use it, and exclude others from its use.

(1) Constructive Possession. [§ 3–11]

Constructive possession is recognized when one who had actual possession no longer has such possession but still intends to exercise control over the object (e.g., an owner of lost goods, not yet found and not abandoned by the owner, still has constructive possession).

(2) Custody: Physical Control Without Intent to Possess. [§ 3–12]

"Custody" is physical control without any intent to exercise control in any way inconsistent with the interests of one with superior rights to the items of personal property in question. The most common example is the physical control by an employee of goods used in his employment but owned by the employer and entrusted by the employer to the employee. (See Case Squib: *State v. Schingen.*)

4. Possessory Actions. [§ 3–13]

Rights to personal property are based largely on possession. Actions to recover possession, or to recover damages for conversion or injury to personal property, are possessory actions, which may be maintained by one who is not the owner but has prior possessory rights. (See Case Squib: *Armory v. Delamirie.*)

a. One Who Has Possession Has Right to Keep or Recover Personal Property. [§ 3–14]

In general, one who has possession but not ownership has a right to keep or recover the article against anyone except the owner or one with a possessory right prior in time to his own.

Example. [§ 3–15] O owns a diamond ring. The ring is lost, and found by A. B steals the ring from A. A may recover possession from B; B cannot successfully defend the suit on the ground that A is not the owner. It is sufficient that A had prior possession. However, O's rights are superior to A's, so that O may regain possession by intervening in the A–B action or by bringing a separate action against A. (See Case Squib: *Armory v. Delamirie.*)

D. ACQUISITION OF TITLE TO PERSONAL PROPERTY BY ORIGINAL POSSESSION. [§ 3–16]

There are a few tangible things which are capable of being owned but have no owner. The two most common examples are wild animals and chattels that have been abandoned by their previous owners.

1. **Goods Without Owners. [§ 3–17]**

The first person to obtain possession of abandoned chattels becomes their owner. There is no person with a superior right, because the rights of the previous owner are deemed to have been forever extinguished by the act of abandonment.

2. **Wild Animals. [§ 3–18]**

Ownership of undomesticated wild animals is normally acquired through capture, which may consist of wounding or ensnarement. Mere pursuit is insufficient. It must be clear that the animal cannot escape. (See Case Squib: *Pierson v. Post.*)

Escape. [§ 3–19]

If a wild animal is captured, but escapes from possession and returns to its natural habitat, the rights of the first possessor are lost. An exception is made if the animal returns periodically to the prior possessor, or if the prior possessor is in pursuit. (See Case Squib: *Mullett v. Bradley.*)

3. **Exception for Trespassers. [§ 3–20]**

If a trespasser finds property or captures and kills a wild animal on land of another, ownership is frequently awarded to the owner of the land upon which the find or capture occurred based upon a theory of constructive possession where the landowner is regarded as being in possession of wild animals on his land while they are on his land (i.e., the landowner is the prior possessor). (See Case Squib: *Favorite v. Miller.*)

E. ACQUISITION OF TITLE TO PERSONAL PROPERTY BY ADVERSE POSSESSION. [§ 3–21]

Title to chattels may be acquired by adverse possession, just as title to land may be so acquired. The doctrine of adverse possession as it relates to both real and personal property is discussed in detail in Chapter XI (Adverse Possession).

F. FINDING LOST ABANDONED AND MISLAID GOODS. [§ 3–22]

1. **Abandoned Chattels. [§ 3–23]**

Goods are abandoned when the owner throws away or leaves her property with the specific intention of permanently giving up all rights to that property. A chattel may also be abandoned when it has been lost and the owner has given up all intention and effort to recover it. While ownership rights in chattels may be extinguished by abandonment, real property cannot be "abandoned" for purposes of either terminating the owner's title or transferring the owner's title. [Note that, at least in theory, ownership of real property cannot be abandoned.]

a.   Previous Owner Has No Rights to Abandoned Goods. [§ 3–24]

Once goods are abandoned, the prior owner no longer has any rights in them; she stands in the same position as any other individual.

b.   Ownership Goes to First Possessor. [§ 3–25]

Ownership of abandoned goods goes to the first possessor (i.e., the finder) subject to the rules concerning landowners and employers discussed below.

2.   Lost Goods. [§ 3–26]

Property is lost when the owner has involuntarily parted with it and does not know where to find it.

a.   Rights of a Finder. [§ 3–27]

One who finds lost or mislaid goods does not, by virtue of taking possession, acquire rights against the owner or a prior possessor. As to everyone else, however, the finder's possession gives him superior rights, which are tantamount to ownership. For example, A finds goods owned by O. The goods are in turn lost by A and found by B. A may recover possession from B, and O may recover from A (or from B if he proceeds against him first. (See Case Squib: *Armory v. Delamirie*.)

b.   Obligations of Finder. [§ 3–28]

A finder has the obligation to return lost goods to the owner, if the owner is ascertainable. Failure to do so may make the finder guilty of tortious conversion. If the identity of the true owner is unknown to the finder, statutes generally require the finder to publish notice of the find and/or turn the property over to the police until a diligent search has been made for the true owner. A finder is a gratuitous bailee of the goods. As such, he must exercise reasonable care, and may be liable for his negligent treatment of the found chattel. The finder may recover reasonable compensation for his services in caring for the article, and he may also be able to recover a reward if one has been offered, as a matter of contract law. (See Case Squib: *Ganter v. Kapiloff*.)

c.   Goods Found on Land Belonging to Another. [§ 3–29]

If lost goods are found on land belonging to someone other than the finder, courts are in conflict as to whether the finder or the owner of the land is entitled to possession. In many jurisdictions, the finder is entitled to possession against everyone except for the owner of the goods. Some jurisdictions consider the circumstances under which the goods were lost. For example, some jurisdictions will consider whether the goods were lost on private property or whether they were embedded in private property. In such cases, some jurisdictions will award possession to the owner of the land as against the finder under a theory of constructive possession (as owner of the private property, the owner is in possession of everything on or attached to the land). (See Case Squib: *Hannah v. Peel.*)

Two rules are relatively well settled:

(1) Goods Found "Under" the Soil. [§ 3–30]

Possession of goods found "under" the soil is generally awarded to the landowner. Where treasure trove (§ 3–34) is recognized as a separate category of lost property, most often it is awarded to the finder, even if found "under" the soil.

(2) Trespassers. [§ 3–31]

If the finder is a trespasser, the court nearly always awards possession to the landowner.

d. Goods Found by an Employee. [§ 3–32]

When property is found by an employee while he is acting within the scope of his employment, possession is awarded to his employer if it is part of the employee's assigned duties to turn such articles over to the employer (e.g., as is usually the case with maintenance and cleaning personnel). (See Case Squib: *South Staffordshire Water Co. v. Sharman.*)

3. Mislaid Goods. [§ 3–33]

A mislaid article is an article the owner has intentionally put in a particular place and failed to reclaim. The person who mislays property is not deemed to have lost it, and the discoverer is not generally considered a finder. When goods are mislaid, rather than lost, courts generally award custody to the owner of the property on which the goods were mislaid on the theory that the true owner of the goods is likely to return and reclaim them. (See Case Squib: *Bridges v. Hawkesworth.*)

4. Treasure Trove. [§ 3–34]

Historically, in England, treasure-trove (gold, silver, or money intentionally hidden in a secret location) belonged to the King. In most American states, however, treasure-trove is treated like any other type of found property. It is classified as lost, mislaid, or abandoned even though the analogy to **mislaid** property may be more appropriate.

G. BAILMENTS. [§ 3–35]

The traditional definition of a bailment is Professor Williston's: "the rightful possession of goods by one who is not the owner," (e.g., when you leave your car at the repair shop or leave your suit at the cleaners). Many bailments are created by express contracts and their study usually occurs in contracts courses. Bailments examined in property courses are generally those where the contractual relationship is implied or even non-existent (i.e., involuntary). (See Case Squib: *Allen v. Hyatt Regency*.)

1. Basic Characteristics. [§ 3–36]

The principles of bailment law covered in property courses generally are those relating to the state of the title to the bailed chattel and the rights and duties of bailees vis à vis bailors and third parties.

a. Title Remains in Bailor. [§ 3–37]

In a bailment, title to the goods remains in the bailor. A bailment implies the obligation of the bailee (person to whom the chattel is given) to return those identical things, in the same or altered form. Thus, if A delivers logs to B so that B can saw them into lumber for A, there is a bailment.

b. Special Problem of Fungible Goods. [§ 3–38]

Special problems arise when several persons give fungible goods (those whose units are interchangeable) to the same person to store in a common facility. For example, the operator of a grain elevator does not promise to return the very kernels of corn left with him by each farmer; he merely promises to return a like quantity and quality of corn. Some courts have taken the position that such a transaction must be considered a sale, but the better view is that bailment of fungible goods is permissible.

c. Bailment Distinguished From a Sale. [§ 3–39]

If the obligation is to pay money, perform services, return other goods, or to do some other act, the transaction is a sale, not a bailment. However, if property is delivered with an option to buy, the transaction may be a bailment, if the option is not exercised.

d. Possession and Physical Control by Bailee. [§ 3–40]

The bailor must surrender exclusive physical possession and control over the property to the bailee. Thus, at common law, there is no bailment when

A places a bag in a coin-operated locker in a railroad station waiting room, since the proprietor of the locker had not assumed possession.

e. Intent to Assume Custody and Control. [§ 3–41]

Actual physical possession by the bailee must be accompanied by an intent on his part to assume custody and control.

(1) Examples. [§ 3–42] The owner of a store that furnishes unattended parking spaces for customers is not a bailee. On the other hand, assume that the owner of a restaurant provides parking spaces for her patrons and an employee of the restaurant drives the patron's car to the parking place and retains custody of the keys. Here there is a bailment because the restaurant owner has possession, control, and the intent to possess and control the patron's car. A hotel guest's parking his car in an indoor, multi-story garage operated by the hotel was held to create a bailment. (See Case Squib: *Allen v. Hyatt Regency*.)

(2) Control Distinguishes Bailment From Mere Custody. [§ 3–43]

A bailment should be distinguished from a grant of mere custody, where actual possession is temporarily surrendered, but there is no intent on the part of the deliverer to part with actual control. For example, if goods are handed over in a store to a customer for him to inspect in the presence of a clerk, the goods have not been bailed to the customer. Similarly, it has been traditionally held that a transfer of goods by a master to a servant confers mere custody upon the servant.

(3) Bailment Need Not Be Voluntary. [§ 3–44]

The intent to take possession and exercise control need not be voluntary. Thus, a bailment is created when A's horse strays onto B's land if B undertakes to look after the animal until A reclaims possession.

2. Standard of Care. [§ 3–45]

In the absence of an agreement to the contrary, various standards of care of have been imposed on the bailee by the courts. (See Case Squib: *Peet v. Roth Hotel Co.*)

a. Older View of Standard of Care. [§ 3–46]

Under the older view, the standard of care of the bailee depended upon how the court classified the bailment.

(1) Bailments for the Benefit of the Bailor. [§ 3–47]

Unless such a bailment is pursuant to a contract which specifies otherwise, the bailee in a bailment for the benefit of the bailor is held only to liability for "gross negligence," meaning the duty of care is slight. For example, if A leaves her cat with a neighbor, B, while she goes on vacation, the bailment is for the benefit of A. If the cat dies while in B's care, B would be liable only if she were grossly negligent.

(2) Bailments for the Benefit of the Bailee. [§ 3–48]

One who borrows goods from another (a bailment for the benefit of the bailee) is required to use extraordinary care with respect to borrowed goods. For example, if B borrowed A's snowmobile for the weekend, the bailment would be for the benefit of B, and B would be liable for injury caused even by B's slightest negligence.

(3) Bailments for the Mutual Benefit of Both Parties. [§ 3–49]

When the bailment is for the benefit of both parties, the bailee is liable only for ordinary negligence. For example, if A boards his dog at a kennel which charges him for the service, the bailment is for the benefit of both. The kennel owner will be liable only if he fails to exercise ordinary care under the circumstances.

b. Modern View of Standard of Care. [§ 3–50]

The modern view is that a bailee must exercise ordinary care under the circumstances. This applies regardless of whether the bailment is solely for the benefit of the bailor, solely for the benefit of the bailee, or for the mutual benefit of both. Note, however, that the court using the modern standard might reach the same result as a traditional court because the modern standard includes "circumstances" and therefore whether the bailment is gratuitous or for money, who derives benefit from the bailment, and the nature and value of the goods bailed are all factors to be considered.

Example. [§ 3–51] A asks B to keep his dog while he goes on vacation. This is a gratuitous bailment for the benefit of A, the bailor. If B negligently leaves the gate open and the dog escapes, the older cases would hold B liable only if he was grossly negligent. The modern view would hold B to a standard of ordinary care under the circumstances, but the circumstances to be considered would include the fact that the bailment was gratuitous and for A's benefit.

c. Contractual Variation of Bailee's Duties. [§ 3–52]

To the extent that the bailment results from a contract, the parties are free to vary their common law rights and duties by any contractual provision that is not contrary to public policy. If a bailee makes an attempt to limit her liability, she must show that the bailor accepted these terms as part of the contract of bailment. Most courts hold that it is contrary to public policy for a bailee to attempt to exclude all liability for negligence. She may, however, be able to exempt herself by contract from damage arising from specific causes.

3. Duty of the Bailee to Redeliver. [§ 3–53]

It is the essence of bailment that the bailee has a duty to redeliver the bailed goods to the bailor. When the time for the redelivery set by the parties arrives, the duty to deliver arises when the bailor demands the goods. If no time was set for redelivery, all that is required is a demand on the part of the bailor.

a. Demand May Be Unnecessary. [§ 3–54]

Demand by the bailor is excused where it would obviously be unavailing (i.e., when the bailee informs the bailor that the goods bailed have been destroyed). Also, any wrongful termination of the bailment by the bailee triggers the bailor's right to recovery of the chattels without the necessity of a demand.

b. Liability Implied by Failure of Bailee to Return Goods. [§ 3–55]

It is not necessary for the bailor initially to prove negligence on the part of the bailee. By simply proving the bailment and the failure of the bailee to redeliver in accordance with its terms, the burden of going forward with the evidence is shifted to the bailee. If the bailee is then able to show that the goods were destroyed, lost, or damaged by virtue of circumstances over which he had no control and which show no neglect on his part, the burden of proof is then put back on the bailor to prove by a preponderance of the evidence that this was not so.

c. Conversion. [§ 3–56]

The bailee is liable for conversion if he transfers possession of the bailed chattel to a third person without authorization or if he fails to redeliver the goods to the bailor upon proper demand.

4. Bailee's Rights. [§ 3–57]

a. Bailee's Rights to Possession and Use. [§ 3–58]

Normally, the extent of the bailee's rights to use the bailed property will be found in the contract between bailor and bailee.

(1) Intent. [§ 3–59]

If there is no contract, the courts will look at the presumed intention of the parties.

(2) Inconsistent Use. [§ 3–60]

If the bailee makes use of the bailed goods in a manner inconsistent with the bailor's rights (e.g., by destroying them, pledging them, selling them, consuming them, or allowing others to do any of these things), he is guilty of conversion. Unintentional or trifling deviations from the terms of the bailment will not normally be found to be conversion or a breach of duty, if there is no damage.

b. Bailee's Right to Compensation and Expenses. [§ 3–61]

As a general rule, the bailee is not entitled to compensation, unless there is an express or implied agreement that the bailee is to be paid. Note that such an agreement will be implied, when the bailee has expended labor and skill on the goods bailed pursuant to an agreement. When there is no express or implied agreement with respect to compensation for the bailee, the bailee may be entitled to recover any necessary and reasonable expenses that he has incurred.

c. Bailee's Lien. [§ 3–62]

A bailee entitled to compensation or expenses may exercise a lien on the goods, if they are still in the bailee's possession.

d. Bailee's Right to Sue Third Parties. [§ 3–63]

The bailee has a right to sue third parties for the full loss or amount of the damage to the bailed goods or for the full value of the bailed goods which are taken, damaged, or destroyed by the third party while the goods are in the third party's possession. The bailee may also recover the goods from a third party that has wrongfully taken them. In such an action, the bailee appears on behalf of the true owner, and any sum the bailee receives by way of damages which goes beyond her special and limited interest may be recovered from her by the bailor.

5. Rights of the Bailor Against Third Parties. [§ 3–64]

The bailor's rights against the bailee are discussed above. (§§ 3–45—3–56) As owner of goods, the bailor also has rights against third persons. The bailor may assert her title against third persons even though they have acquired their rights by virtue of a sale from the bailee. This right generally extends even to bona fide purchasers for value from the bailee who take without notice of the bailor's title if the bailee does not, in its ordinary course of business, deal in goods of the kind that were entrusted to him.

Example. [§ 3–65] A (bailor) leaves his classic car with B (bailee) who is a cake designer so that B can make a cake that looks exactly like A's car. Instead,

B sells the car to C who is one of B's customers. In a suit by A against C to recover the car or the value of the car, A would win. Selling cars is not B's ordinary course of business. C therefore ought to have been on notice that B might not have good title. Through the exercise of due diligence, C possibly could have discovered that the car did not belong to B. Thus, as between the owner and C, the owner, A, likely will win and take without notice of the bailor's title. In contrast, if A entrusts the classic car to B, a body car dealer and auto repair shop, for a new paint job and B wrongfully sells the car to C who is a bona fide purchaser for value. C would prevail against A. In this case, A entrusted the car to a merchant who one would ordinarily expect to be in the business of dealing with cars; under such circumstances, the law protects the bona fide purchaser for value. Of course A could recover damages from B for the conversion.

Similarly, the bailor has a right to sue third persons who damage or destroy his goods. However, if the bailee has already recovered a judgment, the bailor is barred from bringing an action unless the bailee has recovered only to the extent of his limited interest.

H. GIFTS OF PERSONAL PROPERTY. [§ 3–66]

A gift is a voluntary transfer of property to another without consideration or compensation in return. If consideration is present, the transfer is a sale and not a gift.

1. Three Requirements for a Valid Gift. [§ 3–67]

The three basic requirements of a gift are intent, delivery, and acceptance.

a. Intent to Presently Transfer an Interest. [§ 3–68]

The donor must have the intention to presently transfer an interest in his property. An intention to transfer an interest at some future time is insufficient.

b. Delivery. [§ 3–69]

Transfer must be accomplished by delivery of the property by the donor or by delivery of an instrument of gift. Delivery is an act by which the donor surrenders dominion and control over the thing given, with the intention of divesting herself of all power of disposition over the property item. (See Case Squib: *Hocks v. Jeremiah*.) The law recognizes several forms of delivery:

(1) Actual Delivery. [§ 3–70]

Actual delivery involves actual transfer of possession to the donee, without any conditions. Most gifts are made this way.

(2) Constructive Delivery. [§ 3–71]

A constructive delivery occurs when there is delivery of some tangible thing or writing which provides a means of access to the subject matter of the gift and which confers dominion and control over the article (e.g., a key to the container in which the item is located or a writing authorizing a bailee to deliver the good to the donee). Constructive delivery is sufficient only if actual physical delivery of the thing is impossible, impractical, or inconvenient (e.g., the actual subject matter is bulky, or the donor is ill, or the article is in another place). (See Case Squib: *In Re Cohn*.)

(3) Delivery to a Third Party. [§ 3–72]

A donor may satisfy the delivery requirement by transfer to a third party, when the third party is not the agent of the donor or is not otherwise to remain under the continuing control or instruction of the donor.

(a) Third Party an Agent of Donor. [§ 3–73]

If the article is given by the donor to his own agent, and, pursuant to the donor's instruction, the agent physically delivers the article to the donee; an effective gift is made at the time of the "second" delivery. The donor can, of course, revoke his instructions prior to the second delivery, and this agency, like all others, will be revoked, automatically, upon the donor's death.

(b) Third Party Not an Agent of the Donor. [§ 3–74]

If the article is given to a third party who is not an agent of the donor with a surrender of further control by the donor, the delivery to the donee is effectuated at that time, and the gift (unless *causa mortis*) (§ 3–77) can not be revoked.

c. Acceptance. [§ 3–75]

Acceptance by the donee is an essential requirement for any gift, but if the gift is beneficial, acceptance will be presumed. Hence, a gift may be made even though at the time of delivery, the donee is wholly unaware of it. The donee may, upon learning of the gift, refuse to accept it. In such a case, no gift has been made.

2. The Inter Vivos Gift. [§ 3–76]

An inter vivos gift is irrevocable once delivery occurs. In some states, an inter vivos gift can be made subject to a divesting condition subsequent. For this to be valid, the condition must be expressly stated. Other states hold that an inter vivos gift subject to a divesting condition is invalid.

3. Gift Causa Mortis. [§ 3–77]

A gift causa mortis is a gift of personal property made by a donor in fear of approaching death from a present infirmity or peril, on the express or implied condition that the property shall belong absolutely to the donee only if the donor dies of the infirmity in question. (See Case Squib: *In Re Nols' Estate.*) Thus, if an explorer says "I want you to keep my watch if I don't return from climbing Mt. Everest," the gift is causa mortis. The donor's statements may indicate that the gift is made in fear of imminent death, and he or she must expressly state that the donee is to take only if the donor dies of the infirmity. Delivery is also necessary. (See Case Squib: *Newman v. Bost.*) Because the gift causa mortis is really a will substitute, courts strictly adhere to the requirements for a valid gift causa mortis.

a. Existing Infirmity. [§ 3–78]

In most American jurisdictions, there is a rebuttable presumption that a gift made in anticipation of death from an existing infirmity is intended to be a gift *causa mortis*, whether or not such an intention is expressly stated. A donor in such circumstances may indicate an intent to make an inter vivos gift, but the presumption is to the contrary.

b. Revocability of Gifts Causa Mortis Distinguished From Revocability of Inter Vivos Gifts. [§ 3–79]

A gift *causa mortis* is fully revocable until the donor's death and is automatically revoked if the donor recovers from the peril or infirmity that motivated the gift. For example, O physically delivers a Georgia O'Keeffe painting she owns to A, with instructions to deliver it to B if O dies from hepatitis (with which she is afflicted). O recovers, but shortly thereafter dies of a heart attack. In litigation between B and O's heirs, B will most likely lose, because the court will consider the gift to have been revoked upon O's initial recovery.

4. Gifts Upon the Death of the Donor. [§ 3–80]

When a donor during her lifetime (i.e., not in a valid will), indicates an intention that the donee shall take "upon my death," two interpretations are possible. (1) The donee is to take no present interest, and the gift is to take effect only at the donor's death. In this case the purported gift is testamentary and void. (2) The donee is intended to receive a presently owned interest which will become possessory in the future, which is a valid gift of a future interest. (§ 6–2) (See Case Squib: *Gruen v. Gruen.*)

5. Gifts of Choses in Action. [§ 3–81]

Choses in action are intangible rights which are usually evidenced by written instruments which, as a matter of law or custom, are deemed representative of the obligation itself (e.g., bonds, bills of exchange, checks, promissory notes, stock, savings accounts, life and life insurance contracts). Gifts of choses in action may be made in the same manner as gifts of tangible chattels. Delivery of the written instrument (stock certificate, etc.) with the requisite intent is sufficient. Gifts of choses in action may also be made by delivery of a written instrument of gift or assignment. (See Case Squib: *In Re Cohn.*)

6. Particular Problems of Bank Accounts. [§ 3–82]

The law's difficulty with bank accounts placed in whole or in part in the name of one other than the depositor is created by the fact that people use different names on accounts for a number of reasons unrelated to donative intent (e.g., convenience, fraud, tax avoidance, etc.). Hence the fact that there is a different or additional name on a bank account is not in itself strong evidence of donative intent on the part of the depositor.

a. Deposit by the Donor in an Account Solely in the Name of Another Person. [§ 3–83]

If donative intent is clear and if the passbook is delivered to the donee, a deposit in such an account is generally held to constitute a valid gift. If there is no passbook delivery, there may still be a valid gift if the donative intent is clear—the transaction with the bank may serve as a delivery.

b. Deposit by Donor in an Account in His Own Name to be Paid on Death to a Specified Person. [§ 3–84]

Apart from the donative intent problems discussed above, the purported gift of a deposit in an account payable to another on the donor's death is frequently held testamentary and void, in large part because of the donor's ability to withdraw the funds during his life. If this is a savings account, and the passbook is delivered to the donee, some courts hold that the gift is valid as a present transfer of a future interest.

c. The Joint Bank Account. [§ 3–85]

Deposit by the donor in the name of himself and another persona as joint tenants, payable "to either during the lifetime of both, balance to survivor," is a joint account. Statutes in some states establish a rebuttable presumption that a gift arises when a joint tenancy bank account is established. The gift is effectively revocable because the donor may withdraw the entire sum during his lifetime. (See Case Squibs: *Wiggins v. Parson* and *In Re Estate of Thompson.*)

d. Totten Trusts. [§ 3–86]

In most jurisdictions, a valid, non-testamentary inter vivos trust is created by a bank account in the name of the depositor as trustee for another person, even though the depositor may withdraw the funds at any time until death. The other person may claim only those funds remaining in the account upon the depositor's death. The case generally recognized to have established the validity of such trusts (and which gave its name to them) was *Matter of Totten.* (See Case Squib: *Matter of Totten.*)

I. ACCESSION. [§ 3–87]

Accession is the adding of new value to a chattel, commonly by either the addition of skill and labor (e.g., a wood carving from a tree) or by the addition of other goods (e.g., a new engine placed in an old automobile) or by both combined. Courts have identified several types of accession and apply differing rules accordingly.

1. Accession by Natural Growth. [§ 3–88]

Generally, in the case of accession by natural growth, ownership follows title to the principal good, absent an agreement (express or implied) to the contrary. For example, a calf is owned by the owner of its mother.

2. Accession by Labor. [§ 3–89]

The doctrine of accession is most commonly applied when the chattel of one person is improved by the labor of another, or by the addition or annexation of chattels owned by another. When the "improver" is employed by the chattel owner to improve the chattel, title to the improved good remains in the owner of the chattel. For example, A owns a stand of timber, and employs B to cut the timber and convert it to boards. A owns the boards. The principle of accession is called into issue when the individual supplying the labor is a willful wrongdoer, or is acting in the good faith, but erroneous, belief that the chattel which he is improving belongs to him.

a. Willful Wrongdoer. [§ 3–90]

If one who adds value to a chattel is a willful wrongdoer (e.g., B steals timber from A and converts it to boards), title to the improved chattel remains in A. The same result follows if B knows the chattels are not his when he improves them. In most states, if the converter has acted willfully, knowing of his wrong, the owner of the chattel may elect to re-obtain possession or sue for conversion and recover the value of the good "as improved," without compensating the wrongdoer for the value of the labor which has been expended.

b. Innocent Wrongdoer. [§ 3–91]

If one who adds value to the chattel is an innocent wrongdoer (i.e., believes the chattel is hers, or does not know that the chattel belongs to another), title to the chattel is in the converter if the value which has been added to the chattel is sufficiently out of proportion to the value of the unimproved chattel as to make any other result grossly unjust. (See Case Squib: *Wetherbee v. Green.*) An additional requirement often stated is that an innocent wrongdoer obtains title only if the identity of the chattel has been substantially changed (the doctrine of specification), although great disparity in value may override this requirement. An exception to this rule exists when the public interest overrides such recovery; for example, if A takes trees from a national forest (whether innocently or with the intent to steal) and makes curios out of the wood, the federal government's interest in protecting national forests will enable it to re-obtain possession of the wood in its improved condition without compensating A.

(1) Owner's Remedy if He Retains Title. [§ 3–92]

If the value added is not out of proportion, or there has been no significant change in physical identify, title to the improved goods is in the original chattel owner. If the owner elects to re-obtain possession, the improver may not recover the cost of his improvements; however, if the owner sues for money damages, he may recover only the value of the chattel before improvement.

(2) Owner's Remedy if Innocent Wrongdoer Gets Title. [§ 3–93]

If title is in the innocent wrongdoer under the rules set out above, the original owner of the chattel may sue for conversion and recover the value of the unimproved chattel.

3. Addition of Goods Owned by Another. [§ 3–94]

Generally, doctrines of accession do not apply if the goods of each party can be separated without damage to the principal chattel. If the chattels of two persons are incorporated and cannot be separated, the resulting product is owned by the owner of the principal good. This is so even if the owner of the principal good wrongfully and willfully converted the other's property (i.e., if A paints his boat with paint stolen from B, B has no ownership interest in the improved boat).

4. Accession to Realty by Trespasser. [§ 3–95]

If a trespasser makes improvements on real property owned by another, either by his labor or by annexing chattels to the land, such improvements become part of the realty. For example, if A erects a building on the land of B without B's permission, the building is B's.) At common law, no relief was awarded to a trespasser, even if she were an innocent wrongdoer. Today, the landowner can be required to pay the innocent wrongdoer for the value of the improvement, or to allow the innocent wrongdoer to remove the improvement, or to sell the land to the innocent wrongdoer for the value of the unimproved land. (See Case Squib: *Hardy v. Burroughs*.) A trespasser who acted in bad faith (with knowledge that she was a trespasser) generally recovers nothing.

J. CONFUSION. [§ 3–96]

Confusion is the intermixing of the goods of one person with those of another in such a manner that the goods cannot be distinguished. Problems of confusion generally arise when the goods are fungible (e.g., A mixes his pine boards with B's pine boards). Unlike in the case of accession, the goods of each remain physically separable, but cannot be identified and separated.

1. Share of Fungible Goods Known. [§ 3–97]

If the goods are completely fungible, and the shares of each are known, each will be given his proportionate share, even though specific physical items cannot be identified. A willful wrongdoer does not lose his share if the share can be identified.

2. Share of Fungible Goods Unknown. [§ 3–98]

When shares cannot be determined or even approximated, courts generally use the following rules.

a. Innocent Confusion or Confusion With Consent. [§ 3–99]

If the intermixing is with the consent of the parties, by an act of nature, or by accident, the owners become co-owners (tenants in common) on an equal basis.

b. Wrongful Confusion. [§ 3–100]

If goods are commingled by a deliberate and wrongful act of one of the parties, the wrongdoer forfeits all rights and the entire mass becomes the property of the other. The wrongdoer may recover no compensation. The burden to identify the goods, or his share, is thus upon the wrongdoer.

THE LAW OF PERSONAL PROPERTY

REVIEW PROBLEMS

Since very few property courses cover all of the personal property issues just reviewed, it must be re-emphasized that the student's first step in exam preparation on this topic is to be certain of the areas of responsibility for the exam. The following brief checklist of possible topics may be of help in that regard:

1. Ownership, Possession and Custody of Chattels

2. Found Property (i.e., Lost, Mislaid, Abandoned Property and Treasure Trove)

3. Wild Animals (i.e., Obtaining Ownership thereof)

4. Adverse Possession of Personal Property

5. Bailments

6. Gifts of Personal Property

7. Accession

8. Confusion of Goods

The most frequently encountered examination questions in this area are designed to permit (require) the student to discuss possession concepts as they relate to obtaining or defending "ownership" of personal property items. Many professors do this with fact situations involving "found" property and bailment principles applied thereto.

CHAPTER IV

FRAGMENTATION OF OWNERSHIP: THE DEVELOPMENT OF TENURE

A. ORIGIN OF COMMON LAW REAL PROPERTY OWNERSHIP. [§ 4–1]

According to the magnificent myth upon which our common law real property law is based, it all began with the Battle of Hastings in 1066. The victor of that battle, William, Duke of Normandy, or William the Conqueror, as his friends called him, theoretically obtained ownership of most of the land of England. William was flat broke and was indebted to the vast retinue of knights, advisors, priests, servants, and camp followers who had assisted him in wresting the Crown from Harold, the chosen successor of the previous king, Edward the Confessor. [Note that conquest and discovery are considered the origins of land ownership in the United States. See Case Squib: *Johnson v. M'Intosh.*]

B. FEUDALISM AND FEUDAL TENURES ESTABLISHED IN ENGLAND. [§ 4–2]

William, or his advisors, decided to pay his debts with his newly gained lands. Instead of following concepts of outright conveyances of land, William borrowed, but greatly modified, feudal concepts from his native Normandy and established a structure of land use and ownership rights which formed the basis for the establishment of English government and society and gave birth to our common law real property law.

1. Allodial and Tenurial Ownership. [§ 4–3]

Under the feudal system instituted by William, he, as king, retained the ownership of all land and only gave to others a right to use the land for a specified period of time. The persons given tenure were called tenure holders or tenants. If your professor uses the latter term, be careful not to confuse it with tenant in landlord-tenant relations. The king thereby retained allodial ownership (i.e., he was the only absolute owner). Those to whom the right to use the land was given were not owners in the allodial sense, but merely held (tenir, in French) a right to use the land, and were therefore considered to have "tenure" (the right to hold the land of the king). As the centuries went by, tenure, which originally was only a possessory right and not an ownership right, became what we mean by "ownership" under the common law system. Even though in theory the State still today can be said to be the allodial or absolute owner, the modern consequences of tenure lie in the concept of fragmentation of ownership that it began.

2. Types of Tenure and Their Services. [§ 4–4]

William not only paid his debts by creating tenure in regard to land but also extracted future services and payments. The types of services to be performed were the basis for categorizing the tenures. (Note: Neither the labels for the various tenures nor their spelling is uniform so do not be bothered by variations among the various property books.) The major tenures were:

a. Knight's Fee or Military Tenure. [§ 4–5]

Persons given this tenure were obligated to supply the king with a specified number of Knights to fight for him for a specified period of time each year.

b. Sergeanty Tenure. [§ 4–6]

Persons given this tenure were obligated to perform personal or professional services for the king such as being an advisor (grand sergeanty) or serving as his falconer (petit sergeanty).

c. Frankalmoign or Religious Tenure. [§ 4–7]

Religious orders or ecclesiastical corporations were given this tenure in return for the obligation to perform future religious services such as saying mass.

d. Socage Tenure (Also Called Economic or Agricultural Tenure). [§ 4–8]

Persons given this tenure were obligated to perform one or more of a large variety of services not included in any other tenure, for example, supplying food, repairing castles, paying rent. Eventually, all tenures were converted in England to this category.

3. Incidents. [§ 4–9]

Persons given tenure of land were subjected to liability for incidents in addition to the services discussed above. There was considerable variation in the incidents based upon the type of tenure. For example, the incidents for knight's tenure were as follows:

a. **Homage and Fealty. [§ 4–10]**

Tenure obligated those given it to swear allegiance to the king. Breach of that oath of loyalty could cause forfeiture.

b. **Forfeiture. [§ 4–11]**

Breach of fealty obligations often gave the king the right to terminate the tenure and regain possession of the land.

c. **Aids. [§ 4–12]**

The king or overlord was entitled to financial aid from those with military tenure in time of economic need such as needing to raise ransom money or the marriage (dowry) expenses of his daughter.

d. **Wardship and Marriage. [§ 4–13]**

Upon the death of a tenure holder, his interest in the property was subjected to the right of the king or overlord to be guardian during the minority of the tenure holder's heir (eldest son). Unlike modern guardianship, the Guardian got nearly all rents and profits of the land for his personal use. The king or overlord also had the right to sell the right to marry the heir of a tenant holder.

As stated above, different tenures had different incidents. One of the advantages of socage tenure to tenure holders was that it was free of the incidents of wardship and marriage.

e. **Relief. [§ 4–14]**

When a tenure holder died, his heir had to pay a fee in order to inherit the tenure. Many see this as an early version of inheritance taxes.

f. **Escheat. [§ 4–15]**

If a tenant holder died without heirs, the right of possession of the land returned to the king. The concept of escheat exists still today since the real property of those who die without heirs or devisees goes to the State or entities designated by State Legislatures as recipients of such property.

g. **Subinfeudation. [§ 4–16]**

Tenure holders were soon recognized to have the right to transfer their interests in land to others. Such transfers could take place originally either by substitution or subinfeudation. If the latter method was chosen the transferee did not replace the transferor but instead had tenure from (i.e., held of) the transferor who continued to hold of the king. In a surprisingly short period of time the land ownership picture took a complicated pyramid-like form in which E might hold Blackacre of D who held Blackacre of C, who held Blackacre of B who held Blackacre of A who held Blackacre of the king. The value of the king's feudal incidents usually got destroyed in the process. At the king's request, Parliament, in 1290, enacted the Statute Quia Emptores which restricted subinfeudation and made transfer by substitution the norm—as it continues to be today.

C. COPYHOLDS. [§ 4–17]

Peasants (also called villeins) were originally "outside" the feudal system since they did not "hold" land but occupied it at the pleasure of their lord. Their status is sometimes referred to as "unfree tenure" which distinguished it from the "freeholds" of those with true tenure. [Note: Do not confuse "unfree" tenure—i.e., copyhold, with nonfreehold (landlord and tenant) estates. See § 5–4.] As the centuries passed, the peasants were recognized as holding by custom and their "rights" were eventually recorded in manor records of which they were given a "copy." At this point, they were often referred to as "copyholders."

D. SIGNIFICANCE OF TENURE TODAY: OWNERSHIP CONSISTS OF RIGHTS AND RESPONSIBILITIES. [§ 4–18]

Although most scholars contend that the common law retains the concept of tenure even today, the only frequently encountered vestige of it is the concept of escheat. However, the principle upon which it was based continues to be accepted—ownership of land in our common law system involves both rights and responsibilities.

E. EXAMPLES OF FRAGMENTATION OF OWNERSHIP. [§ 4–19]

As you move through the chapters that follow, remember that a unifying theme of real property law is the fragmentation of ownership so as to create an incredibly flexible system which allows many different people to be owners of interests in the same tract of land at the same time. You should be prepared to encounter the following examples of fragmentation of ownership:

1. Allodial versus tenurial ownership (just examined in § 4–3).

2. Freehold and non-freehold estates.

3. Present and future interests.

4. Concurrent estates (co-ownership interests).

5. Legal and Equitable interests.

6. Possessory and Non-possessory interests.

REVIEW

The following chart should help you review the types of tenure:

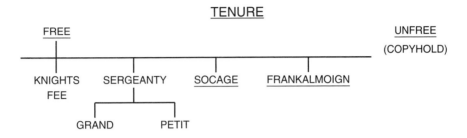

Chapter V

ESTATES IN LAND [FREEHOLDS]

A. CONCEPT OF ESTATES. [§ 5–1]

One of the principal tenets of the common law is that one does not own land directly; one owns an estate in land (often referred to as an estate). Ownership of an estate entitles one to various possessory and/or use rights of the land. For example, a possessory estate entitles the owner of the estate to possess the land in which the estate is owned. Possessory estates are measured and classified in terms of their duration (i.e., the length of time that the owner of the estate is entitled to possession of the land). The ownership, or possessory right, is thereby projected onto an imaginary plane of time. Conceptually, the durational plane is a line. The line is divided into line segments, according to the various estates carved out of the infinite possessory right.

B. CLASSIFICATION OF ESTATES. [§ 5–2]

Estates in land are classified according to whether they are (1) possessory or non-possessory and whether they are (2) legal or equitable. Most estates concepts relate to possessory estates, which are divided into freehold and non-freehold estates.

1. Freehold Estates. [§ 5–3]

The fee simple, the fee tail, and the life estate are characterized as the freehold estates. One of the characteristics of these three estates is that they may be cut short, or defease, under certain conditions. The three defeasable fees are the fee simple determinable, the fee simple upon condition subsequent, and the fee simple subject to executory limitation.

2. Non–Freehold Estates. [§ 5–4]

The tenancy for years, periodic tenancy, and tenancy at will are characterized as the non-freehold (i.e., leasehold) estates, and are discussed in depth in Chapter VIII (Landlord And Tenant Law). Traditionally, in property law, the distinction between freehold and non-freehold estates was significant. For example, non-freehold estates were classified as "chattels real" and passed on at the death of their owner as personal property rather than as real property.

3. Seisin: The Conceptual Distinction Between Freehold and Non–Freehold Estates. [§ 5–5]

Pursuant to feudal principles, holders of freehold estates were said to be "seised" of the land, or to have "seisin", as the freehold estate came along with the intangible concept of seisin. Seisin is perhaps best understood as the possessory use of land in exchange for a pledge of feudal duties (called feudal services and feudal incidents). Holders of non-freehold estates, although they also had a possessory interest, did not have seisin, and were therefore not bound to perform feudal duties. Various manifestations of the significance of the mysterious and mystical concept of seisin (sometimes spelled seizin) will be seen throughout the study of property. For example, traditionally, the ownership of a freehold estate was transferred at a symbolic ceremony called the "livery of seisin." No such concept existed in regard to creation or transfer of non-freehold estates.

4. Chart Illustrating Freehold Estates. [§ 5–6]

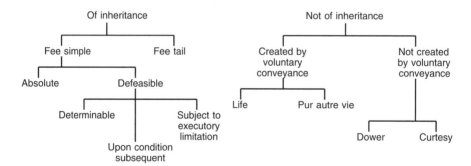

C. THE FEE SIMPLE. [§ 5–7]

1. Greatest Aggregate of Rights in Land. [§ 5–8]

The fee simple is the greatest and most common estate. The word "fee" designates an estate. The word "simple" indicates that the estate is inheritable by general (i.e., lineal and collateral) heirs (as determined by the laws of intestacy) and fully alienable (i.e., transferable and devisable).

2. Fee Simple Absolute. [§ 5–9]

When the fee simple is absolute (i.e., not subject to defeasance), the holder of such an estate has the greatest aggregate of rights that the law recognizes in a piece of land, both from a use and a durational point of view. It may help to picture ownership of land as an aggregate of rights and to think of those rights as a bundle of sticks. Only the holder of an unencumbered fee simple absolute possesses the entire bundle. Also, the duration of a fee simple absolute is infinite (i.e., its owner occupies the entire plane of time or, as some would say, owns a line rather than a line segment). [Caveat: The fee simple absolute should always be called by its full name to distinguish it from a defeasible fee (§ 5–60), but judges, lawyers, and even professors often refer to it as a "fee simple" or even a "fee."]

3. **The Fee Simple Absolute and the Calculus of Estates. [§ 5–10]**

Central to the classification of estates is the idea that at any point in time, the totality of the estates created in a given piece of land must be equal to a fee simple absolute.

Example. [§ 5–11] O, owner of Blackacre (a fictional estate used as an example throughout this book) in fee simple absolute, conveys Blackacre "to A for life." O did not transfer the entire durational interest that he had, and, therefore, A did not receive a fee simple absolute (A only got a life estate.). In this example, O retains ownership of some of the durational rights (a reversion).

4. **Creation of the Fee Simple Absolute. [§ 5–12]**

Originally at common law, a fee simple absolute could be created only by use of the words "and his heirs" (i.e., "to A and his heirs"). A conveyance in any other terms was insufficient to create a fee simple absolute. For example, a simple grant "to A," created only a life estate in A, with the grantor retaining a reversion. Today, words of inheritance are no longer necessary to create a fee simple absolute.

a. **Words of Purchase and Limitation. [§ 5–13]**

In a conveyance "to A and his heirs," the words "to A" are words of purchase and the words "and his heirs" are words of limitation. Words of purchase identify the taker of the estate (whether by sale, gift, devise, or inheritance); words of limitation describe (delimit) the type of estate given. In the basic conveyance of a fee simple absolute, "to A and his heirs," "to A" are words of purchase that designate A as the possessor of the present estate and the words "and his heirs" are words of limitation describing the present estate A is seised of, the fee simple absolute. A's heirs take no estate. A's heirs obtain no interest in the property involved because they are mentioned only to identify the estate which A is taking. While they may eventually inherit the property, they will do so only if A neither conveys it during his lifetime nor devises it to another at his death.

b. **Technical Words of Limitation Abolished. [§ 5–14]**

The common law rule requiring the use of technical words of limitation ("and his/her heirs") to create a fee simple absolute has been abolished by statute in most jurisdictions. These statutes are frequently called "fee simple presumption" statutes. Pursuant to them, a conveyance by the owner of a fee simple absolute is presumed to transfer a fee simple absolute absent an indication that a lesser estate is intended. Thus, today, if A has a fee simple absolute and grants the estate "to B," B receives a fee simple absolute estate, and A, having transferred her entire durational interest, retains nothing.

D. THE FEE TAIL. [§ 5–15]

1. Creation. [§ 5–16]

At common law, a grant from O "to A and the heirs of his body" created a fee tail, an estate which could pass by descent only to A's lineal descendants. The fee tail thus differs from a fee simple absolute, which could descend to both collateral and lineal heirs. The word "fee" once again denotes the estate, while the word "tail" is from the French "tailler" which means to carve and signifies the carving out of an estate in order to satisfy the grantor's wishes. The fee tail estate is a lesser estate than a fee simple absolute, because the fee simple absolute is of infinite duration, but the fee tail terminates when its owner (the tenant in tail) dies without lineal descendants.

Example. [§ 5–17] O grants an estate "to A and the heirs of his body." A receives a fee tail and upon A's death, his oldest child, B, takes the property. If B then dies without lineal descendants, the fee tail would terminate and the property would revert to O or his heirs. [Note for future reference that a future interest (a reversion) is created whenever the grantor owns a fee simple and conveys away only a fee tail.]

2. Traditional Purpose of a Fee Tail. [§ 5–18]

During feudal times, land represented power and wealth to the English aristocracy. Large landowners, seeking to preserve the economic and social position of their families, created the fee tail as a method of ensuring that their land would always remain in the family. [Attempts of the landed class to restrain the alienability of their lands is a recurring theme throughout our property law.] The key characteristic of the fee tail for these landowners was that any individual who possessed land under a fee tail (the tenant in tail) could not convey away the interest that their lineal heirs had in the land. Through the fee tail, these landowners could ensure that future lineal descendants would always have land, regardless of how the ancestor of these future descendants used the land.

Example [§ 5–19] O, owner of a fee simple absolute in Blackacre, conveys a fee tail to A. Even if A conveys his interest in the property to C, upon A's death, the estate would descend to A's heir [eldest son under primogeniture]. C would receive what is in effect a life estate *pur autre vie* (§ 5–35) which ends on A's death.

3. Evolution of Fee Tail at Common Law. [§ 5–20]

The fee tail was not the first attempt at restraining the alienation of family lands. The fee simple conditional, a grant of a fee simple whose alienability was contingent on the grantee having offspring, was the first attempt. This estate was often created as a wedding gift from O "to A and the heirs of his body by his wife, W." In this example, A would receive a fee simple conditional estate, and O would retain a reversion. If A and W had a child born alive, the courts held that A could convey a fee simple absolute and thereby destroy O's reversion and the inheritance rights of his child. If, however, A died without a child having been born alive to him, then O's reversion would become possessory. If A did not convey a fee in the property, then the child would take the property on A's death.

Statute de Donis Conditionalibus. [§ 5–21] In 1285, British Parliament enacted the Statute de Donis Conditionalibus which abolished the fee simple conditional estate and created a new estate, the fee tail. The fee tail was more effective than the fee simple conditional in allowing large landowners to accomplish their restrictive goals, because birth of issue had no effect on the rights of the owner of a fee tail.

4. Future Interests Following a Fee Tail. [§ 5–22]

Because a fee tail does not descend to the broadest class of heirs recognized at law, it is not regarded as an estate of potentially infinite duration (only the fee simple absolute is regarded as having such duration). If a grantor has a fee simple absolute, this fee simple absolute is not totally exhausted by the grant of a fee tail. The grantor, not having granted her entire durational interest, retains a reversion, which becomes possessory when the fee tail terminates. Thus, a father could split his land among his three sons by granting each a fee tail, thereby insuring that if any of those sons' bloodlines ever died out, the land will remain in the family by reverting to the grantor (the father) or his successors (presumably the other two sons and their lineal descendants). The creation of a fee tail does not always create a reversion; a fee tail may be followed by a grant of a remainder or executory interest to a third party. You can be certain of this rule. If the future interest following a fee tail is held by the grantor or the grantor's heirs, it is a reversion. If the future interest following a fee tail is held by someone other than the grantor or the grantor's heirs (a third party), it is a remainder or an executory interest. Every fee tail must be followed by a future interest, and that interest will either be a reversion or a remainder.

Example. [§ 5–23] O owns a fee simple absolute in Blackacre and conveys it to A and the heirs of his body, then to B and his heirs. B or his successors are entitled to possess the land at the termination of A's fee tail estate. They have a vested remainder in fee simple and O retains no interest.

5. A Fee Tail Must Be Precisely Created. [§ 5–24]

A fee tail was created at common law only when the conveyance specifically indicated an estate whose duration was contingent on an indefinite failure of issue. The words "and the heirs of his body" were generally considered to be necessary for the creation of a fee tail estate.

6. Modern Approaches to the Fee Tail Estate. [§ 5–25]

The fee tail as it existed at common law has been abolished or greatly modified by statute and/or judicial decision in most American jurisdictions. These changes fall into several patterns, with the majority of states following the first or second approach.

a. Approach 1: Fee Simple Presumed, Remainder Void. [§ 5–26]

Many states today treat a grant "to A and the heirs of his body, and if A should die without issue then to B and his heirs" as granting to A a fee simple absolute estate. The attempt to create a fee tail is ineffective, and the attempted grant of the remainder interest to B and his heirs is therefore void. Because the grant is construed as conveying a fee simple absolute, no future interest can follow.

b. Approach 2: Fee Simple Presumed, Remainder Valid for One Generation. [§ 5–27]

Other states today treat the grant "to A and the heirs of his body, and if A should die without issue then to B and his heirs" as granting a fee simple but with one qualification; if A does not leave surviving issue then the grant to B is given effect and B has a fee simple absolute. If A does leave surviving issue at his death, B's interest is forever destroyed and A's heirs or devisees take a fee simple absolute.

c. Approach 3: Grantee Takes Life Estate, Lineal Descendants (Issue) Take a Remainder. [§ 5–28]

In a few states, a grant that attempts to create a fee tail estate creates a life estate in the grantee and a remainder in fee simple absolute in the grantee's issue. This approach allows a grantor to accomplish to a lesser degree some of the original goals of the fee tail in that the land is preserved for at least one generation in the family.

d. Approach 4: Fee Tail Allowed but Weakened. [§ 5–29]

In a very few states, a fee tail can still be created. However, the characteristics of the estate have been greatly modified, and the holder of a fee tail estate can convey away a full fee simple absolute estate by deed executed during the life of the fee tail tenant. This process of conveyance by deed is called barring the entail. In these states, the entail cannot be barred by will or by intestate succession.

E. THE LIFE ESTATE. [§ 5–30]

1. Definition. [§ 5–31]

A life estate is an estate whose duration is measured by the life of its owner. A life estate simply lasts for the life or lives of one or more persons. A life estate may be granted for the duration of one life, for the joint lives of one or more persons, or until the death of the last surviving of two or more persons. If an estate is granted "for the lives of A and B," it is normally presumed that the estate continues until the death of the survivor of A and B. To avoid the inherent structural ambiguity, a better worded conveyance would read "for the lives of A and B and the survivor." A conveyance for the "joint lives of A and B" would probably be construed as terminating on the death of either A or B. When a holder of a fee simple absolute chooses to convey away only a life estate, the holder has not conveyed away her entire durational interest and retains (or can simultaneously convey to a third party) a future interest in the property. You can be certain of this rule. If the grantor retains the future interest following a life estate for the grantor or for the grantor's heirs, that future interest is called a reversion. If the future interest following a life estate is held by a third party, it is a remainder. Every life estate must be followed by a future interest and that interest will either be a reversion or a remainder.

2. Creation. [§ 5–32]

While a life estate is normally created by a conveyance from O to A "for life," no specific language is required as is the case with a fee simple absolute and a fee tail. Any language manifesting an intention to create a life estate is sufficient. Life estates may also be created by operation of law, as is the case with the marital property life estates of dower and curtesy. (§§ 5–41 & 5–42)

3. Conventional Life Estates. [§ 5–33]

Most life estates are created voluntarily. They are frequently referred to as "conventional" or "regular" life estates to distinguish them from those created by operation of law. There are two types of conventional life estates: the simple or regular life estate (usually just called "life estate") and the life estate *pur autre vie*.

a. Regular Life Estate. [§ 5–34]

The duration of a simple life estate is measured by the life of the grantee. Assume that O, owner of a fee simple, conveys "to A for life." A has a life estate, which will terminate at A's death. A has no interest which can descend to heirs or be devised, although her life estate is alienable. O, not having granted the entire fee simple, has a reversion which will become possessory in O or his successors at A's death. At common law, a conveyance from "O to A" without any words of limitation created a life estate. Today, such a grant is presumed to convey whatever estate the grantor had. (§ 5–14)

b. Life Estate *Pur Autre Vie.* [§ 5–35]

An estate measured by the life of a person other than the owner of the life estate is a life estate *pur autre vie* (for the life of another).

(1) Creation by Grantor. [§ 5–36]

A life estate *pur autre vie* may be created by the grantor. For example, assume O conveys property "to A for and during the life of B." A has a life estate *pur autre vie* in the property which will terminate upon B's death. O has a reversion which will become possessory on B's death. If B dies before A, O's reversion becomes possessory, even though A is still alive. It is B's life that determines the duration of this life estate, not A's.

(2) Creation by Transfer. [§ 5–37]

A life estate *pur autre vie* may also be created when the grantee of a regular life estate conveys her interest to another.

Example. [§ 5–38] O conveys "to A for life," and A then conveys her interest to B. B now holds an estate for the life of A, and O has a reversion. B's estate ends at A's death, and O's reversion then becomes possessory.

(3) Inheritability of Life Estates *Pur Autre Vie.* [§ 5–39]

Suppose that A owns a life estate for and during the life of B, and that A dies before B. At common law, courts took the position that a life estate was a freehold, but not an inheritable estate, and, until B's death, viewed the property as belonging to the "first taker," (i.e., the first person who took possession upon A's death). [The heir of A seems usually to have been considered the first taker.] Today, this pretense has been abandoned, and a life estate *pur autre vie* is considered to be inheritable and devisable. The estate will still terminate upon B's death, of course.

4. Life Estates Created by Operation of Law. [§ 5–40]

Unlike conventional life estates which are voluntarily created, legal life estates are created by operation of law, without regard to the intention of the parties.

The two legal life estates of greatest significance are the marital estates—curtesy and dower.

a.   Curtesy. [§ 5–41]

The common law was rather generous to husbands. During life, husbands had an estate for the life of the husband and the wife in all the lands in which the wife held a present legal freehold estate, during the marriage. So, the husband had a life estate measured by his life and his wife's life in all estates in which the wife held either a fee simple, a fee tail, or a life estate. If the marriage resulted in a child capable of inheriting from the wife, the common law gave the husband an estate that was called curtesy. Curtesy was the right of the husband on his wife's death to a life estate in all real property of which she was seised during her lifetime, whether legal or equitable, provided that issue of the husband and wife, capable of inheriting the property, had been born alive. In most states, the common law rules have been modified and the husband has been made an heir of the wife in case of her death intestate; also the husband is usually given the right to waive his share under his wife's will and take a statutory forced share in the estate, both real and personal, which his wife owned at her death. Curtesy has been abolished in all states which have abolished dower and in some which have not.

b.   Dower. [§ 5–42]

Dower, at common law, was the wife's right to a life estate in one-third of the lands of which her husband had been seised at any time during marriage and it attached at the moment of marriage. A wife could only claim dower in an estate that was capable of inheritance by issue of the marriage. The husband's estate had to be a legal estate because he could not be seised of an equitable estate. Moreover, the wife could only claim dower over an estate in which the husband held sole seisin. Thus, a wife could not claim dower in lands in which her husband had a life estate, a joint tenancy with right of survivorship, a reversion, a remainder or an equitable estate only (i.e., where the husband was the purchaser under an installment land contract). The husband could not defeat the wife's dower claim by will nor by inter vivos conveyance, even to a bona fide purchaser for value, unless the wife consented to the conveyance. Moreover, the husband's creditors could not defeat the wife's dower claim by sale on execution or seizure. The wife could release her dower claim to a grantee of the husband. However, by making provisions in his will for his wife "in lieu of dower," the husband could force her to elect to take either dower or inherit whatever he left her in the will.

(1)   Requirements. [§ 5–43]

Common law dower requires a valid marriage and the husband having been beneficially seised of the land during the marriage (the

45

widow has no dower right in remainders or reversions, because her husband was not seised of such future estates). Similarly, the widow has no dower in equitable interests of the husband, nor in legal estates of which the husband was not beneficially seised (as where the husband holds a fee as trustee for another).

(2) Derivative Rights. [§ 5–44]

A widow's dower is generally derivative (i.e., she takes subject to limitations on the estate of her husband and can be in no better position than her husband occupied). The wife, therefore, has no dower in property held by the husband as a joint tenant, since on his death the surviving joint tenant takes the whole estate. (§ 7–4) If property acquired by the husband during the marriage is already subject to a mortgage or creditor's claims, the wife's dower is also subject to such claims. (Note, however, that if the husband's creditors attach the land, or a mortgage is granted by the husband during the marriage, the dower right is generally superior, because the creditors and mortgagees are presumed to know of and take subject to the wife's dower right.)

(3) Inchoate Dower. [§ 5–45]

During the husband's lifetime, the wife was said to have inchoate dower. This inchoate right could be released, but could not be defeated by action of the husband alone, even when he conveyed to a bona fide purchaser for value. On the husband's death, the widow was entitled to receive a life estate in one-third of the property in which she had inchoate dower.

(4) Barring of Dower. [§ 5–46]

Dower rights may be barred (i.e., defeated) by: (a) release by the wife (i.e., joining with the husband in a conveyance); (b) divorce; (c) agreement (either before or after marriage, so long as the agreement was fair); (d) estoppel; or (e) third-party mortgage (i.e., where the lender gives the husband money for the sole purpose of purchasing the property, the lender's interests are not subject to dower rights).

(5) Statutory Changes. [§ 5–47]

Most states have abolished dower and, in its place, have given a widow the right to take an intestate share as an heir of her husband and/or have given her a forced share as against her husband's will. In some jurisdictions, she may have to elect between her dower, her intestate share, or her statutory forced share.

5. **Rights and Duties of Life Tenants. [§ 5–48]**

   a. **In General. [§ 5–49]**

   A life tenant, one who is in possession of property through a life estate, is entitled to make all normal uses of the land and to take the profit from such use. Unlike the holder of a fee, however, the holder of a life estate must accommodate his rights to those of a future estate holder (either a reversioner or a remainderman). The presence of a future estate prevents the holder of the life estate from using the property in a wasteful manner.

   b. **Must Pay Taxes. [§ 5–50]**

   Life tenants must pay all taxes which might become a lien on the property for as long as they hold the estate. Special assessments for improvements of a permanent character are apportioned on an equitable basis between life tenants and the holder of the future estate. Life tenants are solely responsible for assessments on improvements which have an anticipated duration that is shorter than the expected duration of the life estate. The life tenant's obligation is limited to the rents and profits the life tenant receives or to the fair rental value if the life tenant occupies the property for his own purposes instead of renting it to others.

   c. **Must Pay Interest on Mortgages and Other Carrying Charges. [§ 5–51]**

   The life tenant must pay interest on all encumbrances to which both the life estate and future estates are subject, to the extent of the gross income from the land, or, if there are no profits, to the extent of the land's fair rental value. Conversely, the reversioner or remainderman must pay the principal on such encumbrances. If the property is mortgaged after the creation of the life estate by the present and future estate holders joining together to execute the mortgage, then both are liable for the payment of principal and interest in amounts that are proportional to the value of each estate.

   d. **Responsible for Repairs, Maintenance, and Waste. [§ 5–52]**

   (1) **Repairs. [§ 5–53]**

   The life tenant's primary duties with respect to maintenance of the property are to make repairs necessary to avoid diminishing the value of the property and to refrain from committing any act which would have the effect of diminishing the value of the property. These duties are expressed as the duty to avoid waste. If a life tenant violates this duty, waste is a basis for recovery of damages or for injunctive relief by the remainderman or reversioner. The life tenant is not required to rebuild in the case of destruction by fire or storm when rebuilding rather than repairing is necessary in order to restore the property. See Chapter VIII (Landlord And Tenant Law (Non–Freehold Estates)), § 8–1.

(2) Maintenance. [§ 5–54]

The life tenant must preserve the land and structures in a reasonable state of maintenance, to the extent of income derived from the land, or if no income is derived from the land, to the extent of the reasonable rental value of the land. Life tenants need not make improvements; if they do, they generally cannot compel the reversioner or remainderman to pay any part of the cost, even though the benefit may inure to the future estate holder.

(3) Natural Resources. [§ 5–55]

Life tenants are limited in their ability to remove and use natural resources. Generally, they can remove minerals, etc., only: (a) to the extent they were granted that right; or (b) in reasonable amounts for the maintenance of the land; or (c) where the grantor was exploiting the resources at the time of the grant (open mines rule); or (d) where the land has no other use.

e. Not Responsible for Insurance. [§ 5–56]

The majority rule is that the life tenant is not obligated to insure the property. If the life tenant decides to insure, the life tenant is entitled to all insurance proceeds upon a loss to the property if the life tenant insures the property in the life tenant's own name, for the life tenant's own benefit, and if the life tenant pays the insurance premiums from his own funds. There are several commonly recognized exceptions to the majority rule. The life tenant must provide insurance for the benefit of the reversioner or remainderman if the instrument creating the life estate expressly provides, if the life tenant agrees with the reversioner or remainderman to provide insurance, or if there is a fiduciary relationship between the life tenant and the reversioner or remainderman apart from the tenancy.

If there is a mortgage on the property, and if the mortgage provides that improvements such as buildings shall be kept insured for the benefit of the mortgagee/lender, then the life tenant must maintain the insurance at the life tenant's expense. In this instance, the insurance is a carrying charge like mortgage interest or taxes.

f. Alienability. [§ 5–57]

The life tenant's interest is freely alienable and may be mortgaged, leased, etc., unless alienability was restricted in the original grant of the life estate. Of course, a purchaser takes only the interest that the life tenant has (i.e., the transferee of the entire interest gets a life estate *pur autre vie*, which terminates upon the death of the original life tenant).

6. Life Estate Followed by a Future Interest. [§ 5–58]

Remember that a future interest (either a reversion or a remainder) is always created simultaneously with the creation of the life estate (as is the case with the conveyance of any estate other than a fee simple absolute).

F. DEFEASIBLE ESTATES. [§ 5–59]

Any estate (whether freehold or non-freehold) may be made defeasible, meaning subject to the possibility of being "prematurely terminated" (forfeited) at a future time. There are three types of defeasibility: (1) determinable, (2) upon condition subsequent (also known as subject to condition subsequent), and (3) subject to an executory interest (also known as subject to an executory limitation). The concepts and rules for defeasibility originally developed in regard to fee simple absolutes, and, therefore, they will be first discussed in that way.

G. DEFEASIBLE FEES. [§ 5–60]

The two most common defeasible fees (sometimes called "base" or "qualified" fees) are: (a) the fee simple determinable; and (b) the fee simple defeasible upon condition subsequent (or fee simple subject to condition subsequent, as it is also called). Both estates are freely inheritable, alienable, and devisable, as indicated by the beginning terms "fee simple."

1. Fee Simple Determinable. [§ 5–61]

The hallmark of the fee simple determinable is that upon the occurrence of some specified event, the fee simple determinable automatically terminates. Once the event occurs, the fee will revert back to the person who originally created it, the grantor, or his heirs or successors. The future interest retained by the grantor is called a possibility of reverter. If the grantor wants to put the right to enforce the defeasible estate in a third party, the grantor can create a present estate which is called a fee simple subject to an executor interest (also referred to as an executor limitation) followed by a future interest in the third party called an executory interest.

a. Example. [§ 5–62]

A, owner of a fee simple absolute, conveys Blackacre "to B and her heirs for so long as the property is used as a school and when it is no longer so used, the property shall revert to A." The limits set on the use of the property "as a school" and the words of termination ("so long as . . . and when it is no longer so used . . .") indicate that B did not receive the full bundle of rights that A possessed as owner of the fee simple absolute. These words indicate that B received a fee simple determinable, which will terminate automatically if Blackacre is not used as a school and that A retained a possibility of reverter.

b. Flag Words. [§ 5–63]

Certain flag words indicate that a fee simple determinable is created. They include durational language such as: "so long as," "while," "during," and "until" and are contained in the granting clause. Traditionally, these words are used to create a fee simple determinable estate. Unfortunately, the use of these words without more is not dispositive, and sloppy drafting often leaves the question of which estate was created to the courts. (See Case Squib: *Mahrenholz v. County Board of School Trustees).*

2. Fee Simple Defeasible Upon Condition Subsequent. [§ 5–64]

The hallmarks of the fee simple defeasible upon (or subject to) a condition subsequent are that the grantor has the right and power to terminate the estate of the grantee if a specific event occurs. Notice that the exercise of this power is optional and does not occur automatically as is the case with the fee simple determinable. The future interest following a fee simple defeasible upon condition subsequent is always retained by the grantor or the grantor's successors and is called a right of entry or a power of termination. If the grantor wants to put the right to enforce the forfeiture of the defeasible estate in a third party, the grantor can create a present estate which is called a fee simple subject to an executory interest (or subject to an executory limitation) followed by a future interest the third party called an executory interest. The only distinction between the fee simple defeasible upon condition subsequent and the fee simple subject to executory interest is who holds the future interest. **(§ 5–71)**

a. Example. [§ 5–65]

The classic creation of the fee simple defeasible upon condition subsequent occurs when A conveys "to B and his heirs provided that the property is used solely for residential purposes and if the property is ever used for any nonresidential purpose then A has a right to re-enter and take possession of the premises." B takes a fee simple defeasible upon condition subsequent and A retains a future interest called a right of re-entry or power of termination. Note that for B's estate to terminate, two conditions must occur: (a) a nonresidential use must be made of the property, and (b) A must affirmatively exercise his right to re-enter.

b. Flag Words. [§ 5–66]

Again, traditionally, there are certain flag words that indicate the creation of a fee simple defeasible upon condition subsequent. They include: "upon condition that" and "provided that."

3.   Rules of Construction. [§ 5–67]

Language is not always absolutely clear, and the flag words are not definite in and of themselves. Suppose there is a conveyance by O to "to A and her heirs so long as the property is used for residential purposes, and should the property be used for any other purpose O or his successors may re-obtain possession." In this grant, "so long as" suggests a fee simple determinable but the language of re-obtaining possession may suggest a fee simple defeasible upon condition subsequent. *Mahrenholtz v. County Board of School Trustees* is an excellent example of the court struggling with this type of construction problem. (See Case Squib: *Mahrenholz v. County Board of School Trustees.*)

Fortunately, the courts have developed several rules of construction to aid in the determination.

a.   Avoid Forfeiture. [§ 5–68]

Courts generally try to avoid forfeiture. Because a fee simple determinable results in automatic termination, while a fee simple defeasible upon condition subsequent requires the affirmative exercise of the right of entry, ambiguous language will generally be construed to create a fee simple defeasible upon condition subsequent.

b.   Construe in Favor of Grantee. [§ 5–69]

Courts will generally construe ambiguous language in favor of the grantee since it is normally the grantor who drafts the conveyance. Normally, the grantee will prefer the "upon condition subsequent" classification to "determinable."

c.   Distinguish From Covenants. [§ 5–70]

Be alert to language that creates neither a fee simple determinable nor a fee simple defeasible upon condition subsequent, but is simply a covenant such as "A conveys Blackacre to B, and B promises to continue to use the land for residential purposes." Here, courts attempting to favor the grantee and avoid forfeiture may simply construe the language as a covenant. If this occurs, B will take a fee simple absolute and A will have no future interest in Blackacre. If B violates this covenant, A's only remedy may be a suit for breach of the covenant but B will not be in jeopardy of forfeiting title as would be the case when a condition of a defeasible estate is breached. See Chapter VIII (Landlord And Tenant Law).

4.   Fee Simple Defeasible Subject to an Executory Interest. [§ 5–71]

With the enactment by Parliament in 1536 of the Statute of Uses (§ 6–86), a third type of defeasibility was created: subject to an executory interest. The important and obvious distinction between this newcomer and the two original types (determinable and upon condition subsequent) is that executory interests can be created in third parties.

Example. [§ 5–72] O conveys to A for so long as the land is used for residential purposes and if it ever ceases to be so used, title to the land shall pass automatically to X. With the determinable and upon condition subsequent types of defeasibility, title to the land could only go back to the Grantor (O) or her heirs. After the Statute of Uses, A has the present estate of a fee simple determinable and X has a shifting executory interest. If the land ever ceases to be used for residential purposes, A's interest will automatically be divested by the executory interest in X.

5. Other Defeasible Estates. [§ 5–73]

As indicated above, (§ 5–59), all estates can be made defeasible and in the same three ways in which the fee simple estate can be made defeasible: (1) determinable, (2) upon condition subsequent, and (3) subject to an executory limitation. Now that the creation and characteristics of the three types of defeasibility have been examined using defeasible fees as examples, other types of defeasible estates will be illustrated.

a. Defeasible Fee Tail. [§ 5–74]

If, or when, a fee tail could be created, the following conveyance should have been held to create a fee tail determinable in the grantee, A, and a possibility of reverter in fee simple absolute in the grantor, O.

Example. [§ 5–75] O, owner of Blackacre in fee simple absolute, conveys it to "A and the heirs of his body for so long as the land is used for residential purposes and if it ever ceases to be so used then title to the property shall automatically revert to O or his heirs."

b. Defeasible Life Estate. [§ 5–76]

The following conveyance should be held to create a life estate upon condition subsequent in the grantee, A, and a reversion in fee simple absolute in the grantor, O.

Example. [§ 5–77] O, owner of Blackacre in fee simple absolute, conveys it to "A, for life, upon the condition that A use the land solely for agricultural purposes and if A uses it for any other purposes, O or his heirs may reenter and terminate A's estate.

c. Defeasible Non–Freehold [Estate for Years]. [§ 5–78]

The following lease should be held to create a determinable term of years in the tenant, T, and a reversion in fee simple absolute in the grantor/landlord, O.

Example. [§ 5–79] O, owner of Blackacre, leases it to T for ten years. The lease contains the following clause: "If T shall ever fail to pay the rent specified herein within 15 days of its due date, all of T's rights herein shall automatically terminate and L shall have sole rights to possession of the property."

6. Defeasible Estates Result in Creation of Future Interests. [§ 5–80]

Defeasible estates are also important because their creation also results in the creation of one of the following future interests: the possibility of reverter, the right of entry/ power of termination, or the executory interest. The Chart in Chapter VI (Future Interests), § 6–96, illustrates this concept.

H. RESTRAINTS ON ALIENATION. [§ 5–81]

One of the most important attributes of ownership of an estate in land is the right to transfer or alienate it to another person (i.e., the right to sell or make a gift of it). The right to alienate is considered part of the bundle of sticks which constitute ownership. Even the owner of a fee tail could generally sell a life estate *pur autre vie*, even though he could not sell any greater interest. Nonetheless, grantors sometimes try to deprive their grantees of the full power of alienation. Over the centuries, common law courts have taken the position that a restraint on alienation is repugnant to a fee and therefore invalid. Unfortunately, courts have been inconsistent and confusing in the way they have dealt with this issue in regard to other estates, as the following principles indicate.

1. Direct Versus Indirect Restraints. [§ 5–82]

Many covenants and conditions (e.g., building and use restrictions, allowing construction of only single family residences) affect alienability indirectly by limiting or even destroying marketability, but such restrictions are indirect, depend upon market factors, and their effect on marketability may be purely coincidental. Direct restraints, on the other hand, have the restraint on alienability as their primary, or even exclusive, purpose. The common law rules prohibiting or restricting restraints on alienation apply only to direct restraints. There are other principles which may restrict indirect restraints. See Chapter X (Covenants Running With The Land And Equitable Servitudes).

2. Total Versus Partial Restraints. [§ 5–83]

Restraints may be total (e.g., "to A and his heirs on the condition that A may never assign or alienate the estate granted"). Restraints may also be partial (e.g., "to A and his heirs on the condition A may never mortgage the estate granted").

3. **Types of Direct Restraints. [§ 5–84]**

    a. **The Disabling Restraint. [§ 5–85]**

    A disabling restraint withholds power in the grantee to alienate the estate. The effect of an attempted alienation in violation of such a clause would be to nullify the attempted conveyance.

    b. **The Promissory Restraint. [§ 5–86]**

    The promissory restraint is in the language of a covenant. A conveyance violating the covenant not to convey would be valid, but the party who ignores the restraint would be liable for breach of contract.

    c. **The Forfeiture Restraint. [§ 5–87]**

    The forfeiture restraint terminates the estate upon attempted alienation and vests the property in someone else (e.g., "to A and his heirs, but should A attempt to alienate the estate, to B and his heirs").

4. **Direct Restraints on Fee Simple Estates. [§ 5–88]**

    Direct restraints on fee simple estates are, as a general rule, void and unenforceable, regardless of whether they are disabling, forfeiture, or promissory restraints. There are two generally recognized exceptions.

    a. **Spendthrift Trust. [§ 5–89]**

    The spendthrift trust can be regarded as an exception to the general rule. A spendthrift trust is a trust created to provide a fund for the maintenance of a beneficiary, and, at the same time, to secure it against his improvidence or incapacity.

    b. **Preemptive Rights. [§ 5–90]**

    A condition or a covenant that a given individual has the right to buy if the owner of the estate offers it for sale (called a right of first refusal) is not within the general rule and is generally upheld.

5. **Direct Restraints on Alienation of Life Estates. [§ 5–91]**

    a. **Disabling Restraints on Life Estates Are Generally Void. [§ 5–92]**

    Disabling restraints are not generally allowed by the courts in conjunction with life estates.

    b. **Promissory and Forfeiture Restraints May Be Valid. [§ 5–93]**

    Promissory and forfeiture restraints on life estates are valid if reasonable, taking into account the purposes and extent of the restraint. In some measure, such restraints may be designated to protect future interest holders.

6. Direct Restraints on Leasehold [Nonfreehold] Estates. [§ 5–94]

Restraints on leasehold estates (e.g., covenants against assignment or subletting in leases) are normally upheld. See Chapter VIII (Landlord And Tenant Law (Non–Freehold Estates)), § 8–103.

I. ESTATES IN PERSONAL PROPERTY [CHATTELS]. [§ 5–95]

Originally in our common law system, the concept of "estates" was applied only to ownership of land. Personal property or chattels were owned absolutely and directly. Personal property "ownership" was similar (if not identical to) the King's allodial ownership of land. Because personal property was not subjected to tenure or the concept of seisin, (§ 5–5), there was never any need or basis for projecting ownership on to an imaginary plane of time and describing the owner's rights in terms of the duration of a possessory right. (§ 5–1) Nonetheless, we common law lawyers have become so enamored of our estates concepts that—for better or worse—it is more and more common to find references to "estates in personal property." At least some judges believe that personal property can be owned in fee simple absolute, fee simple determinable, or fee simple defeasible upon condition subsequent. Recognition of "life estates" has become common for tangible and non-consumable personal property items such as paintings—but not a basket of strawberries! What about a fee tail of personal property? The fee tail ceased to exist in most jurisdictions before the "estates" invasion of personal property law and so the question of whether personal property can be held in fee tail really does not arise very often.

REVIEW PROBLEMS

On both essay and multiple choice exams, estates and future interests issues are almost always combined. Consequently, these two areas should be reviewed together at the end of Chapter VI (Future Interests).

For review purposes, prior to your study of future interests, the following list of the most important estates with examples of the language normally used in their creation, should help you consolidate your knowledge before moving on.

FREEHOLD ESTATES IN LAND

I. FEE SIMPLE

A. FEE SIMPLE ABSOLUTE

"TO A AND HIS HEIRS"

B. FEE SIMPLE DEFEASIBLE

1. FEE SIMPLE DETERMINABLE

"TO A AND HER HEIRS FOR SO LONG AS THE LAND IS USED FOR RESIDENTIAL PURPOSES AND IF IT SHALL EVER CEASE TO BE SO USED IT SHALL AUTOMATICALLY REVERT TO THE GRANTOR OR HIS HEIRS"

2. FEE SIMPLE UPON CONDITION SUBSEQUENT

"TO A AND HER HEIRS UPON THE CONDITION THAT THE LAND BE USED ONLY FOR AGRICULTURAL PURPOSES AND IF IT CEASES TO BE SO USED, THE GRANTOR MAY REENTER AND TAKE POSSESSION OF THE PROPERTY"

3. FEE SIMPLE SUBJECT TO AN EXECUTORY LIMITATION [INTEREST]

"TO A AND HIS HEIRS AND IF IT EVER CEASES TO BE USED FOR SCHOOL PURPOSES THEN TITLE TO THE PROPERTY SHALL AUTOMATICALLY PASS TO X AND HIS HEIRS"

II. FEE TAIL

A. FEE TAIL

"TO A AND THE HEIRS OF HIS BODY"

III. LIFE ESTATES

A. LIFE ESTATE

"TO A FOR LIFE"

B. LIFE ESTATE *PUR AUTRE VIE*

"TO A FOR AND DURING THE LIFE OF B"

CHAPTER VI

FUTURE INTERESTS

A. INTRODUCTION TO FUTURE INTERESTS. [§ 6–1]

It is central to the doctrine of estates that interests in land may be divided by the owner into any number of smaller interests in terms of duration, but that the sum total of these parts must equal the duration of a fee simple absolute. Whenever a grant conveys something less than a fee simple absolute, the remaining interest, which does not presently entitle its owner to possession of the land, is a future interest. Such conveyances result in consecutive rights of possession that are either (1) present possessory interests or (2) interests that will become possessory in the future. It is the second type of interest, interests that will become possessory in the future, that this chapter addresses.

1. Definition of Future Interest. [§ 6–2]

"Future" in "future interest" refers to the time of possession. Thus, a future interest is an interest in land which does not entitle the holder of the interest to possession of the land at the present time, but may become "possessory" in the future. "Future" does not relate to ownership. Future interests are ownership interests immediately when they are created (i.e., even before they become possessory).

Example. [§ 6–3] O conveys Blackacre to A for life; remainder to B. As soon as the conveyance occurs, B owns a future interest even though she is not entitled to take possession until A's life estate has ended. For a case involving the current monetary value of a future interest, see *Ink v. City of Canton.* (See Case Squib: *Ink v. City of Canton.*)

2. Types of Future Interests. [§ 6–4]

a. Designation of Six Future Interests. [§ 6–5]

There are only six future interests: (a) the reversion; (b) the possibility of reverter; (c) the right of entry (sometimes called the power of termination); (d) the vested remainder; (e) the contingent remainder; and (f) the executory interest. If an interest in land is not one of these six, it is not a future interest.

57

b. Categorization by Whether Created in Grantor or Grantee. [§ 6–6]

Every future interest problem will involve a grantor (one who conveys the interest) and one or more grantee(s) (those who receive the interest). Among the six kinds of future interests, three can only be retained by grantors and three can only be created for grantee(s). The analysis of transfers of land which may create future interests should commence by examining each transfer to first identify the present interest. The second step is to identify what interest(s), if any, will follow the present interest. The grantor and/or the grantee(s) may have a future interest that will follow the present interest.

(1) Grantor's Future Interests. [§ 6–7]

The future interests that may be retained by a grantor (or her estate, if the disposition is testamentary) are: (a) the reversion (following only a grant of a fee tail, a life estate, or a leasehold estate); (b) the possibility of reverter (following only a grant of a fee simple determinable); and (c) the right of entry (following only a grant of a fee simple upon condition subsequent). If a future interest is not one of these three, it cannot be a future interest held by the grantor.

(2) Grantee's Future Interests. [§ 6–8]

The future interests that can be received by a grantee are: (a) the vested remainder (usually following a grant of a life estate or a fee tail); (b) the contingent remainder (usually following a grant of a life estate or a fee tail); and (c) the executory interest (following any vested estate—usually a fee simple subject to an executory interest (or limitation) or a vested remainder subject to complete or partial divestment). If the future interest is not one of these three, it cannot be created in a grantee.

3. Future Interests Formulae. [§ 6–9]

In addition to the six types of future interests, the law of future interests involves four rules or formulae that may be applied to those interests. The four formulae are: (a) the Doctrine of Merger; (b) the Rule in Shelley's Case; (c) the Doctrine of Worthier Title and (d) the Rule Against Perpetuities. These rules operate either to change the nature or determine the validity of the future interest.

4. Analytical Approach. [§ 6–10]

Whenever there is a future interest problem, it should be broken down into separate sets of questions and procedures:

Step 1: Identify the Present Interest. [§ 6–11]

Identify the present interest (i.e., the current possessory estate). If it is any estate other than a fee simple absolute, there is at least one future interest.

Step 2: Identify the Future Interests. [§ 6–12]

Identify which one or more of the six future interests have been created.

Step 3: Apply the Four Rules. [§ 6–13]

Test whether any of the four rules or formulae apply.

Step 4: Check for Powers of Appointment or Restraints on Alienation. [§ 6–14]

See if either one of these special issues is present which could alter the analysis in step 2 or step 3.

B. IDENTIFYING FUTURE INTERESTS: GRANTOR'S POSSIBLE FUTURE INTERESTS. [§ 6–15]

1. Reversion. [§ 6–16]

When the grantor conveys a fee tail, a life estate, or a leasehold estate and creates no future interests in third parties, there is something left over; this "something" is a reversion.

a. Example. [§ 6–17]

The classic reversion situation occurs when A, owner of Blackacre in fee simple absolute, grants Blackacre "to B for life." Clearly B did not receive all that A could have granted of her fee simple absolute. B received only a life estate which entitled B or her successors in interest to possess Blackacre during B's lifetime. A's retained interest in Blackacre is a reversion. At B's death, A's reversion becomes possessory and A again owns Blackacre in fee simple absolute.

b. Reversion Always Vested. [§ 6–18]

The reversion is always vested. It is vested because (a) the person who has it is ascertainable (it is always the grantor); and (b) there is no express, unmet, condition precedent to the reversion taking effect (e.g., at the death of the life tenant or termination of the fee tail or leasehold it automatically and naturally goes back to the grantor without any action by anyone and without any other event having to occur).

c. Distinguishing Reversions from the Possibility of Reverter and the Right of Entry. [§ 6–19]

The reversion becomes possessory on the inevitable termination of an estate less than a fee simple absolute. The possibility of reverter and the right of entry become possessory upon the termination of two defeasible estates: (1) the fee simple determinable and (2) the fee simple upon condition subsequent.

2. Possibility of Reverter. [§ 6–20]

When the defeasible event specified at the time of the creation of a fee simple determinable occurs (§ 5–61), the right to possession transfers automatically back to the grantor if the grantor has retained the future interest. The future interest pursuant to which this transfer occurs is called a possibility of reverter.

a. Example. [§ 6–21]

O, owner of a fee simple absolute in Blackacre, conveys Blackacre to A and her heirs for so long as the land is used for residential purposes and if it shall ever cease to be so used Blackacre shall revert to O or his heirs. A receives a fee simple determinable (or determinable fee, as it is sometimes called) and O retains a possibility of reverter.

b. Distinguished From a Reversion. [§ 6–22]

A reversion is a vested future interest in the grantor or the grantor's successors that follows estates of limited duration and definitely will become possessory upon the termination of the preceding estate. The possibility of reverter is a vested future interest in the grantor or the grantor's successors that follows an estate of potentially infinite duration. Because a fee simple determinable legally could last forever, there is only a possibility that the grantor's retained interest will ever become possessory.

c. Alienability. [§ 6–23]

In most states, the possibility of reverter is transferable inter vivos. But, this is the modern trend and you should remember that some states still follow the common law where the interest was not transferable inter vivos. The possibility of reverter is devisable and inheritable. *Mahrenholz v. County Board of School Trustees* discusses the alienability of the possibility of reverter. (See Case Squib: *Mahrenholz v. County Board of School Trustees.*)

3. Right of Entry. [§ 6–24]

When the contingency specified in the creation of a fee simple upon condition subsequent occurs and if the grantor has retained the power to terminate the estate, this power in the grantor is called the right of entry (also known as the power of termination or right of re-entry). The exercise of this power is optional with the grantor (usually exercised by entering the property and demanding possession), and does not operate automatically as is the case with the possibility of reverter. It may be waived if not exercised in a timely manner and a grantor who fails to timely exercise the power may end up losing all retained interest in the property.

a. Example. [§ 6–25]

O, owner of a fee simple absolute in Blackacre, conveys Blackacre to A and her heirs provided that the land be used solely for residential purposes and if it ever ceases to be used, O and his heirs may enter and terminate the estate conveyed to A. A receives a fee simple upon condition subsequent (or fee subject to a condition subsequent, as it is sometimes called) and O retains a right of entry (or power of termination, as it is also called).

b. Alienability. [§ 6–26]

In most states, the right of entry is transferable inter vivos. But, this is the modern trend and you should remember that some states still follow the common law where the interest was not transferable inter vivos. The right of entry is devisable and inheritable. *Mahrenholz v. County Board of School Trustees* discusses the alienability of the right of entry. (See Case Squib: *Mahrenholz v. County Board of School Trustees*.)

C. IDENTIFYING FUTURE INTERESTS: GRANTEE'S POSSIBLE FUTURE INTERESTS. [§ 6–27]

1. Remainders: In General. [§ 6–28]

A remainder is a future interest created in a person (other than the grantor or her estate) which can become possessory upon the inevitable expiration of a prior estate granted by the same instrument to another person. In this way, it is like a reversion, but unlike the reversion, a remainder is always created in a third party.

a. Example. [§ 6–29]

O, owner in fee simple absolute, conveys to "A for life, remainder to B and his heirs." B has a vested remainder which will become possessory at the termination of the preceding estate (at A's death in this example).

b. Creation. [§ 6–30]

While a reversion is seldom expressly created, a remainder must be expressly created. At common law, a remainder could follow only a life estate or a fee tail. Today, in some jurisdictions, a remainder may also follow a vested non-freehold estate such as a leasehold estate.

Example. [§ 6–31] O, owner of Blackacre leases Blackacre to A for a term of one year, beginning on January 1, 2009 and ending on December 31, 2009 remainder to B and his heirs. A has the present estate of a term of years leasehold estate (one of the types of non-freehold estates) and B has a vested reminder in fee simple absolute. When the term of the lease expires, B's remainder will become possessory.

c. Remainders May Be Created Until the Fee Is Exhausted. [§ 6–32]

O, the owner of a fee simple may convey Blackacre "to A for life, remainder to B for life, remainder to C for life, remainder to D and his heirs." In such a case, B, C, and D all have valid vested remainders, each to become possessory on the natural expiration of the preceding estate. B and C, of course, have remainders for life while D has a remainder in fee simple absolute. Note that after the grant to D, O has granted everything she could under her fee simple absolute estate, but if O had granted D only a remainder for life, then O would have retained a reversion.

d. Alienability. [§ 6–33]

Vested remainders have always been regarded as alienable, devisable, and inheritable; today, contingent remainders are similarly transferable in most states.

2. Vested Remainders. [§ 6–34]

A vested remainder is a remainder to an ascertained and existing third party that will become possessory whenever and however the preceding estate comes to an end. The only event necessary for possession by the holder of a vested remainder is the expiration of the preceding estate. In other words, there are no express, unmet, conditions precedent to the remainder becoming possessory (other than the termination of the preceding estate which is a natural termination and does not defeat the vested quality of the remainder).

a. Remainders Absolutely Vested. [§ 6–35]

A remainder is absolutely vested when it is granted to [a] an existing, ascertained person or persons; [b] without an express, unmet, condition precedent; and [c] is not subject to a divesting condition subsequent. Absolutely vested remainders are usually referred to simply as "vested" remainders. Vested remainders are alienable, devisable, and inheritable.

Example. [§ 6–36] O, owner of a fee simple absolute, conveys "to B for life, remainder to C and his heirs." C has a vested remainder. O has no reversion; her fee has been exhausted. C's interest will become possessory on B's death. If C conveys his interest to D during B's life, D takes on B's death. The same result would follow if D received the remainder during B's lifetime through C's will or through inheritance as C's heir.

Example. [§ 6–37] O, owner of fee simple absolute, conveys "to B for life, remainder to C for life." C has a vested remainder for life even though he might not survive B. The only condition precedent to C's estate becoming possessory is the natural expiration of the preceding estate (§ 6–34). Of course, if C does not survive B, C's devisees and heirs get nothing because C's interest in Blackacre was extinguished before ever becoming possessory. O retained a reversion in fee simple absolute.

b. Vested Remainders Subject to Complete Divestment (Total Divestment or Complete Defeasance). [§ 6–38]

A remainder vested subject to complete divestment (also called vested subject to total divestment or vested subject to complete defeasance) is a remainder to an ascertained and existing person or persons, not subject to a condition precedent but subject to divestment upon the occurrence of a condition subsequent.

Example. [§ 6–39] Divesting Executory Interest. O, owner of a fee simple absolute, conveys "to A for life, remainder to B and his heirs, but if B dies without a daughter surviving him, to C and his heirs." B has a vested remainder subject to complete divestment; C has a shifting executory interest. O has no reversion, as the whole fee has been granted. If B dies without a surviving daughter while A is alive, C would "take over" B's vested remainder.

Example. [§ 6–40] Power of Appointment. O, owner of a fee simple absolute, conveys "to A for life, remainder to those persons B shall appoint, but in default of such appointment to C and his heirs." C's remainder is viewed as vested subject to divestment if B exercises his power of appointment. B has a shifting executory interest.

c. Distinguishing Vested Remainders Subject to Complete Divestment From Contingent Remainders. [§ 6–41]

The distinction between a vested remainder subject to complete divestment and a contingent remainder is often difficult, but it is of some importance, because a remainder once vested is no longer subject to the Rule Against Perpetuities (§ 6–116) or to the Doctrine of Destructibility of Contingent Remainders (§ 6–72). Note that in each of the above examples (§ 6–39 & § 6–40), the remainderman's interest can become possessory whenever A's life estate expires. If it can become possessory even though the remainder interest may be "taken away" subsequently, then the interest is a vested remainder subject to complete divestment. If the remainder interest cannot become immediately possessory because some express condition precedent has yet to occur (is unmet), then it is a contingent remainder.

d.   Vested Remainder Subject to Partial Divestment (Subject to Open). [§ 6–42]

A vested remainder subject to partial divestment (sometimes called subject to open) is a remainder to a group of persons, at least one of whom is ascertained and in existence, subject to diminution as other members of the group come into existence or can be ascertained. The most common example of a vested remainder subject to open is a remainder to children of a living person; upon birth of the first child, the remainder is vested, but the birth of additional children will diminish the interest (share) of the then living children proportionately.

Example. [§ 6–43] O conveys "to A for life, remainder to A's children and their heirs." At the time of the grant, A has two children, B and C. B and C have a vested remainder subject to partial divestment (or open). Their interest is vested, because it will become possessory whenever and however A's life estate ends, because it is not subject to an express, unmet, condition precedent. If, prior to his death, A has a third child, D, then B's and C's individual interests are partially divested and vested in D. If this occurred, B, C, and D would all hold equal shares in a vested remainder subject to partial divestment which will become possessory on A's death. Upon A's death, the class will close because no children can any longer be born to A and all of A's children and the devisees or heirs of any children who predeceased A will share in the present estate of a fee simple absolute.

e.   Alienability. [§ 6–44]

All vested remainders (even those subject to complete or partial divestment) are regarded as alienable future interests. Thus, the person owning the remainder may transfer his interest inter vivos or by will and the interest will descend by intestate succession if it still remains at the time of the remainderman's death. Of course, the transferee of a remainder not absolutely vested takes subject to the same possibilities of divestment as the transferor had.

3.   Class Gifts. [§ 6–45]

A class gift is a gift to a group of persons undefined in number when the gift is made, which persons will be ascertained at a time subsequent to the making of the gift, and with the share of each being dependent on the ultimate number of persons within the group. From the foregoing definition, it can be seen that a vested remainder subject to partial divestment (open) is a form of class gift.

a.   Identifying a Class Gift. [§ 6–46]

A class gift is present only when the gift is to a group, not to individuals. Thus, O's gift to B, C, and D, who happen to be all of A's children, is not a class gift to A's children. Class gifts generally use such designations as "children," "heirs," "cousins," etc. If both designations are used (i.e., "to B, C, and D, A's children"), no class gift usually results unless there is some other manifestation of such intent.

b. **Opening of the Class. [§ 6–47]**

A class opens when the creating instrument, deed, or will becomes effective. Note that in the case of a will, this is at the time of the testator's death.

Example. [§ 6–48] Eligibility. O conveys by deed "to A for life, remainder to B's children." B is living, and has one living child, C. D, another child of B's, died before O's conveyance. C is within the class but D (more accurately, perhaps, D's heirs) is not entitled to any part of the gift. O would not ordinarily wish to include a child who O knew was dead at the time of the conveyance. The class opens on the effective date of the conveyance and only children in existence on that date or later may qualify as class members.

Example. [§ 6–49] Eligibility. Same facts as previous example, except that O makes the gift by will and has died. D was alive when the will was executed but predeceased O. Because C survived O and was alive when the class is opened, C is within the class. D is not within the class as such, but his interest is likely to be saved under state probate law by an applicable anti-lapse statute which gives the property devised to devisees who predecease the testator to their descendents (unless there is an express or implied condition of survivorship in O's will).

c. **Closing of the Class. [§ 6–50]**

Closing of the class does not necessarily mean that only members of the class surviving at this point in time can take. Closing of the class refers only to the point after which no new members may enter the class. Survivorship is required only if it is stated as a condition precedent, or if such condition is implied (which is not normally the case). Generally, heirs, devisees, or grantees of non-surviving class members may take their predecessor's share.

(1) **Description of the Class Often Sets the Time When the Class Is Closed. [§ 6–51]**

For example, maximum membership of a class gift to A's heirs, issue, descendants, children, etc., must be determined at A's death, at the latest (recognizing the gestation period when necessary). Thus, if O conveys "to B for life, remainder to A's children," and A dies before B, the class closes at A's death. If A survives B, the rules discussed below apply.

65

(2) Closing of the Class in the Case of an Immediate Gift. [§ 6–52]

(a) When There Are Members of the Class in Being and Ascertained. [§ 6–53]

If there are members of the class in being and ascertained at the time the gift is made immediately to the class (meaning at the time the class is given a present estate), the class opens and closes immediately. This is the "Rule of Convenience" and allows for the immediate distribution of all the property which was the subject of the gift.

Example. [§ 6–54] A's will leaves property "to B's children." At A's death the will becomes irrevocable. B is alive and has one child, C. C takes alone. Even though B is still alive, later-born children cannot share (except that any child of B conceived prior to A's death would be included in this class and would not be treated as a later-born child). We close the class at the testator's death because we assume the testator's intent was to have an immediate distribution.

(b) No Members of the Class Are in Being and Ascertained. [§ 6–55]

If there are no members of the class in being and ascertained when the gift is made, nor born within the period of gestation, and if the gift is of a lump sum or specific property to be divided among members of the class (e.g., $100,000 to be divided equally among B's children), the class will remain open as long as persons can qualify (e.g., in the above example, until B's death). The reason is that otherwise the entire gift would fail. The distribution of the $100,000 to the children will be held up until B dies and all the children are ascertained but the remainder of the testator's estate can be distributed.

However, if the gift is not a lump sum of money or specific property but is instead per capita (e.g., $50,000 to each of B's children), the gift will fail if, when the gift is made, there are no members of the class in being and ascertained or born within the period of gestation thereafter, unless a contrary intent is clearly stated. The reason for this outcome in the second situation is the difficulty in determining how much money to set aside to satisfy the bequest. To let in all children as in the preceding example would unduly delay distribution of the entire estate.

(3) Class Gift With Enjoyment Postponed. [§ 6–56]

Suppose O conveys or devises "to A for life, remainder to B's children and their heirs." We have seen that the class opens on the effective date of the gift. Thus, if the gift is by deed, a child of B who dies before that date is outside the class. Any child then born after the class opens and before the class closes is within the class, regardless of whether this child survives until the closing date (there being no condition of survivorship). But when does the class close? In the case of postponed gifts to a class, there is typically no inconvenience involved by permitting the class to remain open until the time of distribution. In the case of postponed gifts, the Rule of Convenience provides that the class closes on the date fixed for the first distribution, if there are class members at that time (unless a contrary intent is expressed). Thus, in the above example, the class will close on A's death if B has any children, even though B is still alive, because the remainder is immediately conveyed to B's children. If B has no children at A's death, the class will normally remain open until B's death.

(4) Summary for Class Gift Closing. [§ 6–57]

The class includes all those who enter after the opening of the class and before its closing, whether they survive until the later date or not, unless there is an express or implied condition of survivorship.

Example. [§ 6–58] O conveys "to A for life, remainder to the children of B who attain the age of 21." At the time of O's conveyance, B has one child, C, who has attained 21 and two other children, D and E, who are under 21. B is still living. The class closes at A's death. No children born after the conveyance can be within the class. D and E are within the class along with C, although they must attain 21 to take (at A's death C will take possession of the property and will be partially divested of her interest if D or E reach 21—note that if C predeceased A, C's heirs would take in C's place because the remainder had vested in C and vested remainders can pass by devise or by descent).

4. Contingent Remainders. [§ 6–59]

A contingent remainder is a remainder (a) subject to an express, unmet, condition precedent; or (b) to be taken by an unborn person; or (c) to be taken by an unascertained person.

a. Remainders Subject to an Express, Unmet, Condition Precedent. [§ 6–60]

A remainder subject to an express, unmet, condition precedent is contingent because the remainder cannot become possessory if the preceding estate immediately ends unless the condition precedent has also occurred.

(1) **Example. [§ 6–61]** O, owner in fee simple absolute, conveys "to A for life, remainder to B and her heirs if B attains 21." A has a life estate; B, age 18, has a contingent remainder in fee simple absolute, and O has a reversion in fee simple absolute. Note that the reversion is necessary to account for the whole fee, since there is no assurance B's estate will ever become possessory. Now there are three factual patterns that could occur:

(a) B attains 21 during A's lifetime: the remainder immediately becomes vested in B because the condition precedent is satisfied and if B subsequently predeceases A, B's heirs or devisees will take the property upon A's death because vested remainders are freely devisable and inheritable;

(b) B dies under age 21 before A's death: B's contingent remainder fails and O's reversion becomes possessory on A's death; and

(c) B fails to attain 21 before A's death: at common law there could be no gap in the seisin; if the contingency were not completely satisfied at the time the preceding estate terminated, the contingent remainder was destroyed and O's reversion would become absolutely possessory. However, under modern statutes in most jurisdictions this "Destructibility of Contingent Remainders" (§ 6–72) no longer applies and B's contingent remainder will be saved as a springing executory interest (§ 6–88)—thus O's reversion would become possessory but subject to divestment if B attained 21. O would have the present estate of a fee simple subject to an executory interest (or executory limitation); B's springing executory interest would divest O of his possessory interest when B turns 21.

(2) **Example. [§ 6–62]** O, owner in fee simple absolute, conveys "to A for life, remainder to A's surviving children." A's children have a contingent remainder, survivorship of A being an express, unmet, condition, precedent. O has a reversion in fee simple absolute (A may outlive all her children).

b. Remainders to Unborn Persons. [§ 6–63]

Suppose O, owner in fee simple absolute, conveys "to A for life, remainder to A's children." At the time of the grant, A has no children. The remainder is contingent and O therefore retains a reversion. If A, being alive, now has a child, the remainder is vested in this child subject to partial divestment if A has other children; O's reversion is divested when the contingent remainder vests and cannot come back into being.

c.   **Remainders to Unascertained Persons. [§ 6–64]**

Suppose O, owner in fee simple absolute, conveys "to A for life, remainder to the heirs of B." B is still living; the remainder is contingent and O has a reversion. The remainder in the heirs of B is contingent because the heirs are unascertained persons. B's heirs cannot be ascertained until B dies. A remainder to "heirs" of a living person is always contingent, unless a court can be induced to construe "heirs" as "children" or "issue," in which case the remainder is vested subject to partial divestment (assuming there are children in being).

If B survives A, the remainder will still be contingent and O's reversion will become possessory—note that the estate O will have depends on whether the relevant jurisdiction has abolished the doctrine of Destructibility of Contingent Remainders. If the doctrine has not been abolished then O has a fee simple absolute; contingent remainders that do not vest at or before the termination of the preceding freehold estate are destroyed under the doctrine. If the doctrine does not apply then at A's death being survived by B, O has a fee simple subject to an executory interest that will be divested at B's death by B's heirs, who have executory interests.

d.   **Successive and Alternative Contingent Remainders. [§ 6–65]**

(1)   **More Than One Remainder Can Be Granted to Follow a Freehold Estate. [§ 6–66]**

(a)   **Remainders May Be Successive. [§ 6–67]**

Contingent remainders may be successive (e.g., "to A for life, remainder to B for life if he is married at A's death, remainder to C and his heirs if C marries X").

(b)   **Remainders May Be Exclusive and Exhaustive, (i.e., *alternative*). [§ 6–68]**

Alternative remainders are exclusive and exhaustive of each other. In such cases, only one remainder can become possessory. The event which vests one remainder defeats the others. For example, O conveys "to A for life, remainder to B and his heirs if B marries before the age of 25, but if B does not marry before he is 25, to C and his heirs." B and C have alternative contingent remainders in fee simple absolute which are mutually exhaustive. If one vests, the other cannot vest.

(2)   **Two Contingent Remainders Following the Same Life Estate May Not Always Be Alternative. [§ 6–69]**

Suppose O conveys "to A for life, remainder to A's children for life, remainder to B's children for life." Assume A and B are both

69

childless at the time of the conveyance. A has a life estate; A's children have a contingent remainder in a life estate; B's children have a contingent remainder in a life estate; and O has a reversion in fee simple absolute. The contingent remainders in the children are not alternative. If A and B both have children, the life estate will vest in A's children upon A's death and it will vest in B's children upon the death of A's children.

Suppose O conveys "to A for life, remainder to A's children but if A leaves no children surviving him, to B and her heirs." Assume A presently has no children. The limitation to A's children is a contingent remainder in fee simple absolute (to unborn persons). The limitation to B and her heirs is a contingent remainder in fee simple absolute (express, unmet, condition precedent). O has a reversion in fee simple absolute. If A has a child, what is the state of title? A still has a present life estate. A's child now has a vested remainder in fee simple absolute subject to open and subject to complete divestment. The remainder in A's children becomes vested because there are no express, unmet, conditions, precedent although it is subject to partial divestment (A may have more children) and it is subject to a condition subsequent that could result in a total divestment (if none of A's children survive him). B's possibility of taking possession has not been destroyed, but she now has a shifting executory interest.

(3) Alternative Contingent Remainders Accompanied by Reversion in Grantor. [§ 6–70]

Alternative contingent remainders are always accompanied by a reversion in the grantor should neither contingent remainder vest, a fact of consequence given the destructibility rule which applies in a minority of states (§ 6–72).

e. Alienability, Devisability, and Inheritability. [§ 6–71]

Under very early common law rules, a contingent remainder was not regarded as an estate and it could not be alienated. Today, however, a contingent remainder may be alienated and devised in most states and in the case of intestacy will descend to heirs, subject to the contingency inherent in the estate.

f. Destructibility of Contingent Remainders. [§ 6–72]

(1) Common Law Rule. [§ 6–73]

A contingent remainder which failed to vest before or at the moment the preceding possessory estate terminated or expired was destroyed under common law. For example, O conveys "to A for life, remainder to B's heirs." If A dies before B, the remainder, being contingent until B's heirs can be ascertained at her death, is destroyed. O's reversion becomes possessory, and B's heirs would not take when B later died. The reason for the destructibility rule was that the common law could not tolerate a gap in seisin; thus, in the above example, O's reversionary interest had to become possessory to prevent this gap as B's heirs were unascertainable when A died, and since remainders cannot divest possessory interests, any contingent remainders were destroyed when O regained possession.

(2) Most States Have Abolished the Destructibility Rule. [§ 6–74]

Almost all states have abolished the destructibility rule and thus the contingent remainder will take effect if the contingency occurs even after the preceding life estate terminates. In the example "O to A for life, remainder to B's heirs" now when B survives A, O's reversion will still become possessory but the interest of B's heirs will be treated as an executory interest and will operate to divest O's interest when they can be ascertained at B's death. (§ 6–84)

5. Rules of Construction Applicable to Remainders. [§ 6–75]

a. Constructional Preference for Vested Remainders. [§ 6–76]

It is often difficult to determine whether a remainder is subject to a condition subsequent (and therefore vested) or subject to an express, unmet, condition precedent (and therefore contingent). For example, O conveys "to A for life, remainder to C and his heirs when C attains 21, but if C fails to attain 21, to D and his heirs." The language of the remainder alone sounds like a condition precedent; the divesting language sounds like a condition subsequent. There is a strong constructional preference for vested remainders (at common law they were freely alienable and not subject to destruction) so that the court would probably hold that C has a vested remainder subject to complete divestment, and D has an executory interest.

b. Distinguishing Alternative Contingent Remainders From Vested Remainders Subject to Complete Divestment Coupled With an Executory Interest. [§ 6–77]

The most common constructional problem with vested remainders arises in distinguishing alternative contingent remainders from a vested remainder subject to complete divestment followed by an executory interest.

71

(1) Example 1. [§ 6–78] Contingent Remainders. O conveys "to A for life, remainder to C and his heirs, if and only if C attains the age of 21, but if C fails to attain 21, to D and his heirs." C and D have alternative contingent remainders because neither's rights will vest until a condition precedent is met.

(2) Example 2. [§ 6–79] Vested Remainder Subject to Complete Divestment Followed by an Executory Interest. O conveys "to A for life, remainder to C and his heirs, but if C fails to attain 21, to D and her heirs." C has a vested remainder subject to complete divestment (i.e., there is no express, unmet, condition, precedent, only conditions subsequent) and D has a shifting executory interest.

c. Characterization of First Remainder Determinative. [§ 6–80]

(1) Rule 1. [§ 6–81] Contingent Remainder in Fee Simple Absolute Followed by a Future Interest in a Third Party. If a contingent remainder in fee simple absolute is created and is followed by a second future interest in a third party, that future interest will be a contingent remainder also. (§ 6–69)

(2) Rule 2. [§ 6–82] Vested Remainder Subject to Complete Divestment Followed by a Future Interest in a Third Party. If the first future interest following a life estate is a vested remainder in fee simple absolute, the second future interest in a third party will be an executory interest.

(3) Example. [§ 6–83] Consider the following devise and ask yourself why the above two rules do not apply. O devises Blackacre to A for life, then to the survivor of A's children for the life of the survivor, then to A's grandchildren in fee simple upon the death of the last surviving child of A. Assume A has children living at the time of the devise but no grandchildren.

A has a life estate. A's children have a vested remainder in a life estate subject to open (because there are no unascertained persons nor are there express, unmet, conditions, precedent; there is a divesting condition subsequent though). A's grandchildren have a contingent remainder in fee simple absolute (because they are unborn). O has a reversion in fee simple absolute. Rule 2 does not apply to the characterization of the grandchildren's interest because the vested remainder is in a life estate, not in a fee simple absolute.

6. Executory Interests. [§ 6–84]

An executory interest is a future interest in a party other than the grantor (a third party) which can become possessory only by divesting another grantee of a vested remainder or a defeasible fee. Thus, while a remainder may only follow upon the natural termination of an estate of lesser duration than the interest of the grantor, an executory interest is the name given to a future interest in a third party that (a) will only vest on the happening of a condition or the occurrence of an event that is certain to take place, and (b) with the exception of the fee simple subject to an executory interest and the fee simple determinable, vests in derogation of a vested interest.

a.   **Example. [§ 6–85]** O conveys Blackacre "to A for life, then to B, but if my son S marries then to S." A has a life estate, B has a vested remainder subject to complete divestment, and S has a shifting executory interest. If S marries before A dies, S divests B of the vested remainder and will take Blackacre at A's death in fee simple absolute. If A dies before S is married, B's remainder becomes possessory. B will have a fee simple subject to an executory interest. B's estate will still be subject to complete divestment by S's shifting executory interest. If S later marries, S will take possession of Blackacre in fee simple absolute.

b.   **Prior to the Statute of Uses. [§ 6–86]**

Prior to the Statute of Uses (1536), "executory interests" were not allowed and remainders were the only future estates which could be created in a person other than the grantor. Keep in mind that a remainder could only become possessory upon the natural termination of a prior estate less than a fee simple (i.e., a fee tail, a life estate).

c.   **Modern Rule. [§ 6–87]**

The Statute of Uses legitimized executory interests. Today, with the Statute of Uses as part of our common law, executory interests are valid future interests.

d.   **Springing and Shifting Interests. [§ 6–88]**

Executory interests can be broadly classified as springing (cutting off a grantor's possessory interest) or shifting (replacing the interests of another grantee). Note that all of the following examples would have been void prior to the Statute of Uses, and that all are valid today.

73

(1) Example. [§ 6–89] O conveys "to B and his heirs one year from today." O has a fee simple subject to an executory interest. B has a springing executory interest which will divest O of her estate one year from the creation of the interest.

(2) Example. [§ 6–90] O conveys "to A for life, remainder to B and his heirs one year after A's death." A has a life estate, O has a reversion in fee simple subject to an executory interest and B has a springing executory interest (because of the gap between the life estate and future interest, B's interest is not a valid remainder). Once again, it is a "springing executory interest" because at A's death, O's reversion becomes possessory and a year later, B's executory interest will divest O of her estate.

(3) Example. [§ 6–91] O conveys "to A and his heirs, but if A dies without leaving children surviving him, to B and his heirs." Here there could be a "shifting" of the fee. This shifting could not be accomplished under early common law without a new livery of seisin ceremony. Today, it is a valid interest. A has a fee simple subject to an executory interest; B has a shifting executory interest.

(4) Example. [§ 6–92] O conveys "to A and his heirs so long as the property is used for residential purposes for the next 20 years but if it is not so used, to B and his heirs." This is also a "shifting" interest as B's executory interest will operate, if at all, to divest A of the possessory fee simple determinable estate.

(5) Example. [§ 6–93] O conveys "to A for life, remainder to C and his heirs, but if C fails to attain 21, to B and his heirs." Again, this shifting interest, invalid prior to the Statute of Uses, is valid today. A has a life estate; C has a vested remainder subject to complete divestment in fee simple absolute (the reason is because there is a condition subsequent to C's taking); and B has a shifting executory interest (B will divest C of the fee simple absolute if C fails to attain the age of 21).

e. Executory Interests Are "Indestructible." [§ 6–94]

The Doctrine of Destructibility of Contingent Remainders (§ 6–72) does not apply to executory interests nor is there any comparable limitation placed on executory interests. Consequently, the termination of one or more preceding estates has no effect on an otherwise valid executory interest. Caveat: Unlike the case with remainders, there is no possibility for an executory interest to vest prior to it becoming possessory.

Consequently, an executory interest is always a contingent interest and therefore always subject to the Rule Against Perpetuities. (§ 6–116)

f. Executory Interests Are Freely Alienable. [§ 6–95]

In most states, executory interests are freely alienable, can be devised, and will descend if the owner dies intestate.

7. Chart of the Common Permissible Combinations of Present and Future Interests. [§ 6–96]

PRESENT INTEREST	FUTURE INTEREST	
	Created in Grantor or His Estate	Created in Third Person
Fee simple absolute	None	None
Fee simple determinable	Possibility of reverter	None
Fee simple upon condition subsequent	Right of re-entry (Power of termination)	None
Fee simple subject to an executory interest (or limitation)	None	Executory Interest
Life Estate	Reversion	Vested remainder or Contingent remainder
Defeasible life estate	Reversion	Executory Interest

D. FUTURE INTERESTS IN PERSONAL PROPERTY (CHATTELS). [§ 6–97]

As noted earlier (§ 5–95), originally, in our common law system, the concept of estates and therefore future interests were applied only to ownership of land. Personal property or chattels were owned absolutely and directly. Personal property "ownership" was similar if not identical to the King's allodial (meaning free from the tenurial obligations attaching to feudal lands) ownership of land. Since personal property was not subjected to tenure or the concept of seisin, (§ 5–5), there was never any need or basis for projecting ownership on to an imaginary plane of time and describing the owner's rights in terms of the duration of a possessory right. Nonetheless, we common law lawyers have become so enamored of our estates concepts that—for better or worse—it is more and more common to find references to "estates in personal property." At least some judges believe that personal property can be owned in fee simple absolute, fee simple determinable, or fee simple upon condition subsequent. Recognition of life estates, remainders, and executory interests have become rather frequently encountered for tangible and non-consumable personal property items such as paintings—but not a basket of strawberries!

E. THE FOUR FUTURE INTERESTS RULES (FORMULAE). [§ 6–98]

After analyzing a conveyance for the six types of future interests, the grant should be analyzed to see if one of the four formulae apply: (a) the Doctrine of Merger; (b) the Rule in Shelley's Case; (c) the Doctrine of Worthier Title; and (d) the Rule Against Perpetuities. Note that the Doctrine of Destructibility of Contingent Remainders is often included in this list. It has already been discussed, (§ 6–72).

1. The Doctrine of Merger. [§ 6–99]

a. Present and Future Successive Estates May Merge. [§ 6–100]

The Doctrine of Merger states that present and future successive estates merge when they are held by the same individual. If two vested, consecutive, legal estates in land come to be owned by the same person, after their creation, the lesser estate is merged into the larger and is terminated. The Doctrine of Merger does not apply if another vested estate intervenes between the two estates.

(1) **Example 1. [§ 6–101]** O conveys "to A for life, remainder to B and his heirs." A has a life estate; B has a vested remainder in fee simple absolute. B now conveys his estate to A. A's successive estates merge, and he has a fee simple absolute. This result may also occur if B died, leaving A as his heir.

(2) **Example 2. [§ 6–102]** O conveys "to A for life, remainder to B for life, remainder to C and his heirs." A has life estate; B has a vested remainder in a life estate; C has a vested remainder in fee simple absolute. If C conveys his remainder to A, the estates of A do not merge because of the existence of the intervening vested remainder for life owned by B.

b. Intervening Contingent Remainders. [§ 6–103]

Under common law, thanks to the Doctrine of Destructibility of Contingent Remainders (§ 6–72), merger of the preceding possessory estate and reversion destroyed the intervening contingent remainder, since the remainder failed to vest when the preceding estate terminated.

(1) **Example. [§ 6–104]** O, owner in fee simple, conveys "to A for life, remainder to such of B's children who attain 21." B has no children. A has a life estate; B's children have a contingent remainder in fee simple absolute (unborn persons); O has a reversion in fee simple absolute. During A's lifetime, O conveys his reversion to A. A's life estate and his vested remainder (obtained from O) merge and the

terminated. As a result, A would hold this property in fee simple absolute. At common law, contingent remainders were often deliberately destroyed in this manner. With the abolition of the Destructibility Rule in most states, intervening contingent remainders now prevent merger in those states. In these states, A would have a present life estate and a reversion following the contingent remainder in B's unborn children. If B has a child who attains the age of 21, then A has a life estate and the child of B has a vested remainder subject to open. The reversion is destroyed because the life estate and the vested remainder in fee simple equal a fee simple absolute.

2. The Rule in Shelley's Case. [§ 6–105]

a. The Rule. [§ 6–106]

If an instrument conveys a freehold estate to an individual, and a remainder to the same individual's heirs, that individual takes both the freehold estate and the remainder. While the only impact of the Rule in Shelley's Case is on the remainder, the Doctrine of Merger may then be applied in certain cases. The purpose behind the Rule in Shelley's Case seems to have been to prevent tax avoidance since gifts were not taxed and if an individual's heirs took from the grantor rather than inheriting the property they thereby avoided the payment of inheritance taxes.

(1) Example. [§ 6–107] O conveys "to A for life, remainder to A's heirs." Under the Rule in Shelley's case, A has a life estate and a vested remainder in fee simple absolute. Applying the Doctrine of Merger, these estates then merge, so A ends up with a fee simple absolute.

(2) Example. [§ 6–108] The life estate may be a remainder. Assume O conveys "to A for life, remainder to B for life, remainder to B's heirs." A has a life estate. Under the Rule in Shelley's Case and the Merger Doctrine, B has a vested remainder in fee simple absolute (thus note that the Rule in Shelley's Case applies even where a vested future interest is followed by a grant of a remainder to the vested future interest holder's heirs).

(3) Example. [§ 6–109] O conveys "to A for life, remainder to B for life, remainder to A's heirs." A has a life estate, and under the Rule in Shelley's Case, a vested remainder in fee simple absolute. These estates do not merge, however, because B has a vested remainder for life which comes between them.

b. Rule in Shelley's Case Abolished in Most States. [§ 6–110]

The Rule in Shelley's Case has been abolished in most states, so that, in the above examples, A would have a life estate and the heirs of A would have a contingent remainder.

3. The Doctrine of Worthier Title. [§ 6–111]

At common law, an individual could not grant or devise to his own heirs the same estate that the heirs would take by descent; the devise was void and the heirs took the interest by descent. Once again, taxes were the driving force behind this rule as the English monarch collected an inheritance tax but not a gift tax. Thus without the Doctrine of Worthier Title a grantor could avoid taxes by presently giving a future interest to his heirs; upon the grantor's death the property would not pass through his estate and be taxed but would "pass" according to the gift.

    a. Example. [§ 6–112] O grants Blackacre "to A for life, remainder to O's heirs." The remainder is void, O has a reversion and the heirs of O take this reversion by descent if O predeceases A (thus the Doctrine of Worthier Title plugged the loophole whereby feudal inheritance taxes could be avoided).

    b. Doctrine of Worthier Title Obsolete as Applied to Wills. [§ 6–113]

    The only real impact of the Doctrine of Worthier Title as applied to wills was to make the heirs take by descent (rules of descent govern intestate succession when one dies without a will) rather than devise (in the above example if O had instead devised Blackacre, O's heirs would still take by descent and not by devise). Since this is a matter of little consequence today, the Doctrine of Worthier Title as applied to wills is normally regarded as obsolete.

    c. Application to Inter Vivos Conveyances. [§ 6–114]

    While the Doctrine of Worthier Title is obsolete as applied to wills, it is still in use in some jurisdictions in connection with inter vivos conveyances. The result of the Doctrine of Worthier Title is that the grantor cannot make an enforceable inter vivos transfer of a future interest to his own heirs. Thus, the heirs take only if the grantor has not conveyed or devised the interest prior to death.

    d. Present Status of The Doctrine of Worthier Title. [§ 6–115]

    Some states have abolished the rule. However, in most states which retain the Doctrine of Worthier Title it is viewed today as a rule of construction, and does not apply if the grantor in some other way manifests an intent to make a gift to his heirs. Thus, if it appears that the grantor did not use "heirs" in its technical legal sense (i.e., he really meant "children"), the Doctrine of Worthier Title is inapplicable.

4. The Rule Against Perpetuities "RAP." [§ 6–116]

The Rule Against Perpetuities seems to confound students more than any other principle of law. It is not really that difficult if each element is analyzed individually. Try to master the RAP, but do not panic if you cannot. The chances are that you can get most examination questions correct by simply memorizing a few examples involving the applicability of the RAP. Also, you should recognize that less and less time is devoted to the RAP in first year property courses. Before you agonize over the material which follows, be sure to understand from your professor what aspects of the RAP you are responsible for leaning. You may be able to skip all or major portions of the RAP coverage below.

Also, you should be aware that many states have made significant statutory changes to the RAP. The material which follows, except when indicated to the contrary, discusses the RAP as it existed at common law. Be sure you know what statutory changes, if any, you are responsible for on the exam.

a. The RAP. [§ 6–117]

"No interest is good unless it must vest, if at all, not later than twenty-one years after some life in being at the creation of the interest." As you can see from the statement of the RAP, it really has nothing to do with "perpetuities" (long lasting interests). Instead it concerns itself with delays in vesting. Consequently, many scholars prefer to rename the RAP—the Rule Against Remote Vesting. If a future interest is already vested it is not subject to the RAP. Thus, the only future interests that are contingent for purposes of the RAP are contingent remainders, executory interests, and vested remainders subject to open (class gifts).

b. Six Steps for Working Any RAP Problem. [§ 6–118]

If you follow these six steps with any RAP problem, you will find that working through the RAP becomes easier. Professors and scholars have developed numerous methods and devices for solving RAP problems. This six step method is just an example of such approaches that have been useful to students over the years. Professor Peter T. Wendel, in his book, A Possessory Estates and Future Interest Primer, created the "create, kill, and count" approach that makes the six step method so useful. Professor Caryl Yzenbaard also made valuable contributions to the six steps and thus we have the six step method which we believe will be invaluable to you as you approach RAP problems. Professor Wendel's work is used with the permission of Thomson Reuters.

(1) Define all of the present and future estates.

(2) Determine all of the future interests that are subject to the RAP.

(3) List all of the possible validating lives (sometimes referred to as measuring lives). Only persons alive at the time the conveyance becomes irrevocable can be a possible validating life. If the conveyance is an inter

vivos transfer, it must be someone alive at the time of the transfer. If the conveyance is by will, it must be someone alive at the testator's death. If there is a validating life to be found, you can be certain that it will be within one of these four groups: (a) the holder of any life estate; (b) the holder of any contingent interest; (c) any person who can affect the identity of the taker of a contingent interest; (d) any other person who can affect vesting. If we cannot find any person who can prove that the RAP will not be violated, then we do not have a validating life. If we find a person who can be used to prove that the RAP will be satisfied, this person is the validating life.

(4) Create a new life if it helps (someone who can affect the vesting or failure to vest).

(5) Kill the possible validating lives.

(6) Determine whether the future interests subject to the RAP will be certain to vest or fail to vest for all time, within 21 years after the deaths of all the possible validating lives.

(7) **Example. [§ 6–119]** O conveys "to A for life, remainder to A's children who attain the age of 30." At the time of the conveyance O and A are alive and A has two children, B and C, ages four and six respectively. Assume the destructibility of contingent remainders has been abolished. Step 1: Under the grant, A takes a life estate and A's children appear to get a contingent remainder in fee simple absolute (express, unmet, condition precedent). O has a reversion in fee simple absolute. Step 2: Only the contingent remainder in fee simple absolute is subject to the RAP. (§ 6–117) Step 3: The possible validating lives are A, B, C and O. Step 4: Assume that A has an afterborn child D. Step 5: For purposes of testing the RAP, kill off A, B, C, and O. Step 6: Ask, must D either turn 30 (vesting) or die before reaching 30 (failure to vest) not more than 21 years after the death of A, B, C, and O? The answer is no. The key to analyzing these problems is to think hypothetically and identify the possible validating lives. If we find a person or persons, alive at the creation of the interest, during whose lifetime or within 21 years thereafter, the interest **must** vest or fail to vest, then we have a validating life and the conveyance is valid under the RAP. In this question, only O, A, B, and C are possible validating lives. Look at these four and see if you can find any possible way that the interest to A's children will not vest or forever fail to vest within their lifetime or 21 years thereafter. The analysis follows this approach:

> O: O could die tomorrow, and then the interest to A's children will not vest or fail for at least 24 years (or more if B and C die and A has another child, D). Therefore O cannot be the "validating life" which saves the grant.

A: A is essentially the same as O for the purpose of this example; A could die tomorrow, and the interest to A's children would not vest for 24 or 26 years or more in the case of D. A cannot be the validating life.

B and C: B and C could also die tomorrow, the interest in A's afterborn child, D, may not vest for another 30 years. Thus, neither B nor C can be the validating life. Note that if A died the day before the conveyance, then the interest would be valid as B and C would be the only children who could ever attain the age of thirty. In other words, they could be their own validating lives. In this case, during the lifetime of either B or C the interest would have to vest (or fail at the death of the survivor if neither attained 30) (note that property law considers a life "in being" from the time of conception; if D was conceived the day before A died, the analysis for B, C, and D as the validating lives would not change).

Because the conveyance to the children violates the RAP, we strike that provision ("remainder to A's children who attain the age of 30"). The conveyance now is simply "to A for life," which leaves A with a life estate and O with a reversion in fee simple absolute.

c. Elements of the Rule. [§ 6–120]

(1) No Interest Is Good. [§ 6–121]

Any interest which violates the RAP is void. The RAP traditionally applied principally to contingent remainders, executory interests, and vested remainders subject to open (the problem of class gifts). Today, it may also apply to contingent personal property interests and to equitable contingent interests (i.e., trusts), as well as to legal interests. The whole grant, however, is not necessarily void. Other interests created by the same instrument which do not themselves violate the RAP are valid.

(a) Example. [§ 6–122] O devises "to A for life, remainder to A's children who attain the age of 22." A has a valid life estate and O has a reversion which will become possessory at A's death. Assuming the abolition of the destructibility of contingent remainders, the remainder to A's children violates the RAP and is therefore void.

(2) Must Vest, If at All. [§ 6–123]

A future interest subject to the RAP is void unless it is absolutely certain to vest or fail within the perpetuities period. The fact that an interest may vest within the necessary period is wholly irrelevant. If at the time the interest is created there is any possible way in which the interest will not vest, or be destroyed within the perpetuities period, the interest is void.

(a) Certainty of Vesting Present at Date of Creation of Interest. [§ 6–124]

This absolute certainty of vesting must be present from the date on which the interest is created. It is not a rule satisfied by proof that the contingencies have, in fact, occurred within the necessary period. The RAP, unless it has been changed by statute, looks to possibilities at the time of creation, not subsequent actualities, and any interest which violates the RAP is void from the date of its creation (i.e., it is never valid).

(b) Contingency Must Be Resolved During the Period. [§ 6–125]

Note that the RAP does not say that the contingent interest must vest within the period. If the RAP so stated, virtually any contingent interest would be void, for there is always the possibility that the contingency will not occur. The RAP states that the interest must vest, if at all, within the period. The RAP, then, simply demands that the contingency must be resolved, one way or another, during the period.

(i) Example. [§ 6–126] O conveys "to A for life, then to the first of A's children to attain the age of 22." At common law, A received a life estate, O retained a reversion, and the contingent remainder to A's child was valid. Why? The destructibility of contingent remainders applies to literally "save" the contingent remainder. Remember, a contingent remainder is destroyed if there is not an ascertained, ready-to-take individual at the termination of the preceding estate. Using A as the validating life the interest is valid under the RAP because at A's death only two events can occur: either A has a child who has attained 22 and therefore will immediately take possession, or A does not have any children who have attained 22 in which event the contingent remainder is destroyed (the interest fails) and O's reversion becomes possessory. Note that with an "indestructible" contingent remainder (one that will turn into an executory interest if it is still contingent when the preceding estate terminates) the interest would be void upon creation. (A could have a child after the conveyance, and then A and all other lives in being could die while that child was six months old). You must be careful on examinations to know whether you are to assume (or discuss) the applicability of the Doctrine of Destructibility because all but a few jurisdictions have abolished this destructibility concept. If a question states "At common law . . .", you should assume contingent remainders are destructible when performing a RAP analysis. Try to clarify this matter with your professor prior to the examination.

(c) Contingent Interest Need Not Become Possessory Within the Period. [§ 6–127]

The RAP is satisfied if the contingency is resolved within the period (i.e., if there is a vesting in "interest" within the period); the interest need not become possessory within the period.

(i) Example. [§ 6–128] O conveys "to A for life, then to A's oldest living child at A's death for life, then to B's children who attain the age of 22." Assume the abolition of the destructibility of contingent remainders, that A has no children at the time of the conveyance, that B is dead at the time of the conveyance, and that B has one child, C, age five months. Under this conveyance: Step 1: A receives a life estate, A's oldest living child at her death receives a contingent remainder for life (express, unmet, condition precedent), and C has a valid contingent remainder in fee simple (express, unmet, condition precedent) which we know can only vest in C because B is dead and therefore cannot have more children. Step 2: A's oldest living child at A's death and C are the contingent interest holders subject to the RAP. Step 3: The possible validating lives are A, C, and O. Step 4: Assume that A has a child, D. Step 5: For purposes of testing the RAP, kill off A,C, and O. Step 6: Must the interest in D vest or fail within the RAP? The answer is yes. A is the validating life. At the moment of A's death if A is survived by D, then D immediately takes the present life estate and the interest is deemed vested. If A is not survived by children, the interest fails for all time in A's children at A's death. Both of these events will occur well within the perpetuities period.

Must the interest in C vest or fail within the RAP? The answer is yes. C is his own validating life. If C lives to reach 22, the interest will vest in C as either a vested remainder in fee simple absolute if A and/or a child of A are then alive or as a fee simple absolute if neither A nor a child of A are alive when C reaches 22. If C dies before reaching 22, the interest will fail to vest for all time. Both of these events will occur well within the perpetuities period. C will either live to be 22 or die before reaching 22 and one of these two will occur well before 21 years after C's death.

Note that if D survives C and if C dies at age 22, C's heirs would still have a vested remainder in fee simple absolute which may not become possessory until well after 21 years after the death of all lives in being at the time of the conveyance. All that the RAP requires though is a vesting or a failure within the RAP period.

(ii) Must Vest in an Existing, Ascertained Person. [§ 6–129]

To vest, the interest must become owned by an existing, ascertained person and not subject to an express, unmet, condition precedent. (e.g., O conveys "to A for life, remainder to B and his heirs if, and only if, B attains 21." B is now 18. He has a contingent remainder. If B now attains 21 while A is still living, B's interest vests, even though he will not get possession until A's death.)

(iii) Class Gifts. [§ 6–130]

There is a special problem in connection with class gifts. The interest may be held by an ascertained person, subject to no further express, unmet, condition precedent and still be void because the RAP requires that the exact interest of all class members must be determined before the interest of any is held to satisfy the RAP.

(iii–a) Example. [§ 6–131] General Class Gift. O devises "to A for life, remainder to A's children who attain the age of 30." At the time of the devise (O's death), A is alive and has two children (B and C), both over 30. Step 1: A has a life estate; B and C have a vested remainder subject to open in fee simple absolute; there is an executory interest in any child of A who is after born as this child will become a part of the class and will dilute the

interests of B and C. Step 2: The vested remainder subject to open in fee simple absolute must be tested against the RAP and the executory interest. Step 3: The possible validating lives are A, B, and C (O is dead and can't be a possible validating life). Step 4: Assume A has an afterborn child D. Step 5: For purposes of testing the RAP, kill off A, B, and C. Step 6: Must D either turn 30 (vesting) or die before turning 30 (failure to vest), not more than 21 years after A, B, and C have all died? The answer is no. Imagine that A, B, and C all die when D is one year old. If D lives to be 30, the interest will vest 29 years after their deaths which would be outside of the RAP period. Assume A, B, and C all die when D is one year old and D only lives to be 29 years old. The interest in D would fail to vest upon D's death before reaching 30 but it would fail 28 years after the deaths of A, B, and C which would be outside of the RAP period.

At common law, the entire gift to A's children is void, even though the interest of the two existing children is no longer subject to a condition precedent. The reason given for this rather peculiar result is that the class gift is thought of as a single unit and the RAP must be satisfied for each member of the class in order for the conveyance to satisfy the RAP. Because D's interest might not vest or fail within the perpetuities period, the entire unit is invalid. The share of each child thus cannot be determined until the number of takers is established. The class gift, then, is entirely void.

(iii–b) **Example. [§ 6–132] Specific Gift to Each Member.** If, in Example 1 preceding, the gift was $1,000 "to each of A's children who attain the age of 30," the gift would be good as to each child in being when the gift was made as the exact sum to be received by each was immediately determinable and was not dependent on the number of members in the class (note that each child's interest would be valid under the RAP when measured with themselves as the validating life). Under the common law RAP, any children born after the effective date of the gift would be out of luck (they could not be their own validating lives).

Today, under the Rule of Convenience contained in many statutory revisions of the RAP, the class would close at the death of O. This is the dilemma of the postponed per capita gift. Courts tend to construe language creating a postponed per capital gift to mean that the class closes at the death of the testator regardless of whether there is a member of the class in existence. The rationale is that, to do otherwise, would hold up distribution of O's entire estate because it would not be possible to know how much of O's estate to set aside for the class until A's death. So, in this case, the same result is reached under the common law and under the Rule of Convenience. The gift is good as to A's two children (B and C) who are alive at the time of O's death.

(iv) Distinction between Contingent and Vested Remainders May Be Crucial. [§ 6–133]

Because the RAP is predicated upon vesting of interests, the distinction between contingent remainders and vested remainders subject to complete divestment may be crucial in a given case.

(iv–a) Example. [§ 6–134] Condition Precedent (Contingent Remainder). O devises "to A for life, remainder to B's children who attain 25." B is presently living, and has two children under age 25. The contingent remainder in B's children is void; there is a possibility that vesting in interest will occur beyond the perpetuities period. How? As a review, if B's children die tomorrow, B has another child, and then when this child is one year old B dies, the interest in this last child will not vest for 24 years after B's death; thus the grant is void. Clearly any person other than B used as the possible validating life could also die when the child was 1; since the RAP deals in possibilities this "could" standard is all that is required to show the grant violates the RAP. (We are assuming the

abolition of the destructibility of contingent remainders rule.)

(iv–b) Example. [§ 6–135] Condition Subsequent (Vested Remainder). O devises "to A for life, remainder to B's children, but if any child of B fails to attain 25, his share shall pass to the survivors." B is living and has two children under 25. Step 1: A has a life estate, B's living children have a vested remainder subject to open and subject to complete divestment; O's heirs have shifting executory interests. Step 2: The contingent interests are the vested remainder subject to open in B's children and the executory interest in O's heirs. Step 3: The possible validating lives are A, B, and B's living children. Step 4: Assume B has an afterborn child, E. Step 5: For purposes of testing the RAP, kill off A, B, and B's living children. Step 6: Test the RAP against the vested remainder subject to open and against the executory interest. Could the interest in E vest or fail to vest outside of RAP? The answer is yes. A, B, and B's children who were alive at the time of the grant could die while E is 1 year old. If E lived to be 25 years old, this vesting would occur 24 years after the death of A, B, and B's other children which violates the RAP. If E only lived to be 24 and died, this failure to vest would also occur too remotely for purposes of the RAP. The executory interest in O's heirs also violates the RAP. If, as demonstrated above, the interest could vest or fail remotely in E, then the interest in O's heirs would also fail, or vest remotely.

The portion of the devise that violates the RAP must be stricken. So, the revised devise is: O devises "to A for life, remainder to B's children." A has a life estate and the children have a vested remainder in fee simple absolute. The divesting condition and executory interest are void, so the interest of the children is absolutely vested and no right of survivorship exists.

(3) At the Creation of the Interest. [§ 6–136]

If the interest is created by will, the moment of creation, for the purposes of the RAP, is at the testator's death. If the interest is created by deed, the interest is generally deemed to be created when the deed becomes effective; however, a fully revocable inter vivos transfer is not deemed to create any interest, for the purposes of the RAP, until the transfer has become irrevocable (i.e., normally at the death of the transferor).

(4) Within 21 Years After Some Life in Being. [§ 6–137]

(a) The 21 Year Period May Be in Gross. [§ 6–138]

If it is absolutely certain that an interest must vest, if at all, within 21 years after its creation, the interest is valid without considering "lives in being" (i.e., "in gross"). For example, O devises "to A for life, remainder to O's grandchildren living 21 years after O's death." Even if A predeceases O, the remainder interest is valid for the contingency will be resolved within 21 years after the date on which the interest was created; here, O's death.

(b) The 21 Year Period May Not Precede Validating Lives. [§ 6–139]

Validating lives must be "in being" when the interest is created; it is not sufficient that they are in being 21 years after the interest is created.

(c) Identifying Relevant Validating Lives. [§ 6–140]

(i) Transferor May Identify Validating Lives. [§ 6–141]

The transferor may in effect identify the validating life or lives himself.

(i–a) Example. [§ 6–142] Specifically Named Person. O devises "to those of my descendants living at the death of Barack Obama, now President of the United States." The interest is good, for it must vest if at all at the death of an identified life in being.

(i–b) Example. [§ 6–143] Easily Ascertainable Person. O devises "to those of my descendants living at the death of the last surviving member of the United States Supreme Court, as constituted at my death." This gift is valid. Any reasonable number of lives in being may be used.

(ii) Any Relevant Validating Life May Be Used. [§ 6–144]

Absent any identification of a validating life by the transferor, the law permits the use of any life in being as a validating life. However, unless the life used is in some way connected with the grantor, it is not tied to the vesting of the interest and it will not be useful.

(ii–a) Example. **[§ 6–145]** O devises "to my grandchildren who attain the age of 21." This interest is valid. The validating lives, though not mentioned, would logically be O's children. Since the interest is created at O's death, all of his children are lives in being. The interest of each grandchild must vest, therefore, no later than 21 years after a life in being.

(ii–b) Example. **[§ 6–146]** O conveys inter vivos "to my grandchildren who attain the age of 21." This interest is void. O is still living, the interest might vest in the child of a child of O not yet born, and therefore not in being. Be wary of the different effects on this grant of a will (where it is known that O is dead) and a conveyance (where he is not).

(ii–c) Example. **[§ 6–147]** O devises "to my grandchildren who attain the age of 25." This gift is void. Even though the children of O are lives in being, vesting in interest need not occur, if at all, within 21 years after the death of the last surviving child. (O's last surviving child might die the day after O leaving a one-year-old son.) While we might try to use any validating life to sustain this gift, no life will work. (Try using the life X, a newborn infant selected at random. Might he not die tomorrow?)

(iii) "Life in Being" Can Include a Period of Gestation. [§ 6–148]

A "life in being" can be the life of a person in gestation at the time of the creation of the interest subject to the RAP.

d. The Effect of Voiding a Gift under the "RAP." [§ 6–149]

(1) Language Stricken. [§ 6–150]

If a portion of a grant or devise is void under the RAP, that language is stricken, but the remaining interests are valid. If a divesting condition is voided under the RAP, the preceding interest may be made absolute.

(a) Example. [§ 6–151] O devises "to A for life, remainder to A's children who attain the age of 30." A's life estate is good; O has a reversion which will become possessory at A's death. The remainder to A's children is void.

(b) Example. [§ 6–152] **Fee Simple Subject to an Executory Interest (or Executory Limitation).** O conveys "to A and his heirs, but if liquor is sold on the property, to B and his heirs." The executory interest in B is void under the RAP (liquor may be sold on the property 200 years later—beyond the RAP period). Striking the divesting language, A will probably be recognized as having a fee simple absolute.

(2) Language of Special Limitation. [§ 6–153]

If the grant uses language of special limitation (i.e., typically the language creating a fee simple determinable), the estate preceding the void interest will remain defeasible.

(a) Example. [§ 6–154] O conveys "to A and his heirs so long as no liquor is sold on the premises; but if liquor is sold, then to B and his heirs." The executory interest is void, but the interest of A will probably still be considered defeasible so that A will have a fee simple determinable; O has a possibility of reverter.

e. Interests Not Subject to the RAP. [§ 6–155]

The RAP is designed to discourage the creation of contingent future interests and the uncertainties they create in regard to transfer of the entire ownership interest in the property. Consequently, the RAP does not apply to vested future interests.

(1) Reversions and Other Reversionary Interests. [§ 6–156]

Future interests in the grantor—reversions, rights of entry, and possibilities of reverter—are not subject to the RAP.

(2) Vested Remainders. [§ 6–157]

The RAP does not apply to vested remainders. It applies primarily to contingent remainders and executory interests. Vested remainders subject to partial divestment (class gifts) are a special case and the RAP does apply to them.

(3) Charitable Gifts Are Generally Subject to the RAP. [§ 6–158]

The RAP does apply to transfers to charities. However, the RAP is "bent" to provide special treatment for charitable gifts in a few circumstances.

(a) Shift to a Charity. [§ 6–159]

If a shift from a private purpose to a charitable purpose might occur beyond the period, the charitable interest is void.

(b) Shifts Between Charities. [§ 6–160]

The RAP does not apply, in many jurisdictions however, to shifts between charities.

Example. [§ 6–161] A gift "to charity X, but if the property ceases to be used for specified charitable purposes to charity Y," is valid, even though the shift may occur beyond the perpetuities period.

f. Application of the RAP in Special Circumstances. [§ 6–162]

(1) Class Gifts. [§ 6–163] (See also § 6–130)

(a) General Rule. [§ 6–164]

The basic common law rule is that if it is possible that the interest of any member of the class might vest beyond the perpetuities period, the entire class gift is invalid. Also, you should be aware that many states have made significant statutory changes to the RAP. The material which follows, except when indicated to the contrary, discusses the RAP as it existed at common law. Be sure you know what statutory changes, if any, you are responsible for on the exam.

(b) Exception: Gift of a Specific Sum. [§ 6–165]

Where there is a gift of a specific sum to each member of the class, so that the share of each is not dependent on a determination of total membership, then the gifts to some members of the class may be void while the gifts to others may be valid.

(2) Purchase Options. [§ 6–166]

An option in gross (an option to buy granted to one having no other interest in the property) is void if it can be exercised beyond the perpetuities period. On the other hand, options to purchase lands leased by the party holding the option or options to renew leases are valid so long as they must be exercised during the term of the lease, even though this may be beyond the perpetuities period.

(3) Trusts. [§ 6–167]

The RAP has no direct application to a trust in which all interests are vested. It is agreed that charitable trusts can be of unlimited duration.

By analogy to the RAP, however, it is sometimes said that a private trust cannot be made indestructible for longer than the perpetuities period.

5. Special Common Law Rule Against Perpetuities Examples. [§ 6–168]

a. The Fertile Octogenarian. [§ 6–169]

O conveys Blackacre "to A, my wife, for life, then to A's grandchildren." A is 80 years old and has two children, ages 56 and 58, and four young grandchildren. The interest to A's grandchildren is invalid under the RAP. Why? The law treats everyone the same for the purpose of having more children (age and infertility are irrelevant); therefore, A, age 80, could have another child after the conveyance. This child could later produce issue well after the expiration of the perpetuities period. (See Case Squib: *Jee v. Audley.*) Note that if the law treated A as if she could have no more children, the conveyance to the grandchildren would be valid with A's two living children as the validating lives.

b. The Slothful Executor. [§ 6–170]

O conveys "to A for life, then to B and C if then living, if either does not survive A, then his share shall pass to the administrator or executor of his estate to be distributed in accordance therewith." B and C have a valid contingent remainder. However, the apparent alternative contingent remainder to their estates is invalid, and if either does not survive A his interest will go to O because O retained a reversion. Even though normally an administrator or executor of an estate is appointed soon after an individual's death and the estate is closed within several years, there is no guarantee that an administrator or executor will be appointed within 21 years of the person's death. Thus, the possibility exists that the administrator or executor is not a life in being at the time of the conveyance, and will not be ascertainable for more than 21 years after the death of any life in being.

c. The Unborn Widow. [§ 6–171]

O conveys "to A for life, then to A's widow for life, then to the then living children of A and his widow." A's widow has a valid contingent remainder for life (the "widow" of A is not ascertainable until A's death but with A as the validating life it does not violate the RAP), but the children's interest violates the RAP. There is the possibility that A's widow is not a life in being at the time of the conveyance, that A and his widow could have a child after the conveyance, and the interest to this child would not vest or fail until after the termination of the perpetuities period. Note that if the conveyance specifically identified A's current wife as the "widow," the interest to the surviving children would be valid because then the widow could be used as the validating life.

F. POWERS OF APPOINTMENT. [§ 6–172]

In addition to the six future interests already discussed, a grantor may modify the future estate he grants by creating a power of appointment. CAVEAT: It is less and less frequent that powers of appointment are covered in first year property courses. Before spending review time on this topic make sure you are going to be held responsible for it.

1. Authorization to One Not the Owner to Determine Transferees. [§ 6–173]

A power of appointment is an authorization given by a property owner (called the donor) to another (called the donee) to determine the transferees of the property (called the appointees) and the shares which they take (e.g., O conveys "to A for life, then to such persons as B shall select," B has a general power of appointment).

a. Power Not an Estate in the Donee. [§ 6–174]

A power is not regarded, for most purposes, as an estate in the donee; his status is more like that of an agent for the donor. Upon exercise of the power, the property is said to pass directly from the donor to the appointee.

b. Powers Are Usually Created in Wills. [§ 6–175]

Powers are usually created in wills in cases where the donor does not know what the best disposition of his property may be. Thus, a woman with three young children might give her husband a life estate, with a special power to appoint thereafter among their children, recognizing that he may better be able to determine, at a later time, which child is in greatest need. Powers may also be created by inter vivos conveyance.

2. Types of Power. [§ 6–176]

a. General Power. [§ 6–177]

A power which contains no restrictions on possible appointees is a general power. Where such power is given, the donee may select any appointee, including himself, his estate, or his creditors. Where the general power is presently exercisable (i.e., there are no unfulfilled conditions precedent) the power closely resembles absolute ownership (the fee simple absolute).

b. Special Power. [§ 6–178]

A special power is a power which can be exercised in favor of one or more specifically identifiable persons other than the donee, his estate or creditors. Typically, a special power restricts appointment to a designated class of appointees (e.g., "the power to appoint among my children"). The members of the class, however, must be reasonably identifiable.

(1) Exclusive versus Non–Exclusive Special Powers. [§ 6–179]

A special power may be "exclusive," so that the donee may choose among the class, excluding some altogether if she desires (e.g., "to such of my children and in such shares as A shall appoint"). A special power may be "non-exclusive" in which case the donee must give some share to each. Generally, a special power is presumed exclusive unless a contrary intent clearly appears.

(2) May Create Power of Appointment in Appointee. [§ 6–180]

A special power may be exercised by creation of a new general or special power of appointment in a qualified appointee.

c. Presently Exercisable and Postponed Powers. [§ 6–181]

A presently exercisable power may be exercised by the donee during his lifetime or by his written will at any time after its creation and does not include a postponed power. A postponed power may be exercised by the donee only after the expiration of a stated time or after the occurrence or non-occurrence of a specified event.

d. Testamentary Power. [§ 6–182]

The donor may specify that the donee may exercise the power only by his will (this is called a testamentary power). In such cases, an attempted inter vivos transfer is not valid.

e. Imperative versus Discretionary. [§ 6–183]

A power of appointment is imperative (sometimes called powers in trust) when the terms of its creation impose on the donee a duty to exercise it under some circumstances and within some period of time. No general power can be a power in trust. A power of appointment which is not imperative is discretionary.

3. Exercise and Non–Exercise of Powers of Appointment. [§ 6–184]

Statutory regulation of powers, particularly as to releases, are fairly common; but the common law prevails in most jurisdictions as to most problems concerning powers.

a. Proper Manner of Exercise. [§ 6–185]

A power can be exercised only by a written instrument complying with the requirements of the instrument creating the power. Thus, a power exercisable by deed only must be exercised by deed; one exercisable by will only must be exercised by will.

(1) Exercising the Power. [§ 6–186]

A power of appointment is exercised where: (a) there is some reference in the exercising instrument to the power; or (b) there is reference to the property which is subject to the power; or (c) the provisions in the instrument executed by the donee would otherwise be ineffectual or a nullity.

(2) Formalities. [§ 6–187]

Normally, the power must be exercised pursuant to the legal formalities. The donor may, however, require more formalities than are required by law for the execution of a particular instrument, but it is unlikely that a court would sanction the use of lesser formalities than those required by law.

(3) Residuary Clause in Donee's Will Does Not Exercise Power. [§ 6–188]

By the weight of authority, unless there is a statute to the contrary, a residuary or similar clause in the donee's will is presumed not to exercise powers.

(4) Testamentary Power. [§ 6–189]

The donor may specify that the power may only be exercised by will (this is called a testamentary power). In such cases, an attempted inter vivos transfer is not valid.

b. Failure to Exercise Power. [§ 6–190]

(1) Failure to Exercise General Power. [§ 6–191]

If a general power is not exercised, is defectively exercised, or is properly released, the property subject to the power goes as follows:

(a) To Designated Takers in Default. [§ 6–192]

Where takers in default are named by the donor, the interest goes to such takers (e.g., "to such persons as A shall appoint, and in default of such appointment, to B and his heirs"). Takers in default are those who take in the event the power of appointment is not exercised.

(b) To Donor. [§ 6–193]

In the absence of a gift in default, the property generally belongs to the donor of the power (or his estate). However, under some circumstances where the donee has clearly attempted to exercise the power in the donee's will, but his appointment was invalid (i.e., it violated the Rule Against Perpetuities), the property goes to the donee's estate.

(2) Failure to Exercise a Special Power. [§ 6–194]

If the donee of a special power fails to exercise the power, exercises it defectively, or releases it, the appointive assets go as follows:

(a) To Designated Takers in Default. [§ 6–195]

To takers in default if such are named by the grantor.

(b) Equal Shares to Living Members of Class. [§ 6–196]

In the absence of such a gift in default of the power, the appointive assets go in equal shares to living members of the designated class, unless the instrument creating the power indicates that the property shall not go to the appointive donees if the power is not exercised. In the latter case, the property remains in the grantor or his estate.

4. Subject to the Rule Against Perpetuities. [§ 6–197]

Powers of appointment are subject to the RAP.

a. Validity of the Power. [§ 6–198]

(1) General Power Must Be Exercisable Within the RAP. [§ 6–199]

A general power that is presently exercisable (meaning a power to appoint by deed or will) is valid if it is certain that the donee can exercise the power, if at all, within a life in being plus 21 years from the date of its exercise. The rationale is that such a power is equivalent to ownership and once exercisable, alienation is no longer restrained. Thus, the donee must acquire the power within the perpetuities period.

(2) Special Power Is Void if Capable of Being Exercised Beyond RAP Period. [§ 6–200]

A special power, or general testamentary power, is void if it is capable of being exercised beyond RAP period. The mere fact that such a power can be exercised within the RAP period is not sufficient if it is possible that it might be exercised beyond the period. If the power is special, the moment of the creation of the power is the beginning point for measuring the period of time for purposes of the RAP (as opposed to measuring from the time of its exercise which is the case for general powers).

b.   **Validity of the Appointment: Contingent Interests. [§ 6–201]**

Not only must the power itself be valid, but the validity of the contingent interests created by exercise of the power must similarly satisfy the RAP.

(1)   **Interest Made Pursuant to a Presently Exercisable General Power. [§ 6–202]**

When an appointment is made pursuant to a presently exercisable general power, the validity of the appointed interest is determined by reference to a perpetuities period beginning with the exercise of the power.

(2)   **Interest Made Pursuant to a Special Power. [§ 6–203]**

When an appointment is made by the donee of a special power, or of a general testamentary power, the perpetuities period is computed from the date the power was created in the donee by the donor.

(a)   **Facts Existing at Time of Appointment Will Be Considered. [§ 6–204]**

In determining the validity of the appointed interest, facts existing at the time the power was exercised will be taken into account.

(i)   **Example. [§ 6–205]** O devises "to A for life, remainder to such issue of A as A shall appoint." A appoints the remainder to his son B for life, remainder to B's children. Suppose that B was born after O's death. The remainder to B's children is then void since A's issue (the requisite validating lives) were not necessarily lives in being at the time of the creation of the power. However, if at the time A made the appointment we know that B had been born before O's death, the remainder appointed to B's children is valid since B is an appropriate validating life under the RAP.

5.   **Scope of Power in the Donee. [§ 6–206]**

a.   **Cannot Assign or Delegate Power. [§ 6–207]**

As a general rule, the power of appointment is personal to the donee; he cannot assign or delegate it. However, a donee can frequently exercise the power by creating new powers. General powers of appointment that are unrestricted as to the mode of their execution and as to the beneficiaries are an exception to the general prohibition on assignment and delegation. The power of the donee is deemed equivalent to fee simple absolute ownership. Thus, in this situation, the donee may delegate the execution of the power.

b.   Contracts to Appoint. [§ 6–208]

(1)   Presently Exercisable General Power. [§ 6–209]

The donee of a presently exercisable power can contract to make an appointment as long as neither the promised appointment nor the contract confer a benefit upon a person who is not an object of the power of appointment. The rationale is that such a contract by such a donee of a power of appointment, presently exercisable, to make a future appointment that the donee could make immediately does not create the potential of accomplishing purposes indirectly that the donee could not accomplish directly.

(2)   General Power Not Presently Exercisable. [§ 6–210]

The donee of a power not presently exercisable (i.e., testamentary powers (powers which can be exercised only by will) or powers that can only be exercised at a specified future time) cannot contract to make an appointment because the contract, if enforceable, would be like an inter vivos exercise. If the donee of a power enters into a contract even though he may not lawfully do so, the promisee cannot enforce the contract at law, through a damages award, or in equity, through specific performance. The promisee can obtain restitution of the value that the promisee gave to the donee.

(3)   Contracts to Exercise Special Powers Are Invalid. [§ 6–211]

Contracts to exercise special testamentary powers are void, as is the case for general testamentary powers; such a contract would be like an inter vivos exercise. If the special power is presently exercisable, the contract to appoint may be valid as long as the appointment does not benefit a non-object of the power. Usually, the donee in these situations derives some benefit from the use of his power; such appointments are generally held to be void.

c.   Donee May Release Powers. [§ 6–212]

Any power (other than a power in trust) can be released or given up by the donee of the power; the release may be of all or only a part of the assets.

Many statutes provide, and courts have held, that the donee of any general power can release his power at any time. Some statutes forbid release though if the donor of a general power provides that the donee cannot release. As for special powers, there are some state statutes that allow for the donee to release though there is not much case law on the matter. Again, if the donor prohibits the donee from releasing the special power, the constraint will be effective under some state statutes. Furthermore, a donee may generally reduce or limit the persons or classes in whose favor the power can be exercised by release. Such partial releases are not uncommon.

(1) **Contract Between Donee and Affected Party. [§ 6–213]**

A contract between the donee and someone who would be affected by the appointment (e.g., a taker in default or the heirs of the donor) not to exercise the power will effectuate a release.

(2) **Effect of Release. [§ 6–214]**

Some things can be accomplished by a release which otherwise could not be done.

(a) **Example: Testamentary Limitation Avoided. [§ 6–215]** The donee of a testamentary power cannot appoint by deed but he can release the power during his lifetime and thus effectively determine, inter vivos, the disposition of the property. Though it seems inconsistent to permit a donee of a testamentary power to release the power but to prohibit the donee from contracting as to the exercise of the power, this is the direction the law has followed.

(b) **Example: Class Limitation Avoided. [§ 6–216]** The donee of a special power cannot appoint outside the class of permissible objects, but if there is a taker in default who is not within the class of objects, the donee can release the power and in effect direct the disposition of the property to the taker in default. In such instances, the interests of the takers in default are no longer subject to being defeated by the exercise of the power of appointment.

6. **Ramifications of the Exercise of the Power of Appointment. [§ 6–217]**

Normally, the exercise of a power by the donee is said to transfer title from the donor to the appointee; thus, it is often said that the donee really has no interest in the property at all. This statement is relatively accurate if the donee holds a special power, but if the donee holds a general power (which can be exercised in his own favor), some qualification is necessary in regard to taxes and claims by creditors. For instance, donees of general powers of appointment are treated as owners of the property subject to the power of appointment under the federal tax laws.

Absent a statutory provision, a donee's creditors typically cannot reach an unexercised power of appointment. Courts have held that the power of appointment is not property; the exercise of the power is personal to the donee. While the creditors of the donee of a special power cannot reach the appointive assets, the holder of a general power may be treated, to a limited extent, as owner of the appointive assets, and thus subject to claims of his creditors. If the donee exercises a general power by will in favor of a creditor or volunteer and dies insolvent, his creditors can reach appointed property to satisfy their claims. If the donee of a presently exercisable general power exercises his power inter vivos, his creditors can reach the appointed property if the appointment is fraudulent as to them. If the donee of a presently exercisable interest becomes bankrupt, the trustee in bankruptcy can reach property subject to the power.

FUTURE INTERESTS

REVIEW PROBLEM—ESTATES AND FUTURE INTERESTS

Nearly all Property (or Property I, if the course is split) exams include questions which combine estates-in-land and future interests issues. The questions normally involve three steps: (1) Identification of the estates created by an inter vivos or testamentary transfer, (2) Identification of the estates created according to whether they are present or future interests and identification of the future interests according to their type, and (3) Application of the relevant future interests' doctrines to the future interests.

> O owner of a fee simple absolute estate in Blackacre conveys it to A for life and then to B and her heirs if B attains the age of 21. At the time of the conveyance B is 19 years old. What estates and future interests are created?
>
> > **Answer:** The estate given to A is specified to be for life and is therefore a life estate. A's life estate is the present interest since no delay or precondition was established in regard to A's right to immediate possession. Since it is the present interest, all other interests are by definition, future interests. The interest given to B is a remainder, a future interest, in a fee simple absolute since O indicates an intent to give the entire interest to B after A's life estate and also because O used the words "and her heirs" which are the words of limitation describing a fee simple. Remainders are either vested or contingent. This remainder is contingent at the time of its creation since a condition precedent to its becoming possessory is indicated (i.e., B must attain the age of 21 and on the date of the conveyance B is only 19). Since a life estate plus a contingent remainder in fee does not "add up" to a fee simple absolute, O has retained a future interest by operation of law and that future interest is a reversion in fee simple absolute. Since B's interest is a contingent remainder you must apply the Rule Against Perpetuities to make sure it is not violated by the contingent remainder. The most remote date at which B's interest could vest (i.e., the contingent remainder become a vested remainder) is on her 21st birthday. That is within a life in being at the creation of the interest (B is the validating life) and therefore the RAP is not violated and the contingent remainder is valid.

CHAPTER VII

CONCURRENT ESTATES AND MULTIPLE OWNERSHIP

A. BASIC CONCURRENT ESTATES. [§ 7–1]

The fragmentation of ownership of interests in real property through creating successive interests (i.e., present interests followed by future interests) was discussed in the previous chapter. Our common law system not only allows more than one person to own an interest in the same piece of property on a successive (one follows the other) basis, but also allows more than one person to own the same interest or estate at the same time—concurrently.

> **Example.** [§ 7–2] 0, owner of a fee simple absolute in Blackacre, can transfer Blackacre to A and B for life, and the remainder in fee simple to C and D and their heirs. A and B are concurrent owners of a life estate and C and D are concurrent owns of a vested remainder in fee simple absolute.

At common law, concurrent ownership was confined to the three concurrent estates discussed below. There was also once a fourth, coparceny, the tenancy for daughters when a decedent left no male heirs. It no longer exists. In addition, some view partnership as a concurrent ownership concept but, even if it technically belongs on the list, it is a subject for business organization courses, and not property law. Recent statutory enactments in most jurisdictions have expanded the possible ways for two or more people to own an interest in the same piece of property. These new statutorily created concurrent ownership concepts, of which condominium, cooperative, and timeshare ownership are the best examples, are usually referred to as "multiple ownership arrangements" to distinguish them from the traditional common law concurrent estates.

There are three basic concurrent estates: (1) the joint tenancy; (2) the tenancy by the entirety; and (3) the tenancy in common. In each estate, holders have concurrent rights. The modern trend seems to be to recognize these concurrent ownership concepts in both personal and real property.

1. Joint Tenancy. [§ 7–3]

A joint tenancy can be created between two or more cotenants. The joint tenants own one interest together, each having the same rights in that interest as his fellow joint tenants. The right of survivorship is a basic characteristic of the joint tenancy and is, in a sense, simply a recognition of this basic unity.

a.   Right of Survivorship. [§ 7–4]

The right of survivorship is the best known and most important characteristic of the joint tenancy. On the death of one joint tenant, his interest "passes" to the remaining joint tenant or tenants, and does not pass to the deceased joint tenant's heirs or under his will. His wife can assert no dower interest. (See § 5–42)

Example. [§ 7–5] Suppose A, B, and C are joint tenants. A dies and his will leaves all his property to X. B and C now are joint tenants; their shares enlarged from one-third to one-half, X takes nothing. If B now dies, C becomes the sole owner of the fee simple absolute.

b.   Creation of Joint Tenancy at Common Law. [§ 7–6]

The common law required the presence of the four unities to create a joint tenancy.

(1)   Unity of Time. [§ 7–7]

The interests of joint tenants must have been created at the same time.

(2)   Unity of Title. [§ 7–8]

Interests had to be created by the same instrument. Because of the time and title requirements, a holder of an estate could not create a joint tenancy in herself and another without a conveyance to a "straw" (a third party who agreed to reconvey the property immediately after receiving it) and a reconveyance back to the original owner and her donee as joint tenants. For a case discussing whether it is now possible to create and/or destroy a joint tenancy unilaterally (without the use of a straw), see *Riddle v. Harmon*. (See Case Squib: *Riddle v. Harmon*.) Many states that allow unilateral creation and severance of a joint tenancy have done so by statutory modification. (§ 7–11)

(3)   Unity of Interest. [§ 7–9]

The shares taken by the joint tenants had to be equal under the common law. Today, the requirement of holding equal shares is increasingly ignored by courts in construing agreements, so that in a conveyance to A and B as joint tenants with right of survivorship, and not as tenants in common, if A provides one-fourth of the purchase price and B three-fourths (intending to split profits from the same in the proportion to their contributions), and if the other unities are met, most courts would construe the tenancy as a joint tenancy.

(4) Unity of Possession. [§ 7–10]

Each joint tenant's rights of enjoyment had to be the same.

c. Creation and Recognition of the Joint Tenancy Today. [§ 7–11]

Many states recognize the joint tenancy in both real and personal property if the intent to create a joint tenancy is clearly expressed, but the presumption today is in favor of a tenancy in common. Many states require by statute that survivorship be specified and that if it is not, a tenancy in common is created even if the word "joint" is used. In many states today, the only way to be sure that a joint tenancy will be recognized is to use the following language "to A and B as joint tenants with the right of survivorship and not as tenants in common."

At common law, this presumption ran the other way—any conveyance was presumed to create a joint tenancy, unless contrary intention was clearly expressed. The old common law policy reflected the English common law's displeasure with fragmentation of land into small parcels with multiple owners. In some jurisdictions today, an individual holding a fee simple can create a joint tenancy in himself and another without resorting to a straw and a reconveyance. Such direct conveyances are sometimes authorized by statute, and may also apply to estates by the entirety.

d. Conveyance. [§ 7–12]

The interest of each joint tenant can be freely alienated without the consent of the other joint tenants. However, the conveyance severs the joint tenancy with respect to the conveyed interest.

e. Severance of Joint Tenancy. [§ 7–13]

The consequence of a severance is the termination of the joint tenancy (and, of course, the right of survivorship), with respect to the severed interest. Thus, when a joint tenancy is severed, the grantee takes as a tenant in common. A severance can be accomplished in a number of ways including alienation, mortgage, contract of sale, and, in some jurisdictions, lease.

(1) General Examples of Severance of Joint Tenancy [§ 7–14]

When a joint tenancy is severed, the grantee takes as a tenant in common.

Example. [§ 7–15] A and B are joint tenants. A severs by selling her one-half interest to C. B and C are now tenants in common. A's death does not affect the estate. On C's death, with B surviving, C's heirs become tenants in common with B. If B predeceases C, B's heirs become tenants in common with C.

Example. [§ 7–16] A, B, and C are joint tenants. A severs by granting her one-third interest to D. D has a one-third interest as tenant in common with B and C who hold two-thirds interest as joint tenants. On D's death intestate, her heirs take her one-third interest. B and C have no right of survivorship with respect to D's interest, but remain joint tenants as to each other. Thus, if B dies, C has a two-thirds interest held as a tenant in common with D's heirs (who have a one-third interest).

(2) Severance by Alienation. [§ 7–17]

Alienation by one joint tenant of her interest severs the tenancy. (See Case Squib: *Riddle v. Harmon.*) This is true of involuntary and voluntary conveyances. Note that sale of the joint tenant's interest makes the purchaser a tenant in common.

(3) Severance by Mortgage. [§ 7–18]

In states following a title theory of mortgages, a mortgage by one joint tenant is generally held to sever the tenancy (this is true because "title mortgage" states treat a mortgage as an alienation of the land). In a lien theory jurisdiction, a mortgage by one joint tenant generally does not act as a severance; a mortgage simply imposes a lien on a defeasible interest. This is very significant difference, because the lien will terminate upon the death of the mortgagor when her interest in the joint tenancy terminates. In other words, the survivor who was not the mortgaging co-tenant will acquire the entire estate free of the mortgage, if the mortgagor dies first. (See Case Squib: *Harms v. Sprague.*)

What if, in a lien theory jurisdiction, the mortgagor survives and his non-mortgaging joint tenant dies first? Does the mortgage "expand," so that it now is a lien upon the entire estate, or does it only attach to the undivided one-half interest held by the mortgagor at the time the mortgage was put into place? Following the classical theory of joint tenancies, the surviving joint tenant owned the entire estate all along. Because in a lien theory jurisdiction, a mortgage does not destroy a joint tenancy, the mortgage stays with the mortgaging joint tenant and expands and contracts with the joint tenant's interest.

Thus, in a situation like this, when the mortgagor's estate "grows" at the death of the non-mortgaging joint tenant, the mortgage attaches to the mortgagor's entire interest, now the entire estate.

Now, assume one is in a title theory of mortgages jurisdiction, so that the mortgage destroys the joint tenancy. When the loan is paid off and the mortgage is released, is the joint tenancy restored? Technically, the release does not restore the four unities, though a court might hold that the mortgage only created a temporary suspension of the four unities, rather than a permanent destruction. Other courts might consider the intentions of the parties and use this as a basis for finding that the joint tenancy was restored upon release of the mortgage. The result will vary by court.

(4) Severance by Contract of Sale. [§ 7–19]

A sales contract by one joint tenant severs his interest. In most jurisdictions, a sales contract executed by all joint tenants does not sever the joint tenancy, and the right of survivorship survives the execution of the contract. Thus, if A and B hold Blackacre as joint tenants and execute a contract to sell to C, and if A then dies before the proceeds are received, B, under the majority view, is entitled to all of the proceeds (under the minority approach, the contract severs the joint tenancy, abolishing the right of survivorship, and A's heirs or devisees and B would each receive one-half of the proceeds).

(5) Severance by Lease. [§ 7–20]

There is a split of authority on whether a lease by a joint tenant severs the joint tenancy in the reversion. (See Case Squib: *Swartzbaugh v. Sampson.*)

2. Tenancy by the Entirety. [§ 7–21]

The tenancy by the entirety (also called tenancy by the entireties) is a marital estate which can exist only between husband and wife. It carries a right of survivorship, like the joint tenancy, but unlike the joint tenancy, the right of survivorship cannot be destroyed unilaterally. Only a joint conveyance by the husband and wife can destroy the tenancy by the entirety. Caveat: Many states have abolished this form of concurrent ownership as part of their reform of marital property rights. (See Case Squib: *Sawada v. Endo.*)

a. Status Today. [§ 7–22]

Today, the tenancy by the entirety in both real and personal property is recognized in many, but not all, states.

b.   Creation of Tenancy by the Entirety. [§ 7–23]

At common law, the four unities required for a joint tenancy were required for an estate by the entirety. Today, in some jurisdictions, a husband (or wife) can create the estate by direct conveyance to himself and his spouse, without a straw man.

(1)   Valid Marriage Necessary. [§ 7–24]

The estate can be created only in a validly married husband and wife. An attempt to create the estate in persons other than husband and wife will usually result in a tenancy in common. (See Case Squib: *Beal v. Beal.*)

(2)   Conveyance to Husband and Wife Presumed to Create Tenancy by the Entirety. [§ 7–25]

Theoretically, a husband and wife can hold as tenants in common or as joint tenants. However, in those states which recognize the tenancy by the entirety, unless a contrary intent appears, a conveyance to persons who are husband and wife will be presumed to create a tenancy by the entirety.

c.   No Separate Interest. [§ 7–26]

In most states recognizing an estate by the entirety, neither husband nor wife has a separate interest which can be conveyed or encumbered. Both, acting together, may convey or encumber, and creditors may proceed against the property only for their joint debts. Neither spouse can compel partition without the consent of the other spouse. If the husband and wife convey the property and take back a purchase money mortgage, or enter into a contract for sale, the right of survivorship inherent in the tenancy by the entirety attaches to the proceeds. Note that at common law, a husband had full possessory rights during the marriage and could lease and convey the estate, but if he predeceased his wife, the entire title and possessory rights vested in her at the moment of his death.

d.   Termination. [§ 7–27]

A tenancy by the entirety (and its right of survivorship) may be terminated only by: (a) conveyance of the estate by husband and wife, or execution by a creditor of both (See Case Squib: *Sawada v. Endo.*); (b) death of either spouse (leaving the survivor with the fee); (c) mutual agreement in the form of a conveyance by one spouse of his interest to the other (See Case Squib: *Knell v. Price.*); or (d) divorce (unless the divorce decree provides otherwise, the estate is converted to a tenancy in common).

3. Tenancy in Common. [§ 7–28]

A tenancy in common is a concurrent estate without any right of survivorship. Each tenant has a separate interest which can be alienated, devised, and will pass to his heirs if the co-tenant dies intestate, even though each has a right to possess the whole. There are no "unities of interest" as with the joint tenancy; tenants in common may hold unequal shares. The interest of each may be attached by his personal creditors. At common law, heirs taking by descent took as tenants in common, as they do today. In most states, a conveyance to two or more persons is presumed to create a tenancy in common, unless a contrary intent clearly appears.

B. RIGHTS AND DUTIES AMONG CO–TENANTS. [§ 7–29]

1. Partition. [§ 7–30]

A joint tenant or a tenant in common has a unilateral right to partition, which may be accomplished voluntarily (e.g., by exchange of deeds) or by court action. A tenant by the entirety does not have a unilateral right of partition. Partition means the property can be physically divided or the court may order that the property be sold and the proceeds divided. A partition action is an equitable action and the court has a wide range of devices for adjusting the equities of the co-tenants. Partition is thought to be the normal relief for co-tenants who can no longer agree.

2. Possession. [§ 7–31]

Each co-tenant has the right to possess the whole and no co-tenant has the right of exclusive possession as to any part. Exclusive possession by one co-tenant is not unlawful and is itself no grounds for an action by other co-tenants. But if one co-tenant: (1) denies another co-tenant a right to equal possession and enjoyment and refuses a request by the co-tenant to be admitted into common possession, or (2) purports to convey exclusive title to another under a claim of exclusive right in a manner that gives notice to his co-tenant then, there has been an "ouster". Once ousted, the tenant out of possession can maintain a possessory action in ejectment which will restore to the ousted co-tenant his right to possession in common with the ousting co-tenant. Recovery of mesne profits (the reasonable value of the use and occupation of the property) is incidental to the judgment in ejectment. Thus, no co-tenant has the right to unreasonably interfere with the right of another co-tenant to possess the whole. Before a co-tenant in possession can adversely possess her co-tenants, the co-tenant in possession must oust the other co-tenants. Without ouster, the co-tenant in possession is holding in a manner that is not hostile to the interests of her co-tenants as each co-tenant has a right of possession in the entire estate.

3. Accountability and Contribution. [§ 7–32]

Our common law courts have had great difficulty formulating rules in regard to the rents and profits received by, or expenses incurred by, one tenant and whether or not co-tenants can share in those profits or must pay their share of expenses. Originally, the law seemed to have been that there was no accountability, unless the tenants receiving rents and profits had ousted the other tenant(s). Contribution under any scenario seems to have been rare.

a. Rents and Profits From Third Parties. [§ 7–33]

In 1705 (Statute of 4 Anne c. 16), Parliament sought to change the law and establish a principle of accountability among tenants in common and joint tenants—even absent ouster—for rents and profits received from third parties by a co-tenant in excess of his share. The Statute does not require the co-tenant in possession to pay her co-tenants for the reasonable rental value of the property, only for the rents and profits actually received from third parties. The Statute is considered part of the common law in most states, but it receives a wide range of interpretations. Most jurisdictions interpret profit to mean "net" profit, but many jurisdictions depart from the traditional interpretation of the Statute and require accounting for imputed rental value of the property used by the possessing co-tenant. Even without the Statute, if profits are received from an activity which substantially reduces the value of the land (e.g., mining), most courts require the co-tenant in possession to account to his co-tenants.

b. Accounting for Co–Tenant's Own Use if There Is No Ouster. [§ 7–34]

A co-tenant in possession generally is not liable to his co-tenants for any profit he derives from the exclusive use and occupation of the property, as long as the co-tenant in possession has not ousted the other co-tenants. (See Case Squib: *Spiller v. Mackereth.*) The reason is that each co-tenant has an equal and several right to entry and to possession.

A co-tenant in exclusive possession may be liable to his co-tenants for the reasonable rental value of his use under certain circumstances such as: (a) where the co-tenant has agreed to pay the other co-tenants for the exclusive possession and use of the property (i.e., the co-tenant makes a lease with the other co-tenants); or (b) if the co-tenant in possession has a fiduciary obligation to make productive use of the property as a result of a trustee or guardian relationship. (§ 7–41)

c. Accounting if There Is Ouster. [§ 7–35]

An ousting co-tenant must account for the reasonable rental value of the property, as well as rents and profits actually received from third parties.

Example. [§ 7–36] A and B own Blackacre as joint tenants. A decides to fulfill her lifelong dream and study winter butterflies in northern Alaska for four years. During this period B leases a part of Blackacre to C for $1000 a year (purporting to have the sole right to convey the exclusive right of possession), mines the profitable Blackacre uranium mine and receives $25,000 per year, and farms Blackacre's north forty and makes $500 per year. If A returns from her frozen butterfly hunt and demands to be let into possession. B refuses and C, the lessee, refuses. If A demands an accounting of the profits of Blackacre, what can she hope to recover? First, has A been ousted? The answer is yes. (§ 7–31) The general rule prior to the Statute of Anne and after the Statute of Anne is that A, having been ousted, A is entitled to mesne profits. Thus: A would be entitled to recover from C one-half of the annual rent. If B made a bad deal with C and is renting for less than fair rental value, A can disaffirm the lease and sue C for one-half the fair rental value of the portion leased. B would have to account for the net amounts received from operating the uranium mine and B would have to account for the net profits from farming Blackacre.

If A wants to come into physical possession, A has a couple of options. A can seek a partition in kind of Blackacre. If possible, B would likely receive the portion of Blackacre leased to C. But, A may not want to destroy the joint tenancy with B. In this case, A can seek to recover possession in common with C of the leased part of Blackacre. After all, B only had the authority to lease his share of Blackacre and so the lease would only be valid as to B's share. (See Case Squib: *Swartzbaugh v. Sampson.*)

4. **Expenses. [§ 7–37]**

   a. **Improvements. [§ 7–38]**

   In the absence of a contract, the prevailing view seems to be that a co-tenant cannot require his other co-tenant to contribute a share of the costs of improvements which he has made, although in a partition action in the final settlement of accounts and in a suit for an accounting for rents and profits, the court may take such expenditures into account.

   b. **Contribution for Repairs. [§ 7–39]**

   If co-tenants cannot agree to share the cost of repairs and if the co-tenant in possession is the one making the repairs, courts will first inquire whether the co-tenant in possession has been compensated by the value of his enjoyment and possession. If the co-tenant is obligated to account for rents and profits to his co-tenants, he may deduct the cost of reasonable repairs. If neither of these options work, the final remedy is partition and in the final accounting, the co-tenant making repairs can receive a credit for his expenditures.

   c. **Recoupment for Taxes and of Interest and Principal Due Under Mortgages. [§ 7–40]**

   A co-tenant who pays more than his proportionate share of taxes (or principal or interest on a mortgage encumbering the property where his co-tenants have no personal obligation) is entitled to contribution from his co-tenants, which is enforceable by an in rem action, rather than by a personal affirmative action for contribution. Absent any personal obligation, none of the co-tenants owe any duty to the other for such payments. When one co-tenant pays (often to save the property from loss by foreclosure of a mortgage or tax lien), courts may force contribution by applying the equitable doctrine of subrogation when enforcing the mortgage against the land. Essentially, the co-tenant who pays more than his share can step into the shoes of the mortgagee/lender, foreclose the mortgage and seek to recover the amount of contribution to which he is entitled from the foreclosure sales proceeds. Also, enforcement can be had in the form of recoupment in a partition proceeding.

5. Fiduciary Relationship Between Co–Tenants. [§ 7–41]

In most cases, co-tenants are in a quasi-fiduciary relationship. Therefore, if one co-tenant acquires an outstanding title, mortgage, or lien which affects the interests of all, it is deemed to be an acquisition for all and all must be given an opportunity to share in the acquired interest by contributing their pro rata share of the cost within a reasonable amount of time. Not every co-tenancy gives rise to a fiduciary relationship. If one co-tenant has ousted another and is therefore claiming adversely or if the co-tenants are strangers except for the unity of possession, courts may find that no fiduciary obligations are owed.

C. MULTIPLE OWNERSHIP: COOPERATIVES AND CONDOMINIUMS. [§ 7–42]

Caveat: Many professors omit coverage of multiple ownership (condominiums and cooperatives) from the basic property course. Be certain you are responsible for these concepts before spending review time on them.

Techniques for the multiple ownership of buildings may be divided into two general categories, cooperatives and condominiums. In the cooperative, a single entity generally owns and finances the land and the building through a master mortgage, with the individual units being subjected to exclusive occupancy through a lease or easement arrangement. In the condominium, the units are separately owned and financed, with the ownership of each unit also containing as an appurtenance thereto an undivided interest in the underlying land and areas used in common by all the unit owners.

1. Cooperatives. [§ 7–43]

a. Types of Cooperative Ownership. [§ 7–44]

The most practical and common types of cooperative ownership are as follows:

(1) Co–Ownership. [§ 7–45]

Under this plan, the occupants collectively own the entire project as tenants in common. Each occupant acquires by agreement the right to occupy exclusively a designated apartment or unit. Theoretically, the co-owners could own in joint tenancy with exclusive rights to occupy designated apartments or units, but because of the survivorship characteristic and the requirement of the four unities, such type of ownership is not practical. In the tenancy in common scheme, covenants running with the land or equitable servitudes are employed to enforce each co-tenant's financial obligations in the maintenance and operation of the building.

(2) Massachusetts or Business Trust. [§ 7–46]

Under this plan of organization, title to all of the premises is vested in the trustees of a Massachusetts type business trust. Certificates of beneficial interest are issued to the individual owners or cooperators, and each beneficial owner is also assigned an exclusive right of occupancy in a particular unit under a proprietary lease or similar arrangement with the trust. The rights and obligations of the individual owners and beneficiaries of the trust are set forth in the declaration of trust, and limited liability of the cooperating beneficiaries is attained, as long as control of the enterprise is vested in the trustees.

(3) Corporate Ownership. [§ 7–47]

Corporate ownership is the most commonly used form of cooperative organization. In this type of organization, title to the entire premises is vested in a corporation, and the corporation then leases specific apartments or units to the tenant stockholders. This lease is usually a proprietary lease, the unique feature being that the lessee must own a specified number of shares of the lessor corporation both in order to acquire the lease and to continue as tenant. Ownership of shares as such confers no right of occupancy, such occupancy right being conferred by the lease which is obtainable only by owners of shares.

b. Restriction on Sale. [§ 7–48]

Because of a desire to create and maintain a closely knit community of compatible persons, restrictions on the sale of shares of stock are common, and the shares must always be sold in the original block (number) in order to maintain the relative position of each owner as a proportionate owner in the cooperative enterprise. The shares of stock and the lease must be transferred together; they cannot be transferred

113

separately. Other restrictions normally take the form of prohibitions against assignment and subletting without the corporation's approval and this approval generally can be withheld for any permissible reason no matter how minute.

c.   **Rent. [§ 7–49]**

The rent in a proprietary lease includes the following elements: (a) a fixed annual sum which may be nominal if the building and the apartment are free and clear of mortgages and similar encumbrances; (b) a further amount fixed annually based on the maintenance and operation costs of the building, mortgage payments and tax assessments; and (c) an additional sum which may be levied against the individual tenant if that tenant fails to maintain properly the interior of his apartment necessitating the corporation to perform work, and, when applicable, assessment to cover special expenses such as the construction of a new recreational facility.

d.   **Unitary Financing: Interdependence of Cooperators. [§ 7–50]**

In a cooperative enterprise, the entire project is owned by a single legal entity, and if financing is employed, the entire building is covered by the mortgage or mortgages. Similarly, taxes are assessed against the entire building. Thus, the success of the venture depends upon the continued solvency and cooperation of all the cooperators. If one or more defaults on one or more periodic payments, the others must satisfy mortgage and tax payments or run the risk of having the building sold to satisfy such obligations. This financial interdependence is a chief disadvantage of the cooperative, but also the characteristic which allows cooperative owners to selectively choose their co-owners.

2.   **Condominiums. [§ 7–51]**

a.   **Condominiums Generally. [§ 7–52]**

(1)   **Condominium as a Form of Ownership. [§ 7–53]**

As a system of ownership, "condominium" denotes a plan of organization whereby the separate units of a multi-unit building or improvement of real property are subject to ownership by different owners, and there is appurtenant to each unit an undivided share in the underlying ground and in the areas used in common, these latter interests generally referred to as the common elements.

(2)   **Building or Project. [§ 7–54]**

The term "condominium" as applied to a building or project, simply refers to the building or land which is subject to the condominium form of ownership.

114

(3) **Apartment or Unit.** [§ 7–55]

As applied to the individual apartment or unit, the term "condominium" simply means a unit or apartment which is subject to individual ownership, together with an undivided interest in co-tenancy in the common elements or those parts of the realty which are used in common and are owned collectively by all the unit owners in the project.

b. **Basis and Organization.** [§ 7–56]

(1) **Statutory Basis.** [§ 7–57]

Most condominium projects are organized pursuant to statutory authority since statutes authorizing such projects now exist in all states. The provisions of the statutes vary considerably but they all envision the separate ownership of parts of a building or project.

(2) **Leasehold.** [§ 7–58]

Unless the statute directly or indirectly provides otherwise, a condominium regime can be constructed on a long-term leasehold estate.

(3) **Creating Documents.** [§ 7–59]

Four basic documents are required to create a condominium form of ownership: (a) a declaration of condominium; (b) a set of by-laws for governing the association of owners and the operation of the building; (c) a deed for conveying the individual unit or apartment; and (d) articles of association or incorporation organizing the association of owners.

(a) **Declaration of Condominium.** [§ 7–60]

The declaration of condominium is recorded by the owner or owners of the land involved, and is the means by which the property is subjected to or brought under condominium use. The contents of the declaration are usually prescribed by the applicable statute, but such contents would usually include, and in most instances would seem necessarily to include, the following: (a) a legal description of all the land, a legal description of each unit, and a description of all the common elements, along with appropriate plats or drawings; (b) restrictions against partition; (c) sale and occupancy restrictions imposed as covenants designed to preserve a closely knit community of compatible individuals; (d) designation of the

115

shares of each unit or fractional interest in the common elements appurtenant to each unit; (e) provisions for liens on each unit to enforce payment of common expenses; (f) casualty loss and rebuilding provisions; easements for pipes, wires and similar essential services; (g) voting rights of owners; and (h) any methods of amending the declaration and by-laws. [Note that restrictions, however, cannot be imposed to discriminate on the basis of race, color, religion, sex, handicap, familial status or national origin, and care should be taken not to violate the rules pertaining to restraints on alienation.]

(b) Individual Deeds. [§ 7–61]

The deed to an individual unit or apartment must conform to local conveyancing statutes and must sufficiently designate the unit conveyed, the easiest method of which is to incorporate by reference the recorded plan or plat incorporated in the declaration of condominium. The deed frequently includes other matters also, such as covenants and use restrictions which are commonly incorporated by reference; the percentage of interest owned in the common elements, transfer restrictions; and similar items.

(c) Separate Financing. [§ 7–62]

After construction, financing is accomplished by separate mortgages on each unit and its accompanying co-ownership interest in the common elements; each unit is also taxed separately (thus condominiums are treated as separate units while cooperatives remain a single unit in the eyes of the law, and this cooperative "unit" is privately divided into multiple residences).

3. Timeshares. [§ 7–63]

A third type of multiple ownership is a timeshare. This concept is usually grafted on to condominium ownership and divides ownership into a number of fixed periods of time—for example the first week of December each year. Each timeshare owner has an exclusive right of possession for that period of time.

REVIEW PROBLEMS—CONCURRENT ESTATES

Multiple choice and essay questions concerning concurrent estates usually involve identification of those three estates and the meaningful differences among them.

Thus if O, owner of Blackacre, conveys it to A and B, the first problem is to identify which of the three possible concurrent estates is created.

Answer: Today there is a presumption in favor of tenancy in common even though at common law there was a presumption in favor of joint tenancy (tenancy by the entireties for married couples). Today, therefore, clear language must be found to indicate that the grantor intended the right of survivorship to apply to the interest given the co-owners before the courts will find a joint tenancy. In fact in some jurisdictions one must use "right of survivorship" in the conveyance in order to create a joint tenancy.

The next issue tested usually relates to destruction of the right of survivorship by actions of one of the co-tenants.

For example, if A and B are joint tenants and A conveys her interest to C, when A dies, does B take her share?

Answer: No. because her conveyance to C destroyed the joint tenancy and turned it into a tenancy in common.

CHAPTER VIII

LANDLORD AND TENANT LAW (NON–FREEHOLD ESTATES)

Even before coming to law school, nearly every law student is familiar with the law of landlord and tenant—or the law of leases, as it is also called. Most people today think primarily of the contract-type relationship which it establishes and may be surprised to encounter it as a topic in property law, but originally landlord and tenant arrangements were primarily a means of creating an ownership interest in real property, called a non-freehold estate, with relatively minor contract-type characteristics. In fact, the original purpose of non-freehold estates may have been to create security interests—somewhat equivalent to modern mortgages—rather than to provide housing. To fully understand the current dynamic state of this area of property law, it is necessary to examine its origins in estates in land concepts. Landlords and tenants are also known as lessors and lessees, and the terms may be used interchangeably in this chapter.

A. THE NON–FREEHOLD ESTATE CONCEPT. [§ 8–1]

1. Leasehold. [§ 8–2]

The leasehold is a possessory, non-freehold estate. The tenant has the exclusive right to possession. His estate is assignable (unless the lease provides to the contrary), devisable, and capable of descent. Under the laws of intestate succession, it descends like personal property.

2. Reversion Held by Landlord. [§ 8–3]

Because a landlord does not transfer her entire estate to the tenant, the landlord retains a reversion which becomes possessory upon termination of the leasehold. In most leases, the landlord also retains a right of re-entry (i.e., in the lease, the landlord will usually retain the right to enter and terminate the lease upon tenant's failure to pay rent or for breach of other covenants or conditions).

3. Property versus Contract Approach. [§ 8–4]

While a lease is a contract, the common law historically considered a lease as a conveyance of an estate in land. Emphasis on the conveyance characteristics has led to a "property," rather than a "contract," approach to leases. As will be discussed in detail throughout this chapter once the original estates aspects of leases has been explained, the current trend is to replace the old property law rules applied to leases with contract concepts. The student should be forewarned at this point of the most significant differences between the property law and contract law approaches to leases:

a. Dependency of Covenants. [§ 8–5]

In contract law, covenants are mutually dependent and therefore a substantial breach of a material covenant generally excuses the other party from the duty to perform any further. In property law, covenants of a lease are considered independent, and, consequently, the nonperformance of a covenant by one party does not excuse the other party from performance of her obligations under the lease. So, for example, destruction of a house that is being leased does not absolve the tenant from the obligation to continue paying rent. Likewise, the landlord's breach of his duty to make repairs is not a defense in an action of rent.

b. Implied Warranties. [§ 8–6]

Contract law, particularly modern contract law, implies various warranties or guarantees into contracts to give mutual protection to the parties, even if they do not specifically contract for such protection. The most common and most important implied warranty is that of marketability or merchantability. The traditional property law view was that virtually no warranties are implied into a lease, so that there was no warranty of habitability unless it was specifically stated in the lease.

c. Mitigation of Damages. [§ 8–7]

Under contract law, a party has a duty to mitigate (lessen as much as possible) the damages that he will suffer and for which he can hold the other party liable. No such duty was recognized at property law, and, consequently, a landlord had no duty to relet premises wrongly vacated by a tenant.

d. Anticipatory Repudiation (Breach). [§ 8–8]

Under contract law, a "wronged" party can bring suit for the total damages he will suffer without waiting for the supposed dates of performance. Property law recognized no such concept and consequently landlords could not sue for the rent due under a broken lease until the date it would have been paid under the lease.

e. Frustration of Purpose. [§ 8–9]

Contract law has long recognized that the strict performance of contract obligations may be excused if the purpose of the contract is totally frustrated. Property law recognized no such flexibility for leases.

B. TYPES OF LEASEHOLD ESTATES. [§ 8–10]

1. Tenancy for Years. [§ 8–11]

A tenancy for years is an estate for a fixed, ascertainable period of time. The time need not be measured in specific numbers of years and can be for more or less than a year (e.g., a grant in February of 2011 "until March 31, 2011" is an estate for years). If the termination date is uncertain, the tenancy is not an estate for years.

a. Created by Written Instrument. [§ 8–12]

Estates with a duration of more than one year must be created by a written instrument signed by the grantor in order to comply with the Statute of Frauds and conveyancing statutes. Thus, an oral lease is valid only if its term does not exceed one year.

b. Termination. [§ 8–13]

An estate for years terminates naturally upon expiration of the stated term or pursuant to a landlord's reserved right of re-entry. Neither the death of the landlord nor of the tenant terminates the tenancy for years.

2. Periodic Tenancies. [§ 8–14]

A periodic tenancy is a tenancy which will continue for successive stated periods, unless the lease is terminated at the end of a given period by proper notice from either landlord or tenant. This "automatic renewal" is the chief characteristic of the estate.

a. Creation. [§ 8–15]

A periodic tenancy may be created:

(1) by express agreement;

(2) by implication where the lease between the parties is silent about duration, but the parties have agreed that rent shall be paid at specific periods; or

(3) by operation of law if there is either possession under an invalid lease with rent paid on a periodic basis or if the tenant becomes a "holdover tenant."

b. Establishing Length of Period. [§ 8–16]

When the lease is silent about duration, and if the parties agree on an annual rent, the lease will be treated as a tenancy from year-to-year. If the lease does not reserve rent on an annual basis, but provides for monthly rental, the leasehold will be month-to-month. In the case of an annual rental to be paid in monthly installments, the lease is generally viewed as creating an estate from year-to-year. Thus, rent reservation contained in the lease, up to a maximum of one year, determines the period where rent is paid with reference to the rent reservation.

c. Inferential Establishment. [§ 8–17]

If the tenant has entered into possession, and rent has been paid on a periodic basis, this may be sufficient evidence of a periodic tenancy, even where no written lease exists.

d. Terminated at End of Period With Giving of Proper Notice. [§ 8–18]

At common law, a periodic tenancy could be terminated at the end of any period by either party, upon the giving of proper notice. The notice had to specify the date of termination, which had to be the end of the period. To terminate a year-to-year tenancy, notice had to be given six months before the end of the period. If the tenancy was less than one year, notice had to be given equal to the length of the term of the lease but not to exceed six months. Thus, for example, one month notice was needed to terminate a month-to-month tenancy, one week notice to terminate a week-to-week tenancy. Any attempted termination that did not comply with the respective notice requirements was ineffective. Death of the landlord or tenant does not terminate the periodic tenancy.

3. Tenancy at Will. [§ 8–19]

A tenancy at will is an estate terminable at the will of either landlord or tenant without fixed duration. If the lease gives the landlord the right to terminate at will, a similar right is implied in the tenant, and the tenancy is at will. If the lease gives only the tenant such a right, the cases are split. Some cases hold that the estate is a defeasible life estate; others hold that it is a tenancy at will for both parties. (See Case Squib: *Garner v. Gerrish.*) A tenant at will has a sufficient estate to maintain a trespass action against third parties and thus has the right to exclusive possession of the property (at least until the landlord terminates the lease).

a. Creation. [§ 8–20]

A tenancy at will can be created by express agreement, but more commonly it arises when the parties enter into a lease without agreement as to duration, and without agreement that rent is to be paid on a periodic basis, so that a periodic tenancy cannot be inferred. It may also arise following entry under a void lease.

b. Termination. [§ 8–21]

A tenancy at will continues until terminated by one of the parties. At common law, notice was not required. A tenancy at will could also be terminated by the death of either party, by conveyance of the landlord's reversion, or by the attempted conveyance of the leasehold.

4.   Tenancy at Sufferance: The Holdover Doctrine. [§ 8–22]

A tenancy at sufferance is created where a tenant holds over after the expiration of his leasehold (i.e., he refuses to vacate after the expiration of the lease). Where a tenancy at sufferance arises, the law favors the landlord and gives her two choices. (See Case Squib: *Crechale & Polles, Inc. v. Smith.*)

a.   Landlord May Treat Holdover Tenant as Trespasser. [§ 8–23]

If a tenant wrongfully holds over, the landlord may elect to treat him as a trespasser and take appropriate steps to evict him by bringing a common law action of ejectment or by pursing available statutory remedies such as summary proceedings.

b.   Landlord May Elect to Hold Tenant to New Tenancy. [§ 8–24]

The landlord may, in the alternative, elect to hold the tenant to a new tenancy. The landlord's election to hold the tenant to a new tenancy may be shown by express statement, but it is more commonly implied upon the landlord's continued acceptance of rent from the holdover tenant.

(1)   The Election to Hold the Tenant Is the Landlord's. [§ 8–25]

Generally, the holdover tenant may be held to a new tenancy, even though it is clear he does not want such an arrangement. The harshness of this rule (e.g., a tenant could be forced to pay rent for another year long term, etc.) has been modified by recognition that the landlord may not use a holdover as the basis for a new tenancy, if the holdover is for a brief period and due to unavoidable circumstances.

(2)   Periodic Tenancy Created. [§ 8–26]

In the majority of states, the period of the new tenancy is determined by the manner in which rent is reserved in the original lease. If the original lease reserved an annual rent (even if payable in monthly installments), the new tenancy estate is for a year; if the rental reserved is by the month, the period of tenancy is one month. However, the holdover period may not be for longer than one year.

c.   Rights of Subsequent Tenant. [§ 8–27]

If the landlord had leased the land to another for a period beginning immediately after the expiration of the term of the tenant who is now holding over, the new tenant has a sufficient interest in the land to justify his own action for removal of the holdover.

5. Entry Under an Invalid Lease. [§ 8–28]

In most states, a parol lease (meaning an oral lease) for a period not to exceed one year from the making thereof is valid (some states consider only whether the lease itself is more than one year). Parol leases for periods in excess of one year, on the other hand, are generally invalid or ineffective to create a tenancy for years, because of the Statute of Frauds. If the tenant takes possession with the permission of the landlord, some sort of tenancy is created, even if only a tenancy at will, by fact of the tenant's possession with the landlord's permission (though not by formal or informal instrument).

a. Tenancy at Will or Periodic Tenancy Created. [§ 8–29]

Entry under an ineffective parol lease creates a tenancy at will until rent is paid. Thereafter, if the tenant pays periodic rent, the relationship converts into a periodic tenancy (by implication). If the rent is paid monthly, the tenancy is from month-to-month; if yearly, then the tenancy is from year-to-year.

b. Statute of Frauds Affects Only Duration. [§ 8–30]

The invalidity of the parol lease generally relates only to the duration. In the case of a parol lease for longer than one year, the agreement as to the duration exceeding the one year is void. The other covenants and conditions agreed upon, such as the amount of rent and other obligations of the parties, control the relationship while it continues and are enforceable.

C. RENT. [§ 8–31]

Rent is a basic obligation of the landlord-tenant relationship, though it is not essential to the existence of a leasehold estate. Leaseholds, like the freehold estates, can be transferred gratuitously. Absent an agreement against rent, one who permissively occupies the land of another generally has a duty to pay rent in the amount of reasonable use value and the duty arises even when the parties have not agreed on the rent to be paid. Normally, however, the amount and obligation to pay rent are contained in the lease. [CAVEAT: Federal statutes and constitutional law principles in regard to rent control and racial and ethnic discrimination are attracting more and more attention in various rent controversies. Two leading cases on these points are *Marable v. H. Walker* and *Pennell v. City of San Jose* (See Case Squibs: *Marable v. H. Walker* and *Pennell v. City of San Jose*.), but constitutional law review materials should be consulted for these issues in their proper context.]

1. Payment of Rent. [§ 8–32]

At common law, rent was due at the end of the tenancy period. The typical lease today makes rent payable in advance of a particular use period. The common law took the position that rent is not apportionable (e.g., if rent is payable monthly at the end of each month, and the tenancy terminated in the middle of the month, not at the fault of the tenant, the tenant owed no rent for the half month he was in possession after the last rent payment). In most states today, the tenant must pay a proportion for the period he is in possession.

2. Non–Payment of Rent. [§ 8–33]

At common law, failure to pay rent did not permit the landlord to recover possession; the rent covenant was independent and was not a condition to the right of possession. The modern lease typically gives the landlord a right of re-entry which may be exercised on failure to pay rent (in some states the landlord has a statutory right to terminate for failure to pay rent, whether or not the lease gives such a right). Thus, by agreement or statute, the rental obligation today typically is both a covenant and a condition. The failure to pay rent, therefore, gives the landlord an election: he may evict or he may hold the tenant for the rent due, until the proper termination of the lease.

a. Eviction. [§ 8–34]

The landlord may remove the tenant in those cases where the landlord has the right (by lease or statute) to retake possession. The landlord may have such a right for failure of the tenant to pay rent or for other reasons (e.g., the tenant has breached a covenant and the lease makes such a breach grounds for termination).

(1) Self–Help Evictions Not Permitted. [§ 8–35]

The landlord is not authorized to use self-help in evicting a tenant. Even entry by use of a key in the tenant's absence is unauthorized in many jurisdictions. (See Case Squib: *Berg v. Wiley.*)

(2) Summary Eviction. [§ 8–36]

The landlord may recover possession by resorting to either unlawful detainer or summary eviction statutes in most jurisdictions. To evict under these summary proceedings, a notice in writing demanding the payment of overdue rent or possession of the premises must be served on the person owing the rent. The procedure for eviction and the length of notice are governed by statute.

(3) Eviction Terminates Tenant's Obligations. [§ 8–37]

Eviction by the landlord terminates the tenant's obligations under the lease, including the duty to pay rent for the balance of the term, unless the lease expressly provides to the contrary.

(4) Rent Acceleration Clauses. [§ 8–38]

To avoid the termination of the tenant's obligations upon eviction, rent acceleration clauses in the nature of a covenant are usually included in the lease. Rent acceleration clauses commonly provide that upon failure to pay rent, all the rent for the remainder of the term shall become due. Generally, such clauses have been invalidated as unwarranted penalties, if the landlord seeks both acceleration and recovery of possession. Some courts will uphold such clauses, if the language is sufficiently explicit based upon the freedom of parties to contract in advance for liquidated damages in the event of the tenant's default.

b. Suit for Rent Without Eviction. [§ 8–39]

If the tenant fails to pay rent due, the landlord may leave him in possession and simply sue for rent as it becomes due.

(1) Doctrine of Anticipatory Repudiation Not Applicable. [§ 8–40]

In the absence of an acceleration clause, the common law property rule was that rent can be sued for only as it becomes due. Thus, even though the tenant has not paid his monthly rent for three months, the landlord may not presently sue for future rent; he may sue only for the rent currently due. The current trend is to apply the contract law principle to leases, even though they contain no acceleration clause. The contract Doctrine of Anticipatory Repudiation provides that if one party to a contract, unequivocally and positively repudiates the contract, the other party to the contract can sue for breach of contract without waiting for the time of performance to arrive.

3. Abandonment and Surrender. [§ 8–41]

The question of abandonment and surrender commonly arises in a suit for rent where the landlord asserts that the tenant has failed to pay rent and has abandoned the leased premises (and thus continues to be liable for rent as it comes due), and the tenant counters with the argument that no rent is due because the leasehold has been surrendered (by mutual agreement of the landlord and tenant to end the lease) and all obligations thereunder terminated.

Abandonment occurs when a tenant simply vacates the leased premises, without justification and with no intention to return, coupled with a default in rent payments. Abandonment is an implied offer to surrender the leasehold. Such abandonment, standing alone, is not sufficient to terminate the lease prior to its normal termination date. The issue is whether the landlord has accepted the tenant's offer. Courts will consider the landlord's conduct in resolving the matter. If the landlord's conduct after the abandonment is inconsistent with the rights of the tenant under the lease, the landlord may be deemed to have accepted the abandonment, thereby terminating the tenancy.

A lease may be terminated and the liability for rent may cease prior to the normal termination date by surrender. Surrender is a means of terminating a leasehold agreement early either by mutual agreement of the parties or by operation of law. An express surrender is a conveyance. Some courts hold that all surrender agreements, to be enforced, must be in writing, regardless of whether the original lease had to be written to satisfy the Statute of Frauds. Just as in the case of abandonment (an implied offer of surrender), the surrender must be accepted by the landlord in order to terminate the leasehold estate. Only an express surrender need comply with the Statute of Frauds; acceptance of the surrender may occur by implication from the landlord's conduct or by operation of law.

When a tenant either abandons or surrenders, a landlord has three options. First, the landlord can accept the tenant's offer and re-enter for his own account. The lease is terminated and no future rent is due. The landlord can still recover past, unpaid rent and possibly damages measured as the loss of value for the remaining time on the lease. Second, the landlord can reject the tenant's offer and do nothing and keep the tenant on the lease. Subject to the landlord's duty to mitigate, if any, the tenant would still be obligated for the rent under the lease. Third, the landlord can re-enter and re-let (mitigate on the tenant's behalf) the leasehold premises for the benefit of the tenant or for the tenant's "account". The tenant would remain liable on the lease and the landlord could charge the tenant for the difference between the agreed rent and the rent the landlord receives from the new tenant.

a. Generally No Duty at Common Law to Mitigate Damages in Case of Abandonment. [§ 8–42]

When a tenant abandons the premises, at common law the landlord could simply leave the premises vacant and sue the tenant for rent as it fell due. In a majority of jurisdictions, the landlord is now under a duty to mitigate by reletting. This is part of the new contract law approach to leases. (See Case Squib: *Sommer v. Kridel.*)

b. Effect of Resumption of Possession or Re-letting by Landlord. [§ 8–43]

At common law, any re-letting by the landlord operated as a surrender. Today, however, there is no formula answer for the effect of resumption of possession or re-letting by the landlord. The court will carefully scrutinize the facts in making a determination of whether a surrender has occurred.

(1) Resumption of Possession for Landlord's Benefit. [§ 8–44]

In a majority of states, resumption of possession by the landlord for his own benefit (i.e., the landlord occupies the land himself) following abandonment operates as a surrender by operation of law and terminates the lease.

(2) Landlord's Intent Significant in Re-letting. [§ 8–45]

Doctrines concerning the ability of the landlord to re-let without losing his right to hold the tenant for the balance of the term vary from state to state. In most states, surrender in these circumstances is a matter of the landlord's intent and the landlord may generally re-let and sue the tenant for deficiencies for the balance of the term. This is especially true where the re-letting is for a shorter term than is left on the lease, and the tenant is notified that the re-letting is for his account.

c. Liquidated Damages, Penalties, and Prepayments. [§ 8–46]

(1) Good–Faith Liquidated Damages Are Valid. [§ 8–47]

Provisions for liquidated damages are generally valid and upheld. However, the court will scrutinize such provisions to determine whether the provision is a good-faith effort to liquidate damages before breach or whether, in fact, it is a penalty for the purpose of inducing performance.

(2) Penalties Are Void. [§ 8–48]

Penalty provisions are void and unenforceable. Thus, if the liquidated damages provisions are construed as a penalty, the provision is unenforceable and the landlord must prove all damages. If the sum is already on deposit, the tenant must wait until the end of the term to recover such sum less the damages actually proved by the landlord.

(3) Advance Rental Payments Not Recoverable by Tenant. [§ 8–49]

Where the tenant has made advance rental payments and then defaults, such advance payments may not be recovered by the tenant. For this reason, a landlord may believe it to be in his best interest to describe the security deposit as an advance payment of rent. Based upon the rule of non-apportionment of rent, some courts may allow a landlord to keep an advance rent payment upon forfeiture of the lease by the default of the tenant.

(4) Security Deposits Recoverable by Tenant. [§ 8–50]

A security deposit, in the absence of a lease provision or statute to the contrary, simply creates a debtor-creditor relationship. The landlord is obligated to return a security deposit, less actual damages, to the tenant at the end of the lease.

4. Defenses to Rent. [§ 8–51]

a. Illegality. [§ 8–52]

(1) Illegal Purpose. [§ 8–53]

Where a lease is expressly made for an illegal purpose, the lease is unenforceable; the landlord may regain possession, but may not recover rent. There is a split of authority on the question of whether or not a lease is unenforceable because of the landlord's mere knowledge of the tenant's illegal purpose at the time the lease is made.

(2) Particular Use Subsequently Becomes Illegal. [§ 8–54]

Where the lease limits the tenant to a particular use, and the use subsequently becomes illegal, liability for rent ends. The landlord recovers possession.

b. Frustration of Purpose. [§ 8–55]

If the lease limits the tenant to a particular use that is legal at the inception of the lease but later government restrictions make that purpose impossible or substantially interfere with it, the tenant may be discharged from rent liability (e.g., if the only permitted use of the property is as a saloon and the state prohibits all sale of alcoholic beverages a few months after the signing of the lease, the tenant may terminate the lease). This result is drawn from contractual frustration of purpose rules. However, some courts have refused to apply frustration doctrines to leases, viewing the lease under property law only as an estate and not as a contract (note that the current trend is to treat a lease as a contract and apply contractual theories). (See Case Squib: *Albert M. Greenfield v. Kolea.*)

c. Taking of the Leasehold by Eminent Domain. [§ 8–56]

(1) Taking of Entire Leasehold. [§ 8–57]

If all of the leased land is taken by eminent domain (see Chapter XVI § 16–45), the leasehold and reversion merge in the taker; the leasehold is terminated and the obligation to pay rent ceases. The tenant is entitled to receive from the condemnation award an amount equal to the present fair market value of the unexpired term less future rent due (which, of course, he need not pay). Practically speaking, in these cases, the tenant will only receive a share of the condemnation award if the value of the lease for the remainder of the term is greater than the cost of the tenant's remaining obligations under the lease.

129

(2) Temporary Taking. [§ 8–58]

If the taking is for a time shorter than the balance of the term, liability to pay rent continues, but the tenant is entitled to receive from the condemnation award an amount equal to the value of the portion taken.

(3) Taking of Part of the Leased Property. [§ 8–59]

If part of the leased property is taken, the majority rule is that the tenant's obligation to pay the rent reserved is not diminished. The tenant is entitled to receive, out of the condemnation award, the present market value of the unexpired term of the part taken. There is no deduction for rent that is unaccrued, because the tenant has continuing liability for the reserved rent under the lease. Under the minority view, rent is abated in proportion to the amount of the property taken.

d. Destruction of Premises. [§ 8–60]

In the absence of a covenant to the contrary, the common law rule is that destruction of the premises without the fault of the landlord does not excuse the tenant from payment of rent. A recognized exception is if the leased property is an office or apartment within a building and the building itself is destroyed; in such a circumstance the rent liability is extinguished. Under modern contract oriented decisions, destruction of premises is held to terminate the rental payment obligation. (See Case Squib: *Albert M. Greenfield v. Kolea.*)

e. Eviction and Constructive Eviction. [§ 8–61]

Basic to an understanding of actual and constructive eviction is the implied covenant of quiet enjoyment. Implied in a lease is a covenant by the landlord that neither he, nor anyone claiming under him or having paramount title, will substantially interfere with the tenant's quiet enjoyment of the leased premises. Breach of this covenant may give rise to an action for damages. Yet, more important, breach of this covenant amounting to an eviction or constructive eviction is a defense to an action for rent, if the tenant vacates and chooses to assert that defense. (See Case Squib: *Reste Realty v. Cooper.*)

(1) Actual Eviction: Denial of Possession to Tenant by Landlord or His Privy. [§ 8–62]

The most obvious actual eviction occurs when the landlord, or someone claiming through him or representing him, physically removes the tenant and his goods from the leased premises or denies the tenant possession (e.g., by padlocking). Actual eviction may also occur if the tenant is deprived of possession by one having title paramount to the landlord (e.g., O mortgages his property to A and subsequently leases to B; if A now forecloses and B is dispossessed, B is evicted and B's estate is terminated).

(a) Partial Actual Eviction. [§ 8–63]

If the landlord physically evicts the tenant from any part of the leased premises, under common law rules, the obligation to pay all or any part of the rent ceases; the rent is not apportioned. If there is a partial eviction by one holding paramount title, the tenant generally continues to be liable for the rental value of the balance of the premises. However, where loss of the portion seriously impairs the tenant's ability to use the rest, the tenant may be excused entirely from the obligation to pay rent.

(2) Constructive Eviction. [§ 8–64]

(a) Lease Covenants Generally Are Independent. [§ 8–65]

Traditionally, courts have taken the position that lease covenants are independent of each other (i.e., breach of a covenant by one party does not excuse performance by the other). Remember that this has its roots in the estates' concept of leaseholds. Today, however, the trend is to treat lease covenants as dependent and to permit contract doctrines to be applied to breaches.

(b) Implied Covenant of Quiet Enjoyment and Obligation to Pay Rent Are Dependent. [§ 8–66]

Even those courts which adhere to the traditional doctrine of the independence of lease covenants make an exception in the case of the implied covenant of quiet enjoyment and the obligation to pay rent, holding that these two covenants are dependent. The covenant of quiet enjoyment is breached if the tenant's possession is disturbed by the landlord or by one with paramount title during the term of the lease.

(c) Constructive Eviction Is Landlord's Interference With Tenant's Beneficial Enjoyment. [§ 8–67]

A constructive eviction consists of conduct (or failure to perform where the landlord is under a duty to act) by the landlord which substantially interferes with the tenant's beneficial enjoyment (quiet enjoyment) of the leased premises such that the premises become "untenantable". The conduct or breach of the duty must be by the landlord and the tenant must vacate the premises within a reasonable time.

(i) Example. [§ 8–68]

L leases an apartment to T. L occupies an adjacent apartment. L uses his apartment for purposes of prostitution and loud music is played constantly. This conduct by L has been held to be sufficient for constructive eviction. L, by his affirmative act, has substantially interfered with T's quiet enjoyment.

(ii) Example. [§ 8–69]

Same facts as prior Example, but the adjacent apartment has been rented by L to A who runs and uses the premises as a brothel. T complains to L, who does nothing about A's conduct. Courts have found no constructive eviction in this situation, because the acts are not those of L, nor is L under a duty to act. There must be a duty, not simply a power in L, to act.

(iii) Example. [§ 8–70]

L leases an apartment to T. L permits other tenants to act raucously in the hallways, disturbing T. T complains to L, who does nothing. These facts might support constructive eviction even though the acts are not those of L, since L controls the common areas.

(d) Tenant Must Vacate Within Reasonable Time. [§ 8–71]

In order to defend a claim for rent on constructive eviction grounds, the tenant must vacate the premises within a reasonable time after the wrongful acts occurred. Failure to vacate constitutes a waiver of constructive eviction.

(e) Breach of Duty Imposed by Covenant May Constitute Constructive Eviction. [§ 8–72]

The constructive eviction doctrine has increasingly been used to achieve results similar to the contract doctrine of mutually dependent covenants. This has been accomplished by treating a breach of a duty imposed by covenant which causes the premises to become untenantable as a constructive eviction, which in turn, is a defense to rent.

(i) Example. [§ 8–73]

L leases to T, L covenanting to keep the plumbing in good repair. The plumbing becomes so defective that the property is untenantable. L refuses to repair, and T vacates. This is a constructive eviction in some states, predicated on failure to perform a duty imposed by the lease. Courts are very accommodating to residential tenants when a landlord's failure to provide fundamental essentials such as heat, water, or electricity renders the premises unfit for human habitation (in residential leases the warranty of habitability may also give a tenant some options).

(ii) Example. [§ 8–74]

L leases a drugstore to T. L covenants not to rent any other portion of the same building for another drugstore. L subsequently rents another portion of the building for another drugstore and T vacates. On these facts, some courts have relieved T of his rent obligation on the grounds of contractual dependence of covenants.

f. Exam Hint: Consider Implied Covenant of Habitability. [§ 8–75] Whenever the question of constructive eviction arises, consider the applicability of the implied covenant of habitability (§ 8–89) which many states have imposed on residential tenancies. (See Case Squib: *Javins v. First National Realty Corp.*)

D. CONDITION OF THE PREMISES. [§ 8–76]

In the preceding section, we discussed the duty of the tenant to pay rent and the reciprocal duty of the landlord to give the tenant quiet enjoyment of the premises. The remaining duties of landlord and tenant to one another involve the allocation of the responsibility for maintaining the premises.

1. Tenant Has Duty to Avoid Waste. [§ 8–77]

The tenant has the duty to avoid waste and he may be held liable for resulting damages if this duty is breached.

a. Voluntary Waste. [§ 8–78]

Voluntary waste is negligent or intentional conduct by the tenant which damages the property (e.g., tenant's negligence causes the building to burn down; tenant substantially alters the building; tenant cuts timber or takes minerals without landlord's consent). Clearing land and removing minerals involve special aspects of the law of waste in many instances. For example, if the lease does not prohibit mineral extraction and if mineral extraction was an ongoing operation at the time of the leasing, many courts will find that it is not waste for the tenant to continue to work the same pits or mines. The tenant may even be allowed to expand existing operations, though the tenant cannot open new pits or mines on the leasehold premises. Likewise, many courts hold that cutting timber to promote "good husbandry" is not waste and these courts may also permit cutting timber for fences and building repairs.

b.   Permissive Waste. [§ 8–79]

Permissive waste occurs when the tenant, by failing to make timely minor repairs, allows serious damage to result. The tenant is under a duty to make minor repairs in order to preserve the property in substantially the same condition as when leased. For example, if a window breaks, the tenant must repair it or he will be liable for water damage.

c.   Ameliorating Waste. [§ 8–80]

Ameliorating waste is conduct by the tenant substantially altering the leased premises so that the freehold estate is permanently changed. The term "waste" can be misleading, because the land's value is increased (e.g., replacing an old structure with a new one; converting farmland into an industrial park or residential subdivision; cementing part of property for a parking lot). Such conduct was strictly prohibited by the old common law, even where the changes enhanced the value of the property. The theory was that the landlord has the right to receive the property back in the same form as when leased. However, because of the hardships which arose in areas of rapid industrialization, most courts have come to permit beneficial structural changes, when long-term leases are involved, although the tenant may still be liable for increases in taxes or insurance generated by his changes.

2.   Duty to Repair in the Absence of Express Covenant (Apart From Waste). [§ 8–81]

As a general rule at common law, in the absence of an express covenant or statute, neither landlord nor tenant owes the other any duty to maintain, repair, or rebuild the property. The following are exceptions to this general principle:

a.   Either Causing Intentional or Negligent Damage Is Liable. [§ 8–82]

If one or the other (landlord or tenant) intentionally or negligently causes damage, he may, of course, be held liable.

b. Undertaking to Act. [§ 8–83]

In line with the law of torts, a party who undertakes to repair the premises is liable for injury if he makes the condition worse or lulls others into believing that a dangerous condition has been repaired.

c. Landlord Has Duty to Maintain Common Areas. [§ 8–84]

The landlord is under a duty to maintain common areas under his control (e.g., driveways, common hallways, gardens which are not a part of the leasehold).

d. Landlord Responsible for Hidden Defects. [§ 8–85]

If the landlord leases property containing a defect of which he knows or should know, but which a reasonable inspection by the tenant would not reveal, the landlord may be liable for injuries caused by the defect to the tenant and the tenant's guests.

3. Express Covenants to Repair or Surrender in Good Condition. [§ 8–86]

a. Landlord's Covenant to Repair. [§ 8–87]

When the landlord has covenanted to repair, he will be liable for any injury resulting to the tenant or the tenant's guests. The landlord is normally under no duty to act, however, until notice of the need for repairs is given.

b. Tenant's Covenant to Repair. [§ 8–88]

A covenant to repair (or surrender in good condition) by the tenant requires only that the building be maintained (or surrendered) in as good a condition as when it was leased, normal wear and tear excepted.

4. Residential Tenancies: The Implied Covenant of Habitability. [§ 8–89]

There is a significant trend to expand the duties of the landlord in the area of residential leasing—most states have implied a covenant of habitability which requires that leased premises be suitable for living purposes during the entire term of the lease. Note, however, that often there is no similar covenant implied in commercial leases (thus the doctrine of caveat emptor (buyer beware) is alive and well with respect to commercial leases in many jurisdictions). (See Case Squibs: *Javins v. First National Realty Corp.* and *Hilder v. St. Peter.*) In order to bring a cause of action for breach of the implied covenant of habitability, the tenant has to show that he notified the landlord of the defect, not already known to the landlord, and that the tenant allowed the landlord a reasonable time to correct the defect.

135

a. Landlord Has Duty to Make Premises Comply with Codes. [§ 8–90]

A common test of habitability is that the premises comply with all housing, building, safety, and health codes. Although such codes are usually embraced in local ordinances rather than in statutes, the courts are likely to require the landlord make the premises comply, when the codes are properly pleaded and put in evidence.

b. When Habitability Required. [§ 8–91]

(1) Beginning of the Lease. [§ 8–92]

Obviously, habitability must be satisfied at the beginning of the lease. Otherwise, the court may regard the lease as an illegal one and preclude the landlord from enforcing it. (See Case Squib: *Brown v. Southall Realty.*)

(2) Throughout the Lease. [§ 8–93]

The obligation to provide habitable premises throughout the entire lease period may also be imposed on the landlord, at least insofar as the duty to comply with applicable housing and related codes is concerned. Note that any holding to the contrary undermines the policies which support the warranty of habitability.

c. Remedies for Breach. [§ 8–94]

(1) Tenant May Withhold Rent. [§ 8–95]

Jurisdictions implying a covenant of habitability hold that when the landlord breaches this covenant, the tenant need not pay the agreed upon rent. In some jurisdictions, however, the tenant is liable for the reasonable rental value of the premises so long as he or she remains in occupation.

(2) Retaliatory Evictions Prohibited. [§ 8–96]

Some tenants, attempting to compel the landlord to comply with minimum housing standards by reporting such violations to the proper authorities, have been met with a notice to terminate the lease and an eviction proceeding. In such circumstances, the courts have developed the rule that if the tenant can prove that retaliation is the basis of the landlord's termination of the lease, the landlord will not be permitted to evict the tenant. (See Case Squib: *Edwards v. Habib.*) Some states aid the tenant with a presumption that attempted evictions and/or rent increases within a short period (e.g., 90 days) of the reported violation are improperly motivated.

(a) **Example. [§ 8–97]**

L leases residential property to T for five years. T complains to the proper authorities for existing code violations in the premises. L attempts to terminate the lease because of T's breach of one or more covenants in the lease. The retaliatory eviction defense could be asserted, but T would have to show that the reason for the eviction was his reporting to the authorities and not the violation of his lease covenants.

(b) **Example. [§ 8–98]**

T leases property from L on a periodic tenancy. T informs authorities of building code violations and L serves notice of termination and then initiates eviction proceedings. In this situation, the landlord might terminate the lease for any reason or no reason at all, but he cannot terminate it in retaliation for the tenant's informing public authorities of violations of codes.

(3) **Rent Strike May Be Appropriate. [§ 8–99]**

As a group, tenants have been authorized to withhold rent and pay it into court, until housing violations by an uncooperative landlord are corrected. Under such circumstances, a good-faith requirement is imposed on both parties and rent is made apportionable. Often, rent strikes are statutorily regulated.

d. **Constructive Eviction Compared. [§ 8–100]**

For breach of an implied covenant of habitability, the tenant need not vacate the premises in order to assert a breach. Thus, alleging a breach of an implied covenant of habitability is much more advantageous than alleging a constructive eviction where the tenant must vacate the premises to preserve the benefits of that doctrine. This remedy has been especially effective in the area of slum dwellings (and arose in response to the plight of tenants in run-down tenements).

5. **Landlord's Tort Liability for Habitability. [§ 8–101]**

Traditionally, the tort liability of landlords vis à vis tenants was quite limited. Courts generally found such liability only if they found (or the lease created) a specific duty and the landlord negligently breached that duty. Today, however, some courts have greatly expanded tort liability by coupling it with the implied warranty of habitability and thereby recognizing a general standard of care for landlords pursuant to all aspects of the landlord tenant relationship. In *Kline v. 1500 Massachusetts Ave. Apartment Corp.*, the landlords' standard of care was extended to taking steps to protect tenants from criminal acts of third parties. (See Case Squib: *Kline v. 1500 Massachusetts Ave. Apartment Corp.*)

6. Fitness of the Premises. [§ 8–102]

Generally, a lease contains no implied covenant that the leased property is fit or suitable for the purpose for which it is leased. Thus, in the absence of fraud, the doctrine of caveat emptor is still applied, with the very large exception of the covenant of habitability discussed above. (§ 8–89) In residential leases this exception may have swallowed the rule.

E. ASSIGNMENT AND SUBLETTING. [§ 8–103]

In the absence of a covenant to the contrary, a tenant may either assign or sublet his leasehold.

1. Assignment is Transfer of Entire Remaining Duration. [§ 8–104]

When a tenant transfers the entire remaining interest (generally the concern is with the duration (i.e., time)) left on the lease, retaining no reversion in the event of default, the lease has been assigned, and the transferee is an assignee.

Example. [§ 8–105] L leases to T for ten years. T transfers his leasehold to A one year later, A takes the entire remaining nine years of the leasehold and T retains no right to enter or terminate A's interest. A is an assignee and will be so regarded regardless of the label attached to the transfer by the parties.

a. Retention of Possession of Part of the Premises. [§ 8–106]

It should also be noted that the assignor may relinquish possession of the entire premises or of part of the premises for the full remaining time on the term. If this occurs, there has been a partial assignment.

b. Retention of Right of Termination. [§ 8–107]

The majority holds that the reservation of a right to terminate the transferred interest prior to the end of the term does not make the transfer a sublease rather than an assignment. So long as nothing in point of time is reserved, even with a right of re-entry, the transfer is an assignment.

Example. [§ 8–108] L leases to T for ten years at a $400 per month rental. T immediately transfers the whole term to A. A agrees to pay $500 per month and agrees that T has the right to terminate A's estate if the rent is not paid. The entire term having been transferred, this is an assignment.

A minority of courts hold that the reservation of a power of termination, such as in the above example, makes the transfer a sublease and not an assignment.

c.   **Other Terms. [§ 8–109]**

An assignment need not contain terms identical to those in the main lease. Thus, as indicated in the example above (§ 8–108), a transfer is not a sublease merely because the transferor charges different rent than he himself was obligated to pay to the landlord.

d.   **Rights and Liabilities of the Parties. [§ 8–110]**

(1)   **Assignee in Privity of Estate with Landlord. [§ 8–111]**

If the tenant assigns the leasehold, the assignee is liable to the landlord for rent accruing after the assignment. The assignee is in privity of estate (i.e., bound by obligations stemming from the ownership of a property interest) with the landlord. The assignee has the present estate of a leasehold (non-freehold) estate followed by a reversion in the landlord. Thus, the burden and benefit of covenants in the lease runs to her as long as she remains in privity of estate, but she is not liable for rents accrued before the assignment was made. Without more, the assignee is not in privity of contract (i.e., not bound by provisions of the lease) with the landlord. Because of the privity of estate between the landlord and the assignee, the assignee is liable to the landlord to perform all of the tenant's covenants in the lease that run with the leasehold, including the covenant to pay rent.

(2)   **Assignee Can Assume the Lease's Obligations. [§ 8–112]**

If the tenant's assignee assumes the obligations of the lease (in addition to taking the assignment), the assignee becomes liable to the original tenant for rent due thereafter, even if the assignee reassigns. Today this contract between the tenant and the assignee may also be enforced by the landlord pursuant to the contracts law theory that he is a third-party beneficiary of the contract.

Example. [§ 8–113] L leases to T for five years. T holds the property for a year and then assigns to A. A holds the property for a year and then assigns to B, who holds until the end of the term. A is liable to L only for rent for the one year he was in possession. B is liable to L only for the rent due for the remaining three years he was in possession. (T is, of course, liable by contract for any rent not paid.) If, when T assigns, A assumes the obligation of the lease, in most states A will be liable to L for all rent while A and B are in possession or have the right thereto.

(3)   **Tenant Who Assigns Leasehold Remains in Privity of Contract. [§ 8–114]**

Where a tenant assigns the leasehold, she is no longer in privity of estate with the landlord. However, the original tenant remains in privity of contract and therefore is liable to the landlord for all obligations during the term, irrespective of assignments or reassignments.

(4) Assignee Is Primarily Liable for Rent. [§ 8–115]

The tenant's liability for rent accruing subsequent to assignment is secondary; the assignee is primarily liable. Hence, if the landlord recovers such rent from the original tenant, the tenant may in turn recover damages from the assignee in whose term the rent accrued.

2. Sublease is Transfer of Less Than Remaining Estate. [§ 8–116]

A sublease is created when the tenant transfers less than the entire remaining duration of time left in the lease. For example, L leases to T for ten years. One year later, T transfers an estate to A for five years. T has retained a reversion (four years). This is clearly a sublease.

a. Sublessee Not in Privity of Estate or Contract with Landlord. [§ 8–117]

When the tenant sublets, the sublessee is liable to the tenant but is not directly liable to the landlord for rent or for other covenants in the original lease. The sublessee is neither in privity of estate nor privity of contract with the landlord. After a sublease, the sublessee has the present estate of a leasehold estate, the tenant has a reversion in the leasehold for the remainder of the term and the landlord has a reversion usually in a fee simple absolute. Because of the tenant's intervening reversion between the sublessee's present estate and the landlord's reversion in fee simple absolute, the sublessee and the landlord cannot be in privity of estate.

b. Landlord's Remedies. [§ 8–118]

(1) Sublessor Still Liable for Rent and Other Covenants. [§ 8–119]

The tenant/sublessor who sublets remains liable for rent accruing after the sublease and for other covenants in the lease. The tenant/sublessor may pursue any remedies against a defaulting sublessee for breach of contract.

(2) Sublessee Liable to Landlord if Assumed Obligation. [§ 8–120]

If the sublessee assumes the obligations of the main lease, the landlord may be able to hold the sublessee to rent or other covenants under a third-party beneficiary doctrine.

(3) Landlord May Terminate Main Lease Upon Breach. [§ 8–121]

The sublease is dependent upon the viability of the main lease. Therefore, while the landlord may not seek performance directly from the sublessee, failure of the covenants of the master lease may result in a lien against the property or the termination of the main lease upon which the sublease is dependent.

3. Summary. [§ 8–122]

An assignment is a transfer of all of a tenant's leasehold; if any interest is retained in terms of duration, the transfer is a sublease. The primary impact of the distinction is that an assignee is in privity of estate with the landlord and hence owes a duty directly to the landlord to pay the reserved rent and perform other covenants running with the leasehold. A sublessee is neither in privity of estate nor privity of contract with the landlord, and cannot therefore be held by the landlord to the performance of covenants in the original lease, including payment of rent. Courts often speak of a two part test to determine whether an arrangement is an assignment or a sublease: 1) intent of the parties, and 2) transfer of the entire interest, but overlap the two tests in their decisions. (See Case Squib: *Ernst v. Conditt.*)

4. Covenants Against Assignment or Subletting. [§ 8–123]

The courts reflect their bias in favor of free alienability of estates, even when such an estate is a leasehold, in the way they interpret covenants against assignment or subletting.

a. Strictly Construed. [§ 8–124]

Such covenants in the lease are valid, but strictly construed. Thus, a covenant against assignment without the landlord's consent is not breached by the tenant granting a sublease. Many courts now require that consent to assignment or sublease not be withheld by the landlord unreasonably. (See Case Squib: *Kendall v. Ernest Pestana.*)

b. Voidable but Not Void. [§ 8–125]

An assignment or sublease in violation of such a covenant is not void, although the breaching tenant may be sued for breach of covenant. The assignment or sublease is voidable at the election of the landlord if a right to terminate in case of breach of the covenant has been reserved.

c. Rule in Dumpor's Case. [§ 8–126]

Many states apply the rule laid down by *Dumpor's Case*: if the landlord consents to an assignment by the tenant, the covenant against assignment is thereafter waived and the assignee may in turn assign without regard for the covenant. In essence, the assignee is not bound by the covenant.

F. TRANSFER OF REVERSION BY LANDLORD. [§ 8–127]

Although most controversies over transfers of interests pursuant to leases concern transfers (subleases and assignments) by tenants, it is also important to consider transfers by landlords of their reversions.

Example. [§ 8–128] L, owner of a fee simple absolute in Blackacre, leases it to T for 10 years. Five years later, L sells Blackacre to B. What relationships now exist between L, T, and B?

1. Common Law Rule. [§ 8–129]

At common law, the new owner, B, did not become T's landlord unless T consented to such a relationship. The act of consent was referred to as attornment. The Grantees of Reversions Act was enacted in the 1500's and was designed to make automatic the substitution of the grantee of the reversion for the original landlord.

2. Modern View. [§ 8–130]

The prevailing, if not unanimous, view today is that B steps into L's shoes and becomes T's landlord. B is entitled to the benefit of all covenants in the lease (unless one or more fail to meet all of the requirements for covenants to run with the land, see § 10–7). B takes subject to the lease and T's rights unless there is a notice problem. In order for B to take free of T's lease: (1) the lease would have to be of such a duration that it is required to be recorded to protect T's priority; (2) the lease would have to be unrecorded; (3) B would have to have paid value for L's interest; (4) B would have to be able to prove he had no notice of T's interest which, practically speaking, would mean that T was not in possession as this would give B inquiry notice of the tenancy. (See § 14–58 for an indepth discussion of the notice problem discussed here). In sum, B and T normally have the same rights and responsibilities vis à vis each other as did L and T prior to L's transfer to B.

G. FIXTURES. [§ 8–131]

1. Definition. [§ 8–132]

A fixture is something which was originally a chattel (personal property), but which, by reason of its annexation to, or use in connection with land, is regarded as a part of real property. The treatment of a thing as a fixture is relevant to several areas of real property law but most fixtures problems these days arise in connection with landlord and tenant law.

2. General Issues and Examples. [§ 8–133]

a. Does the Ownership of an Item Pass on Transfer of the Land? [§ 8–134]

Normally, a fixture passes with the property to which it is annexed, when that property passes by deed, will, or descent. For example, O owns

Blackacre, which has a house on it. O installs a furnace in the house. Thereafter, O conveys Blackacre to A. If the furnace is a fixture, it goes to A as part of the realty and O cannot remove the furnace and take it with her.

b.   Divided Ownership. [§ 8–135]

In cases involving divided ownership (land owned by one, chattel owned by another), the question is whether the owner of what began as a chattel has a right of removal. This is most commonly a problem in landlord-tenant cases where the tenant, having made improvements, seeks to remove them. If the article has become a fixture and no right of removal was reserved by the tenant, it cannot, as a general rule, be removed.

c.   Cases Involving Third Parties. [§ 8–136]

The characterization of something as a fixture may be of import in cases involving third parties (e.g., where both the holder of a security interest in the chattel/fixture and the mortgagee of the real property on which it is located may claim it).

3.   Conversion of Chattel to a Fixture. [§ 8–137]

a.   Old Cases Emphasized Physical Annexation. [§ 8–138].

The old English cases placed heavy emphasis on physical annexation to the land.

b.   American Courts Look to Intention. [§ 8–139]

American courts have made the question primarily one of intention. The intention is an objective fact and is often phrased in terms of what the usual reasonable buyer or mortgagee would expect. In determining whether a chattel was intended to be made a permanent accession to the land, the courts have considered:

(1)   Degree of Actual Physical Annexation. [§ 8–140]

The greater the degree of physical annexation, the more likely a finding that an article is a fixture. Thus, if an article is attached to the floor or to the walls or is embedded in the soil, there is a high degree of annexation. Extreme weight also suggests annexation.

(2)   Ease of Removal Without Damage to the Property. [§ 8–141]

If the chattel may be easily removed without damaging the property, the article is probably not a fixture.

(3) Adaptation to the Use of the Particular Realty (Constructive Annexation). [§ 8–142]

Articles are sometimes said to be constructively annexed where the degree of physical annexation is slight, but the article is peculiarly adapted to the realty (e.g., storm windows and screens, or window shades, which are specifically fitted to windows of the building) or where the article is incorporated in something which is itself clearly a fixture (e.g., a new burner unit, installed in the furnace, which is normally regarded as a fixture, is "constructively annexed").

(4) How Essential Is the Fixture to the Use of the Property? [§ 8–143]

Machinery which is essential to the use of a particular building's use will normally be regarded as a fixture. Conversely, an article which may appear to be annexed may not be a fixture because it does not relate to the normal use of the property.

(5) Local Custom. [§ 8–144]

Certain kinds of articles today are clearly fixtures (e.g., furnaces, hot water heaters); this is in part a matter of local custom.

4. Severance: Conversion of a Fixture to a Chattel. [§ 8–145]

As a chattel may be converted to a fixture, a fixture may be severed from the realty, becoming a chattel again. If the article is severed before a conveyance or sale contract, it does not pass as realty. Whether or not there has been a severance is primarily a matter of intent.

a. Physical Removal is Likely to Constitute a Severance. [§ 8–146]

If the landowner has physically removed the chattel before the sale of the land, he no longer regards it as part of the realty. However, temporary removal for repairs is not a severance, nor is involuntary removal, such as pursuant to a health and safety regulation.

b. Sale as Chattel Is a Severance. [§ 8–147]

Sale of the article as a chattel is a severance, although as to a BFP of the realty, the article may still be treated as a fixture.

c. An Article May Be Severed by Agreement of the Parties. [§ 8–148]

The land sale contract, deed, or mortgage can specify who has title to the article. If otherwise a fixture, the article has been converted back to personalty. This is especially important in landlord-tenant cases where the tenant may reserve the right to remove improvements—a reservation which will be given effect.

5. Special Landlord and Tenant Rules. [§ 8–149]

The lease itself may make express provision for removal of fixtures and improvements. In the absence of such a governing provision, the following rules apply.

a. General Rule. [§ 8–150]

Items which are incorporated into the lease premises so that their separate identity is lost (e.g., bricks in a wall, or lumber in the structure) are part of the realty. Similarly, if the article is so annexed that removal would cause substantial damage, it is a fixture and cannot be removed.

b. Trade Fixtures. [§ 8–151]

A trade fixture is a chattel brought to the premises by the tenant for use in her particular business or trade. The courts have consistently held that the tenant clearly does not intend to make articles which are part of her business realty; the tenant clearly means to take them with her.

(1) Must Be Removed Before Tenancy Ends. [§ 8–152]

If trade fixtures are not removed from the premises within a proper amount of time, typically before the end of the term, they become realty and cannot be removed thereafter. However, if the tenant holds for an indefinite term, he is given a reasonable time after termination for removal.

(2) Tenant Must Repair Damage. [§ 8–153]

The tenant must repair any damage caused by removal of the fixture.

c. Other Chattels. [§ 8–154]

The rationale of the trade fixture doctrine has been expanded to other types of chattels which can be removed, are usable any place, and are related to the particular uses or tastes of the tenant. Thus, ornamental fixtures are frequently judicially subjected to the same basic rules applied to trade fixtures.

6. Miscellaneous Rules. [§ 8–155]

a. Life Tenant and Remaindermen. [§ 8–156]

The rules applied to life tenants and remaindermen are similar to those in landlord-tenant cases, although courts generally find in favor of remaindermen more often than tenants.

b.   Licensees. [§ 8–157]

It is normally assumed that a licensee does not intend to confer a benefit on the licensor; licensees are permitted to remove chattels within a reasonable time after termination of the license. They must repair injuries caused by removal.

c.   Trespassers Lose Their Annexation. [§ 8–158]

Trespassers normally lose their annexations. Thus, buildings erected by a trespasser cannot be removed, even in those cases where the actor honestly believes he is the owner of the land. In a few states, the equity courts have ameliorated this rule somewhat in the case of innocent trespassers by requiring the landowner to pay the trespasser the "value added." These "betterment" statutes permit the defendant in ejectment to recover the value of improvements where he believed that the title under which he was possessing was valid.

d.   Fixtures Which Are Annexed After the Giving of a Mortgage on the Realty are Normally Within the Mortgage. [§ 8–159]

Even fixtures which are obtained after the creation of the mortgage are reachable by the mortgagee in the event of foreclosure.

LANDLORD AND TENANT LAW

REVIEW PROBLEMS—LANDLORD AND TENANT

Landlord and Tenant law is a dynamic area of property law in which the rules have changed dramatically in the last twenty-five years. Multiple choice exam questions still stress some of the less dynamic parts of the subject area such as the distinctions between sublease and assignment or the differences between the creation and termination of the types of leasehold estates.

Most essay questions these days stress the changes from old property rules to contract approaches (see § 8–4) and the new concepts of implied warranties of habitability (§ 8–89), illegal lease (§ 8–52), and retaliatory eviction (§ 8–96). The object of these questions is for the student to compare the possibility (very bad) the tenant has of winning a dispute over, for example, needed repairs of the premises, under the old property law approach and the possibility (very good) the tenant has of winning if the contract doctrines are applied. (The following question illustrate these types of issues in an exam format.)

> **Question:** L owns a residential duplex and rents apartment #1 to T1 and apartment #2 to T2. Neither lease contains any reference to the responsibility of either landlord or tenant to make repairs. A hurricane damages the roof over both apartments and the roof leaks badly when it rains. Both T1 and T2 inform L of the problem and request repairs. L refuses and T1 moves out and stops paying rent. T2 remains in possession and stops paying rent. L sues both T1 and T2 for unpaid rent. What result?
>
> > **Answer:** T1 can probably prevail against L's claim by using the defense of constructive eviction (i.e., the idea that even though L had no duty at common law to repair, his failure to make such an essential repair as that needed here is tantamount to evicting the tenant). An eviction, actual or constructive, terminates the lease and T1's rental payment obligations. It is usually a prerequisite to asserting the constructive eviction defense that T1 vacated the premises which is the case here. T2 is also likely to prevail but since he has remained in possession he can not use the constructive eviction defense but instead must use modern contract principles to imply into the lease a covenant of habitability and then use the contracts doctrine of mutual dependency of lease (contract) covenants to assert that L's failure to repair excused T2 from performance of his rental payment obligation. It is possible, even likely, that the court will find some rental value left to the unit and require T2 to pay whatever that value is (i.e., reduce the rent originally due down to the rental value of a dwelling unit with a leaking roof).

CHAPTER IX

EASEMENTS, PROFITS AND LICENSES

A. OVERVIEW. [§ 9–1]

Easements, profits, and licenses, along with real covenants and equitable servitudes which are discussed in Chapter X (Covenants Running With The Land And Equitable Servitudes), are devices that permit the holder of the easement, profit, or license to make use of the land of another that is subject to them. In so doing, easements, profits, and licenses must, in some way, restrict or limit the uses which the owner of the land might otherwise make of it. Viewed from the perspective of the other land owner, easements, profits, and licenses are encumbrances, burdens, upon the other land owner's estate. Viewed from the perspective of the holder of the easements, profits, or licenses, they are benefits that give the holder the right to use or to remove something from land belonging to another. Easements, profits, and licenses are property rights that are enforced against the owner of the land burdened by them and also against others.

Although these various devices have different historical roots, there is a growing tendency in the law to consolidate and rationalize them under the generic label "SERVITUDES." The more traditional grouping (i.e., easements, profits, and licenses in one group and real covenants and equitable servitudes in a distinct group) is followed in this Quick Review because a majority of law professors and courts probably still follow such an organization and because it is usually easier to learn these devices if one sees their original roles and origins.

B. EASEMENTS. [§ 9–2]

An easement (and a profit, as we shall see later) is distinguishable from an estate in land (which is discussed in Chapter V (Estates In Land)). Thus far, the estates in land we have covered have been possessory interests (i.e., their owner (or their successors in interest) is or may be entitled to take possession of the property). Easements and profits are conceptually different from estates in land because they are not capable of becoming possessory. They give the holder the right to use or restrict the use of the land that is burdened by the easement, without the right to take possession of the land. (Note: Sometimes it can be difficult to distinguish use rights from possessory interests. Just remember that the strength of common law property is its responsiveness to precedent and historical development and not its ability to define terms!)

1. Classification of Easements: Affirmative and Negative. [§ 9–3]

One way of classifying easements is according to whether they are affirmative or negative.

a. Affirmative Easements. [§ 9–4]

Most easements are "affirmative," (i.e., they permit the easement holder to make use of land whose possessory estates belong to other person(s)). The classic example of an affirmative easement is a "right of way."

Example. [§ 9–5] O, owner of Blackacre, grants to B the right to use Blackacre by driving across it in order to get from B's land, Whiteacre, to a public road. B's right to use Blackacre is considered an "affirmative" easement because B can make an actual physical use of the land subjected to the easement.

b. Negative Easements. [§ 9–6]

An easement may also be "negative" in that it is created so as to limit or restrict the use that the owner of the possessory estate can make of her own land rather than to give a use right to the grantee of the easement. A classic example of a negative easement is an easement for light or view whereby the grantor of the easement restricts her rights to use her own land (Blackacre) in order to benefit the grantee of the easement by guaranteeing light or view for his land (Whiteacre). For example, a landowner restricts her right to build on her own land in a way that would block her neighbor's view.

c. Restrictions on Creation of Negative Easements. [§ 9–7]

English courts arbitrarily and illogically limited the creation of negative easements to four fact situations. The easement holder can prevent the owner of the burdened land from: (1) interfering with the flow of water in artificial streams to the easement holder's land, (2) removing the support of the easement holder's building, (3) blocking the easement holder's windows, and (4) blocking the flow of air to the easement holder's land. American courts have, for the most part, accepted these restrictions on creating new types of negative easements. Nevertheless, American courts have recognized new forms of negative easements. For instance, conservation easements, developed to preserve scenic areas, open space, and historic landmarks, are a relatively new form of negative easement and are extremely popular. One reason for the broadened use and recognition of negative easements is doubtless the enactment by many state legislatures of statutes specifically authorizing negative easements designed for environmental conservation and historic preservation purposes.

2. Characteristics of Easements and Their Terminology. [§ 9–8]

Not only are easements divided into affirmative and negative easements but they are also characterized according to whether they are appurtenant or in gross. The latter categorization revolves around the concept of dominant and servient tenements.

a. Servient Tenement. [§ 9–9]

An affirmative easement is a right to use the land of another. The land that is to be used, the "burdened" land, is normally referred to as the "servient tenement" or the "burdened parcel." In our previous examples illustrating affirmative and negative easements (§§ 9–5 & 9–6), Blackacre is the servient tenement since under the affirmative easement it is "burdened" by the use which B is allowed to make of it and in the negative easement example it is burdened by the restrictions placed on the use which its owner, A, is allowed to make of it. Because all easements, affirmative and negative, are by definition non-possessory interests in land, any time either type of easement is created there will always be a servient estate whose possessory estate(s) will belong to someone other than the owner of the easement.

b. Dominant Tenement. [§ 9–10]

Originally in the common law, the purpose of both affirmative and negative easements was to benefit land owned by the grantee of the easement. Thus, in our previous examples of typical affirmative and negative easements, the purpose and effect of both easements of which Blackacre was the servient tenement was to benefit Whiteacre. More precisely, the purpose and effect of the easements was to benefit B's ownership interest in Whiteacre and not just B as a person. Whiteacre is correspondingly called the "dominant tenement" or the "benefited parcel." Today, the common law recognizes that under certain restricted circumstances an easement may solely benefit an individual even if the individual owns no land or no land that is benefited by the easement. Once this development occurred, it was necessary to distinguish between those easements that benefited other land (easements appurtenant) and those that benefited only the individuals who owned (were granted) the easement (easements in gross).

c. Easements: Appurtenant or in Gross. [§ 9–11]

The distinction between easements in gross and appurtenant easements relates to whether or not the benefit created by the easement "benefits" a tract of land or only the individual(s) granted the easement.

(1) An Appurtenant Easement Has Both a Dominant Tenement and a Servient Tenement. [§ 9–12]

An appurtenant easement is an easement whose benefit (the right to assert the easement) becomes part and parcel of another parcel of land—the dominant tenement. An appurtenant easement is granted to an individual in his capacity as a landowner and benefits his land or the use of his land. Some easements are almost always deemed appurtenant (e.g., right of way easements always benefit the land to which they give access). Both affirmative and negative easements can be appurtenant and our previous examples (§§ 9–5 & 9–6) illustrate appurtenant easements since Whiteacre is benefited by both easements and will be considered the dominant tenement. Blackacre is burdened by both easements and will be considered the servient tenement.

(2) An Easement in Gross Does Not Have a Dominant Tenement; It Only Has a Servient Tenement. [§ 9–13]

An easement is classified as "in gross" (not "appurtenant") if it does not benefit a specific tract, but is solely for the use or benefit of an individual or business and is unrelated to any land owned by the individual or business. Commonly encountered examples of easements in gross are public utility easements, water company pipes, gas lines, telephone lines and cables. These easements are generally viewed as easements in gross since the easement which allows the utility to run the pipes or lines across the servient estate benefits only the utility business and not the land, if any, owned by the utility company.

Example. [§ 9–14] Let us assume that A, owner of a fee simple absolute in Blackacre, grants an easement to the EKG Oil Transmission Co. whereby EKG Co. is permitted to lay an oil pipeline across Blackacre to connect with a pipeline that runs across hundreds of miles of land between the Texas oil fields and the City of New Orleans. Let us further assume that EKG Co. owns no land anywhere and that the oil is to be exported to foreign countries. The easement is an affirmative easement per our previous analysis and Blackacre is the servient tenement. Where is the dominant tenement? There is none. Various persons are benefited by the gas line and some of them may in fact be landowners but no particularly identifiable parcels of land are intended to be benefited. Since there is no "dominant tenement" the easement is classified as "in gross" meaning that the benefit is not attached to a piece of land.

(3) Intent of the Parties Determines Whether Easement Is Appurtenant or in Gross. [§ 9–15]

Whether an easement is in gross or appurtenant rests ultimately on the intent of the parties who created the easement, the surrounding circumstances, and the language used to create the easement. Intention to create an appurtenant easement is determined by reference to such matters as the purpose of the easement and its relation to the use of other land (is there a benefited/dominant estate?). One approach, for example, is to consider whether the easement holder would have any use for the easement other than a use in connection with a specific piece of land. Whether an easement is appurtenant or in gross typically is only of consequence when one is trying to determine whether the easement is assignable or whether the easement passes with the title of the benefited estate.

(4) Constructional Preference for Appurtenant Easements. [§ 9–16]

There is a strong constructional preference for appurtenant easements because the ownership of appurtenant easements is more easily determined.

d. Alienation of Appurtenant Easements. [§ 9–17]

(1) Transfer of the Servient Tenement. [§ 9–18]

Unless the duration of an easement is expressly or implicitly limited, or the easement is extinguished by reference to one of the doctrines subsequently discussed (§ 9–76), the easement will continue to burden the servient tenement even though the possessory interests to the burdened land are conveyed or devised, or descend to another person.

(2) Transfer of Dominant Tenement Transfers Easement. [§ 9–19]

Ownership of an appurtenant easement is annexed to, or part of, ownership of the dominant estate. Transfer of the dominant tenement thus transfers ownership of the easement as well, even if the conveyance did not expressly include the easement. One exception is the case in which the owner of the servient tenement acquires ownership of the dominant tenement. If the dominant and servient tenements come into common ownership, the appurtenant easement is terminated by merger. (§ 9–79)

(3) May Be Apportionable. [§ 9–20]

If ownership of the dominant tenement is divided, the easement is deemed part of each portion of the dominant tenement and may be exercised by the owner of each such portion, unless the result is to burden the servient tenement beyond the burden contemplated when the easement was created or unless the parties to the easement have prohibited this result by the terms of the easement agreement.

Example. [§ 9–21] O, owner of Blackacre, is granted a right of way easement over adjacent Whiteacre. O now subdivides Blackacre into three tracts; she retains one, and conveys one to X and one to Y. O, X, and Y all have the right to use the right of way, unless it can be demonstrated on the facts of the particular case that the burden on the servient tenement will be increased significantly beyond that originally contemplated.

(4) Not Severable. [§ 9–22]

An appurtenant easement cannot be severed from the dominant estate in such a way as to permit the easement to become one in gross or appurtenant to another dominant tract. It can be prevented from passing with the dominant tenement but this normally has the effect of extinguishing the easement.

e. Alienation of Easements in Gross. [§ 9–23]

At common law, easements in gross were personal to the grantee and could not be alienated or devised unless the grantee was expressly granted a power to do so. It is now firmly established, however, that commercial easements in gross (i.e., one granted for the principal purpose of economically benefiting the grantee) are alienable unless a contrary intent has been manifested; many jurisdictions still prohibit the assignment of non-commercial easements in gross but the trend is toward free alienation.

3. Creation of Easements. [§ 9–24]

Easements may be created in several ways.

a. Easements Created Expressly by Written Grant or Reservation. [§ 9–25]

An easement may be created expressly by a written grant or deed of easement. (Note the old terminology for the document creating an easement by transfer was "grant" but in more and more jurisdictions the document is now called "deed of easement.") Another way to create an easement through writing is by reservation in a written conveyance. Thus, a landowner may convey her land by deed, but retain (reserve) an easement over it. The easement she retains is said to have been created by reservation. Traditionally, courts would not allow easements to be created in third parties by reservation but the rule seems to be changing so as to allow creation in third parties by reservation. (See Case Squib: *Willard v. First Church of Christ*.)

(1) Statute of Frauds Applies. [§ 9–26]

Because easements are interests in land, they normally must be created in compliance with the Statute of Frauds. However, the methods of creation discussed below indicate the willingness of courts to overlook Statute of Frauds requirements.

b. Easements Created by Implication. [§ 9–27]

Easements by implication are created where the parties have not expressly reserved or granted easements in writing. Because these easements are created by operation of law, no writing under the Statute of Frauds is necessary. Easements by implication arise only when land under common title is severed (e.g., A owning a large tract conveys part of the tract to B). If there is no severance of common ownership, there can be no easement by implication, even in the case of strict necessity. All implied easements are appurtenant.

(1) Easements Implied From Necessity. [§ 9–28]

The easement implied from necessity is discussed here because it is actually a type of implied easement which requires both common ownership and strict necessity. To create an easement implied from necessity, both the dominant and servient tenement must at one time have been under common ownership and there must have been strict necessity for the easement when the tract was severed. (See Case Squibs section, *Othen v. Rosier*). "Strict necessity" does not require absolute impossibility of solving the problem in some other way but only substantial impracticability or unreasonable expense. Note that even if there is no strict necessity, an easement by implied grant (§ 9–31) may arise so long as there is reasonable necessity and additional requirements are met.

The elements of an easement implied from necessity are: (1) previous common ownership of land; (2) a conveyance of a physical part of the land, creating two or more parcels, that severs the common ownership; (3) as a result of the severance, it is "necessary" (strict necessity) to impose an easement appurtenant over one or more parcels (servient tenements) to secure rights necessary for the reasonable enjoyment of one or more parcels (dominant tenements). The necessity must exist at the time of the severance; a subsequent necessity will not have any effect.

(a) Right of Way Easements. [§ 9–29]

Easements implied from necessity almost invariably involve right of way easements.

155

Example. [§ 9–30] O owns a large tract, Blackacre. It is bounded by a public highway on the south. O conveys the northern half of Blackacre to X. X has no means of access to a highway from his tract, either directly or across any other land which he owns. On these facts, X will have an implied easement of necessity by grant across the southern half of Blackacre.

(b) Can Be Created by Implied Grant or Implied Reservation. [§ 9–31]

An easement implied from necessity may be created by implied reservation (i.e., on behalf of the grantor) as well as by implied grant (i.e., on behalf of the grantee). In the above example, if O had conveyed the southern half of Blackacre to X, O would retain an implied easement of necessity by reservation. Note, many courts profess to be reluctant to recognize implied reservations unless there is strict necessity. One reason for this reluctance by courts probably is the principle that a grantor cannot derogate from his own grant and the companion rule that a deed is construed against the drafter. The implied reservation in favor of the grantor contravenes the express language of the grant to the detriment of the grantee who receives less than what the grantor expressly conveyed to the grantee in the deed and less than what the grantee paid to receive. (See Case Squib: *Othen v. Rosier.*) Courts have not taken a unified approach to the distinction between granted and reserved implied easements. It is fair to say that most courts may require stronger proof of a reserved as opposed to a granted implied easement.

(c) Continues Only as Long as Necessity Continues. [§ 9–32]

According to most but not all courts, an easement implied from necessity continues only so long as the strict necessity continues to exist. Thus, if in the above example a new highway is constructed adjacent to X's parcel of land, the easement implied from necessity is terminated and X loses her right of way over O's property.

If the dominant and servient tenements come together under common ownership, the easement implied from necessity is extinguished because the necessity no longer exists. If the now united title is again divided, a new easement implied from necessity could arise if the circumstances give rise to the elements of the easement. (See § 9–28)

(2) Easement Implied From Prior Use—The Quasi–Easement. [§ 9–33]

Many courts recognize a second category of implied easements—the quasi-easement, which is an easement implied on the basis of one portion of the relevant parcel of land having been used for the benefit of another portion of the relevant portion of land prior to the division of the land into two or more parcels. (See Case Squib: *Van Sandt v. Royster*.)

The elements of an easement implied from prior use are: (1) once common ownership of land; (2) a conveyance of a physical part of the land, creating two or more parcels, that severs the common ownership (the grantor retains part that usually adjoins the part conveyed); (3) prior to the conveyance, the grantor used part of the land for the benefit of the other so that had the parts then been severed, the usage could have been the subject of an easement appurtenant; (4) the use of part for the benefit of the other to which it is appurtenant is "reasonably necessary"; (5) the use, prior to the severance, was apparent; and (6) the use was continuous, meaning more than merely temporary or casual.

(a) Example. [§ 9–34] O is the owner of Blackacre. During the period of his ownership, O installed a drainpipe to carry surface water from the northern part of Blackacre across the southern part of Blackacre to a public storm sewer. O now conveys the northern part of Blackacre to X. The granting deed says nothing about the drainpipe. Assuming that the drain is "apparent" (i.e., it was visible, or knowledgeable, people in O and X's situation would have realized its possible existence), X will have an easement implied from prior use by grant across the southern part of Blackacre even though it is still owned by O. Assume that instead of conveying the northern part of Blackacre to X, O conveys the southern part of Blackacre to X and retains the northern part. O will have an easement implied from prior use by reservation across the southern part of Blackacre which is now owned by X. The same concerns about implied reservations of easement implied from necessity pertain to easements implied by prior use.

(b) Common Ownership. [§ 9–35]

Both dominant and servient tenements must have been under common ownership which has since been severed. The severance may be voluntary or involuntary.

157

(c) **During the Period of Common Ownership, the Owner Must Have Used One Part for the Benefit of the Other Part. [§ 9–36]**

The use which allegedly becomes an easement must have been present before, as well as at, the time of severance. This use of one tract for the benefit of another tract owned by the same person is called a "quasi-easement." The quasi-easement becomes an implied easement when the common ownership is severed.

(d) **Characteristics of Quasi–Easements. [§ 9–37]**

In order for an easement by implication to arise, the quasi-easement must have certain qualities. The quasi-easement must be apparent (i.e., the existence of the quasi-easement must be ascertainable from a reasonable inspection of the dominant estate—note that this requirement is usually met in the case of rights of way which tend to be highly visible. The courts have more difficulty with underground pipes where the "apparent" requirement is normally satisfied if the appliances to which the pipes are connected are obvious and visible). (See Case Squib: *Van Sandt v. Royster.*) The use must be continuous (the continuity test is met if the quasi-easement has some degree of permanence and regularity of use, which continuity can be observed in the case of a right of way by the amount of wear). Today, many courts do not mention continuity as an element or they find that intermittent use is sufficient or they treat the element of apparent/visible use as being important with continuity as an aspect of visibility. Also, the use must be reasonably necessary to the use of the dominant tenement.

(3) **Quasi–Easement and Implied Reservation. [§ 9–38]**

(a) **Distinguished From Implied Easement by Grant. [§ 9–39]**

An implied reservation of an easement is created in favor of the grantor on severance of the common ownership, whereas an implied grant of an easement arises in favor of the grantee at the time of severance.

(b) **Requires Strict Necessity. [§ 9–40]**

The requirements for an implied reservation are essentially the same as those for an implied grant. However, because the implied reservation of an easement is being given to the grantor (who should not be allowed to keep what he apparently sold), a number of court decisions hold that there is a requirement of strict necessity, rather than reasonable necessity, before an easement will be implied.

c. Easements by Prescription (Adverse Use). [§ 9–41]

An easement may be acquired in much the same way that title to a possessory estate may be secured by adverse possession (discussed in Chapter XII (Adverse Possession)). Title by adverse possession is predicated upon the running of a Statute of Limitations on a claim to regain possession. Doctrines concerning prescription proceed by analogy to adverse possession, but are based on use, not possession, since easements are non-possessory interests in land. For example, if B, owner of Whiteacre, drives across neighboring land, Blackacre, owned by A, day after day, year after year to reach the public road which borders Blackacre and B's use of Blackacre as a right of way is without A's permission. B's adverse use of Blackacre may result in his obtaining a right of way easement across Blackacre. For an easement to be thusly created, the courts have formulated certain requirements which must be met. These requirements have been "borrowed" from the law of adverse possession. These requirements for adverse use (prescription) are discussed below.

(1) Actual. [§ 9–42]

The use must be actual (i.e., the use has really occurred and the use which can be proved is of primary importance in determining the scope (physical extent) of the easement).

(2) Open and Notorious. [§ 9–43]

The use must be of such a character as to give notice to the owner of the burdened parcel.

(3) Continuous for the Statutory Period. [§ 9–44]

The use must continue for the statutory period (which, at common law, was twenty years). The period varies from state to state but is the same as the period for adverse possession in most jurisdictions.

(a) The Running of the Prescriptive Period Begins When the Adverse Use Begins. [§ 9–45]

If a prescriptive easement arises, it is deemed for some purposes to have been created when the use began.

(b) Legal Disability of Owners. [§ 9–46]

The running of the prescriptive period against owners under legal disability is dealt with as disabilities are dealt with in connection with adverse possession (§ 11–16).

(c) Continuous Does Not Mean Every Day. [§ 9–47]

Continuity is a question which often must be considered on a case by case basis, taking into account the nature of the use and the nature of the property. For example, A and B own adjacent lots with summer cottages on them in a resort area. The cottages are vacant except for the period from May through September. Every summer for twenty years, A has used a strip of B's land as his regular means of access to his cottage. Such use would probably be held continuous.

(d) Periods May Be Tacked. [§ 9–48]

The use need not be by one individual for the entire period; the "tacking" doctrine applied in adverse possession cases is equally applicable here. The use of two or more successors in interest may be tacked if the users are in privity. Privity may be established either by reference to the easement in the deed from the predecessor or by parol transfer (an indication, actual or presumed, that the grantee is the successor of the grantor with respect to the use).

(e) Use Which Is Interrupted May Require Period to Start Anew. [§ 9–49]

Continuity may be broken ("interrupted") so as to stop the running of the period and require that it start anew. This may occur in several ways. The owner may physically obstruct the use (such obstruction which results in a cessation of use for any length of time stops the running of the period) or the owner may interrupt the use by a successful legal action, even though the use does not in fact stop. However, mere protest by the owner is not generally held to interrupt the use.

(4) Exclusive. [§ 9–50]

The use must be exclusive. This, however, does not mean that it must be of such a nature that it effectively excludes the landowner. Exclusive use means that the use must be made by the user in an individual capacity and not simply as a member of the general public. Use in common with the public is deemed not to be open and notorious so as to put the owner on notice that the particular use is different from that of the general public.

Most states permit the public to acquire public prescriptive easements by establishing a history of long, open, continuous, adverse use. Because such easements are public, the element of exclusivity is not required.

(5) Adverse or Hostile. [§ 9–51]

The use must be adverse or hostile. This is the most difficult requirement to establish. Generally, this means that the use must be non-permissive. While some cases speak of a "claim of right" requirement, this usually means only that the use is made in a manner indicating indifference toward the rights of the owner.

(a) A Permissive Use Cannot Result in an Easement by Prescription. [§ 9–52]

If a use is permissive at the outset, it can be made non-permissive only by distinct and open communication to the owner that the user is no longer operating with the owner's permission. If the use begins with the permission of the owner, who subsequently conveys to another, the use will be deemed non-permissive against the new grantee unless the grantee informs the user that he will allow the use to continue

In many jurisdictions, a use initially non-permissive cannot be made permissive by the owner subsequently giving unilateral permission without the user's consent. Of course, the parties can execute a formal easement agreement or agree to an informal license, both of which would cause a non-permissive use to become permissive.

(b) Burden of Proof. [§ 9–53]

Use that is open, notorious, and continuous for the statutory period is presumed non-permissive in many states and this is likely the better view. The burden of proving permission is then on the owner. Other states, however, require that the element of adverseness be established by clear and positive proof, thus making the law of prescription conform to that of adverse possession on this important element.

(c) Use Must Be Inconsistent With Owner's Rights. [§ 9–54]

In order to be hostile, the use must be inconsistent with the landowner's rights and must create a cause of action in him. For this reason, it is impossible to create negative easements by prescription. (e.g., the fact that a landowner has received unobstructed light or air across a neighbor's lot for twenty years gives him no right to insist that it continue; he has done nothing against which his neighbor had a right to protest.)

d. Easement by Estoppel. [§ 9–55]

In certain circumstances, a court may estop a landowner to deny that she has created an easement.

161

Example. [§ 9–56] X asks his neighbor Y for the right to lay drain tiles across Y's land. X and Y orally agree that X may lay such tiles. The oral agreement does not suffice to constitute the grant of an easement because the Statute of Frauds requires that an easement be created by a writing. X simply has a license (an oral permission to make a use of land that without permission would constitute a trespass) which can be revoked by Y at any time. (§ 9–103 & § 9–112) X then enters and lays the drain tile. What effect does X's installation of the drain pipes have?

(a) Detrimental Reliance May Create an Irrevocable License or an Easement. [§ 9–57]

In some states, the detrimental reliance by X will make the "license" irrevocable, and the courts may conclude that an easement has in fact been created. To obtain this result, it must be clear that an easement was intended; if only a license was contemplated, reliance is unjustified (note that some states will refer to a license coupled with justified reliance as an "irrevocable license"). The duration of the easement may, however, be limited to the time needed for X to recoup the value of his improvements. (See Case Squib: *Holbrook v. Taylor*.)

(b) Contra View. [§ 9–58]

In other states, the license does not become irrevocable, although X must be given a reasonable time after revocation of the license to remove his improvements.

e. Creation of Easement Rights in the Public by Dedication (Usually Rights of Way). [§ 9–59]

(1) Common Law Dedication. [§ 9–60]

At common law, dedication may be made formally (i.e., typically by deed to an appropriate public body) or by other means manifesting an intent to dedicate to public use, coupled with some degree of actual public use. In the typical case, an intent to dedicate is implied from facts indicating that the owner assisted the public in its use of his land; such conduct is regarded as an offer to dedicate, which may be revoked if not accepted within a reasonable time. Acceptance may of course be by formal act of the public's governing body. It may be found in the assumption of control manifested by the city when it makes repairs. In some cases, public use is itself acceptance, although there is some authority indicating that public use is not itself sufficient acceptance with respect to city streets; some additional act by the city is necessary. Common law dedication transfers only a servitude and may occur even if the requirements for a statutory dedication have not been met. Using either prescription or dedication theory, the majority of courts permit acquisition of servitudes by long-continued public use.

(2) Statutory Dedication. [§ 9–61]

Statutory dedication is the process of dedication to public use by the recording of a plat showing the land intended to be dedicated for streets, parks, etc. Acceptance by a public within a reasonable time is necessary to complete the dedication. Unlike common law dedication, statutory dedication often results in a fee estate being transferred to the public.

4. Scope of Easements: Reconciling the Rights of Easement Users and Owners of the Servient Tenement. [§ 9–62]

a. Physical Location. [§ 9–63]

(1) The Location of an Easement Can Be Changed Only by Mutual Agreement. [§ 9–64]

If the location of the easement is precisely indicated by a written instrument, or by the location of a quasi-easement (in the case of an easement by implication), or by use in the case of a prescriptive easement, its location cannot be changed except by mutual agreement. Neither the dominant nor servient owner may unilaterally relocate the easement in a more convenient place. While this is the established rule, you should be aware that the Restatement (Third) Property does not follow the established rule. The Restatement states that, unless expressly denied by the terms of the easement, the servient owner can make reasonable changes to the dimensions or location of an easement to allow normal use or development of the servient estate as long as the changes do not: (1) significantly lessen the easement's utility, (2) increase the dominant owner's burdens in its use and enjoyment of the easement, or (3) frustrate the purposes for creating the easement.

(2) Deciding Location of General Grants. [§ 9–65]

If the grant is general (i.e., without a defined location), or in the case of an easement implied from necessity, the servient tenement holder may determine the exact location of the easement, subject to the requirement that it be reasonably convenient to the easement holder and suited for the purpose for which the easement was created.

CHAPTER IX

Once fixed, the location may not be changed, without the agreement of the parties.

b. Rights and Duties of Easement Holder. [§ 9–66]

(1) Proper Uses—May Not Over–Burden Servient Tenement. [§ 9–67]

The easement holder may only use the easement for those activities which were reasonably contemplated at the time the easement was created.

(a) Express Grants or Reservations. [§ 9–68]

The scope of use in express grants or reservations is initially determined by reference to the language of the instrument and the subsequent construction put on it by the parties. However, the parties are presumed to have intended a reasonable scope to the easement and to have contemplated reasonable or normal changes in the type of use which might be required and in the character of the dominant estate.

(b) Easements by Implication. [§ 9–69]

In the case of easements by implication, the scope is determined by reference to the nature of the use being made when common title was severed. Again, however, the parties are assumed to have contemplated reasonably foreseeable changes in the dominant estate.

(c) Prescriptive Easements. [§ 9–70]

The scope of prescriptive easements is confined to the nature of the use made during the prescriptive period (and which gave rise to the rights created by prescription) on the theory that the owner might have objected to more burdensome uses. Some variation may be permitted, but the courts have been hostile to any expansion of the scope of prescriptive easements.

(d) Appurtenant Easements May Not Be Used for Other Tracts. [§ 9–71]

The holder of an appurtenant easement may use his easement only for the benefit of the dominant tenement. (See Case Squib: *Brown v. Voss.*)

Example. [§ 9–72] If A has a right of way easement appurtenant to Blackacre over Whiteacre, she may not use the right of way for access to any tract but Blackacre. Use for any other tract automatically over-burdens the servient estate and may be enjoined.

(e) Change in Circumstances. [§ 9–73]

When the language creating the easement is general, the use of the easement may normally be allowed to change to keep up with changes in circumstances that the dominant tenement could reasonably have anticipated. In some cases, a change in situation may be so fundamental that the scope of the easement will be limited. Thus, if the nature of the physical use changes (e.g., if the easement for a right of way was created before 1900, may it now be used for automobile traffic?) or the character of the dominant tenement has changed (e.g., an appurtenant right of way easement was granted when the dominant estate was a residence; it is now a state highway department garage), the easement may be limited. However, reasonable subdivision of the dominant estate (e.g., from one to four residences) is probably allowable and each owner of a part of the dominant estate acquires a right to use the easement. Of course, a subdivision involving 400 condominiums with every owner using the easement would probably be held to over-burden the easement. (§ 9–20)

Similar principles apply to easements created by implication and to easements by prescription; however, the manner of creation of these easements does cause special problems in applying the principles. The primary difficulty is in defining the uses originally permitted by the easement.

(2) Right to Enter and Duty to Make Repairs on Servient Tenement. [§ 9–74]

The easement holder (the dominant tenement) has both the right and the duty to enter the servient tenement to make repairs on the easement. The servient tenement holder has no duty to maintain the easement unless he agrees to do so. The easement holder may not, however, substantially change the nature of an easement in the name of repairs. For example, it has been held that an easement holder may not pave a right of way which has long existed as a dirt road.

c. Rights of Servient Tenement Owner. [§ 9–75]

The owner of the servient tenement may make any use of his property that does not interfere with, or is not inconsistent with, the easement holder's rights. For example, the owner of the servient tenement across which another has a right of way easement may use the right of way himself, or may allow others to do so, as long as he does not interfere with the easement holder's use (assuming that the original grant did not confer exclusive rights of use). Similarly, he may build over the easement, if the use by the easement holder is not obstructed.

5. Termination of Easements. [§ 9–76]

Easements may be terminated in a number of ways:

a. Condition Reached. [§ 9–77]

The easement may simply come to an end, if granted for a limited term (e.g., "until August 24, 2020") or upon the occurrence of a condition (e.g., "until the new road is built").

b. Written Release. [§ 9–78]

An easement may be terminated by a written release which complies with the Statute of Frauds.

c. Merger. [§ 9–79]

An appurtenant easement is terminated by merger if the dominant and servient tenements come into common ownership. The reason the appurtenant easement is terminated is because, as a result of the unity of ownership, the right to exercise the privileges formerly exercised under the appurtenant easement become exercisable as part of the rights of ownership of the servient tenement. If the unity of the dominant and servient tenement is complete, the extinguishment will be complete. If the unity is incomplete, the extinguishment of the easement will also be incomplete.

Example. [§ 9–80] Assume A is the owner of Blackacre, the dominant tenement. B is the owner of Whiteacre, the servient tenement. B grants A an easement for ingress and egress over Whiteacre in order to get to and from Blackacre. Later, A leases Blackacre to B for a term of years. The easement will be extinguished during the term of the lease. At the end of the lease, A who is the owner of the reversion in the dominant tenement, Blackacre, will still have the right to the benefit of the easement.

It is important to note that the easement that is completely extinguished does not automatically revive if the estates are again severed. Revival requires re-creation under the rules stated in this chapter. An easement in gross is terminated by merger when its holder acquires the servient tenement.

d. Non–Use Plus Manifest Intent to Abandon. [§ 9–81]

Any easement may be lost if two elements are present: (1) extended non-use coupled with other acts clearly indicating the user's, (2) intent to relinquish the use (e.g., a railroad company ceased active transportation over a railroad line and removed all of its tracts and other infrastructure necessary to return the line to active service for an extended period. Note that a spoken intent to abandon coupled with non-use is generally not sufficient to terminate the easement). (See Case Squib: *Preseault v. United States*.)

e. Adverse Use, Prescription. [§ 9–82]

Just as an easement may be created by adverse use (prescription), an easement may be terminated by use of the servient tenement which is adverse to the rights of the easement holder and satisfies the elements of adverse use. To accomplish this result, the owner of the servient estate must continuously interfere with or prevent the use of the easement by the easement holder for the full prescriptive period. For example, if X, the owner of the servient tenement, builds a structure across Y's right of way, and the structure remains for the statutory period, Y has lost his easement. The conduct of X must, of course, be non-permissive.

f. Condemnation of Servient Estate. [§ 9–83]

The Restatement (Third) Property states that condemnation (taking of title through the exercise of the power of eminent domain by a governmental entity or its delegate) of the servient estate terminates the easement to the extent that the taking permits a use inconsistent with continuance of the servitude. However, the holder of the easement is entitled to share in the condemnation award. Condemnation of the dominant estate terminates the benefit only if that is the purpose of the condemnation.

g. Destruction of Servient Estate. [§ 9–84]

If the easement is granted within a structure (e.g., an easement in a stairway), the easement is terminated if the structure is destroyed. Obviously, the owner of the servient tenement will be liable to the holder of the easement if the destruction is wrongful. Replacement of the structure does not revive the easement unless a court finds that such was the intention of the parties.

h. Termination by Estoppel. [§ 9–85]

An easement may be terminated by estoppel if: (1) the holder of the easement communicates to the owner of the servient tenement an intent to abandon, by words, deeds, or silence, (2) under circumstances in which it would be reasonable to foresee that the owner of the servient tenement would rely, (3) the servient tenement owner reasonably and substantially relies, to his detriment, on the apparent intent of the easement holder to abandon (e.g., the servient tenement owner makes substantial expenditures in improving the area of his property where the easement exists) and, (4) the easement holder does not object within a reasonable time. Thus, an express oral intention to abandon coupled with non-use does not terminate the easement unless the servient tenement holder relies on this stated intent to his detriment.

i. An Easement Implied From Necessity Ends When the Necessity Ends. [§ 9–86]

As mentioned earlier (§ 9–32), the prevailing view is that an easement implied from necessity will terminate when the "necessity" for the easement is removed such as by the construction of a new road so that the easement is no longer necessary.

j. Limited Purpose for Which Created Can No Longer Be Served. [§ 9–87]

An easement will terminate if it was created for a certain or limited purpose but can no longer serve that purpose. The broader the purpose of the easement, the less likely that it will be terminated because all of the easement's purposes must have permanently ended.

C. PROFITS A PRENDRE. [§ 9–88]

Like an easement, a profit a prendre (literally, a right to take), typically called a "profit," is a non-possessory interest in land. Whereas an easement is a right to use the land of another, a profit is the right to take something or things previously constituting part of the land from the land of another. Consequently, all profits are affirmative. The most common profits are rights to take sand or gravel, minerals, wood, or water. In each case, the holder of the profit is authorized to physically remove something from the land.

Profits are interests in land within the Statute of Frauds.

1. All Profits Necessarily Include an Easement. [§ 9–89]

A profit necessarily includes an easement for access to the material subject to the profit. Thus, if X is granted the right to take sand from the land of O, she is impliedly given the right to enter O's land via a reasonable route. Since a profit includes an easement the rules relating to these two interests overlap so considerably that there is a growing tendency to assimilate the law of easements and the law of profits. Thus, in some jurisdictions, profits are viewed as merely a type of easement.

2. Profits May Be Appurtenant or in Gross. [§ 9–90]

Like easements, profits may be either appurtenant to a particular dominant tract or in gross.

a. Profit Appurtenant. [§ 9–91]

A profit may be granted in a way which makes it clear that its use is limited to a particular tract, thus making it appurtenant. An appurtenant profit is annexed to the dominant tract, passes with it, and cannot be severed from it.

(1) Divisibility of Appurtenant Profits. [§ 9–92]

Appurtenant easements are divisible/apportionable so that when the dominant tenement is divided the owners of each part are presumed to have the benefit of the easement. (§ 9–20) Does the same doctrine apply to profits? Suppose A is the owner of Blackacre, to which an appurtenant profit is attached. A divides Blackacre, conveying one-third to B, one-third to C, and retaining one-third himself. Under what circumstances may B and C claim rights through the profit? Generally, the concern in this area is that allowing the profit to be apportioned may create an additional burden on the servient tenement.

(a) Exclusive Profits. [§ 9–93]

If the profit originally gave A "the sole right" to take all of a substance from the land or to make sole use of the profit, or in some other way indicated that the right was to be exclusive, the profit passes to and is apportioned among all holders of portions of the estate. An exclusive profit precludes even the owner of the servient tenement from taking, and is close to outright ownership. In most cases, division of an exclusive profit does not increase the burden on the servient tenement. In this example, the exclusive profit gave A the right to take all of the substance so regardless of the number of grantees, it would be impossible for the grantees to take more than what was conveyed to A.

(b) Non–Exclusive But Admeasurable Profits. [§ 9–94]

If the profit is nonexclusive, but admeasurable (i.e., measurable in scope by the quantity of land to which it is attached), it may be divided and apportioned by reference to land quantity. A non-exclusive profit which is not admeasurable (e.g., a right to take water for residential purposes) normally cannot be divided, unless it is clear that the division cannot materially increase the burden on the servient tenement.

b. Profit in Gross. [§ 9–95]

Just as is the case with easements in gross (§ 9–11), a profit is in gross if it is created so that its owner is granted the right pursuant to the profits for purposes totally unrelated to any land he might own.

(1) Exclusive or Non–Exclusive. [§ 9–96]

Profits in gross may be exclusive (meaning that even the owner of the servient tenement may not take) or non-exclusive. An exclusive profit in gross is virtually outright ownership of the substance to be taken. Profits are presumed to be non-exclusive; only a clear expression of intent will create an exclusive profit.

(2) Unlike Easements in Gross, All Profits in Gross Are Assignable. [§ 9–97]

Even in those jurisdictions which restrict the assignability of some types of easements in gross, profits in gross are assignable, (i.e., a grantee may transfer them to a third party). This remains one of the few differences between the law of easements and the law of profits.

(3) Not All Profits in Gross Are Divisible. [§ 9–98]

While assignable, not all profits in gross may be assigned to two or more persons unless they exercise the profit jointly as a single unit.

(a) Exclusive Profit in Gross. [§ 9–99]

An exclusive profit in gross is normally divisible, unless an undue increase in the burden of the servient tenement would occur (an unlikely result).

(b) Non–Exclusive Profit in Gross. [§ 9–100]

A non-exclusive profit in gross is not divisible. An exception has been recognized in which courts have held that it is not a division to transfer a profit to multiple persons who will use it as "one stock" (meaning if they use the profit together and take only what the original holder would have taken). *Miller v. Lutheran Conference & Camp Association* exemplifies applying the one stock rule in the context of assignability of easements in gross. (See Case Squib: *Miller v. Lutheran Conference & Camp Association*.) If a profit is improperly assigned or divided, it will likely be held to be destroyed.

3. Creation of Profits. [§ 9–101]

Profits can be created by express grants, express reservation, and by prescription. Unlike easements, they cannot be created by necessity or by implication.

4. Profits Terminate Like Easements. [§ 9–102]

Profits are terminated in the same way as easements. (§ 9–76)

D. LICENSES. [§ 9–103]

A license is a revocable permission given by a landowner to another party which gives that party the right to make some use of the landowner's land that without that permission would constitute a trespass.

> **Example. [§ 9–104]** If A, owner of Blackacre, gives his neighbor, B, oral permission to cross Blackacre to get to the road which borders Blackacre, B has a license or permission which, unless and until A revokes it, would be a defense for B should A seek to sue him for trespass.

1. License Not an Interest in Land. [§ 9–105]

A license is not an interest in land and thus it may be created orally since the Statute of Frauds does not apply to it. You may wonder why licenses are grouped with easements and profits if licenses are not interests in land. Conceptually they should not be. However, they normally are discussed with easements and profits because the circumstances and purposes of their creation so often overlap the circumstances and purposes for the creation of easements that landowners and courts alike have trouble distinguishing them. Consider the example given in § 9–104. Did A intend his oral permission to B to create an easement or a license? The Statue of Frauds, in theory, prevents A from orally creating an easement so we must assume he intended to create a license, but not all landowners who give such permissions understand the Statute of Frauds and the key operative distinction between easements and licenses (i.e., that licenses are revocable and easements are presumed irrevocable). As a result, courts, in their effort to do justice to the parties, often turn oral permissions which are conceptually licenses into easements created by estoppel (or licenses irrevocable because they are coupled with an interest). (§§ 9–55—9–58)

2. Revocable at Will. [§ 9–106]

A license is normally revocable at the will of the licensor even though the licensor may be bound by contract not to revoke (and can perhaps be sued for damages in contract if she does so). A revocable license is automatically revoked by the death of the licensor or the licensee, or by the conveyance of the land subject to the license. Normally, an attempted assignment by the licensee also acts as a revocation.

3. Irrevocable Licenses. [§ 9–107]

There are two major exceptions to the general rule that a license is revocable:

a. The License Coupled With an Interest. [§ 9–108]

A license coupled with an interest is a license in which the licensor consents to the placing of personal property (chattel) of the licensee on his land or the licensee has purchased personal property of the licensor that is located on the licensor's land, and where the exercise of the license is necessary in order for the licensee to make use of his personal property. On occasion, a license may be coupled with a grant of a more durable interest in the property (e.g., the right to build a pier and rent boats on O's lake). In either of these cases, the license may be held to be irrevocable so long as the interest lasts. For example, if B sells A a herd of cattle that are located on B's land, B has impliedly given A a license to go onto B's land to remove the cattle.

b. The Executed License. [§ 9–109]

A license, once granted, may be substantially relied upon by the licensee, who invests substantial sums or effort in making improvements, etc. In this sense, the license has been executed.

(1) Irrevocable License View. [§ 9–110]

In most jurisdictions, such reliance may create an easement by estoppel (an irrevocable license) if the reliance was justified in the belief that a durable interest had been created. (See Case Squib: *Holbrook v. Taylor*.) Other states have reached much the same result by treating oral licenses as contracts which, when partly performed, are outside the Statute of Frauds and specifically enforceable. The meaningful difference between an irrevocable license and an easement is elusive at best.

(2) Minority View. [§ 9–111]

Other states have refused to recognize any estoppel effect from such reliance on the ground that this in effect permits creation of an easement in violation of the Statute of Frauds. While these courts may permit removal of improvements, or may condition the licensor's revocation on payment for improvements, the license remains revocable.

4. Reasonable Time for Removal. [§ 9–112]

Once the license has been revoked, the licensee is given a reasonable time to remove herself and her property from the licensor's land.

REVIEW PROBLEMS—EASEMENTS

Most exam questions on easements combine problems with the creation of easements other than by express grant or reservation with issues concerning the transferability and apportionability of easements.

A owns tract A which is bordered on the north by a public road. A sells the southern one-half of tract A to B. The only access to a public road from the southern one-half of tract A (now called tract B) is across tract A but no mention of a right of way easement was included in the deed from A to B. B sues A seeking judicial recognition of an easement of right of way across tract A. What result?

Answer: Most courts will create (imply) an easement of right of way on the basis of B's necessity for access to a public road.

A grants an easement of right of way across her land to B, an adjoining land owner, so that B will have access to a public road which borders A's land. Two years later B divides parcel B into four lots and sells them to C, D, E and F. A physically blocks the right of way across her land and refuses to allow C, D, E and F to use it. C, D, E, and F sue A in order to establish their rights to use the right of way. What result?

Answer: C, D, E, and F will probably win because an affirmative easement appurtenant (the proper categorization of this easement) is transferable and apportionable unless the owner of the servient estate (A) can show that apportionment on division of the dominant tenant (tract B) would unduly burden the servient tenement so as to unnecessarily and unreasonably interfere with the use of the land by the owner of the servient estate (A).

CHAPTER X

COVENANTS RUNNING WITH THE LAND AND EQUITABLE SERVITUDES

A. OVERVIEW. [§ 10–1]

Real covenants (the popular name for covenants running with the land) are contractually created restrictions placed on the use of land which are created by landowners in order to protect their land from incompatible uses of neighboring land. (Covenant is the old word for contract so today they can be called "real contracts" but seldom are in the classroom.)

Real covenants are of recent origin—primarily early nineteenth century—and their development was necessitated by the fact that when they were developed our current framework of public land use control law (such as zoning and subdivision regulation, see Chapter XVI) was not in existence.

Throughout most of the history of common law property, landowners who wished to protect the character and value of their land by ensuring that neighboring land would not be used in a way that interfered with their use—building a pig sty next to a mansion, for example—had to rely on the law of nuisance or on private arrangements with the other landowners. As used here, a private nuisance is an unreasonable interference with another person's use and enjoyment of his private lands. To commit a nuisance is a tort. The law of nuisance is the antecedent to zoning and other forms of land use regulation. The subject of nuisance law is beyond the scope of this chapter and shall not be addressed in any greater detail than what has already been said; however, you should understand that private land use arrangements exist within the context of public land use control law, of which nuisance law is an important part.

Privately negotiated arrangements typically consisted of easements and profits, just discussed in Chapter IX. They provided a workable means for obtaining affirmative use rights, such as rights of way, over neighboring land, but use restrictions over neighboring land were difficult to accomplish through easements because of the subject matter restrictions arbitrarily placed by the English courts on negative easements (See § 9–7). To overcome the judicially imposed restrictions on negative easements, landowners resorted to contractual arrangements or covenants as they were then called, to agree among themselves on the restrictions on the use of land that would be imposed for mutual or individual benefit in a given neighborhood. As long as the parties to these covenants (contracts) could enforce them under contract law principles, everything worked as planned and outside of the framework of property law. But when the covenants needed to be enforced against non-contracting parties (generally persons to whom the contracting parties conveyed the property), property law had to take over their enforcement. The enforcement of such private land use control agreements is what led to the development of the law of real covenants and eventually to equitable servitudes, which were designed to allow the enforcement of many traditionally unenforceable real covenants.

B. INTRODUCTION TO REAL COVENANTS. [§ 10–2]

1. Real Covenant Defined. [§ 10–3]

Covenants running with the land, or real covenants as they are more commonly called, are contractual obligations relating to the use of land which are enforceable by or against persons who currently own the land in question but who were not a party to the contract which created them. Under contract law, such a result could not be reached because, with certain exceptions, contract law provides that only the parties to a contract may be benefited or burdened by obligations arising under the contract. But under property law, if a covenant meets all of the elements such that it runs with the land at law, the covenant may be enforceable by or against remote parties (individuals who were not party to the contract). The theory is that the original contract created rights and obligations which are attached to the ownership interest or estate in the land in question and those rights and obligations are a part of the ownership interest of the successors in ownership of the original contracting parties.

    a. **Example.** [§ 10–4] Assume that Ann and Bob are neighboring landowners of parcels A and B respectively and they enter into a contract restricting both parcels to residential uses. If the courts will enforce the contract as a covenant which will run with the land (i.e., pass to successive owners) then when Ann sells parcel A to Clara and Bob sells parcel B to Don, Clara and Don can enforce the contract against each other even though neither was a party to the contract. Note: The use of the word "covenant," is traditional but in today's language covenants could just as well be called "real contracts." Although we traditionally refer to the "covenanting" parties who create them, "contracting parties" has the same meaning.

2. Real Covenants Create Real Property Interests. [§ 10–5]

Real covenants create interests in real property. Just like easements and profits (see § 9–1 et seq.), burdens and benefits are created by the covenants and these benefits and burdens attach to the appropriate estate in the land. Covenants can be attached to and therefore can be found in any creation of an interest in real property. Hence, covenants can be found in deeds of possessory interests, leases, and grants of easements. Their creation is subject to the Statute of Frauds and they cannot be created by implication, estoppel or prescription.

3. Current Role of Real Covenants. [§ 10–6]

As discussed above, the need for covenants grows out of the practical problem that many landowners faced in trying to protect property from inappropriate uses of neighboring property prior to the development of a public land use control system. Ironically, real covenants and their liberalized version, equitable servitudes, continue to be used today in conjunction with public land use regulations. The classic situation is the developer of a residential subdivision who wants to make the development attractive to people who wish to purchase or lease the properties. The prospective buyers may want to know, indeed they will often demand, that surrounding land will not be put to uses that adversely affect the value of their property. While other devices may effectively control land usage (e.g., defeasible fees or public zoning restrictions), real covenants are a frequently used means as they lack the harshness of other private methods which normally involve a forfeiture of property (e.g. defeasible fees), and their enforcement, utilizing contract remedies, is very flexible. Unlike zoning, they are within the control of private parties rather than government officials. Additionally, private parties can achieve more aggressive regulation of private property uses with covenants than government can through public land use regulations.

4. Requirements for Real Covenants. [§ 10–7]

The courts exacted a price for agreeing to enforce certain contract rights as real property interests and that price was the formulation of the following requirements which a restriction had to meet before it would be recognized as a real covenant running with the land.

The following chart summarizes the requirements, which are discussed in detail below, that a covenant must meet in order to be enforced as a real covenant at common law:

CHAPTER X

REQUIREMENTS FOR REAL COVENANTS

BURDEN	BENEFIT
Formalities must be met; the Statute of Frauds must be satisfied.	Formalities must be met; the Statute of Frauds must be satisfied.
Intent to burden the future owners of the land	Intent to benefit the future owners of the land
The obligations must "touch and concern" the land and not be "merely personal" obligations.	The benefits must "touch and concern" the land and not be "merely personal" benefits.
Horizontal Privity of Estate: The original contracting parties must have a land ownership relationship when they enter into the covenant. Examples of relationships that create horizontal privity include: (1) landlord and tenant; (2) parties to an easement; (3) life tenants and remaindermen or holders of the reversion; (4) owners of interests in defeasible estates; and (5) parties to a deed. (See § 10–22)	Horizontal Privity of Estate: Not required. (See § 10–22)
Vertical Privity of Estate (Strict): The successor to real property burdened by the covenant must succeed to the entire interest of the covenantor. (See § 10–21)	Vertical Privity of Estate (Relaxed): The successor to the real property benefited by the covenant must succeed to an interest of the covenantor. This interest can be less than the entire interest (e.g. owner of a fee simple absolute transfers a life estate, a fee tail, or one of the defeasible estates). (See § 10–21)
Notice of the covenant. Some courts do not expressly list notice as a requirement for a burden to run; however, failure to provide notice may result in the covenant being unenforceable against a subsequent bona fide purchaser. (See § 10–65)	

a. **Formalities, i.e., a Valid Contract Between the Covenanting Parties. [§ 10–8]**

For a covenant to be enforceable by or against successors to the covenanting parties there must first be a valid enforceable contract between the contracting parties that meets the requirements of the Statute of Frauds.

b. **Intent to Bind Successors. [§ 10–9]**

The contracting parties must intend enforceability of the covenant by or against their successors in interest to the property in question. Courts look to the words of the contract. A well-drafted contract will recite that it is to be enforceable by and against the heirs, successors, and assigns of the parties. If intent is not specified through the use of such language, the courts will imply an intent to bind successors unless the subject matter of the covenant is not yet in existence. While the majority of jurisdictions no longer distinguish between things that are in being and things that are not, be aware of this type of fact scenario as it may be fertile ground for examination. As a practical matter, any well-drafted covenant that is intended to run with the land will contain language of intent to run and the word "assigns" is the classic term used to indicate such intent. (See § 10–49)

(1) **Example. [§ 10–10]** Assume the jurisdiction adopts the minority position and distinguishes between things that are in being and things that are not in being. A contracts to maintain her side of a party wall to be built by adjacent landowner, B. Unless intent that the agreement be enforceable by and against the heirs, successors, and assigns of the parties is specified in the contract, A's successor will not be bound by A's covenant to maintain the wall because intent that the agreement "run" to successors in interest will not be implied since it relates to a party wall not in existence at the time the contract is entered into.

c. **Touch and Concern. [§ 10–11]**

In order that a covenant run with the land (i.e., that it will be enforceable by successors to covenantees and enforceable against successors to covenantors) it must "touch and concern" the land. Consequently, only if the covenant affects the quality or value of the property, or if it affects the use of the property, is it considered to touch and concern the land. The reason for this requirement is that the courts wanted to avoid a return to the practice under feudalism (see § 4–4 et seq.) of tying personal obligations to land ownership. Thus the purpose of this requirement is to assure that purely personal obligations unrelated to the ownership of the land in question do not get enforced as property rights and the movement of property law concepts away from feudalism is not reversed. Although the purpose behind the rule aids considerably in applying it, there is no mechanical test to determine when a promise touches and concerns land so it is helpful to simply remember specific instances in which the promise is said to touch and concern the land.

Example 1. [§ 10–12] A promise not to use property in certain ways or for certain purposes is said to touch and concern the land.

Example 2. [§ 10–13] A promise to repair, maintain, improve, or cultivate land (or structures on the land) touches and concerns that land.

Example 3. [§ 10–14] There are a range of promises that do not involve restrictions on use, building, or cultivation which may or may not be found to satisfy the touch and concern requirement. An example of such a promise is a promise to pay money—a promise to pay rent, a promise to pay taxes, a promise to pay insurance on a specific piece of land. These promises, which are not directly related to the use of the land, have been widely litigated with many different results, and they will be discussed in the following sections detailing the requirements for a benefit or a burden to run with the land.

(1) Covenants That Do Not Touch and Concern the Land. [§ 10–15]

Personal covenants, or covenants in gross (i.e., a covenant where the benefit is personal and there is no benefited piece of land) do not touch and concern the land and are not enforceable as property interests. Any right to damages as a result of a breach of a personal covenant would be determined on a contract theory. (See Case Squib: *Caullett v. Stanley Stilwell*)

(a) Example. [§ 10–16] A covenants to B that he will walk B's horse twice around the track in B's backyard each morning. Although an imaginative mind may find some collateral benefit to B's property, the covenant is unlikely to be held to touch and concern the land.

d. Privity of Estate. [§ 10–17]

"Privity" is a mysterious and seldom precisely defined concept which plays many roles in real property law. In real covenant law it is really nothing more than a "required relationship" and therefore the privity of estate requirement simply means that the parties wishing to enforce a contract as a real covenant and the persons against whom they wish to enforce it must have a relationship to the property in question, in addition to the covenant. Exactly what the courts will recognize to constitute such a relationship is complicated by the fact that there are really two very different privity of estate requirements—i.e., vertical privity and horizontal privity. The terms "horizontal" and "vertical" are simply directional showing the "location" of the parties in a diagrammatic representation of the transactions leading to a controversy over enforcement of a real covenant.

(1) **Example. [§ 10–18]** To illustrate, A and B enter into a contract pursuant to which B agrees to make only residential use of tract B which is contiguous with tract A on which A has already built a mansion. Later, A sells tract A to C and C sells it to D. B sells tract B to X who later sells it to Y. As indicated in the diagram below, the "relationship" required among the parties in the vertical columns is referred to as vertical privity and the "relationship" required between the original parties to the covenant is called horizontal privity.

```
(Covenantor)                                        (Covenantee)
                           Horizontal
   V          A _____ B         V
   E                                                   E
   R          C                            X           R
   T                                                   T
   I          D                            Y           I
   C                                                   C
   A                                                   A
   L                                                   L
```

(2) **Vertical privity. [§ 10–19]**

The relationship required here is succession in interest to the property subjected to a real covenant. In fact, this privity requirement is sometimes called "successive" privity. In most fact situations there is no lack of vertical privity. Two situations where vertical privity may be found lacking is where one or more parties in a vertical column are adverse possessors and where lesser estates have been transferred.

(a) **Adverse Possessors. [§ 10–20]**

As indicated in our discussion of adverse possession (see Chapter XI), a successful adverse possessor obtains a new title or estate to the land rather than succeeding to the estate of the person against whom he adversely possessed. The courts have interpreted this principle of adverse possession law to mean that there is no succession to an interest of a contracting party in a real covenant context and therefore no vertical privity of the adverse possessor.

The Restatement of Property takes a different position. It provides, subject to certain exceptions, that if a covenant meets all of the requirements for it to run with the land, then its burdens and benefits run to adverse possessors. Clearly, not all courts follow the Restatement of Property so you should be aware of the differences in treatment.

(b) Transferees of Lesser Estates. [§ 10–21]

The other problem that sometimes arises in regard to vertical privity occurs when one or more parties in one or both vertical columns transfers a lesser estate than that originally subjected to the covenant. For example, assume A and B both owned fee simple absolutes and conveyed them to D and X respectively but X transferred only a life estate or leasehold interest to Y. The decisions on point are sparse and conflicting but it seems that in most jurisdictions there is vertical privity between grantors of lesser estates and their grantees if the issue is the running of the benefit of the covenant. This is referred to in the chart above as relaxed vertical privity. (See § 10–7) Additional examples of relaxed vertical privity include: a life tenant conveys a leasehold estate and the holder of a fee simple absolute transfers a defeasible estate). Thus, in our example, Y could enforce a benefit if all other requirements are met. In many jurisdictions, however, no privity is found unless the entire servient estate is transferred when the issue is the running of the burden. This is referred to in the chart above as strict vertical privity. (See § 10–7) Examples of strict vertical privity include: a life tenant conveys a life estate pur autre vie, the holder of a fee simple absolute transfers a fee simple absolute. Thus in our example, Y would not take subject to burdens.

(3) Horizontal privity. [§ 10–22]

Horizontal privity, or mutual privity or tenurial privity as it is sometimes also called, relates to the relationship required between the parties to the contract which purportedly creates the real covenant—i.e., A and B in the diagram above. (Note, this is the only place the horizontal privity requirement exists, it does not exist between C and X or D and Y or anybody else.) The original purpose of requiring a "relationship" to the property in question by the parties to the covenant was probably to restrict the use and therefore growth of real covenants since the courts were always reluctant to tie land up with possibly feudal type personal obligations. In fact, at one point in the development of real covenant law, the English courts held that the only relationship that would satisfy the requirement of horizontal privity was that of one of the parties being the landlord and the other a tenant of the same piece of property. Today, especially in the United States, a common ownership interest suffices, for example if A is the grantor and B the grantee of any possessory estate—or for some courts—non-possessory estate (i.e. an easement)—in the same parcel of land. What most courts never accepted as satisfying the required relationship was that the parcels of land involved be merely adjoining or contiguous. Thus if A and B were simply adjoining landowners, they could not create a valid real covenant that runs with the land (i.e., could not satisfy the horizontal privity requirement) without transferring some interest in the property between themselves or through a straw (third person). As will be developed more later, the horizontal privity requirement has fallen into disrepute with the courts, many of which have discarded it altogether or have rewritten the traditional law to make it a requirement for the burden (obligations) but not the benefit (rights) created by the covenant to run.

5. Enforcement of a Real Covenant. [§ 10–23]

a. Rights and Obligations of Covenanting Parties. [§ 10–24]

Even if the covenant does not run with the land, the original parties can enforce the covenant against one another and are obligated to perform the duties required by the covenant. When an original party transfers her interest in the land to a successor, however, she surrenders all rights and obligations under the covenant (except that she may still enforce any personal covenants which are independent of the covenants running with the land).

(1) Example. [§ 10–25] A's covenant to adjoining landowner B to walk B's horse twice around the track in B's backyard each morning is enforceable as a contract by B against A, if contract principles are satisfied (e.g., consideration). However, because the covenant doesn't touch and concern either party's land, successors to A are not bound and successors to B cannot enforce the contract.

b. Rights of Successors. [§ 10–26]

The question of whether the covenant runs with the land does not arise until there is a transfer of interest in land by either the covenantor or the covenantee. If the covenant does in fact run with the land, the successors of the original parties may enforce (or be obligated to honor) the covenants of their predecessors.

c.   **Remedies. [§ 10–27]**

The remedies available for a breach of covenant are the standard contract remedy—money damages. Equitable remedies are discussed in connection with equitable servitudes. (See § 10–66 et seq.)

6.   Components: Burden and Benefit. [§ 10–28]

There are two components to a covenant which must be analyzed separately in determining whether and to what extent it is enforceable: (a) the burden(s) imposed by the covenant; and (b) the benefit(s) conferred by the covenant.

a.   **Burden. [§ 10–29]**

A burden is traditionally characterized by a promisor surrendering a portion of his legal interest in the property or making that legal interest less valuable to him. For example, A covenants (promises) to B that he will only use his property for a single family dwelling. Hence, A has agreed to encumber his property and thereby reduce his legal interest therein.

b.   **Benefit. [§ 10–30]**

A benefit is traditionally characterized by an agreement whereby the value of the land owned by the covenantee or land in which the covenantee has an interest is enhanced. For example, A, the lessee, covenants to B, the lessor, that he will paint the fence on the leased property every third month. B has a legal interest in the property; hence, A has agreed to confer a benefit upon B since the maintenance of the property will enhance its value.

c.   **Difference in Enforceability. [§ 10–31]**

Whether one can be bound by a promise he never made and whether one is the assignee of the benefits owed to another are two fundamentally different questions. While there is little reason why a benefit connected with certain property cannot be assigned to successors, a burden binding someone for a promise that someone else made is virtually unprecedented in our legal system and consequently the courts have thrown up more roadblocks to the running of burdens than to the running of benefits.

d.   **Overlap of Running of Burden and Running of Benefit Issues. [§ 10–32]**

In any given case, the issue may be whether either of the two—the benefit or the burden—has separately run. In many situations, however, both issues will be present. In the great majority of covenants, if either side of the covenant touches and concerns the land, the other necessarily must, because of the physical character of the performance that characterizes the covenant.

(1) Example. [§ 10–33] Building restrictions, the most common type of covenant, will necessarily have some benefit on the covenantee's land. Thus, a burden which restricts A to residential use also benefits adjoining landowner and covenantee B by keeping B's land free from the noise and traffic generated by non-residential uses and enhancing the value of B's property.

e. Exam Hint. [§ 10–34] There are two analytical steps that must be taken in determining whether a covenant runs with the land.

(1) First: It must be determined whether the covenant involves the running of both a benefit and a burden, or whether it only involves one of the two.

(2) Second: If both a benefit and a burden are involved, they should be considered separately since the technical requirements are different.

C. REQUIREMENTS FOR THE BENEFIT TO RUN. [§ 10–35]

1. Benefit Need Not Be Direct. [§ 10–36]

Most jurisdictions hold that it is sufficient for a benefit to run with the land if the covenantee's legal interest in the land is rendered more valuable by the covenantor's performance. The trend has been to relax the requirement of direct benefit on the land of the covenantee.

a. Example 1. [§ 10–37] A covenant to pay rent that contains an acceleration clause as to all rent in the event of a default of payment is held to run with the leasehold estate since the landlord's rights and the tenant's obligations are affected.

b. Example 2. [§ 10–38] Covenants to pay money can run with the land if the payment results in a physical benefit. For example, if money is paid for a future improvement such as the erection of a fence, the enforcement of the covenant will result in a physical benefit to the land. The covenant should be applied at the time the improvement is finished. If, however, the improvement for which the covenantor pays already exists, then the covenant to pay the cost of the improvement is merely an extension of credit; hence, the burden and the benefit are personal and do not run with the land. Having said this, the subdivision cases have held that covenants requiring the owners to pay dues or maintenance assessments to the association are enforceable. These cases recognize that the older English decisions treated a covenant to pay money as a personal affirmative covenant. They apply a broad approach and treat the promise to pay as analogous to a promise to do the thing itself. (See Case Squib: *Neponsit Property Owners' Association, Inc. v. Emigrant Industrial Savings Bank*)

2. Intent of Parties That Benefit Run. [§ 10–39]

The benefit can only run with the land if the original covenanting parties intended that the covenantee's successors in interest have the right to enforce the covenant.

3. Touch and Concern. [§ 10–40]

a. Benefits Which Touch and Concern. [§ 10–41]

In general, the benefit of the covenant will touch and concern the land when it enhances the value of the land in the hands of the covenantee. Perhaps a simpler test is that if only the person who owns the benefited land can benefit from the other landowner's performance, the benefit touches and concerns the land.

(1) Example. [§ 10–42] A sells parcel X to B. B covenants that he will erect a fence on parcel X. A owns no land in the community in which parcel X is located. A cannot enforce the covenant against B since the covenant does not benefit A's land. There must be some benefit, either physical or commercial, in some property of the covenantee in order for him to enforce a covenant that will run with the land. Note, however, that an agreement to erect a fence on parcel X, even though A has no property in the community, can be enforced as a personal obligation between A and B under contract theory. (See Case Squib: *Caullett v. Stanley Stilwell.*)

b. New Restatement Discards Touch and Concern. [§ 10–43]

In the Restatement of Property (Third), the "touch and concern" requirement is discarded and replaced by other tests for enforceability which include restraints on alienation (direct and indirect), restraints on trade, and unconscionability.

4. Privity. [§ 10–44]

Today, the majority view seems to be that the benefit may run with the land even if there was no privity of estate between the covenantor and the covenantee (horizontal privity), so long as there was privity between the party seeking to obtain the benefit and the original covenantee (vertical privity).

a. **Example. [§ 10–45]** A lake covers a portion of both A and B's property. B covenants to pay a share of A's costs of maintaining a dam on A's property to control the level of the lake for the benefit of A and B. Though there was no privity of estate between A and B, A's successor C may enforce the covenant to pay the share of costs against B.

D. REQUIREMENTS FOR THE BURDEN TO RUN. [§ 10–46]

1. Covenantee's Benefit. [§ 10–47]

The prevailing view seems to be that the running of a benefit when the burden is in gross (personal) is not objectionable. However, when the burden runs with the land and the benefit is in gross, there is a serious question as to the wisdom of encumbering property when there is no benefit to other land. The Restatement argues that there is a strong policy against the running of a burden where the benefit is in gross, but not all courts agree with this position. (See Case Squib: *Caullett v. Stanley Stilwell.*)

a. **Example. [§ 10–48]** City sells property to A with a covenant that A must use the land for low-income housing. Some courts hold that the city may enforce the covenant against A's successor though the benefit to the city doesn't touch and concern any specific land and is, thus, a benefit in gross.

2. Intent of Parties That Burden Run. [§ 10–49]

A burden will not run with the land unless the covenanting parties so intended. At common law, if the covenant concerned something which did not presently exist (e.g., if the covenantor agreed to build a fence, as opposed to painting an existing fence), the burden would run only if the covenant stated that X and his assigns agree to do the necessary act. Today, while the use of the words "and his assigns" clearly establishes the intent that the burden run, those words are not required even if the subject of the covenant is not in being if the intent of the parties is clear. (See § 10–9)

3. Touch and Concern. [§ 10–50]

a. **Burdens Which Touch and Concern. [§ 10–51]**

The burden will not run with the land unless it touches and concerns the land. A covenant touches and concerns the land if only the owner of the burdened land can perform the covenanted act.

b. Building Restrictions. [§ 10–52]

The most common type of covenant in which the burden runs with the land is a building restriction. The covenant is not entirely negative in character since its enforcement can enhance either the commercial or the physical value of the covenantee's land. Since the performance of the covenant necessarily requires ownership, it clearly touches and concerns the land. The normal remedy sought for a breach of covenant which imposes a building restriction is an injunction.

c. Covenants Requiring Affirmative Action. [§ 10–53]

At one time, some courts held that affirmative covenants, with specified exceptions, did not touch and concern. Practically speaking, most courts hold that both affirmative and negative covenants may touch and concern. When a covenant requires affirmative action, such as erecting a fence or building a bridge, it is quite common that the covenantee will seek relief in the form of an action at law for breach of the covenant. The covenantee can perform the service prescribed by the covenant and then seek restitution.

d. Covenant to Pay Money. [§ 10–54]

At first glance, it may be difficult to see how a covenant to pay money would touch and concern land, yet courts frequently enforce such obligations. Whether the covenant to pay money touches and concerns land depends on how the payment relates to the land in which the covenantor has an interest. (See Case Squib: *Neponsit v. Emigrant Bank.*) Disputes regarding covenants to pay money are particularly likely to arise in the context of obligations to homeowner and condominium associations.

(1) Example. [§ 10–55]

A covenant to pay money for a fence would touch and concern the land since the money has a direct relationship to the land in which the covenantor has an interest. On the other hand, a covenant for the lessee to pay the lessor's annual dues for the American Bar Association does not touch and concern the land and therefore is enforceable only as a personal obligation between the original parties.

(2) Ultimate Purpose of the Payment. [§ 10–56]

A question arises as to whether an obligation to pay money should be enforced as a covenant running with the land if the money is not ultimately used for purposes related to the land. Thus, a promise to purchase fire insurance on a house may not touch and concern the land if the insured is not bound to use insurance proceeds to rebuild the premises.

(3) Security Deposits. [§ 10–57]

Some courts have found that a security deposit arrangement was collateral to the leasehold agreement since it really did not touch and concern the land directly. The prevailing view, however, is that the security deposit does touch and concern the land since it serves as security and, therefore, it is binding on the covenantor and his successors.

(4) Covenants Not to Assign an Interest in Property. [§ 10–58]

A covenant by a lessee not to assign his interest in property without the express consent of the lessor is generally binding on the covenantor and his successors since it limits the legal interest in the land on the part of the covenantor. Of course, the limitations imposed on the covenantor result in additional legal rights in the land on the part of the covenantee.

4. Horizontal Privity. [§ 10–59]

In addition to privity of estate between the covenantor and the successor, most jurisdictions further require that there be privity of estate between the original covenanting parties for the burden to run.

a. Mutual Privity. [§ 10–60]

In those jurisdictions which take the position that the burden of a covenant can run only if there is privity of estate between the original contracting parties, mutual privity is always sufficient. Such privity is present when, at the time of the contractual undertaking, both parties hold interests in the same piece of land and the covenant touches and concerns those interests. The most common illustrations are leasehold covenants and covenants relating to an easement between the holder of the servient tenement and the holder of the easement.

(1) Example. [§ 10–61] L leases Blackacre to T and T covenants to build a wall on Blackacre. L may enforce T's covenant to build the wall against T's assignee.

b. Grantor–Grantee Privity. [§ 10–62]

In most jurisdictions, grantor-grantee privity (when the covenant accompanies the conveyance of an estate or other interest in land) is sufficient. This is based on the notion that at the exact moment of the conveyance, both parties have an interest in the same land (even though these interests exist simultaneously only for an instant). Thus, if the covenant is entered into after the grant (so that grant and covenant cannot simply be called one transaction) the requisite privity is not present.

(1) **Example 1. [§ 10–63]** O owns Whiteacre and Blackacre. He conveys Blackacre to X, X covenanting at the time to use Blackacre only for residential purposes. Grantor-grantee privity is present. In the few states that require mutual privity the covenant in the above example could not run. In most states, however, this covenantor-covenantee privity requirement is satisfied by either mutual or grantor-grantee privity.

(2) **Example 2. [§ 10–64]** O owns Blackacre. X owns Whiteacre, which is adjacent to Blackacre. O and X sign a contract, with X covenanting to use his property for residential purposes only. In no state requiring covenantor-covenantee privity can the burden of this covenant run at law.

5. Notice. [§ 10–65]

Although notice is not generally listed as a requirement for a real covenant to run at law, the failure to record the covenant (or an instrument containing it) may result in a bona fide purchaser (one who pays value and has no notice) taking free of the covenant as a result of the recording act. (See §§ 10–7, Chapter XIV.)

E. INTRODUCTION TO EQUITABLE SERVITUDES. [§ 10–66]

1. General Characteristics. [§ 10–67]

An equitable servitude is a privately created land use restriction analogous to a real covenant enforced by courts using their equity powers and giving equitable remedies. Many equitable servitudes are intended by their creators to be real covenants but the courts decline to enforce them as such because they do not meet all requirements prerequisite to the creation of such interests. Thus, an equitable servitude, like a covenant running with the land at law, has its genesis in a specific covenant between two parties. Equitable servitudes, however, may be enforced in the absence of privity of estate and therefore offer greater flexibility to landowners who wish to create private land use control arrangements and courts which wish to enforce them.

2. Analogous to Negative Easements. [§ 10–68]

The most common equitable servitudes relate to building and land use restrictions. The analogy between such servitudes and negative easements (see Chapter IX) again indicates that the restrictions placed by English courts on negative easements are the primary reason for their development as well as the development of real covenant law. Some courts have made such a close analogy between negative easements and equitable servitudes that they have concluded that affirmative covenants cannot be enforced as equitable servitudes. Most American courts, however, have taken a contrary position, permitting affirmative covenants to be enforced as equitable servitudes. Note that jurisdiction in equity rests, at least in theory, on a showing that legal damages are inadequate. This presents no problems in the typical case involving building restrictions, but it may present an obstacle to the enforcement as equitable servitudes of covenants to pay money.

3. Requirements. [§ 10–69]

The technical requirements for the creation of an equitable servitude, binding upon subsequent purchasers, are relatively few. Once again, the benefit and burden should be analyzed separately. Briefly, for equitable enforcement of covenants (i.e., for an equitable servitude) there must be:

    a. an intent that the servitude should run;

    b. land which the servitude touches and concerns;

    c. constructive, actual, or implied notice on the part of the purchaser in order for it to be enforced against him.

There is no requirement of privity of estate. Unlike real covenants, equitable servitudes may arise by implication from a preexisting common plan. (see § 10–92)

The following chart summarizes those requirements:

REQUIREMENTS FOR EXPRESS EQUITABLE SERVITUDES

BURDEN	BENEFIT
Formalities must be met; the Statute of Frauds must be satisfied.	Formalities must be met; the Statute of Frauds must be satisfied.
Intent to burden the future owners of the land	Intent to benefit the future owners of the land.
The obligations must "touch and concern" the land and not be "merely personal" obligations.	The benefits must "touch and concern" the land and not be "merely personal" benefits.
Notice, either actual, constructive, or inquiry of the covenant. The notice requirement only applies to purchasers for value. Successors to the burdened land who have not paid value, such as donees, will be bound by the covenant even though the successor does not have actual, constructive, or inquiry notice. (See § 10–77)	

F. RUNNING OF THE BURDEN. [§ 10–70]

The standards used are basically the same as those used on the law side with real covenants.

1. Presence of a Specific Benefited Dominant Estate. [§ 10–71]

In a large number of jurisdictions, the burden of an equitable servitude does not bind successors where the benefit is in gross (or personal) to the promisees; the benefit must also touch and concern the land.

   a. Example. [§ 10–72] The city sells property to A who promises to use the land only for residential purposes. If the city owns no land benefited by A's promise, the city may not enforce the promise as an equitable servitude against A's successor.

2. Intention to Bind Successors. [§ 10–73]

This may be established by use of words like "successors," "heirs," or "assigns," but the use of such technical language is not necessary. More commonly, such an intention may be implied from the circumstances. In the case of standard building restrictions, it can be presumed.

3. Touch and Concern. [§ 10–74]

The burden must be of a type which may only be performed by the owner of the burdened tract.

4. Privity of Estate Is Not Required. [§ 10–75]

Privity of estate between covenanting parties is not necessary for the creation of an equitable servitude. In most cases, such privity is present in any event since covenants normally appear in deeds conveying an estate. Privity of estate between covenantor and the party to be bound likewise is not required in equity, in contrast to the so-called "vertical privity" requirements at law. An equitable servitude may be enforced against any taker of the burdened land who takes with notice of the covenant and against any taker who has not given value (a donee) even though the taker does not hold the estate held by the covenantor. Courts have held, for instance, that even an adverse possessor may be bound.

   a. Example. [§ 10–76] A and B, owners of adjacent lots, enter into a contract where each agrees not to construct an apartment house on his land. B's successor by adverse possession may be enjoined by A from building an apartment house even though horizontal and vertical privity are both lacking.

5. Notice Is Crucial. [§ 10–77]

The very first case recognizing an equitable servitude made it clear that notice is the hallmark of the concept. (See Case Squib: *Tulk v. Moxhay.*) An equitable servitude binds: (1) subsequent takers with notice and (2) subsequent takers who have not given value (donees).

Notice may be actual notice but more commonly notice is imputed because the covenant is in a deed which is properly recorded, or appears as part of a properly recorded subdivision plat. Even in the absence of actual notice or notice through recording, a subsequent taker may be charged with inquiry notice of common building restrictions because the neighborhood physically manifests a common, restricted plan. (See Case Squib: *Sanborn v. McLean*).

a. **Example.** [§ 10–78] Subdivider O conveys lots to A, B, C, and D, all with deeds containing covenants that the grantee will use the lot for residential purposes only. A, B, C, and D all build expensive dwellings on their lots. O then conveys a lot on the same street to X without any restrictions. The residential character of the development places X on inquiry notice of the residential scheme established by the restrictions in A, B, C, and D's deeds. O and her assigns may enforce the residential restriction against X.

G. RUNNING OF THE BENEFIT. [§ 10–79]

1. Touch and Concern. [§ 10–80]

The benefit of the covenant must touch and concern the allegedly benefited tract in order to be enforceable as an equitable servitude by a subsequent taker of that tract. As on the law side, courts have disagreed about the nature of the benefit which must be conferred, some saying the benefit must be physical, others permitting the benefit to run on a showing of commercial enhancement (in the case of covenants not to compete). The typical building restriction is almost invariably viewed as conferring a physical benefit on neighboring land.

2. Intent to Benefit a Specific Tract. [§ 10–81]

The covenant must be made with the intention to benefit the specific tract. If the benefit was intended to be personal to the original promisee, it cannot be enforced by subsequent takers even though their land is physically benefited. In some cases, it may also be necessary to examine intention to determine the tract to which the benefit attaches.

a. **Personal Covenants.** [§ 10–82]

If, at the time the covenant is made, the promisee owns no land in the immediate area of the burdened land, the benefit is normally personal. If the promisee owns land in the neighborhood which is in fact benefited by the promise, a few states create a presumption that the benefit attaches to

193

such land. Other states create no such presumption, and intention to benefit specific land must be proven by reference to language in the deed, by implication from the nature of the benefit conferred, or by an agreement which is part of a general subdivision plan.

b. What Specific Tracts Are Benefited? [§ 10–83]

A given covenant may "touch and concern" lands over a wide area. A building restriction may physically benefit lots blocks away. In such cases, it is often necessary to determine which lots are benefited; this is a matter of intention.

c. Cannot Benefit Lands Owned by Third Parties. [§ 10–84]

Subject to the discussion below concerning enforcement by prior purchasers, the benefited land must be owned by the promisee. A covenant cannot generally be used to confer a benefit on lands owned by third persons.

d. Existence of General Building Plan. [§ 10–85]

If, at the time the covenant is made, it is part of a general building or development plan for a subdivision (also called a common scheme), the benefit will attach to the remaining lots of the subdivider. The existence of such a plan is most readily established where a subdivision plat showing the restrictions has been recorded, but it may also be established by proof that maps and restricted plans were consistently used and followed in selling lots. The existence of a common scheme may also be inferred from the fact that uniform restrictions were in fact placed in the deeds of lots sold before and after the lot in question.

3. Privity Not Required. [§ 10–86]

Subsequent takers may enforce whether or not there was privity of estate between covenanting parties, and whether or not there was privity of estate between the original promisee and the subsequent taker.

a. Example. [§ 10–87]

Enforcement Without Privity: Assume O owns a large tract which he subdivides into 12 lots. O conveys Lot 1 to A, with a covenant limiting A's use to residential purposes. O then conveys Lot 2 to B with a similar covenant. The same covenants are part of the conveyances of Lots 3 and 4. Lot 5 is sold to X without any restrictive covenant in his deed. May B enforce the covenant against A? May A enforce the covenant against B? Who may enforce the covenant against X?

b. B v. A. [§ 10–88]

B may sue A (assuming that a common scheme including this restriction can be established). At the time of A's deed, the benefit of his covenant attached to the grantor's remaining lots, including the lot now held by B. (See § 10–85).

c. A v. B. [§ 10–89]

A's suit against B presents a new difficulty, since the promisee of B's covenant, the common grantor O, did not own Lot 1 when B's covenant was made. Normally, the benefit of a covenant cannot be attached to property not owned by one of the covenanting parties. However, in this case, A will be allowed to enforce the covenant if it can be demonstrated that, at the time he purchased, the grantor represented that subsequent takers would be restricted as A was and that this was relied upon by A. The most common way to establish this expectation in A is by demonstrating that, when A took, the grantor had a developed building scheme (a common scheme) for the area which included the restrictions in question, and that this plan was made known to A. The same result may be reached if the grantor covenants with A to similarly restrict his remaining lots, and in fact does so. (See § 10–85).

d. Theories Allowing A to Enforce the Covenant Against Subsequent Purchasers of Lots From O. [§ 10–90]

A is permitted to enforce the covenant, if the above conditions are met, under one of two theories:

(1) a third party beneficiary contract arising when the grantor and the subsequent taker covenant in A's favor; or

(2) an implied reciprocal servitude which says that when, pursuant to a common scheme, A's lot is restricted, a similar restriction is implied on the grantor's remaining land. Thus, when B takes, his land is already burdened by a servitude in A's favor. (See Case Squib: *Sanborn v. McLean*); (See § 10–92).

e. Does the Covenant Burden or Benefit Lot 5 Owned by X. [§ 10–91]

A suit against X by either A or B to enforce the burden of the covenant presents yet another difficulty since X did not make a covenant to restrict Lot 5. So, no grantee covenant is inserted in X's deed. Also, as O sold Lots 1–4, O did not include an express grantor covenant burdening all other lots in the subdivision that O still owned. A and B may be able to enforce the covenant against X if they can show that prior to X's purchase of Lot 5, O had a common scheme for the area, the restrictions were included in the common scheme, and O orally-implied the existence of the covenant to X. This is the essence of the implied reciprocal servitude; O impliedly covenanted to the purchasers of Lots 1 through 4 that the lots still owned by O were burdened by the restriction and the uniform development of the subdivision, consistent with the restrictions, put X on notice of the restriction. Lots 1 through 4 were expressly restricted before X bought Lot 5 and if Lots 1 through 4 were developed pursuant to the deed restrictions before X bought Lot 5, a court might find a common scheme and determine that Lot 5 is burdened by the covenant. Absent a finding of an implied reciprocal servitude that predates X's purchase of Lot 5, it seems that X is not burdened by the covenant.

Does X as owner of Lot 5 have the benefit of the covenants? The analysis would be the same as in the case of B suing A to enforce the covenant. Assuming a common scheme, at the time of the deeds to A and B, the benefit of their covenants attached to the grantor's remaining lots, which included Lot 5, now held by X. So the benefit of the covenant may run to X.

H. IMPLIED RECIPROCAL SERVITUDES OR IMPLIED RECIPROCAL NEGATIVE EASEMENTS. [§ 10–92]

The doctrine of implied reciprocal servitudes, sometimes called implied reciprocal negative easements, provides a basis for enforcement of an express covenant made by a subsequent taker, as just noted (A v. B). It may also provide a basis for burdening purchasers within a subdivision whose own deeds do not expressly contain the restriction in question. (See Case Squib: *Sanborn v. McLean*) (In the above example, we are now considering the responsibilities of X.) If an implied reciprocal servitude on the grantor's remaining land has been created by the conveyances and covenants with A, B and the purchasers of Lots 3 and 4, X takes his land already burdened by a servitude, without regard to any express covenant in his own deed. (He must, of course, have notice for the burden of the covenant to run.) (See § 10–91).

Reciprocal servitudes implied from a general plan or scheme are legally significant in several ways. Any owner of a lot in a common scheme can sue owners of other lots within the common scheme to enforce a restriction. Also, development pursuant to a pattern of deed restrictions so as to establish the common scheme, on the ground, can be deemed sufficient to put a purchaser on notice that his lot is restricted even though the restriction does not appear in the purchaser's chain of title. Lastly, while real covenants at law cannot be implied, the existence of a common scheme allows courts to imply restrictions in equity that were never expressly imposed. (See §§ 10–5, 10–69)

a. Creation. [§ 10–93]

Some cases suggest that such an implied servitude is created against the grantor's retained land simply by virtue of the restriction in the earlier taker's deeds. If A is restricted, the restriction becomes reciprocal. Generally, however, more is required. An implied reciprocal servitude against the grantor's retained land will arise if

(1) a general plan of development encompassing the restrictions exists when the earlier conveyances are made and this is known to the earlier grantees, or

(**2**) the grantor promises to insert similar restrictions in subsequent deeds.

(a) Minority Position. [§ 10–94]

Note that there is authority indicating that the latter is not sufficient and, indeed, negating the existence of an implied reciprocal servitude, since it is said to indicate that no present restriction is intended. These authorities would hold that if a promise to insert such restrictions is made but not kept, the subsequent taker is not bound.

I. DEFENSES TO AN ACTION TO ENFORCE EQUITABLE SERVITUDES. [§ 10–95]

1. Lack of Notice. [§ 10–96]

Lack of notice is a defense to an action to enforce an equitable servitude, but look closely for notice through recording or inquiry notice from visible manifestations of a common restricted plan.

2. Change in Character of Neighborhood, Changed Conditions Doctrine. [§ 10–97]

An equity court will not enforce a restrictive covenant if, because of changes in the neighborhood, it is no longer possible to secure in any substantial way the benefits which the restrictions were designed to confer. Typically, this means not only that the changes have worked considerable hardship on the burdened land, but also that little benefit is being conferred on the benefited tracts.

In most states, the impact on an individual as a result of changed conditions is not sufficient to relieve him of the covenant. The courts fear a "domino" effect. If A may now use his property for commercial purposes, it is only a matter of time before his neighbor must have the same right. Thus, the change-in-the-character-of-the-neighborhood defense is usually permitted only when the changed conditions are such that even interior lot owners can no longer realize substantial benefit from the restrictions.

a. **Example.** [§ 10–98] All of the lots in a subdivision are restricted to residential use. The area surrounding the subdivision has been converted to commercial use, making each of the lots in the subdivision that border the commercial area less attractive as residential property. If the residential character of the subdivision has not been destroyed by the commercial use and if the purposes of the restrictions can still be achieved for the subdivision, then a court would enforce the restrictions. (See Case Squib: *Western Land Co. v. Truskolaski*).

3. **Equitable Defenses of Unclean Hands, Laches, and Estoppel.** [§ 10–99]

An equity court may deny relief to (a) a particular lot owner whose lot is similarly restricted and who is himself violating the restrictions (unclean hands), (b) one who unreasonably delays in bringing suit (laches), or (c) one whose affirmative statements or actions lead the person bound by the servitude to detrimentally rely on the other party's apparent waiver of the servitude (estoppel).

4. **Acquiescence.** [§ 10–100]

A lot holder otherwise entitled to enforce a covenant may be denied equitable relief because he has failed to seek relief against third parties who have violated the same restrictions, thus lulling others into a belief that the restriction will not be enforced.

5. **Abandonment.** [§ 10–101]

Where the restriction has been violated by those subject to it with sufficient regularity that the benefits created by it are no longer present, equitable relief may be denied. (See Case Squib: *Western Land Co. v. Truskolaski*).

6. **Discriminatory Covenants Unenforceable.** [§ 10–102]

The Supreme Court of the United States held that judicial enforcement of a covenant restricting the transfer of property because of race, creed, color, national origin, or ancestry constitutes state action prohibited by the Equal Protection Clause of the Fourteenth Amendment. (See Case Squib: *Shelley v. Kraemer* and *Barrows v. Jackson*) Distinctions have been drawn, however, between private and public restrictions relating to First Amendment rights. (See Case Squib: *Ginsberg v. Yeshiva.*)

J. SUMMARY OF REQUIREMENTS FOR REAL COVENANTS AND EQUITABLE SERVITUDES. [§ 10–103]

SUMMARY OF REQUIREMENTS FOR REAL COVENANTS AND EQUITABLE SERVITUDES

	Formalities	Intent	Touch and Concern	Vertical Privity	Horizontal Privity	Notice
Real Covenants Burden	Required	Required	Required	Required	Required	*Required
Real Covenants Benefit	Required	Required	Required	Required	Not Required	Not Required
Equitable Servitudes Burden	Required	Required	Required	Not Required	Not Required	**Required
Equitable Servitudes Benefit	Required	Required	Required	Not Required	Not Required	Not Required

* See §§ 10–65, 10–7
** See §§ 10–69, 10–77

CHAPTER X

REVIEW PROBLEMS—REAL COVENANTS AND EQUITABLE SERVITUDES

The typical exam question on real covenants and equitable servitudes sets up a fact situation in which most but arguably not all requirements for a real covenant are established. The student is expected to explain why the agreement in question can not be enforced as a real covenant and to then examine the facts given to see if the restriction on the use of the land can be enforced as an equitable servitude.

> A and B, landowners of adjoining tracts A and B, respectively, enter into a contract whereby each promises to use his parcel for residential purposes only. The contract is in writing and properly describes the parties and the tracts of land. The contract further provides that it is the intent of the parties that the contract be binding upon the heirs, successors, and assigns of A and B. The contract was properly recorded in the land records office. A sells parcel A to C and B sells parcel B to D. D starts to erect a Buffaloburger restaurant on her land and C files suit to obtain either an injunction against D or damages from her. What result?
>
> > **Answer:** The contract meets the following requirements for a real covenant: formalities, intent, vertical privity, and touch and concern. Horizontal privity, required by many courts, is not met because A and B were merely adjoining landowners. There was no ownership interest passed or jointly owned by them. Consequently, C can probably not get damages. However, all of the requirements are met for a valid equitable servitude—(i.e. intent, touch and concern, and notice through recording the contract). Consequently, C should be able to obtain an injunction which is normally the equitable remedy available for enforcement of equitable servitudes.

CHAPTER XI

ADVERSE POSSESSION

At its core, adverse possession considers the circumstances under which mere possession by one, other than the owner of real property, can ripen into title in the adverse possessor and divest the owner of title. Adverse possession plays two very important and interrelated roles in real property law. First, it is a means of obtaining title based upon actual possession. Second, it is a means of "purifying" titles and destroying potential claims that otherwise might make our cumbersome system of land records collapse. Adverse possession also provides the concepts for the comparable doctrine of "adverse use" or prescription applied to non-possessory interests such as easements. (§ 9–41)

A. IN GENERAL. [§ 11–1]

The doctrine of adverse possession has its roots in the common law doctrine of seisin, and in the tradition of courts giving the possessor of land many of the rights of ownership. Adverse possession is based on the theory that once an owner is barred by a Statute of Limitations from proceeding against a trespasser, the trespasser becomes the owner of the land.

> **Example [§ 11–2]** O is the owner of Blackacre. A takes possession of Blackacre, entering wrongfully. In other words, A trespasses upon Blackacre. Next, B wrongfully ousts A from Blackacre without O's permission; so B is also trespassing upon Blackacre. Later, O sues A and B to regain possession. Will O succeed? The answer is yes as long as O has not waited too long. O can regain possession from both A and B because they are both trespassing upon Blackacre; they both entered onto Blackacre wrongfully. What if A sues B to recover possession, will A succeed? The answer is yes. In short, A's rights as a prior possessor are superior to B's rights as a later possessor. The old maxim "first in time, first in right" explains the result. A has a better claim to Blackacre relative to B because A's possession was earlier than B's possession. A's possession was interrupted only by B's wrongful ouster.

If O waits too long, O's opportunity to evict A will expire as the Statute of Limitations on an action for possession will run out. This, of course, assumes that A has regained possession from B. Once O cannot evict A, it is a simple step to call A the owner. Similarly, if B is still in possession and if O waits too long, O's opportunity to evict B will expire as the Statute of Limitations on an action for possession will run out.

1. **Policy. [§ 11–3]**

Today, adverse possession is justified by various policies including protecting the reasonable expectations of the parties to a dispute over possession of land, stimulating land use, clearing land titles of stale claims, and penalizing slothful owners.

2. **Requirements for Adverse Possession. [§ 11–4]**

The courts have formulated a list of requirements that must be met before adverse possession can be claimed. Today, common law rules of adverse possession are supplemented by statute.

   a. **Cause of Action in Owner. [§ 11–5]**

   The owner must have a cause of action for the recovery of land before the Statute of Limitations on the cause of action can begin to run against the adverse possessor. It follows that the possession in question must be without the owner's permission; otherwise there would be no cause of action.

   b. **Adverse Possession Must Continue for the Period of Statute of Limitations. [§ 11–6]**

   The adverse possession must continue for the period of the Statute of Limitations. If the owner regains possession during the period, the owner no longer has a cause of action against which the statute runs. If the owner is again dispossessed, the statute must begin to run all over again on the new cause of action.

   c. **Possession Must Be Actual and Exclusive. [§ 11–7]**

   The possessor must make an actual entry that gives exclusive possession, meaning, possession that is exclusive of the owner. The type of possession that is sufficient to satisfy the "actual" requirement is a function of not only the common law but also of statute. Adverse possession statutes may liberally or conservatively delineate the activities that constitute actual possession for purposes of the adverse possession statute. (See Case Squib: *Van Valkenburgh v. Lutz.*)

   Constructive possession is an exception to the requirement of actual possession. An owner in actual possession of part of the land is also in constructive possession of the remainder of the land. An adverse possessor who is in actual possession of part of the land and who has "color of title" to the whole of the land is in constructive possession of the part of the land not actually possessed.

d. Possession Must Be Open and Notorious. [§ 11–8]

The requirement that actual possession be open and notorious is virtually redundant, for if the possessor has generally behaved as a typical owner his behavior generally is "open and notorious." This element is not always straightforward though.

e. Possession Must Be Hostile and Under Claim of Right. [§ 11–9]

The possession must not be with the permission of the owner but under "claim of right".

3. Acquisition of Title. [§ 11–10]

Upon the running of the statute and the barring of the owner's cause of action, the adverse possessor acquires title. The adverse possessor's title is a new title that is created by operation of law and the title is deemed to relate back to the date on which the cause of action first arose. Assume A adversely enters upon Blackacre in 1985 and remains in possession for twenty years, the statutory period, and meets all of the other requirements of adverse possession. In 2009, A sues to quite the title to Blackacre and is victorious. A is now the owner of Blackacre and the law will treat A as though A has been the owner of Blackacre since 1985.

Until its validity is judicially determined and a recording is made in the probate records, the title obtained by adverse possession is outside the recording act. It usually becomes "marketable of record" only after its validity is judicially determined. Subsequent purchasers, with notice, are bound by the adverse possessor's title even though it has not been recorded.

B. THE STATUTORY PERIOD. [§ 11–11]

The statutory period varies considerably among the states from five to thirty years. (The common law was twenty years.) At very early common law there was no "period" but instead a specified year so that claims brought after that date could no longer be brought before the courts.

1. When the Statute Begins to Run: Possession Without Permission. [§ 11–12]

The statute begins to run when the cause of action first accrues (i.e., when another goes into possession without the permission of the owner).

a. Holder of Future Estate Must Have Immediate Right to Possession. [§ 11–13]

The holder of a future estate generally has no cause of action until he has the immediate right to possession, and the statute does not begin to run against the holder until that time.

(1) Example. [§ 11–14]

A has a life estate, B has a vested remainder in fee simple absolute. During A's lifetime, C goes into adverse possession. The period runs while A is still living. C has acquired A's interest by adverse possession, but has acquired no interest against B. The statute does not begin to run against B until A's death at which time B will first have a right to possess the property and thus first have an opportunity to evict C.

(2) Exception: Change in Ownership During Period of Adverse Possession Does Not Affect Running of Statute. [§ 11–15]

A change in record ownership occurring during the period of adverse possession does not cause the period to begin again. Similarly, the holder of a future interest is not protected if the future interest was created during the time when another was in adverse possession. Thus, if A goes into adverse possession against O, and two years later O conveys the land to B for life, remainder to C, the interests of both B and C will be cut off after eighteen more years of possession by A (assuming a twenty year period and that all other requirements are met).

b. If Record Owner Is Under a Legal Disability. [§ 11–16]

The adverse possession may begin at a time when the record owner is under a legal disability (e.g., he is a minor, legally incompetent, or imprisoned). In such a case, the owner, or those claiming under him, has the additional period, designated in the statute, following the removal of the disability (the disability period) to bring the action, even though the statutory period has run. Suppose O, the owner, is mentally incompetent when A goes into adverse possession in 1960. If O dies intestate, his heirs have the disability period to regain possession, and A does not get title until this additional time has run.

(1) If Disability Period Is Longer Than Statutory Period. [§ 11–17]

Under some statutes, adverse possession for a designated period, usually considerably in excess of the normal statutory period, confers title in spite of any continuing disability in the owner or owners (this rule is strongly supported by the policy favoring free alienation of land by extinguishing stale claims). Assume a thirty year disability period with a twenty year statutory period. If O is incompetent when the disability begins in 1980, title will be acquired by the adverse possessor in 2010, thirty years after adverse possession began. In jurisdictions adhering to this view, it would be immaterial that O's disability has never been removed.

(2) If Disability Period the Same as Statutory Period. [§ 11–18]

Where both the statutory period and the disability period are for the same length of time, any disability present at the time the action accrues (no matter how short-lived), will extend the period required for the acquisition of title by adverse possession. Assume the statutory period and the disability period are both twenty years. If O is fifteen years old when adverse possession starts in 1982 and if the age of majority is eighteen, title will be acquired in 2005, twenty years after O turn eighteen and his disability is thereby removed.

(3) If Disability Period Is Shorter than Statutory Period. [§ 11–19]

In the case of disabilities, the owner gets the benefit of whichever period is longer, the statutory period or the disability period. Assume a twenty year statutory period with a ten year disability period. The age of majority is eighteen. If O is fifteen years old when adverse possession starts in 1982, title will be acquired by the adverse possessor in 2002, twenty years after adverse possession began. Since O's disability of infancy lasted only three years, and ten years after the disability was removed was less than twenty years from the beginning of adverse possession, the twenty year period controls.

(4) Statute Recognizes Only Disabilities in the True Owner at Time Cause of Action First Accrued. [§ 11–20]

A very key concept in this area is that a disability must be present when the adverse possessor first wrongfully possesses the land. A disability in the true owner arising after the adverse possession began has no effect on the statutory period because the owner is not entitled to the benefit of the disability period. Thus, if A goes into adverse possession against O when O is legally competent, O's subsequent insanity will have no effect on the statutory period. Similarly, successive disabilities cannot be tacked. Thus, if A goes into adverse possession against O, the true owner, when O is then fifteen years old, and O dies two years later, leaving B, his five-year-old brother, as his sole heir, B's disability is irrelevant.

2. The Adverse Possession Must Be Continuous for the Statutory Period. [§ 11–21]

Possession must be continuous for the statutory period. Thus, if A goes into adverse possession against O in 2004, leaves the property in 2006, and returns in 2008, the statutory period starts to run beginning in 2008. Note, however, that continuity of possession does not necessarily mean continuity of use. It is enough that the possession is that typical of the usual owner. For example, O owns land used for and suitable only for growing crops. Every year for fifteen years A enters in the spring, plows and plants crops, and ultimately harvests. This possession may be continuous, even though in winter months A is not on the land. (See Case Squib: *Howard v. Kunto.*)

a. Interruption of Possession. [§ 11–22]

If a period of adverse possession is interrupted (i.e., made discontinuous) the statute stops running, and must begin all over again against a new cause of action if possession is resumed.

(1) Abandonment. [§ 11–23]

Abandonment of possession by the adverse possessor is deemed to be resumption of possession by the owner and the continuity is interrupted.

(2) The Owner's Resumption of Possession by Decree Interrupts the Continuity of Possession. [§ 11–24]

If the owner brings suit to regain possession and secures a decree, possession is interrupted, even if actual possession is not obtained.

b. Temporary Dispossession by Third Person Does Not Interrupt Possession. [§ 11–25]

Possession is not interrupted by dispossession of the adverse possessor by a third party if the adverse possessor takes prompt (and successful) steps to regain possession. Thus if A adversely possesses O's property for ten years, and then X ousts A at gunpoint, A does not have to start all over against O if A takes prompt steps to regain possession from X.

c. Tacking. [§ 11–26]

The concept of tacking relates to adding on to or combining the periods of adverse possession of two or more adverse possessors.

(1) Adverse Possession by Several Possessors. [§ 11–27]

Not uncommonly, no single individual is in adverse possession for the entire statutory period, but the periods of adverse possession by several possessors, may be added together ("tacked") when tacking is permitted. Title goes to the final adverse possessor. (See Case Squib: *Howard v. Kunto.*)

(2) Privity Between Successive Holders Necessary. [§ 11–28]

The basic requirement for the tacking of successive (and therefore otherwise continuous) periods of adverse possession is that a privity relationship exist between the successive holders. Privity is present, and tacking therefore permitted, when the successive possessor has taken the possessory interest of the prior possessor by transfer. In the typical case, successive holders are in privity of estate created when one party, the grantor, gives a deed to the other party, the grantee, and the grantee seeks to establish title by adverse possession to more land than is described by the deed. The deed in this case is a voluntary transfer of an estate in land and creates successive privity between the grantor and grantee. Tacking is usually permitted under such facts. In addition to the grantor and grantee relationship, other examples of successive privity of estate include intestate and heir, or testator and devisee. Some jurisdictions also find that privity exists when there is a voluntary transfer of possession from one occupant to another, even in the absence of a deed describing the property in question. These jurisdictions emphasize the existence of a reasonable connection between the successive occupants as the source of privity. (See Case Squib: *Howard v. Kunto.*) In a few jurisdictions, tacking is permitted where there was an ouster or abandonment.

(3) Boundary Case Example. [§ 11–29]

Assume O owns Blackacre, and A owns adjoining Whiteacre. A fences a strip of land belonging to O. A then conveys to B, the description in the deed covering only the lot as actually owned by A. B takes possession up to the fence. A and B's adverse possession may be tacked, even though the deed did not describe the adversely possessed strip, if the parties understood that the right to possess was transferred (this understanding is strongly supported by the existence of the fence).

C. POSSESSION. [§ 11–30]

The amount of land to which an adverse possessor obtains title is determined by whether constructive possession as well as adverse possession is counted.

1. Actual and Exclusive. [§ 11–31]

a. Possession Appropriate to the Property. [§ 11–32]

Actual possession means simply that there has been possession of the kind appropriate to the property (i.e., the alleged adverse possessor has acted with respect to the property the way an owner of such property is expected to act). (See Case Squib: *Van Valkenburgh v. Lutz.*) In essence, whether one is in actual possession may turn on the kind of land it is. For example, assume that Blackacre is suitable for hunting and fishing. A enters, builds a hunting shack, and hunts and fishes the land and its waters during appropriate seasons. The land is not fenced, but A has cut timber and built a roadway. A will likely be held in actual possession. Exclusive means without the presence of the true owner.

b. Facts Facilitating a Finding of Possession. [§ 11–33]

Fencing, living on the premises, or payment of taxes coupled with acts of possession, are facts which facilitate a finding of possession.

2. Open and Notorious Possession. [§ 11–34]

a. "Open and Notorious" General Meaning. [§ 11–35]

The possessor cannot exercise his right to possession in secret, but must openly and notoriously possess the land, in a clearly visible way, so that a diligent owner would know he had a cause of action against the adverse possessor. This requirement is usually uncontroversial, but not always.

b. Common Boundary Exception. [§ 11–36]

Consider the situation of a slight encroachment by a permanent improvement over a common boundary. In one such case, a state supreme court announced what has come to be known by many as the "Common Boundary Rule". The court held that in such cases, the owner must have actual knowledge of the "adverse occupancy" (of the trespass) to meet the open and notorious requirement. Knowledge just of the presence of the improvement was not sufficient. (See Case Squib: *Mannillo v. Gorski.*) In a few cases, usually involving wild and vacant land where sporadic use by various members of the public is expected, the courts may insist on some conduct which distinguishes the alleged possessor from other members of the public.

3. Adverse Possession Under Color of Title: Constructive Adverse Possession. [§ 11–37]

a. Color of Title. [§ 11–38]

Color of title means that the possessor holds pursuant to a written instrument or court decree of judgment which appears to convey record title, but is for some reason defective as a conveyance. For example, A receives a tax deed to Blackacre which is in fact defective. Believing that he has title, A goes into possession. A is an adverse possessor under color of title.

b. Significance. [§ 11–39]

Some state statutes establish different requirements for adverse possession under color of title and for adverse possession without color of title. In some states, the period of time required for adverse possession (the statutory period) may be different. Another significant difference is that the claimant may take advantage of constructive adverse possession if her possession is under color of title.

c. Constructive Adverse Possession. [§ 11–40]

Absent color of title, an adverse possessor geographically acquires only the area of land he actually possesses. (§ 11–32) This may, of course, be determined by fencing, etc. (§ 11–33) However, if the adverse possessor takes possession under color of title, then adverse possession of a portion of the tract described in the instrument which constitutes color of title constitutes constructive adverse possession of the remainder of the tract described in the instrument, at least if the balance of the tract is contiguous and related to the portion actually possessed. Through such constructive adverse possession, actual adverse possession of only a part of a tract will result in title to the whole tract.

(1) Priority of Claims Among Owners and Adverse Possessors [§ 11–41]

Actual possession by the owner defeats constructive possession by an adverse possessor. Moreover, if the owner is in actual possession, it is not possible for the adverse possessor to be in actual possession for purposes of the law of adverse possession. Remember, the adverse possessor must actually *and* exclusively possess the land. By definition, exclusivity requires the absence of the owner.

Constructive possession by the owner defeats constructive possession by an adverse possessor. The rule is supported by the concept of prior in time. The owner is the ultimate "prior possessor."

(2) Limitations on the Doctrine. [§ 11–42]

If a tract has been subdivided (i.e., divided into lots), the possession of any one lot does not constitute possession of any other lot in the tract although the possessor has color of title to the entire parcel. Furthermore, it usually does not apply to a conscious wrongdoer or forger, although an innocent claimant under a forged deed would be protected. Also, it does not apply when the tract is considered too large to constitute practical use or cultivation as an economic unit.

D. HOSTILITY OF POSSESSION (AND CLAIM OF RIGHT). [§ 11–43]

In order to acquire title by adverse possession, the possessor must hold against the right of the owner; otherwise, there is no cause of action against which the statute can run. Thus, a possession which is with the permission of the owner cannot result in the acquisition of title and courts therefore require that the adverse possessor be in possession under a "claim of right," (i.e., not with the permission of the owner). As discussed below, the "claim of right" requirement is probably nothing more than another way of requiring that the possessor's possession be "hostile" (i.e., adverse), but many courts list it as a separate requirement. If the adverse possessor's possession is hostile, the owner may attempt to terminate the hostility element and thereby thwart the adverse possession by granting permission to the adverse possessor. Most courts will not consider after-the-fact permission as interrupting the Statute of Limitations. The owner must physically interrupt the possession or obtain a judicial decision in his favor to stop the adverse possession once it has begun.

1. Permissive Possession Is Not Adverse Possession. [§ 11–44]

In the following situations, possession is permissive and, in the absence of some further conduct by the possessor indicating that she is in fact holding against the owner, will not give rise to any adverse possession claim.

a. Landlord–Tenant. [§ 11–45]

The classic example of permissive possession occurs in the landlord-tenant relationship. The possession of a tenant is not adverse to his landlord. The statute may begin to run if the tenant makes clear to the landlord that she is in fact holding against him as where the tenant repudiates or disclaims the lease in writing or in some other way makes her claim clear to the landlord. Such a repudiation may also be inferred from conduct (e.g., tenant gives a lease to a third party, or physically excludes the landlord from the land where the lease gives landlord a right to enter the land).

b. Co–Tenancy. [§ 11–46]

The possession of one co-tenant is not adverse to the rights of the others. It is presumed that a co-tenant in exclusive possession is there with the consent of the rest. (Remember each co-tenant has the right to possess the whole. See § 7–31) However, the statute will begin to run if the co-tenant in possession ousts or excludes the others. However, this will not be presumed simply because one co-tenant is in exclusive possession, pays taxes, etc.

c. Grantor Remaining in Possession after Conveyance. [§ 11–47]

If a grantor remains in possession after conveyance to a grantee, the grantor's possession is presumed permissive. The statute will begin to run if and only if the grantor openly repudiates the conveyance.

2. Claim of Right Requirement for Adverse Possession. [§ 11–48]

It is commonly stated that the possessor must hold under claim of right in order to acquire title by adverse possession, but the nature of the claim of right requirement is unclear. If claim of right simply means that the holding is non-permissive, the requirement adds nothing to the requirements which have already been discussed.

a. Meaning of "Claim of Right." [§ 11–49]

The modern tendency, found in some cases, is to conclude that the one who openly exerts acts of ownership, and thereby manifests an intent to exclude others, is holding under a claim of right; in these states, it is sufficient, for purposes of the claim of right requirement, that the possessor acts as if she has a right to be there. In some states the presumption, by statute or case law, is in favor of the legal owner, and the adverse possessor has the burden of proving claim of right or claim of title by clear and positive evidence.

b. Claim of Right under Specific Circumstances. [§ 11–50]

(1) Color of Title. [§ 11–51]

If the possessor holds under color of title, he clearly holds under claim of right. This is also true if he holds under a parol grant (oral transfer of title).

(2) Defiant or Bad–Faith Trespasser. [§ 11–52]

The so-called "defiant trespasser"—the possessor who has no color of title, knows he has no title, but by openly acting like the owner clearly indicates that he asserts title—also holds under claim of right.

(3) Passive or Good–Faith Trespasser. [§ 11–53]

If the possessor indicates that he has no title, and that he will move off if the owner comes along and demands possession, some courts would conclude that he does not hold under claim of right. This view is now largely discredited. Courts recognize that such statements are not inconsistent with a claim of right and are irrelevant to the question underlying adverse possession—did the adverse possessor act in such a way as to put a diligent owner on notice that the adverse possessor is making a claim to the title that is inconsistent with the owner's title? If, however, such statements are made directly to the owner or under circumstances which it will clearly be communicated to him, the claim of adverse possession may be denied on the ground that the possessor lulled the owner into inaction.

(4) Trespasser's State of Mind is Irrelevant—The Objective Standard. [§ 11–54]

The position taken by most modern courts is that the trespasser's state of mind is not important when determining if the adverse possessor is acting hostile and under claim of right. Instead of asking whether the adverse possessor was acting as a defiant trespasser or as a passive trespasser, courts following the modern position are simply concerned with whether, from an objective view, there is the type of entry against the owner that will put the owner on notice that the adverse possessor is making a claim against the owner's title.

E. ACQUISITION OF TITLE TO PERSONAL PROPERTY BY ADVERSE POSSESSION. [§ 11–55]

Originally, the concept of adverse possession applied only to land and was grounded in the real property concept of seisin. For better or worse, courts now generally apply not only the same concepts but most of the same rules to many items of personal property (chattels).

1. Requirements. [§ 11–56]

The doctrine of adverse possession of personal property rests on the Statute of Limitations. When the owner is out of possession, and his action to recover possession is barred by the statute, the possessor becomes the owner. The Statute of Limitations for damages or recovery of personal property varies from state to state. In most states it is six years or less, although it may be as long as ten years.

a. Possession Must Be Actual and Exclusive. [§ 11–57]

The adverse possessor must take actual possession of a type that would give the owner a cause of action in replevin (for return of the personal property) or in detinue (to recover the value of the personal property).

b. Possession Must Be Open and Notorious. [§ 11–58]

The requirement that possession, to ripen into ownership, must be open and notorious, has presented peculiar problems in dealing with personal property. In cases involving land, an owner can be charged with notice of the fact that another is in possession of his land; he knows where his land is, and it can be neither moved nor concealed. Personal property, however, can be moved and can be concealed.

(1) Open Possession Starts Statute Running. [§ 11–59]

If a possessor holds openly and notoriously, the statute will run even though the owner does not know of the possession, who the possessor is, or where the personal property is.

(2) Concealed Possession Does Not Start Statute. [§ 11–60]

If, on the other hand, the chattel is secreted or concealed, the statute does not run until the chattel is discovered by the owner or the possession becomes open (the discovery rule). If the possessor is a thief there is a rebuttable presumption that he has concealed the chattel. The same presumption is applied to one who takes from the thief with notice of the illegality. Note that the discovery rule shifts the emphasis from the conduct of the possessor (as is the case with adverse possession of real property) to the conduct of the owner so that the most important issue becomes whether or not the owner has acted and is acting with due diligence in pursuing her chattel. (See Case Squib: *O'Keeffe v. Snyder.*)

c. Possession Must Be Hostile and Under Claim of Right. [§ 11–61]

"Hostility" generally means that the possession must be non-permissive (e.g., the possession of a bailee does not start the running of the statute until the bailee refuses to redeliver). This is one area in which adverse possession of personal property differs somewhat from adverse possession of real property. Generally, a thief can never acquire title to personal property nor can a thief convey title to stolen personal property to a purchaser.

(1) The Case of Voluntary Bailment—Merchants in the Ordinary Course of Business. [§ 11–62]

If an owner voluntarily entrusts personal property to a merchant/bailee who ordinarily deals in goods of the same kind (a bailee in the ordinary course of business) and the bailee, without the owner's permission, transfers the property to a purchaser in the ordinary course of business (a good faith purchaser), the purchaser may acquire title to the personal property. The rationale for courts that follow this view is that, as between the innocent owner and the innocent purchaser for value, the owner was in the relatively better position to check the character of the merchant.

Example [§ 11–63] O is the owner of a precious ring. O, takes the ring to a jeweler to have it appraised. The jeweler appraises rings as part of his ordinary course of business. Instead of appraising the ring and returning it to O, the jeweler sells the ring to A. A was unaware that the jeweler did not have authority to sell the ring. O later sues A seeking either the return of the ring on the value of the ring. A would win because O voluntarily entrusted the ring to the jeweler and A, without notice of any irregularity, purchased the ring from a jeweler who, as part of his business, sells rings.

213

CHAPTER XI

(2) The Case of Voluntary Bailment—Merchants Not in the Ordinary Course of Business. [§ 11–64]

If an owner voluntary entrusts personal property to a merchant/bailee who does not ordinarily deal in goods of the same kind and the bailee, without the owner's permission, transfers the property to a purchaser, not in the ordinary course of business, the owner will not lose title to the purchaser. The rationale is that the purchaser, having notice of the irregularity by the mere fact of purchasing personal property from one who does not ordinarily deal in personal property of that nature, is not a good-faith (bona fide) purchaser. Also, relative to the owner, the purchaser was in the better position to check the character of the merchant and determine whether the merchant had the authority to sell.

Example [§ 11–65] O takes a valuable sculpture to a cake designer. She wants the cake designer to design a cake in the likeness of the sculpture. While shopping for a cake to take to her office party, A sees the sculpture and offers to buy it from the cake designer. The cake designer agrees to sell A the sculpture. O returns only to find the sculpture gone. O sues A seeking the return of the sculpture or the value of the sculpture. O would win. O voluntarily entrusted the sculpture but not to a merchant who normally sells sculptures as part of his business. The purchaser, under such circumstances, would be deemed to be on notice that this is not the type of merchant who ordinarily sells expensive sculptures. As between the owner and such a purchaser, the purchaser had the last and best opportunity to verify the authority of the merchant to sell the sculpture.

d. Possession Must Be Continuous for the Statutory Period. [§ 11–66]

The adverse possession must be continuous for the statutory period, just as with realty. The time period of successive possessors may be tacked if the successors are in privity with each other. For example, A takes possession of a ring belonging to 0 and possesses it for three years. A then makes a gift of the ring to B, who possesses it for eight years. A and B are in privity, and their successive possessions may be added tacked to make up the statutory period.

2. Ownership When Statute Has Run. [11–67]

Once the statutory period has run, the adverse possessor acquires ownership. This ownership may be related back to the time the adverse possession began. Accessions (§ 3–87) to the property during the statutory period are therefore deemed to be owned by the possessor, and he cannot be charged with tortious conduct toward the property occurring during the statutory period.

214

REVIEW PROBLEMS—ADVERSE POSSESSION

O, owner of a fee simple absolute interest in Blackacre, conveys it in 1960, to A for life, remainder to B and his heirs. A moves on the property in 1960 but leaves a few months later. In January, 1961, X takes possession of the property and continually possesses it. In 1985, A dies, and B brings an eviction action against X who is still in possession. There is a twenty year period required for adverse possession in the jurisdiction. Can B evict X?

> **Answer:** Yes. X's entry into possession in 1961 created a cause of action for A to recover possession. A lost the right to bring that action in 1981 and X obtained title to the property but only title to a life estate since that was the interest against which X adversely possessed. X's possession was not adverse to B until 1985 since B was not entitled to possession until A's death. Since B brought an eviction action immediately against X no 20 year period of adverse possession existed vis-à-vis B's possessory rights and therefore B is the owner of Blackacre and X is merely a trespasser vis-à-vis B.

CHAPTER XII

LAND SALES CONTRACTS

A. CONTRACTS FOR THE SALE OF LAND: FORMALITIES. [§ 12–1]

Most real estate transactions include a written contract of sale. The reason for the written contract is the Statute of Frauds, which exists in every state in America. The Statute of Frauds requires that certain contracts be in writing. Contracts for the conveyance of an interest in land are subject to the Statute of Frauds. Certain formalities must be met for such contracts to be valid and enforceable.

As originally enacted in England in 1677, the English Statute of Frauds was entitled "An Act for Prevention of Frauds and Perjuries," which suggests the purpose behind the statute—the prevention of fraud pertaining to land sales contracts.

1. Statute of Frauds. [§ 12–2]

A contract for the sale of land must be evidenced by a writing signed by the party to be charged or by someone authorized to act for him. The "party to be charged" refers to the person who is resisting enforcement of the contract, so it can be either the seller or the buyer. Because it is impossible to know, at the time of the writing, which party might resist enforcement, the best practice is to have both the seller and the buyer sign the sales contract. In several jurisdictions, an agreement for the sale of real property, if made by an agent of the party sought to be charged, is invalid, unless the authority of the agent is in writing and it is subscribed (signed) by the person sought to be charged.

a. Writing Must Contain Essential Terms. [§ 12–3]

The essential terms of the contract must be contained in the writing. These include (a) a description of the property, (b) identification of the parties, (c) words indicating an intention to buy or sell, and (d) a signature. Incidental matters—such as the type of deed, proof of title, proration of insurance or taxes, means of payment, and even the purchase price—should, but need not, appear in writing and can be supplied by reference to local custom, established legal rule, or standards of reasonableness. Such incidental matters need not even have been agreed upon. If, for

217

example, the parties did not agree upon a price, courts will assume that a reasonable price was to be paid. However, if the parties agreed upon a price, courts are badly divided about whether the price must be stated in the contract if the contract is to be enforced. The writing must be signed by the party to be charged or, in some states, by all parties.

b. Parol Evidence. [§ 12–4]

Parol evidence, extraneous oral or written evidence, is generally admissible to resolve ambiguities, although essential terms cannot be supplied by parol.

c. Getting around Statute of Frauds. [§ 12–5]

The Statute of Frauds receives more attention than respect from judges. An oral land sales contract may become enforceable through application of the doctrine of part performance. The doctrine of part performance is a judicially created exception to the Statute of Frauds. When courts apply the doctrine of part performance to enforce a contract otherwise unenforceable because it violates the Statute of Frauds, they usually do so for one of two reasons. First, courts will apply the doctrine of part performance if the court finds that the parties really did enter into an oral agreement (a contract) as the plaintiff alleges and a refusal to enforce the contract would unfairly frustrate the plaintiff's reasonable expectations. The second type of situation in which courts apply the doctrine of part performance is when a plaintiff, in reliance on a contract, makes substantial investments, or materially alters his position such that serious harm can only be avoided by enforcing the contract.

A good example of performance adequate to remove any Statute of Frauds challenge can be seen from the following events: after an oral land sales agreement is reached but before closing occurs, a buyer (1) takes possession of the property, and (2) pays the full contract price or makes substantial improvements.

2. Other Statutory Requirements. [§ 12–6]

The formalities of execution required for the enforceability or recording of land sales contracts depend upon state statutes. Some jurisdictions require both witnesses and acknowledgment for recording, while other states may require only acknowledgment. Usually, a written contract between the parties, if signed by the party sought to be charged, is sufficient for enforcement between the parties. However, contracts for the sale of particular types of property, as, for example, a homestead in some jurisdictions, may have to be witnessed or would have to comply with other formalities in order to be enforced.

B. LAND SALES CONTRACTS: IMPLIED PROVISIONS. [§ 12–7]

Under freedom of contract principles, the parties to a land sales contract are free to agree to any matter they wish, as long as they do not agree to matters that contravene public policy. Over the centuries, however, the courts have formulated a list of provisions that will be implied into land sales contracts, if the parties do not expressly address the issues in the contract or if the contract is ambiguous as to the issue. These implied provisions or policies are discussed below.

1. Risk of Loss. [§ 12–8]

The parties are free to allocate the risk of loss due to casualties occurring between the time that the contract is entered into and the time the land is actually conveyed (i.e., the title transfers). In the absence of contrary provisions in the contract, however, the following rules apply:

a. Equitable Conversion. [§ 12–9]

Under the doctrine of equitable conversion, the vendee (buyer) under an enforceable contract for the sale of realty is regarded in equity as the beneficial owner from the date of the contract and thus has the equitable title to the property. The vendor (seller) has the legal title to the property, until title is transferred by deed, but holds the legal title as trustee for the buyer. The buyer's interest is treated as a real property interest, a right to receive title to the property, and the seller's interest is treated as a personal property interest, a right to the balance of the purchase price. As a result, the common law placed the risk of loss from casualty occurring during the existence of the sales contract on the buyer. The result of this doctrine was to allow a seller to specifically enforce a land sales contract against a buyer even after the contracted-for improvements (buildings) were destroyed. (See Case Squib: *Skelly Oil v. Ashmore.*)

b. Uniform Vendor and Purchaser Risk Act. [§ 12–10]

In those jurisdictions which have adopted the Uniform Vendor and Purchaser Risk Act, if neither title nor possession has passed to the buyer and all or a material part of the improvements are destroyed without the buyer's fault or are taken by eminent domain, the seller cannot enforce the contract and the buyer may recover any partial payment. When the damage or taking affects an immaterial part of the premises, neither the seller nor the buyer loses the right to specifically enforce the contract, but the purchase price is abated to the extent of the destruction or taking. Once title or possession has passed to the buyer, the buyer bears the risk of loss. However, the parties may contractually reallocate the risk.

c. Insurance. [§ 12–11]

Both seller and buyer have an insurable interest in property subject to a sales contract. A pragmatic decision would be that if the seller has insured and the buyer has not insured and if the improvements on the property are destroyed prior to closing, the seller may compel the buyer to perform the contract but the buyer is entitled to the benefit of the insurance proceeds as the insurance proceeds are deemed to take the place of a destroyed building. The result is that the buyer is entitled to a deduction against the sales price to the extent of the insurance proceeds on completing the purchase of the real estate. Recent decisions point in this direction.

2. Type of Deed to Be Executed by Seller. [§ 12–12]

If the contract calls for a certain type of deed (e.g., a general warranty deed, a special warranty deed, or a quitclaim deed), the seller can perform only by delivery of such a deed. (§ 13–40) It is customary, in most states, to convey by a statutory or general warranty deed, but this is usually specified in the contract. The obligation to convey by a statutory or general warranty deed will be implied in the absence of a specific contract provision to the contrary.

3. Marketable Title. [§ 12–13]

The seller is under an obligation to supply the buyer with "marketable title." This is often put in terms of an implied covenant. (See Case Squib: *Lohmeyer v. Bower*.) The duty may be modified by the terms of the contract (e.g., today the buyer may ask for "insurable" title).

a. When Seller Defaults. [§ 12–14]

If the buyer makes proper objection prior to closing, and the seller's title is not "marketable," the buyer cannot be compelled to perform and can recover whatever portion of the purchase price he has already paid. The buyer may also seek damages or specific performance with an abatement of the purchase price.

b. Necessity of Timely Objection by Buyer. [§ 12–15]

The seller satisfies his obligation if defects are removed prior to the time of performance. Thus the buyer's right to object to particular defects may be waived if he knows of the defect and fails to make timely objection. Finally, under the concept of merger by deed, once the buyer has received the deed, he may no longer object that the title is not marketable; the contract merges with the deed (i.e., acceptance of the deed extinguishes any claim the buyer may have had under the contract), and is deemed performed. (§ 13–105). The recognized exceptions to the concept of merger by deed are for fraud and promises that are collateral to the deed.

c. Meaning of "Marketable Title." [§ 12–16]

"Marketable title" is not to be equated with "perfect" or "absolute" title. A title is unmarketable if there is reasonable doubt as to whether it is good or bad. There is no uniform definition of marketable title and the various courts have articulated differing views regarding when title is marketable. Generally, a marketable title is a title free from reasonable doubt in terms of both law and fact, a title which a well-informed, reasonably prudent buyer would be willing to accept. A reasonable buyer would not normally accept a title which is likely to be tested in litigation.

(1) Defects Making a Title Less Than "Marketable." [§ 12–17]

(a) Problems in the Record. [§ 12–18]

Normally, a marketable title must be a title which can be deduced from the land records. See Chapter XV (Recording Acts). Gaps in the record, for example, normally make the title unmarketable (e.g., if A swindled B and sold him a certain bridge in New York and B attempted to sell this bridge to C, a gap in the record would appear as A's ownership of the bridge would never show up and B would not be able to provide C with marketable title). Certain defects which appear in the record, however, may be cured with evidence outside the record. For example, the record may show that title went to X, a married man. The record does not reveal that the wife of X released her dower right when X conveyed. This defect could be cured by proof that the wife was deceased when X conveyed. Erroneous descriptions, variances in names, or other defects which appear on the record may also make title unmarketable.

(b) Encumbrances. [§ 12–19]

Outstanding mortgages, liens, taxes, and assessments will render a title unmarketable if not paid off by the time of performance of the land sales contract. Title may also be unmarketable because of one or more of the following types of encumbrances: dower interests; easements precluding full enjoyment of the premises; pending suits affecting title; use restrictions (covenants); violation of zoning ordinances; and substantial encroachments. However, if such interests are recognized and the contract is made subject to them, title is not made unmarketable. Zoning ordinances do not generally render title unmarketable, their violation will, however, render title unmarketable. (See Case Squib: *Lohmeyer v. Bower*.)

221

(c) Adverse Possession. [§ 12–20]

A title acquired by adverse possession may be marketable, and a seller may rely on matters outside the record to establish his title. Generally, however, courts are reluctant to force adverse possessory title on purchasers and require strict proof to establish such titles. If the contract calls for a marketable title of record, or an abstract showing a marketable title, an adverse possession based title is not sufficient unless its validity has been judicially determined and the decree recorded.

4. Warranty of Marketable Quality. [§ 12–21]

The common law rule in regard to the quality and state of improvements on real property was *caveat emptor* (buyer beware). Thus, unless there was some provision in a land sales contract on point, the seller was under no duty to warrant the quality of the improvements. This rule is now under attack on two fronts:

a. Duty to Disclose defects. [§ 12–22]

In recent years, more and more courts have held that the seller, even absent any provision on point in the land sales contract, is under a duty to disclose facts known to her which materially affect the value of the land and its improvements especially if the seller knows that such facts are not known to or are not within the reach of the buyer. (See Case Squib: *Johnson v. Davis.*)

b. Implied Warranty of Marketability. [§ 12–23]

Today many courts "borrow" the implied warranty of quality concept from contract law and the recently adopted implied warranty of habitability from landlord and tenant law and apply it to land sales contracts as an implied warranty of "marketability" when the seller is the builder or agent of the builder of the improvements. The extension of such implied warranties to contracts for "used" housing is not yet settled. (See Case Squib: *Redarowicz v. Ohlendorf.*)

C. FINANCING. [§ 12–24]

The major concern in most real estate transactions (residential, commercial, industrial or agrarian) these days is financing, because very few individuals or corporations pay for their purchase in cash. In other words, most land is bought with borrowed money. The importance of financing manifests itself in many ways.

1. Financing Contingency Clauses. [§ 12–25]

Most land sales contracts include financing contingency clauses which are designed to make the buyer's obligation to buy contingent upon her ability to obtain mortgage financing. Pursuant to such clauses, if the buyer is unable to obtain financing, the buyer is released from all obligations under the contract and is normally entitled to a refund of any down payment or "earnest" money. It is in the interests of both the buyer and the seller to have considerable specificity in a financing contingency clause in regard to the amount of financing the buyer must obtain, (e.g., 80% of the purchase price), the maximum interest rate that the buyer must pay, the length of the loan, the types of financing entities the buyer must approach to obtain a loan, and a time limit within which the buyer must obtain a commitment for the financing or terminate the contract.

2. Mortgages. [§ 12–26]

A mortgage is a security interest in land created to secure the payment of a debt. When buyers borrow money to purchase land and improvements they are usually required to create a mortgage in favor of the lender to secure their obligation to repay the amount borrowed. Most law schools have separate courses in real estate finance law. In fact, the course is sometimes called "Mortgages." As a result, there is usually little coverage of mortgages in property courses. Mortgage terminology does, however, often occur in cases relating to land sales contracts.

The explanations of the following terms should help in understanding those cases.

1. Ant–Deficiency Statutes. Some states by statute prohibit a deficiency judgment thereby confining the amount the lender (mortgagee) can recover on foreclosure to the amount received at the judicial foreclosure sale.

2. Deficiency Judgment. If the sale price at the judicial foreclosure sale is less than the amount owed to the mortgagee, the mortgagee is entitled to a judgment for the difference and can collect it out of the general assets of the borrower (mortgagor).

3. Due on Sale Clause. Many mortgages contain a due on sale or acceleration clause, as it is also called, which provides that if the mortgagor transfers ownership of the property, the entire balance due becomes payable immediately.

4. Equity of Redemption. The mortgagor's interest after the mortgage is executed is the equity. The equity is the difference between the market value of a piece of property and the current balance due on the mortgage loan (i.e., the actual value "owned" by the mortgagor, free and clear of the mortgagee's interest). After a default by the mortgagor, the mortgagor still has the right to redeem the property and save his equity by paying the amount due; this is called the equity of redemption. The equity of redemption continues until it is cut off by a foreclosure sale.

5. Foreclosure. Foreclosure is the process by which the mortgagee asserts its security interest and obtains repayment when a mortgagor defaults. The mortgagee cuts off the mortgagor's equity of redemption by holding a public sale of the property, conveying title to the property to the purchaser at the sale and applying the sales proceeds to satisfy the outstanding debt owed to the mortgagee. There are three types of foreclosure, judicial foreclosure, power of sale foreclosure, and strict foreclosure. Judicial foreclosure, as its name indicates, involves a lawsuit and judicial oversight. Power of sale foreclosure allows sale of the property by the mortgagee without court supervision. All states provide for judicial foreclosure. Not all states allow power of sale foreclosure and in those states that do allow power of sale foreclosure, many require that the right of power of sale foreclosure must be expressly stated in the mortgage. Strict foreclosure is a foreclosure without a sale of the property. The mortgagor is given a date by which he must pay off the mortgage or lose the property interest.

6. Lien Theory. The lien theory of mortgages, and the one found in the majority of jurisdictions, treats the mortgage as conveying a lien in the property to the mortgagee. The mortgagor retains legal title and the mortgagee gets only a lien (security) interest in the land. Most jurisdictions are lien theory of mortgage jurisdictions. The alternate analysis to the lien theory of mortgages is the title theory, discussed below.

7. Mortgagee. The mortgagee is the lender. The mortgagee can be an entity, such as a financing institution or an individual. Sometimes, sellers finance the sales of their own properties by accepting less than the full purchase price and taking a mortgage to secure the balance of the purchase price. This form of seller financing is referred to as a purchase money mortgage and the sellers are purchase money mortgagees.

8. Mortgagor. The mortgagor is the borrower or debtor who offers land as security for repayment of the debt.

9. Promissory Note. The mortgagor executes a promissory note for the amount of money borrowed from the mortgagee. The mortgage secures the promissory note.

10. Self-amortizing. Most residential mortgages today provide for the borrowed amount to be paid off totally during the life of the loan so that the monthly payment made by mortgagor is part interest and part principal. If a mortgage is not self amortizing (or only partially so) it is referred to as a balloon mortgage because all or part of the principal is paid at the end—a balloon payment.

11. Second mortgage. A mortgagor may borrow money from more than one institution or individual and secure each loan with a mortgage on the same piece of land. The terms "first", "second," "third," etc. relate to the priority of the given mortgage in terms of payment on default or foreclosure. The first mortgage has first priority for payment, the second is paid second and so on until all mortgages are paid off or no money is left.

12.   Statutory Redemption. Many states have passed statutes that give a mortgagor, for a specified period of time after a foreclosure sale, the right to buy back the title to the property from the purchaser at foreclosure. The statutory right of redemption arises after the equity of redemption has terminated and is the last opportunity for the mortgagor to redeem.

13.   Title Theory. In some—but an ever decreasing number—of jurisdictions, the execution of a mortgage is deemed to pass title from the mortgagee to the mortgagor so that the mortgagee has legal title to the land and the mortgagor has only the equity of redemption.

3.   Installment Land Contracts. [§ 12–27]

An informal and risky way for the buyer to obtain financing from the seller is through a land installment contract or "contract for deed" as they are called in many jurisdictions. The buyer makes periodic (usually monthly) payments of principal and interest just as is the case with most mortgage financing. Unlike the situation with a mortgage, the seller retains title until the buyer makes all installment payments. Only then does the seller deliver a deed. Until recently, buyers pursuant to land installment contracts were in a precarious situation. If they made all but the final installment payment, for example, they lost all rights to the land and had no "equity build up" as is the case with a mortgage. Additionally, the seller's obligation to convey marketable title was deemed to apply only to the end of the installment payment period when the deed was to be delivered. This meant that if, in the middle of the installment payment time period, the buyer had reason to doubt the marketability of the seller's title, no remedy was available until the buyer had made all installment payments. Most of these abuses no longer apply because most courts have begun applying equitable mortgage principles to land installment contracts and for most purposes have given buyers many of the same protections they would have received had the transaction been financed through a mortgage. (See Case Squib: *Bean v. Walker.*)

CHAPTER XII

REVIEW PROBLEMS—LAND SALES: CONTRACTS

Many essay questions on land sales contracts concentrate on implied covenants in order to stress newer developments in this area of real property law.

S, a builder of houses, enters into a land sales contract with B, buyer, for the sale of a residence recently constructed by S. The contract contains no reference to the quality of title which S must convey to B nor to the type of deed to be used for the conveyance. A title defect is discovered and B wants out of the contract or perhaps S wants to convey title using a quitclaim deed.

> **Answer:** Even before recent contract law oriented changes in property law a land sales contract silent in regard to quality of title or type of deed to be used for conveyance of title has implied into it a requirement that S have marketable title and that she convey it by general warranty deed.

Soon after B moved in, the roof collapsed due to poor construction. May B sue S?

> **Answer:** Your analysis in regard to potential liability on Seller should center on the new line of cases which borrow from contracts law the concept of an implied warranty of marketability and imply it into land sales contracts which are silent on this point. Real property law is still uncertain as to what to do about implying such warranties of marketability into land sales contracts for used housing as opposed to new housing. There is a new and vastly expanded duty placed on sellers to disclose all information they have or should have about defects in the improvements. This might provide a further basis for liability in the new housing context and in regard to used housing as well.

CHAPTER XIII

DEEDS

A. OVERVIEW. [§ 13–1]

The object of a land sales contract is the transfer of title (ownership) of the land in question from the seller to the buyer. See Chapter XII (Land Sales Contracts). In our system, a deed is normally necessary for the transfer of title to land on an inter vivos basis

B. GENERAL CONSIDERATIONS. [§ 13–2]

1. Transfer of Title. [§ 13–3]

Normally, a deed is used to transfer title to real property interests. There are some occasions when title may be transferred without a deed (e.g., transfers by will or transfers by operation of law such as through adverse possession, death of a joint tenant holding a joint tenancy with right of survivorship, or death of one spouse if the couple is holding as tenants by the entirety, etc.), but the deed is the usual, and in most cases, the only way to transfer such interests.

2. Deed Formalities. [§ 13–4]

A deed must satisfy certain statutory or common law requirements in order to be an effective instrument.

a. The Deed Must Be in Writing, Signed by the Grantor. [§ 13–5]

The Statute of Frauds requires that a deed be in writing and signed by the grantor. The grantee need not sign; his acceptance of the deed is enough in itself to bind him contractually to any covenants in the deed. A seal is not necessary in most states but witnesses and even acknowledgment (certification by a notary public) may be required.

A forged deed is void and cannot be enforced against the grantor whose signature is forged, not even by a subsequent purchaser for value without notice of the forgery (BFP). In contrast, most courts hold that a deed obtained by fraud is voidable, not void, in an action by the grantor against the grantee. As against a subsequent BFP from the grantee, the grantor would not prevail. The idea is that the grantor, by signing the deed, introduced the deed into commerce, making it possible for a subsequent BFP to incur a loss. Even though the grantor's signature was acquired by fraud, as between the innocent grantor and the subsequent BFP, the grantor was in the superior position to avoid the loss.

b. Identification of Parties and Interests Involved. [§ 13–6]

The deed should identify with reasonable clarity the grantor, the grantee, the property involved, and the estate or interest which is to pass. If the parties or the land itself cannot be determined from the deed, the deed may be void for uncertainty. If no estate or interest is defined, it will be presumed that the grantor conveys whatever interest he has.

c. Intention to Transfer. [§ 13–7]

The deed should indicate a present intent to transfer an interest. Words such as "convey" or "grant" are sufficient, though no technical words are necessary.

d. Consideration Not Necessary. [§ 13–8]

The deed need not recite consideration, for consideration is not necessary for a valid deed. Property may be conveyed as a gift.

e. Prerequisites for Recording. [§ 13–9]

Additional formalities may be required in some states for recording (e.g., acknowledgment before a notary public) but are not necessary to make a deed operative as a conveyance between the grantor and grantee.

C. PHYSICAL DESCRIPTION, BOUNDARIES, AND BOUNDARY DISPUTES. [§ 13–10]

The most important part of a deed is the description of the land to which it transfers title.

1. Adequacy and Nature of Description. [§ 13–11]

a. Specific Description Important. [§ 13–12]

The geographic dimensions of land, like other elements of deeds, must be described in writing. The courts have been quick to note that varying the terms of a written description, or supplying a description not set forth in writing through the use of parol evidence, contravenes the policy of the Statute of Frauds. However, in some circumstances, parol evidence may be used to resolve ambiguity, or to clarify the grantor's intent. See Chapter XII (Land Sales Contracts), § 12–4.

b. Methods of Description. [§ 13–13]

The most common, acceptable methods of description are by reference to government survey, recorded plat maps, by metes and bounds (e.g., "from the fence to the river"), or courses and distances.

c. Indefinite Description Void. [§ 13–14]

A description which is wholly indefinite or uncertain, even when construed in the light of circumstances at the time of its execution, is void. However, a court will avoid such a result whenever possible, consistent with the Statute of Frauds.

(1) Example. [§ 13–15] O conveys to A "part of my farm." Such a description is sufficiently indefinite that the grant would be void. Admission of parol evidence would simply be to provide the description outright, and would probably not be allowed.

(2) Example. [§ 13–16] O conveys to A "one acre of" a described ten acre tract. The location of the conveyed acre is not set out, but the deed will probably be treated as the conveyance of a one-tenth interest in the larger tract (which A will own as a tenant in common with O).

d. Ambiguity and Uncertainty in Descriptions. [§ 13–17]

The old common law recognized two types of ambiguity, and the admissibility of parol evidence turned on which was present. However, problems of ambiguity tend to be treated along with other problems of uncertainty as matters of construction.

(1) Cannot Vary a Clear Description. [§ 13–18]

Testimony as to the intent of the parties cannot be used to vary a written description which is in fact clear, even if the description was not as intended (although reformation (judicial rewriting of the contract) may be available). Nor can a deed be construed to transfer an interest if that interest is beyond the boundaries of the permissible construction of the property described in the deed. For example, if O conveys "my hardware store in Miami," and he has two such stores, the deed cannot be construed to convey O's store in Orlando.

(2) May Interpret in Light of Facts Known by Parties. [§ 13–19]

In construing a deed, the court may interpret its language in light of facts and circumstances known by the parties when the deed was executed. This assumes that there is an uncertainty or ambiguity which makes reference outside the deed itself legitimate. In boundary cases, where there is uncertainty or ambiguity which the parties have resolved by their own conduct (e.g., by placing a fence), that conduct is likely to be heavily relied upon in construing the deed.

(3) Rules of Construction. [§ 13–20]

In addition, the court may use certain established rules of construction. These are not rules of law, and will not be used if there is sufficient evidence of contrary intent.

(a) Natural Monuments Prevail Over Man–Made Monuments. [§ 13–21]

Natural monuments prevail over man-made monuments, lines or distances, angles, quantity descriptions, or general generic descriptions. For example, a call to "the big elm tree, one hundred feet south" is construed as going to the tree, even if it is one hundred and ten feet south.

(b) Artificial Monuments and Marked or Surveyed Lines Prevail Over Courses or Directions. [§ 13–22]

Artificial monuments (stakes, markers, buildings, etc.) and marked or surveyed lines prevail over courses or directions, distances, angles, quantity, or general descriptions.

(c) Stated Courses or Directions Prevail Over Distances. [§ 13–23]

(d) All of the Above Prevail Over General Descriptions of Area or Quantity. [§ 13–24]

All of these prevail over statements of quantity or general descriptions ("the Carter place").

(e) Highway and Water Boundaries. [§ 13–25]

References in legal descriptions to water bodies and highways as boundaries are governed by special rules of construction. Monuments, such as highways and public streets that are significantly wide, raise unique problems. Often the underlying fee is owned by a private grantor, subject to an easement in favor of a public agency. The usual rule of construction is that a conveyance describing land with a reference to a monument such as "to Elm Street," will be construed as conveying title to the center of the street, subject, of course, to the easement. A similar rule of construction applies to waterways such as rivers and streams, assuming the grantor owns title to the bed.

Bodies of water also pose additional challenges because their courses can and do change over time. If the course changes slowly over time, the usual policy is to treat the legal boundary as changing with the body of water. If the change is sudden, the boundaries are not affected and the original (previous) boundary line remains unchanged. (See § 13–32).

(4) Presumptions of Conveyance. [§ 13–26]

There is a rebuttable presumption that when a grantor uses a public or private way, or a body of water, as a boundary, he intends to convey the land to the center of the way (or body of water), assuming that he owns to the center. If a way is a boundary, and the grantor owns beneath the entire width of the way, it will be presumed that the entire width of the way had been conveyed. (The grantee normally takes subject to a right of way easement in the public.)

(a) Boundary "Running Along" a Way. [§ 13–27]

If a deed describes a boundary not "as bounded by Street X" but by a call "running along the street," or "by the side of the street," the deed may be interpreted as conveying only to the edge of the right of way and any land beneath the right of way is retained by the grantor. The same rules are applicable to water boundaries. There is a strong presumption however that the boundary extends to the center of the monument when the grantor owns that far, and the presumption has been applied when the conveyance was in reference to a plat and the monument was a street.

(b) Measurements "from" a Monument. [§ 13–28]

Measurement "from" a monument (e.g., 100 feet south from Road X) is normally taken from the "side" of the monument, even though the deed actually conveys to the center.

(5) Variable Water Boundaries. [§ 13–29]

(a) Accretion and Reliction. [§ 13–30]

When land is bounded by a body of water, deposits of soil which build up slowly or imperceptibly ("accretion") belong to the riparian landowner whose land the deposit abuts. Similarly, if the water slowly recedes, the additional dry land belongs to the abutting owner. This process is called reliction. If the riparian owner owns to the center of a stream, a gradual and imperceptible change in the center line will change his boundary.

(b) Erosion. [§ 13–31]

Boundaries may also be changed by the opposite process. Thus, a riparian owner may find that some (or indeed perhaps even all) of his land has been gradually washed away ("erosion"). If his boundary is set by a waterline, (as opposed to a fixed line in a particular place), erosion results in a corresponding boundary line change. (If a boundary is fixed without reference to a waterline the fact that it becomes submerged does not affect the boundary.)

(c) Avulsion. [§ 13–32]

Water boundary lines are not affected by sudden, perceptible changes of the watercourse ("avulsion") as where a river suddenly floods and cuts a new channel. Avulsion often occurs in connection with natural disasters such as hurricanes or earthquakes.

2. Boundary Disputes and Their Resolution. [§ 13–33]

There is perhaps no more common kind of property dispute than the argument over boundaries. The starting point for their resolution is the description in the deed. Relevant doctrines used in resolving boundary disputes are:

a. Construction of the Deed. [§ 13–34]

If there is an element of uncertainty or ambiguity in the deed, its construction is likely to be the primary matter of dispute. Within the range of uncertainty or ambiguity, the court may be willing to look to evidence outside the deed. A most persuasive fact, if present, is the subsequent action of the parties in physically locating the boundary.

b. Reformation of the Deed. [§ 13–35]

The deed may be reformed if there was a mutual mistake.

c. Adverse Possession. [§ 13–36]

In many cases, one landowner has fenced or used land which simply is not his, although he may believe it is. In such cases, adverse possession must be considered.

d. Boundary Line Agreements. [§ 13–37]

A written boundary agreement is normally controlling (as it may be viewed as a conveyance of land). An oral agreement that a certain line will be treated as the true boundary may also be controlling, despite the Statute of Frauds, if (a) there was a bona fide dispute or uncertainty, and (b) both parties treat the agreed line as the true boundary. Some courts require, in addition, that the boundary was fixed on the ground (e.g., by a fence or monument).

e. Boundaries by Acquiescence. [§ 13–38]

A boundary line may also be fixed by acquiescence in a particular location even if the abutting property owners have not explicitly agreed to the location of the boundary. The period of acceptance and recognition (acquiescence) must be lengthy. The majority of courts will likely base the required period of acquiescence on the period of the applicable adverse possession statute. This doctrine requires a boundary dispute and acquiescence, but not a specific oral agreement. Additionally, the asserted boundary must be physically marked on the ground, often with a fence or some other type of barrier. The physical marking must be put in place for the purpose of marking a boundary and not for some other purpose such as complying with a city ordinance or containing animals. Both adjoining owners must know of the marked boundary and both must possess up to the marked line.

f. Boundaries by Estoppel. [§ 13–39]

Courts may apply equitable estoppel principles to resolve the boundary dispute thereby allowing a party to prevail without the necessity of showing a marking on the ground or an agreement between the parties. The elements of a boundary by estoppel are: (a) one owner misrepresents the location of the boundary line to the owner of the bordering land, and (b) the second owner relies on the misrepresentation of the first owner and builds improvements that encroach on the true boundary or takes other actions that are detrimental. The first owner, who misrepresented the boundary, is estopped from denying his representation and the boundary is shifted according to the representation.

D. DELIVERY OF DEEDS. [§ 13–40]

In our common law system, a deed is not effective unless and until it is delivered by the grantor to the grantee with an intent by the grantor that the deed be presently operative. The grantee must accept the deed in order for the delivery to be complete. If the grantee would be benefited by the conveyance, the grantee's acceptance will be presumed. In some cases, courts have presumed the grantee's acceptance of a beneficial transfer even when the grantee did not have knowledge of the deed or of its delivery. If the grantee does not want the conveyance, the grantee may disclaim and title will remain in the grantor. Most of the problems in this area do not concern the grantee's acceptance but rather the question of whether there was an effective delivery.

Delivery is typically accomplished by physically transferring the deed from the grantor to the grantee; however, courts have found an effective delivery in cases in which the grantor expressed, in words, an intention to make a present transfer but did not make a manual delivery. (§ 13–43) The important question in these cases is whether the grantor intended to make an immediate transfer or whether the grantor was attempting to use the deed as a will substitute, in violation of the Statute of Wills. If the latter is the case, courts will find the deed to be invalid and title will remain in the grantor.

1. **Transfer of Interest With Delivery Qualifications. [§ 13–41]**

   A deed does not operate to transfer any interest in land until it has been "delivered." Delivery is a word of art and although a deed may be delivered simply by giving it to the grantee (the usual method), such a physical act is unnecessary to a valid delivery. Conversely, physical transfer alone may not be sufficient for a "delivery." Delivery is essentially an intent requirement, and the delivery requirement is satisfied if the grantor, by some words or acts, has manifested an intention that his deed have a present operative effect (that some interest shall pass immediately and irrevocably to the grantee).

   (1) **Example. [§ 13–42]** O executes a deed to A. He tells A he wants to be ready to convey an interest to A "sometime." O gives the deed to A "for safekeeping." Despite the transfer of the deed, there is no delivery; it is clear O did not intend the deed to be presently operative.

   (2) **Example. [§ 13–43]** O executes a deed to A, but is unable to give it to him because A is out of the country. O has the deed acknowledged and recorded, and places it in his own safety deposit box. Thereafter, he tells people A is the owner, and generally behaves as though this is so. In most states, there has been a valid delivery.

2. **General Presumptions. [§ 13–44]**

   a. **Grantee in Possession. [§ 13–45]**

   Possession of the deed by the grantee creates a rebuttable presumption that it has been delivered.

b. Grantor in Possession. [§ 13–46]

If the grantor has retained possession of the deed, there is a rebuttable presumption that the deed has not been validly delivered. (Note example (§ 13–43) above where this presumption was rebutted.)

c. Recording. [§ 13–47]

Acknowledgment and proper recording of the deed creates a rebuttable presumption that the deed has been delivered.

d. Dating of the Deed. [§ 13–48]

Mere dating of a deed has nothing to do with delivery. If delivery is established, however, it is presumed that the deed was delivered on its date.

3. Delivery in Cases Where the Grantor Has Retained the Deed. [§ 13–49]

While it is possible to establish a delivery when the grantor has retained the deed, the burden created by the presumption to the contrary is very difficult to satisfy.

a. Example. [§ 13–50] If the facts show that the grantor did physically transfer the deed to the grantee with the requisite intent, and the grantee then "returned" the deed to the grantor for safekeeping, the presumption is overcome and there is a valid delivery. Once there has been an effective delivery, title passes to the grantee. If the grantee returns the deed to the grantor, as in the example, this has no effect to either cancel the earlier delivery or to reconvey the title to the grantor. If the grantee wishes to reconvey the title, the grantee will need to execute and deliver a new deed which complies with the Statute of Frauds.

b. Grantor as Co–Tenant. [§ 13–51]

If the deed in question purports to make the grantor and grantee co-tenants and there is some evidence that the deed was intended to be presently operative, the presumption arising from the grantor's retention of possession is overcome. Retention of possession here is as consistent with the grantor's status as a grantee as it is with a finding that the deed was not meant to be presently operative. (Normally, a delivery to one co-tenant is deemed a delivery to all.)

c. Establishing Transfer When Grantor Retains Possession. [§ 13–52]

In cases where the grantor does not physically transfer the deed because of some inability to do so and retains possession himself, it is unlikely that

235

a valid delivery can be established unless: (a) the deed has been acknowledged and properly recorded; and (b) there is some objective evidence of an intent to make the deed presently operative; and (c) the grantor's subsequent conduct indicates his belief that the deed was operative.

4. Delivery Where the Deed Has Been Physically Transferred to the Grantee. [§ 13–53]

There is a rebuttable presumption of delivery when the grantee has possession of the deed. However, the presumption can be rebutted by proof (typically by parol evidence) that the deed was not intended to have any operative effect whatsoever. For example, if A gives a deed to B simply as part of an initiation ceremony or merely for examination, and A did not intend to convey anything at all, there is no delivery.

a. Transfer Through Unlawful Means. [§ 13–54]

The presumption of a valid delivery can be rebutted by proof that the grantor did not physically transfer the deed to the grantee, but that the deed came into the grantee's possession through theft, trickery, or other unlawful means.

b. Conditional Delivery to the Grantee. [§ 13–55]

Suppose O delivers a deed to Blackacre, absolute on its face, to A, telling A that the property is his if O fails to return from a hazardous journey which she is about to undertake. O takes the journey and returns. A insists the property belongs to him. To what extent will a court give effect to parol conditions (oral conditions) attached at the time of delivery?

(1) Majority View. [§ 13–56]

The prevailing view seems to be that when the grantor has physically transferred the deed, absolute and unconditional on its face, to the grantee, parol evidence is not admissible to show that the delivery was subject to a condition. In such a case, the delivery is absolute. On the facts above, A wins. (See Case Squib: *Sweeney v. Sweeney.*)

(2) Criticism of Majority View. [§ 13–57]

The majority view has been subjected to severe criticism, in part because even when an absolute deed has been physically given to the grantee, parol evidence is admissible to establish that the grantor had no intention to make the deed presently operative as a conveyance. The intent to make a conditional delivery and the absence of any intent presently to convey are often very difficult to distinguish.

(3) **Example.** [§ 13–58] O gives A an absolute deed to Blackacre, telling him that the deed is to operate as a conveyance only at O's death (e.g., "this is yours when I die"). Such evidence is likely to be held admissible as going to the question of the type of future estate O intended to immediately convey. Death is certain and A most likely gets immediately a future interest being either a remainder or executory interest with O retaining a present possessory life estate.

(4) **Example.** [§ 13–59] O gives A an absolute deed to Blackacre, stating that it is to be effective if A pays off an existing mortgage within one year. Here the parol evidence is likely to be held inadmissible as this is an attempt to prove a conditional present delivery. Under the majority approach, A takes free of the condition.

The distinction between the prior examples is often not very clear. The true test in every case is in regard to the grantor's intent relative to the present passage of title. In the first example, O's statement evidences an intent to make a present transfer of title, the question concerns the nature of the title O wants to presently transfer. In the second example, the condition shows a lack of a present, immediate intent to transfer either a present or a future estate.

c. **Estoppel in Favor of an Innocent Purchaser.** [§ 13–60]

If the grantee of a deed "absolute and complete" on its face obtains possession of the deed without a valid delivery, the grantor or his successors may be estopped to deny the validity of the delivery against a subsequent BFP who dealt with the grantee. There are two innocent parties—the grantor and the BFP. If the grantor is responsible for entrusting the grantee with a deed absolute on its face, the grantor will lose to a BFP because the grantor contributed most to the loss and, as between the grantor and the BFP, the grantor was in the superior position to avoid the loss.

5. **Delivery Where the Grantor Has Physically Transferred the Deed to a Third Party.** [§ 13–61]

a. **The Commercial Escrow.** [§ 13–62]

Most cases agree that in order to have a valid commercial escrow, there must be an enforceable contract of sale that satisfies the Statute of Frauds. Meaning, the deed must be placed beyond the grantor's control by a contract enforceable in equity. If the contract fails, the grantor can repudiate the contract and compel the escrow agent to return the deed before the escrow agent has delivered the deed to the grantee. Suppose that O, owner of Blackacre, contracts to sell Blackacre to A. O agrees to give the deed to X, with instructions to X to turn the deed over to A when the purchase price has been paid. This is the standard commercial escrow. When O gives the deed to X, it can be said that a valid conditional delivery has occurred. X has made a conditional delivery to a third party (not to the grantee) and has relinquished control over the interest conveyed. Title will transfer automatically when the condition is met; O retains title only if the condition is not met. When O makes the conditional delivery of the deed to X, the effect of the delivery is to bind O upon the instrument meaning that, unless the power of revocation is reserved, the instrument is irrevocable. (See Case Squib: *Sweeney v. Sweeney*.)

(1) Condition Must Be Beyond Control of Grantor. [§ 13–63]

Note that the condition must be beyond the control of the grantor (otherwise the grantor has not given up control of the deed).

(2) Establishing Conditions of Transfer. [§ 13–64]

Conditions and terms upon which the deed is transferred to a third party may be established even though they are oral and the deed is absolute on its face. This is in contrast to the rules applied where the deed is transferred directly to the grantee.

(3) Improper Delivery by the Escrow Agent. [§ 13–65]

Once the condition occurs, title is in the grantee, and he can compel the agent to deliver the deed. On the other hand, if the grantee wrongfully acquires the deed from the escrow agent without satisfaction of the conditions, title does not pass; thus in most states, even a BFP from such a grantee acquires no title (the grantor is not estopped to assert the lack of delivery). In a few states the grantor is estopped against a BFP in these circumstances if the escrow agent was selected by the grantor.

(4) Revocation by the Grantor. [§ 13–66]

The weight of authority is that if the grantor delivers the deed to the escrow agent with no reservation of the power of revocation, the delivery is irrevocable. Under this view, delivery to the escrow agent itself irrevocably transfers a contingent interest to the grantee so that if the grantee satisfies the conditions imposed, the escrow agent must turn over the deed regardless of any protests from the grantor. For the delivery of the deed to the escrow agent to be effective to convey title, the escrow agreement must be irrevocable. If the grantor reserves a power of revocation, no delivery has occurred and no transfer of title results regardless of whether the grantor ever exercises the power. (See Case Squib: *Rosengrant v. Rosengrant.*)

(5) When Title Passes. [§ 13–67]

Under the rules normally applied to commercial escrows, title does not pass until the performance of the stated conditions. However, title will "relate back" to the date on which the deed was deposited with the escrow agent so that the transfer of title to the grantee will be effective even if the grantor dies, becomes mentally incompetent, or otherwise is incapable of conveying property during the escrow period (the title will basically relate back when it is "just and equitable" to do so). Under the relation back theory, at the time of the conveyance by the grantor to the escrow agent, there is a transfer to the grantee of a fee title subject to an interest in the grantor, usually characterized as a life estate, until the occurrence of the condition (in this case, payment of the purchase price) which then terminates the grantor's interest.

The doctrine will not be used to defeat intervening BFPs, mortgagees, or third parties whose claims were known to the grantee before performance of the conditions. But note that if the deed in the grantee's name is properly recorded when placed in escrow, there will be no BFP because the recording of the deed will give record notice of the grantee's interest in the property. Thus, the claims of an intervening third party which have attached to the property during the escrow period may be cut off if the intervening third party had notice of the grantee's interest.

b. Delivery of the Deed to a Third Person in the Gift Context. [§ 13–68]

In general, if O gives a deed to X with instructions to give the deed to A, there will be a valid delivery so long as O has not retained control over the deed (if O retains the power to unilaterally revoke the delivery to X and recover the deed, then no delivery has occurred).

(1) No Delivery if Grantor Retains Control. [§ 13–69]

If the grantor has retained control, or has indicated that delivery to A shall only be made by X upon further instruction from O, there is no valid delivery at this point and O is not bound. (O is, of course, bound if X delivers in accord with his instructions.) If the third party is clearly a continuing agent of the grantor, there is no delivery as control is presumed.

(2) Delivery on the Death of the Grantor. [§ 13–70]

O delivers to X a deed to Blackacre, absolute on its face and naming A as grantee in fee simple. X is instructed to give the deed to A at O's death, a condition certain to occur. In almost all of our states, this is a valid delivery if O has retained no further control over X and has retained no right to revoke. The fact that the stated condition is oral is of little consequence. In most states, this is viewed as the creation of a vested remainder, with reservation of a life estate in the grantor. In other states upholding such a delivery, the grantee is viewed as taking an executory interest. Hence the deed is presently operative as the grantor has presently created a vested future interest in the grantee. (This also avoids the argument that the disposition is testamentary and violates the Statute of Wills).

(3) Delivery on a Condition Not Certain to Occur. [§ 13–71]

(a) No Delivery if Condition Within Control of Grantor. [§ 13–72]

Virtually all courts agree that the grantor cannot effectively deliver a deed by giving it to a third party with instructions to deliver to the grantee upon the happening of an event which is completely within the control of the grantor. If the grantor controls the condition, then the grantor has not given up control of the deed and can in effect revoke the delivery to the escrow agent by preventing the condition from occurring. In some jurisdictions a reservation of a power of revocation may not prevent delivery. (See Case Squib: *St. Louis Bank v. Fielder.*)

(b) Condition Within Control of the Grantee. [§ 13–73]

In a few states, delivery to a third party on a condition exclusively within the control of the grantee is valid, whether or not there is a valid, underlying contract that satisfies the Statute of Frauds (e.g., O gives a deed to B, instructing him to deliver the deed to A "if A marries X"). This is the most obvious analogy to the commercial escrow and states following this view in the gift escrow setting may be expected to conclude that such a delivery is valid and creates an irrevocable right in the grantee to take if the condition is met.

(c) Delivery on an Uncertain Condition Beyond the Control of Grantor or Grantee. [§ 13–74]

Suppose O makes out a deed to A. O gives the deed to B, with instruction to give the deed to A "if he survives me," or "if I fail to return from vacation." The majority of courts view this situation as a retention of control by the grantor over the instrument. Courts following this view use the parol condition to find that the deed was not a valid transfer of an interest and O, the grantor, retains the title even if O dies before A or fails to return from vacation. A few jurisdictions, following the rules developed in death cases, uphold such a conditional delivery in accord with its terms, reasoning that the grantor by delivering the deed to the escrow agent has presently conveyed a contingent future interest (either a contingent remainder or an executory interest).

In contrast, if such conditions accompany delivery to the grantee, the deed is regarded as absolute and the oral condition is not enforceable. (§ 13–56) Thus, if the above example is altered to state that O gave the deed to A with the same instructions, A would hold title in fee simple absolute, free of the conditions.

6. Grantee Must Accept Deed. [§ 13–75]

In order to complete a conveyance, the deed must be accepted by the grantee. This means that the grantee has the option of rejecting the grant within a reasonable period of time. If the grant is beneficial, acceptance is presumed.

a. Relates Back to Date of Delivery. [§ 13–76]

Normally, acceptance is related back to the date of delivery (note how this applies to a situation where the grantee does not know of the delivery until after the grantor's death), although a court may refuse to "relate back" if there are intervening bona fide purchasers or mortgagees.

Example. [§ 13–77] O wishes to give Blackacre to his daughter D for surviving her first year in law school. O executes and records the deed to D. O delivers the deed to D at a party at O's home. D, however, does not want Blackacre because she is insolvent and is about to file for bankruptcy and rejects the deed. When D's creditors try to reach Blackacre because of the recorded deed what is the result? (Assume that simply transferring Blackacre back to O would not help D because as long as the transfer from O to D was effective the creditors would be able to reach the property in O's hands.) D's creditors lose. D never accepted the deed and even though the grant was beneficial and a deed was recorded, the presumption of delivery and acceptance can be rebutted; thus no effective transfer of "ownership" from O to D ever occurred.

E. DEED COVENANTS OF TITLE. [§ 13–78]

1. Title Assurance. [§ 13–79]

Covenants for title are a form of title assurance, providing the means by which a grantee or his successors may hold the grantor responsible for defects in the title. In the absence of such covenants, the grantee who accepts a deed generally has no basis for proceeding back against his grantor if the title is not good, or is encumbered with unknown easements or restrictions. With the growth of title insurance, covenants for title no longer have the significance which once attached to them.

2. Three Forms of Deeds. [§ 13–80]

Deeds today normally take one of three forms: (a) general warranty deeds, (b) special warranty deeds, and (c) quitclaim deeds. The major difference between them is in the title covenants they contain, or do not contain. Covenants of title are not implied at common law. Today, however, in most states there are also statutory short form versions of each of these three types of deeds and the statutes may specify brief language, which results in creating the traditional covenants.

a. General Warranty Deed. [§ 13–81]

The statement that a conveyance is by general warranty deed usually suggests that the deed contains all the covenants of title and some state statutes imply those covenants in such a case, but it should be emphasized that the covenants normally must be expressed in the deed. The general warranty deed places the grantor in the position of guaranteeing that no defects in title are present; the grantor will be liable if any defects are actually present regardless of whether these defects arose before she obtained title or during her period of ownership.

b. Special Warranty Deed. [§ 13–82]

A special warranty deed contains a warranty covenant in which the grantor warrants only that no defects in title arose during her period of ownership (i.e., the grantor did nothing wrong vis-a-vis the title). In most states the use of special warranty deeds is confined in practice to conveyances by fiduciaries.

c. Quitclaim Deed. [§ 13–83]

A quitclaim deed is similar to a release. It conveys whatever estate or interest the grantor owns, but contains no covenants of title. In a quitclaim deed, the grantor warrants nothing and just transfers whatever title she has, if any.

3. Granting Portion of Deed Determines Covenants Given. [§ 13–84]

The granting portion of the deed, not the land-sale contract, determines the estate to which the covenants are applicable. Thus if A conveys to B "subject to a mortgage held by X," none of the subsequent covenants will be breached either by the existence of the mortgage or by steps taken to enforce it. However, if an encumbrance is excepted simply from one covenant, it is not excepted from others. For example, A conveys to B. The present covenant against encumbrances excepts a mortgage held by X. However, if the future covenant of general warranty also does not except the mortgage, eviction of the grantee pursuant to the mortgage will breach the warranty covenant.

4. The Title Covenants. [§ 13–85]

At common law, and in some jurisdictions today, there are six title covenants. These six are divided into two groups of three each—present covenants and future covenants.

a. Present Covenants: The Covenant of Seisin and Covenant of Right to Convey. [§ 13–86]

The covenant of seisin is a covenant by the grantor that he is seized of an indefeasible estate of the quantity and quality which he has purported to convey. In most states, this means he must have both title and possession. The covenant of right to convey is very similar, the differences being that (a) this covenant is satisfied if the grantor has a right to convey even though he has no title (e.g., he has a power of appointment), and (b) there is no requirement that the grantor be in possession.

(1) Breach of These Covenants. [§ 13–87]

These covenants are broken if the grantor lacks the title to all or part of the land which he has conveyed, or if he holds a lesser estate than that which he purported to convey.

(2) Time of Breach. [§ 13–88]

These covenants are broken, if at all, at the time and date of the conveyance (the grantor either has title at that time or does not). This means the Statute of Limitations begins to run on any cause of action for breach at the time of the conveyance. This also means, in many states, that these covenants may be enforced only by the original grantee. Thus, assume that O conveys to A, the deed containing a covenant of seisin. In fact, B was the owner (for example, by adverse possession). A would have a cause of action against O, but if A then conveys to C, under the majority view, C would have no cause of action against O. Many courts today assume that the original grantee assigns the cause of action and allow suits by remote grantees on that basis. (See Case Squib: *Rockafellor v. Gray*.)

(3) Damages. [§ 13–89]

If the grantor lacks title altogether, recovery is usually in the amount of the purchase price plus interest. In the case of partial title, damages are usually a proportion of the purchase price plus interest. Changes in land values are disregarded.

b. **Present Covenant: The Covenant Against Encumbrances. [§ 13–90]**

The covenant against encumbrances is a covenant against the existence of any right in a third party that diminishes the value of the land granted or limits its use. An encumbrance, in general, is an outstanding legal interest which diminishes the value or restricts the use of the land. All encumbrances are either: (a) pecuniary charges against the land such as assessments, tax liens, mortgages, or judgment liens; (b) estates or interests in the land that are less than the fee simple absolute such as leases, life estates, and dower rights; or (c) easements or servitudes affecting the land such as profits, rights of way, water rights, and covenants.

(1) **Breach of the Covenant. [§ 13–91]**

In many jurisdictions, an encumbrance which is visible, or is otherwise known to the grantee, breaches the covenant just as any unknown, invisible encumbrance does. In other jurisdictions, knowledge of a physical encumbrance or an encumbrance on title takes the encumbrance outside the covenant. In a few other states, the covenant does include encumbrances on title which are known to the grantee (the grantee's knowledge is no defense to a claimed breach) but visible physical encumbrances are not within the covenant (open visibility is a defense to a claimed breach). In states holding visible encumbrances, such as easements, are not encumbrances within the meaning of the covenant, the reason is that the parties presumably inspect the land, notice the encumbrance, and impliedly except it from the conveyance and covenant.

Another controversy is the existence of violations of municipal codes such as building and housing codes. The majority of cases hold that violations of municipal codes do not breach the covenant against encumbrances because technically these matters do not affect the title at all. (See Case Squib: *Frimberger v. Anzellotti.*) Some cases create an exception when the municipal code violation is the subject of official enforcement proceedings at the time the covenant is given.

A related question is whether zoning ordinance violations constitute encumbrances. During the executory phase, prior to closing, zoning code violations are often held to make title unmarketable and some courts have extended this idea to deed covenants against encumbrances. (See Case Squib: *Lohmeyer v. Bower.*)

(2) **Time of Breach. [§ 13–92]**

As with covenants of seisin and right to convey, the covenant against encumbrances is a promise that the grantor will pay damages if a certain set of facts did not exist when the conveyance was made. It is a "one-shot" covenant, breached, if at all, when made. The Statute of Limitations begins at that time. In most states, a subsequent taker from the original grantee may not enforce the covenant for the reasons set out in connection with the covenant of seisin. There is a contra minority view. Under this view, the conveyance by the original grantee of the title also works as an assignment of the original grantee's cause of action against the grantor for breach of the present covenants. (See Case Squib: *Rockafellor v. Gray*.)

(3) Damages. [§ 13–93]

Insofar as damages are concerned, the usual rule is that there can be no recovery of more than nominal damages in the absence of a showing of actual damages for breach of the covenant against encumbrances.

c. Future Covenants: The Covenants of Quiet Enjoyment, Warranty, and Further Assurances. [§ 13–94]

(1) Contents of the Covenants. [§ 13–95]

(a) Covenant of Quiet Enjoyment. [§ 13–96]

The covenant of quiet enjoyment is a covenant that the grantee shall peaceably and quietly enjoy possession without interference by the vendor or anyone with lawful claim of title.

(b) General Warranty Covenant. [§ 13–97]

A general warranty covenant is an agreement by the grantor to defend the grantee's possession from all lawful or reasonable claims by a third party. It substantially overlaps the covenant for quiet enjoyment.

(c) Covenant for Further Assurance [§ 13–98]

The covenant for further assurance is not common in the United States. It is an agreement by the grantor to make and execute such assurances for the more effective conveyance of the property as may reasonably be required by the grantee. In many states it is considered to be included in the covenants of general warranty rather than as a separate covenant.

(2) Breached Only Upon Substantial Interference With Possession. [§ 13–99]

The covenants of warranty and quiet enjoyment are not breached by the mere existence of title claims or encumbrances. (See

Case Squib: *Brown v. Lober.*) This is one of the primary differences between these future covenants and present covenants. Warranty and quiet enjoyment covenants are breached only by eviction through outstanding title claims. In short, a grantee cannot use these covenants until the grantee's possession is actually substantially interfered with.

(a) Eviction. [§ 13–100]

Eviction may occur when one exerting a lawful claim actually disturbs the grantee's possession or if the grantee surrenders possession to one having a lawful paramount claim. For example, O conveys by general warranty deed, without exceptions, to A. At the time, B has a valid mortgage on the property. The existence of the mortgage would not violate future covenants (a mortgage is merely an encumbrance) but if the mortgage is foreclosed, and A loses possession as a result, a breach of the quiet enjoyment and warranty covenants has occurred. Eviction may also be "constructive," but unlike the constructive eviction doctrine in landlord-tenant cases, abandonment of possession may not be necessary. The most common "constructive eviction" which breaches a warranty covenant occurs when the grantee is forced to buy out an outstanding adverse, paramount claim in order to retain possession.

(3) Future Covenants Run to Subsequent Grantees. [§ 13–101]

The covenants for quiet enjoyment, for further assurance, and of general warranty are continuing covenants, breached only when a disturbance of possession pursuant to paramount title actually occurs. The Statute of Limitations does not begin to run until there is an eviction. The benefit of these covenants runs with the grantee's estate to subsequent takers. Thus, these future covenants differ greatly from the present covenants of seisin, right to convey, and against encumbrances.

(4) Damages and Subsequent Grantees. [§ 13–102]

Whoever messed up first loses. Suppose O conveys to A by general warranty deed. A conveys to B by general warranty deed. Ultimately B, using a general warranty deed, conveys to C. C is ousted by X, who has a lawful paramount title superior to O's at the time of the first conveyance. It is clear that C may sue A or B or O. The title of X is superior to that of each of these individuals, and each has covenanted that such interest would not harm subsequent takers. (If A had used a quitclaim deed, C could proceed only against B or O.) C may pursue any of these parties until his claim is satisfied. If C sues B, and recovers, B has been "evicted" (even though not in possession) and would be entitled to sue A or O. (If C sued and recovered from O, neither A nor B has any claim.)

(a) Amount of Recovery. [§ 13–103]

In most states, C will recover from O either what C paid to B or what O originally received from A, whichever is less. In suits on such covenants by the original grantee, damages are limited to consideration paid plus interest.

(b) Vertical Privity Required. [§ 13–104]

A remote grantee, in order to enforce such a covenant, must be in vertical privity with the original grantee. A transfer of possession is normally sufficient. (Since such cases commonly arise when the first grantor lacked title, there is no privity of legal estate, but most courts have not insisted that there must be.)

F. MERGER BY DEED. [§ 13–105]

There is an old common law rule to the effect that once a deed is delivered and accepted its terms supersede those of any land sales contract between the parties (i.e., the contract merges into and is replaced by the deed). It seems that the original operation of the rule was confined to title matters. Thus if the land sales contract expressly or impliedly called for the seller to convey a marketable title but the seller delivered a quitclaim deed (i.e., no title warranties) and the purchaser accepted the quitclaim deed then the lack of title obligations in the deed extinguished the title obligations in the land sales contract. Some courts have extended the merger by deed principle to include matters other than title obligations but such extensions and even the rule itself are in disrepute in many jurisdictions today.

G. ESTOPPEL BY DEED. [§ 13–106]

1. Application. [§ 13–107]

Estoppel by deed applies when one without ownership purports to convey an estate which he does not have to another. If the grantor subsequently acquires ownership, title will inure to the benefit of the grantee.

a. Example. [§ 13–108] O conveys by warranty deed to A. At the time, title is in fact held by X. X subsequently conveys to O. Under the doctrine of estoppel by deed, title automatically inures to the benefit of A.

b. Operates to Pass Ownership. [§ 13–109]

According to the majority view, after-acquired title passes by operation of law to the prior grantee as soon as it is acquired by the grantor. Estoppel by deed, then, is something more than mere personal estoppel—it actually operates to pass ownership. This makes the job of the title examiner simpler. A title examiner who discovers a situation raising an estoppel by deed issue can assume that the grantee got title by operation of law without having to be concerned about whether there was a judicial action taken to acquire title.

(1) Cannot Sue for Breach of Covenant. [§ 13–110]

States applying estoppel in this manner generally hold that the grantee may not sue for breach of covenant; his only remedy is to assert ownership of the after-acquired title.

(2) Rights of Intervening Third Parties. [§ 13–111]

The grantor, having subsequently acquired ownership, may in turn deal with third parties. To what extent are these parties cut off by the estoppel doctrine (i.e., by the fact that subsequently acquired title "automatically" passed to the earlier grantee)? This is the problem of competing grantees. If the second grantee does not pay value or if the second grantee has notice of the first grantee, then the first grantee will prevail. But, if the second grantee is a BFP from O, the cases are divided. Some cases emphasize the automatic inurement of the title to the first grantee and hold that the grantor had nothing to pass by deed to the second grantee.

Other cases focus on the estoppel concept and give priority to the second grantee. The reasoning of these cases is that the estoppel by deed concept applies to the grantor. The innocent second grantee is not estopped to assert title in herself. The recording acts may also bring about this result. (§ 14–40). If the first grantee did not record her deed, the deed will be void as against a subsequent BFP who records (the result would be the same in notice, race, and race notice jurisdictions). But even if the first deed is recorded, the second grantee will still prevail, in some cases, especially if the jurisdiction relies upon a grantor-grantee index system. The reasoning is that the first deed, though actually recorded, is a wild deed (an improperly recorded deed). The first deed is a wild deed because it is uncon-nected to an owner in the chair of title. A title examiner, constructing a search of the title, would not find the first deed. Therefore, the first deed must be treated as unrecorded. The first deed would be void as against a subsequent BFP who records first.

c. Minority View. [§ 13–112]

A minority of jurisdictions interpret estoppel by deed as creating only a personal estoppel. The grantor is viewed as a wrongdoer, who is estopped to deny that he acquired title subsequently for the benefit of anyone but the earlier grantee. Under such a view, the earlier grantee may establish title or sue for breach of covenant, at his option. Because this estoppel is viewed as personal, a BFP who takes from the grantor after ownership has been acquired gets good title against the earlier grantee.

2. To What Types of Deed Does the Doctrine Apply? [§ 13–113]

a. Warranty Deed. [§ 13–114]

Today, the doctrine is clearly applicable when the grantor, without ownership, conveys by a warranty deed. At one time, it was thought that a covenant of general warranty was essential to the application of the doctrine. While it may not now be viewed as essential, a warranty deed is clearly sufficient to create an estoppel.

b. Quitclaim Deed. [§ 13–115]

In some states, the doctrine can never be applied to such a deed. In most states, however, the doctrine is applied to any deed which purports to convey an estate, whether or not title covenants appear. While a quitclaim deed in usual form does not purport to convey any estate and cannot therefore create an estoppel, a quitclaim which does represent that a particular estate is being conveyed can create an estoppel.

3. Affected by Recording Rules. [§ 13–116]

Recording statutes have greatly affected the doctrine of estoppel by deed as it relates to the rights of other takers. They frequently operate to give title to subsequent bona fide purchasers rather than to the prior grantee who is entitled to invoke an estoppel against the grantor. (See § 14–40).

CHAPTER XIII

REVIEW PROBLEM—DEEDS

A frequently tested area is deed covenants of title. The basic division of such covenants into present (covenants of seisin, right to convey, and against encumbrances) and future covenants (covenants of quiet enjoyment, warranty, and further assurances) offers many problems since, under traditional real property law theories, present covenants were considered broken, if ever, at the time the deed becomes effective (i.e., time of delivery).

A conveys Blackacre to B by a general warranty deed and B conveys Blackacre to C by a quitclaim deed and C later discovers that JCJ Pipeline company has an easement, created during A's ownership, through C's living room. Can C sue A on one of the present covenants in the deed she gave to B?

> **Answer:** Traditionally the answer was "NO" because present covenants were deemed to have been broken when the deed was delivered to B and therefore unable to run with the land to C. Courts now often reject the old rule and hold that a broken covenant can run or they reach the same result by holding that B impliedly assigned his cause of action against A when she conveyed the property to C. Some courts might be troubled by implying an assignment in this fact situation since the deed from B to C was a quitclaim. C probably could not recover from A on the basis of a future covenant because even though they have run to C they have not yet been broken since the facts do not disclose that C has been disturbed in her possession by the owner of the outstanding interest (the pipeline company). Note also that C could not recover from B because she conveyed by a quitclaim deed which contains no title covenants.

Chapter XIV

RECORDING ACTS

A. ROLE OF RECORDING ACTS IN TITLE ASSURANCE. [§ 14–1]

Title assurance refers to the system we have developed in the United States to establish and prove title to land. The two key elements to our current system of title assurance are deeds (and their title covenants or title warranties) and our land records systems. Lawyers' title opinions (based on abstracts of the land records) and title insurance are dependent upon the land records system for their functioning.

B. DUAL ASPECTS OF THE RECORDING ACTS. [§ 14–2]

1. In General. [§ 14–3]

Recording acts have two functions. First, the recording acts establish priority rules to resolve title disputes which can arise in different contexts such as, for example, when a landowner, either by mistake or intention, conveys the same piece of property to two or more successive grantees or when a landowner conveys an interest in the same property to two or more successive creditors (such as by mortgage or deed of trust). This is the so-called "priorities" aspects of the acts. Second, the recording acts establish land records offices for the public recording of documents which affect the title to land. Each state is responsible for maintaining records of title to land for the land within the state. Most states organize their land title records on a county-by-county basis. There is no federal recording system and the federal government does not maintain land title records.

It is important to remember that recording is not mandatory. As between the original parties to a conveyance, an instrument that is otherwise valid is binding between the parties, regardless of whether it is recorded or not. In this case, recording would protect the original grantee in the event that the original grantor made a subsequent and competing conveyance of the same interest to another grantee. If the original grantee has properly recorded the instrument, then the original grantee will be protected from having his interest destroyed or diminished by the subsequent transfer.

CHAPTER XIV

The interests in real property that law students most commonly encounter in the context of the recording acts are deeds, easements, covenants, mortgages (and deeds of trust), leases, and liens.

a. Priorities at Common Law and Pursuant to Recording Acts. [§ 14–4]

At common law, priority between successive legal transfers of land was determined simply on the basis of time priority—"first in time, first in right." Consequently, the first grantee prevailed over subsequent grantees. Only when doctrines concerning fraudulent conveyances were applicable could priorities be reversed. Thus if O, owner of Blackacre, conveyed Blackacre to X, and then conveyed Blackacre to Y, it was clear at common law that X had good title, even if Y was a bona fide purchaser without notice. (The same rules applied if the first interest created was a legal interest, and the second an equitable interest, or if both interests were equitable.) The recording acts are designed to change the common law rule under specified circumstances and to protect subsequent bona fide purchasers without notice. Note that if a prior conveyance is properly recorded prior to the second conveyance, basic common law priorities are maintained through the concept of notice.

b. Improper Recording Under the Recording Act. [§ 14–5]

If an instrument covered by the recording act is not properly recorded, common law priorities may be reversed (assuming that the subsequent grantee is a bona fide purchaser). Thus, one who takes legal title and fails to record loses priority to a subsequent bona fide purchaser from the same grantor.

c. The Three Issues in Applying Recording Act Priority Rules. [§ 14–6]

In dealing with recording act problems, there are always three questions to consider:

(1) Is the Instrument Within the Act? [§ 14–7]

The deed or other instrument which grants an interest to a previous grantee (whether a purchaser, donee, mortgagee, etc.) must be subject to the recording acts in order for the recording acts to operate so that a bona fide purchaser without notice receives protection; otherwise, the common law "first in time, first in right" applies.

(2) Has There Been a Failure to Record Properly? [§ 14–8]

Unless there has been a failure to record or a defect in recording, there is no merit to a priority claim by a subsequent grantee. Proper recording of the instrument gives notice to all and absolutely protects the first in time grantee against claims by subsequent grantees.

(3) Is There a Subsequent Grantee Entitled to the Protection of the Act? [§ 14–9]

If the subsequent grantee is a donee, or can be charged with notice, the subsequent grantee cannot assert priority because of a failure by the prior grantee to record. Donees are not bona fide purchasers protected by the statute and depending on the statute, judicial creditors are often also not entitled to assert priority against unrecorded interests. Grantees with actual or inquiry notice of the prior transfer cannot qualify as purchasers protected by the act in jurisdictions that require the subsequent purchaser to be bona fide, meaning to have no knowledge of the prior transfer. Statutes that incorporate the concept of notice are the notice and race-notice statutes. Most states are either notice or race-notice jurisdictions. In the very few jurisdictions that adopt the race statute, a subsequent purchaser charged with notice of the prior transfer can still assert priority against a prior grantee who has failed to record. See § 14–10.

2. The Statutes. [§ 14–10]

There are three major types of recording acts which are classified according to the rules they establish for reversing common law priorities: (a) notice, (b) race-notice, and (c) race (or pure race, as it is sometimes called to clearly distinguish it from race-notice). About half of the states have notice type acts and about half have race-notice type acts. Only a handful still have race acts. In considering the variations between them, think about the following example: O conveys Blackacre to A on June 10. O then conveys Blackacre to B on September 1. B pays a valuable consideration, and has no notice of A's interest. On September 15, A records. B records on September 20. The transaction might be expressed like this:

O———A   June 10
O———B   September 1   B = a bona fide purchaser without notice
A Records   September 15
B Records   September 20

a. Jurisdiction With a Notice Statute. [§ 14–11]

(1) A Typical Notice Statute. [§ 14–12]

A statute of the notice type provides in abbreviated form: "No conveyance, transfer or mortgage of real property shall be good and effectual in law or equity against creditors or subsequent purchasers for a valuable consideration and without notice, unless the same be recorded."

(2) Result. [§ 14–13]

Under a notice statute, in the above example B has the superior right. At the time B purchased, A had not recorded. Because B did not have actual notice of A's interest or record notice, B was a subsequent bona fide purchaser without notice and B's priority was established as soon as B purchased. As between A and B, the fact that A ultimately recorded first is irrelevant; thus, this example demonstrates the importance of immediately recording. If A had recorded A's deed before B purchased Blackacre, B would have been put on record notice and would not have qualified as a bona fide purchaser without notice.

b. Jurisdiction With a Race–Notice Statute. [§ 14–14]

(1) A Typical Race–Notice Statute. [§ 14–15]

A race-notice statute typically provides: "Every conveyance of real estate . . . which shall not be recorded shall be void as against any subsequent purchaser in good faith, and for a valuable consideration of the same real estate or any portion thereof, whose conveyance shall be first duly recorded."

(2) Result. [§ 14–16]

Under such a statute, in the above example A prevails. In order to gain priority because of A's failure to record, B must not only be a bona fide purchaser without notice, but must also record before A records. If B had recorded before A, B would have prevailed.

c. Jurisdiction With a Race Statute. [§ 14–17]

(1) Priority to First Instrument Recorded. [§ 14–18]

Such statutes are very uncommon. They simply provide that the first instrument recorded has priority. Notice, or the absence thereof, is irrelevant.

(2) Result. [§ 14–19]

Under a race statute, in the above example, A has priority simply because A recorded first.

C. THE MECHANICS OF RECORDING. [§ 14–20]

1. Record in County Where Land Is Located. [§ 14–21]

Recording begins when the grantee presents his deed to the recorder for the county in which the property is located. The instrument is copied, usually photographically or into computer records, and the copy is entered in a bound volume or electronic file, which is simply kept chronologically. The method of indexing them determines the manner in which the records are used in a title search.

a. Grantor–Grantee (and Grantee–Grantor) Indexes. [§ 14–22]

These are the standard indexes, and title searches in most jurisdictions are directly geared to such indexes. The grantor-grantee index is arranged alphabetically by the name of the grantor in each transaction. The searcher, having found the name of a particular grantor, will then find in the index the name of the grantee, the date of the instrument, a brief description of the property, and references to where in the bound volumes the actual copy of the instrument is located. The grantee-grantor index contains the same information, but the alphabetical listing is in the name of the grantee in the particular transaction.

b. Tract Indexes. [§ 14–23]

A tract index is an index not by name of parties, but an index by lot, block or parcel number. All conveyances—deeds, mortgages, deeds of trust, easements, etc., are then indexed on a page assigned to a particular lot, block or parcel. Title search is easier than with grantor/grantee indexes because all entries affecting a particular tract are located in one place. Such indexes are not in common use in many areas where land is not platted in a manner to facilitate such indexing. Such indexes are in use primarily in urban areas.

2. Title Search. [§ 14–24]

Assume that O has agreed to sell to A. As A's attorney, you must search the title. How is this done?

a. If There Is a Tract Index. [§ 14–25]

If a tract index is available, search is made simply by examining the appropriate lot or parcel pages. All instruments involving the tract which are recorded are entered there. The searcher will also need to examine other public records, for some interests will appear there but not in the land records. For example, the searcher will be charged with examining probate court records and records of the court of general jurisdiction for judgment liens.

b. If There Is Only a Grantor/Grantee Index. [§ 14–26]

Without a tract index, title search is more complicated.

(1) Begin With Name of the Grantor. [§ 14–27]

The searcher will begin with the name in the land sales contract that prompts the title search. By taking the name of the grantor as grantee, the searcher can locate in the grantee-grantor index the deed by which the grantor (O above) took title, the so-called "In" deed to the grantor. Once the deed to the grantor is found, a time period is established; namely, the period from the date on which the grantor took title to the present, when the grantor proposes to convey to your client. Having established that the grantor received record title, the remaining question is whether the grantor has conveyed it away already. Hence the grantor's name will be run through the grantor-grantee index for the relevant time period.

(2) Repeat for Predecessor in Title. [§ 14–28]

Once it is established that the grantor received record title and has not since conveyed it or encumbered it, the same process is then repeated for the grantor's predecessor in title (who is identified by using the grantee-grantor index with the grantor's name as grantee), and so on up the chain of title.

(3) Must Check Other Public Records. [§ 14–29]

As is the case when using a tract index, other public records must be checked for liens, etc. Where gaps appear in the record title, probate court records must be checked to determine whether the property passed by intestacy or will. The buyer is charged with notice of such records, whether the buyer examines them or not.

3. Recorder's Mistakes. [§ 14–30]

While it is not likely that an error will occur in copying the deed itself (today this is done with a photocopy machine or scanner), errors may occur in indexing. What is the effect of an instrument properly copied, but indexed improperly by the recorder so that it cannot be found by a searcher using the indexes in any manner? Cases are divided on this question, some holding that the deed is not recorded and does not give record notice, others holding that since the grantee did all the grantee could do the deed must be regarded as properly recorded even though a subsequent grantee cannot find it. Under the former view, the grantee is charged with the duty of making sure the deed is properly recorded.

4. Consequences of Not Recording. [§ 14–31]

Generally, the mere fact of recording cannot make an invalid deed operate as a valid transfer. Conversely, in most jurisdictions recording is not necessary to make an otherwise valid deed effective as a conveyance between the parties. Recording relates only to subsequent purchasers.

5. **Requirements for Recording. [§ 14–32]**

   a. **Acknowledgment or Witnesses May Be Required. [§ 14–33]**

      In most states a deed must be acknowledged in order to be recorded. Some states further require that the deed be attested by two witnesses in order to be recorded. A seal is not necessary either for the validity of the deed or for recording in most states. In some states, a deed, once recorded, will give notice even if it was defectively acknowledged or witnessed. In other states, a deed that is not entitled to be recorded because it does not meet the statutory requirements of the recording laws affords no constructive notice of its contents, even though actually recorded. (See Case Squib: *Messersmith v. Smith*).

   b. **Improper Recording. [§ 14–34]**

      A deed not meeting these requirements for recording is valid between the parties, but is not entitled to be recorded. In most jurisdictions, if such a deed is physically recorded, it is not deemed properly recorded and gives no "record notice" to a subsequent grantee. (See Case Squib: *Messersmith v. Smith*). In most states, however, actual knowledge of such a deed derived from a title search puts a subsequent purchaser on inquiry notice, and the subsequent purchaser is charged with what a reasonable inquiry would have revealed.

D. RECORDING OUTSIDE THE CHAIN OF TITLE. [§ 14–35]

The most difficult recording problems arise when the prior grantee has in fact recorded his deed before a subsequent purchaser takes, but the recording is such that even with proper indexing it is outside the recorded chain of title. A deed may be said to be outside the chain of title when the court feels it would not be discovered in a reasonable title search. In determining whether a deed is beyond a reasonable title search the courts have presumed the availability of only a grantor-grantee index system; the presence of a tract index may change the results.

1. **Result if a Deed Is Recorded, but Is Outside the Chain of Title. [§ 14–36]**

   In a few states, if the deed is recorded outside the chain of title the deed is still deemed properly recorded, and the subsequent purchaser takes subject to it even though the subsequent purchaser may not be able to find it in the land records. In most states, a deed which is outside the chain of title is simply deemed not recorded (it does not give notice to a subsequent purchaser); hence, a subsequent bona fide purchaser without notice may achieve priority.

2. **Examples of Common Problems. [§ 14–37]**

   (Note: all of the following problems are based on the assumption that only a grantor-grantee index is available to the title searcher.)

a. **Example 1: Lazy Grantor.** [§ 14–38] O conveys to A on June 1. A does not record. On July 1, A conveys to B, who promptly records his deed. On August 15, O conveys to C, who pays value, is without notice and promptly records. As between A, B, and C, who has the superior claim? The answer depends upon the applicable recording statute. Notice state: C wins. While it is true that B recorded before C's purchase, his deed is completely outside the recorded chain of title because the linking deed from O to A is not recorded. There is no way that one making a reasonable title search could find B's deed. B's deed is a wild deed. (Note that here the result might be different if there was a tract index.) Likewise, A's deed is unrecorded and therefore does not provide C with notice. Because C is the last bona fide purchaser without notice, C wins. Race-notice state: The result should be the same, although a few courts have reached a contrary result on the ground that C failed to record before B. However, in most states, B's deed is viewed as not properly recorded, and C is viewed as properly recording first. (See Case Squib: *Board of Educ. of Minneapolis v. Hughes*).

b. **Example 2: Bad Faith Latter Grantee.** [§ 14–39] O conveys to A on April 1. A does not record. On May 15, O conveys to B, who had actual notice of the deed to A. B records immediately. On May 25, A records. On June 15, B then conveys to C, a bona fide purchaser without notice. C promptly records. As between A, B, and C, who has the superior claim? The cases are more difficult and are divided under both kinds of statutes. Notice state: Some cases simply hold that A recorded before C took, and hold that determinative. However, under the approach taken by most courts, C wins. It is true that because B was not a bona fide purchaser without notice, B would have lost in a dispute with A. However, C is a bona fide purchaser without notice and since A's deed is outside the chain of title, it can be said to be not properly recorded. (It is outside the chain of title because a title searcher finding the "out" deed from O to B is not required to search for any "out" deeds recorded thereafter.) Note: If the facts are changed so that B was a bona fide purchaser without notice, C would clearly win as B's priority over A is clear, and C may assert B's rights. Race-notice states: Some authority suggests that A wins simply because C did not record before A. Other authority is contra, taking the position that C wins because C is the first to record within the chain of title. (See Case Squib: Compare *Woods v. Garnett* with *Morse v. Curtis*).

c. **Example 3: Grantor Without Title (Estoppel by Deed).** [§ 14–40] On January 1, O is the record owner and A conveys by warranty deed to B, who promptly records. On February 15, O conveys to A. At this point, the doctrine of estoppel by deed will operate in most jurisdictions to pass title to B. A records. On March 1, A conveys to C, a bona fide purchaser without notice. Now there is a conflict between the estoppel by deed concept and the chain of title (notice) concept. B claims title under the doctrine of estoppel by deed. However, can C be charged with constructive notice of the deed from A to B? A number of courts have said C cannot be charged with notice, and have awarded priority to C. A title searcher, taking A's name as grantee, would find the deed from O to A. Normally he would then search for deeds made by A thereafter, and would not find the earlier deed from A to B. (See Case Squib: *Sabo v. Horvath*).

d.   **Example 4. Deeds Out of a Common Grantor. [§ 14–41]** O owns Blackacre and Whiteacre. On January 1, O conveys Blackacre to A. The deed contains covenants and grants an easement, burdening Whiteacre. A records the deed to Blackacre. O then conveys Whiteacre to B who asserts that under the recording act B takes free of the servitude. The difficulty here is that B, in searching the record for conveyances by O, will not examine an "out" deed to a tract other than Whiteacre. B will find the Blackacre deed in the index, but view it as irrelevant. The cases are split, some say the recording is outside the chain of title and award priority to B. Others say A should win because A has done all A could (note that other factors may be determinative—are the properties adjacent?). (See Case Squib: *Guillette v. Daly Dry Wall*)

E. INSTRUMENTS SUBJECT TO THE RECORDING ACT. [§ 14–42]

1.   Application of the Recording Act. [§ 14–43]

Real property rights that arise outside of the statute of frauds and therefore do not need to be in writing are not subject to the recording acts. Common law priority rules determine priorities disputes regarding these types of interests. In short, failure to record reverses common law priority rules only for instruments subject to the recording act. Interests that are outside of the recording acts include implied easements, title by adverse possession (not extinguished by sale to a bona fide purchaser without notice), rights of dower and curtesy, etc.

2.   Conveyances of Real Estate. [§ 14–44]

The recording acts generally apply to any conveyance, transfer, or mortgage of real property, or of any interest therein and to leases of a term of one year or longer. Executory contracts for the sale of land may be recorded in most jurisdictions, but in some jurisdictions they are not regarded as being included within the statutory provisions so that even if recorded, they do not constitute constructive notice.

3. Does Not Apply to Interests Created by Implication or Operation of Law. [§ 14–45]

The recording acts do not apply to certain interests created by implication or operation of law. Thus, titles derived from adverse possession, and prescriptive easements, are governed by priority rules wholly outside recording acts. (For example, A adversely possesses Blackacre against O, the record owner). Thereafter, O conveys Blackacre to B. B has no claim or priority under the recording acts.

F. PARTIES PROTECTED BY THE RECORDING ACT. [§ 14–46]

1. Effect of Mere Failure to Record. [§ 14–47]

Remember, a mere failure to record in itself means little; there must, in addition, be a grantee who is protected by the act and who can assert the failure to record. If a subsequent grantee is not within the act, common law priority rules apply.

2. Subsequent Bona Fide Purchaser for Value Without Notice. [§ 14–48]

a. Purchaser. [§ 14–49]

Obviously "purchaser" covers any individual who buys an interest for value. In virtually all states, this includes mortgagees who are considered purchasers to the extent of their interest.

(1) General Creditors. [§ 14–50]

In most states, the act does not protect general creditors, even though they may have extended credit in reliance on the record. In a minority of states, once the lien of a creditor is perfected by judgment, the creditor is considered a bona fide purchaser.

(a) Subordinate to Prior Unrecorded Interests. [§ 14–51]

Where the recording act does not specifically include creditors within the category of protected persons, most states afford no priority over unrecorded prior interests to judgment creditors.

(b) Even if Protected by Recording Act, Creditor Must Perfect Lien. [§ 14–52]

Whether the recording act protects "creditors" or "subsequent creditors," it is clear that a creditor cannot get priority over unrecorded instruments until the creditor actually obtains a judgment. The time when the credit is extended would be important in those jurisdictions protecting only "subsequent creditors."

(2) The Purchaser at an Execution Sale Is Protected. [§ 14–53]

The purchaser at an execution sale gets priority if at the time of sale any prior interest covered by the recording act is unrecorded and the purchaser has no notice thereof.

b. For Value. [§ 14–54]

The valuable consideration must be more than a nominal sum; that is, the subsequent grantee must be more than a donee. The court, having found a valuable consideration, will not examine whether it was adequate or equal to market value (otherwise purchasers at execution sales would usually not be protected). Consideration recited in the deed may be contradicted by parol evidence.

(1) Antecedent Debt Insufficient Consideration. [§ 14–55]

Most states do not regard an antecedent debt as valuable consideration. Thus, if an individual takes a mortgage simply to secure a preexisting debt, most states do not regard the mortgagee as a subsequent purchaser for value unless the mortgagee changes its position to its own detriment in exchange for the mortgage by, for example, reducing the interest rate, agreeing to a repayment extension, or forbearing to sue. However, if a deed is taken in satisfaction of an antecedent debt, the majority view is that value has been given.

(2) Mere Promise to Pay Not Payment of Value. [§ 14–56]

In a few states, a negotiable note is viewed as a payment, but the majority view is that the value must have been paid in fact. If a negotiable note is negotiated to a holder in due course, all courts agree it constitutes a payment of value.

(3) Partial Payment. [§ 14–57]

If a subsequent purchaser pays part of the purchase price and gives a note for the balance, the subsequent purchaser is protected only to the extent of actual payment before notice is received. The prior unrecorded grantee must reimburse the subsequent grantee, or the subsequent grantee will be given a lien. Infrequently, the grantees are made co-owners of the property. (See Case Squib: *Daniels v. Anderson*)

c. Without Notice. [§ 14–58]

Except in jurisdictions which have pure race statutes, if a subsequent grantee has actual notice (knowledge) of an earlier unrecorded deed, the subsequent grantee is subject to that deed even though it is unrecorded. A subsequent grantee is also charged with record notice of all instruments which are properly recorded, whether or not the subsequent grantee has actually examined the records. Also, a subsequent purchaser will be charged with inquiry notice if facts the subsequent purchaser knew or should have known would have led a reasonable person to discover the prior unrecorded interest.

(1) Notice After Partial Payment. [§ 14–59]

If the subsequent grantee receives notice after some, but not all, consideration has been paid, the subsequent grantee is protected only to the extent of payments made before notice is received, i.e., on a pro tanto basis. (See Case Squib: *Daniels v. Anderson*)

(2) Inquiry Notice. [§ 14–60]

There may be circumstances where the purchaser is charged with making inquiry. Where such a duty exists, the purchaser will be charged with what a reasonable inquiry would have revealed, whether or not the inquiry was in fact made.

(a) Inquiry Notice From Possession by Someone Other Than the Grantor. [§ 14–61]

Suppose O conveys to A, who fails to record but goes into actual possession. O then conveys to B, who pays value and is without actual notice. Assuming that A's possession is open, B is charged (a) with notice of A's possession, and (b) with notice of what a reasonable inquiry would have revealed (A's title). B is not "without knowledge" even though B has no actual knowledge of A's possession. However, if O conveys to A, O's wife, who does not record but is in possession, A's possession would not charge a subsequent purchaser with notice. Possession by a wife is deemed fully consistent with a record title in O. Inquiry notice arises only from possession inconsistent with record title.

(b) Inquiry Notice From Visible Use. [§ 14–62]

Suppose O grants an easement for a paved right of way over Blackacre to A. The grant is not recorded, but the roadway is established. A subsequent purchaser will be charged with inquiry notice of this visible use.

(c) Inquiry Notice of Documents Referred to in the Subsequent Purchaser's Own Chain of Title. [§ 14–63]

A purchaser is put on inquiry notice of documents referred to in his own chain of title when the unrecorded instrument is identified by a reference in a deed in the record chain of title. The purchaser is charged with the duty to inquire about such transfers. For example, O mortgages to A; the mortgage is not recorded. O then conveys to B, the deed reciting that the property is subject to a mortgage in A. B records. B then conveys to C, who records. C paid value, and is without actual notice of A's interest. A will usually win; C is charged with inquiry notice because a recorded deed in his own chain of title refers to A's interest.

(d) Where the Subsequent Purchaser Takes by Quitclaim Deed. [§ 14–64]

The common law, as applied in some states, took the position that a subsequent grantee whose transfer was by quitclaim either took subject to prior unrecorded deeds or was at least under a duty to make further inquiry. The quitclaim itself was said to create suspicion about the title. In most states, however, the fact that a quitclaim deed is used has no effect on the bona fide purchaser without notice status of the subsequent purchaser.

3. Grantee From a Bona Fide Purchaser Is Protected. [§ 14–65]

A person who takes from a subsequent purchaser for value without notice is entitled to the protection of the recording act even if the person is not a bona fide purchaser without notice. This is sometimes referred to as the shelter rule. Similarly, a person may be a bona fide purchaser without notice even if his grantor has no title.

Example 1. [§ 14–66] O conveys to A, who fails to record. O then conveys to B, who takes without notice and pays value. B records. B then conveys to C, who has actual notice of the deed to A (or C could be a donee). C wins over A even though C is not a bona fide purchaser without notice; priority was established in B, and C takes under this priority. (In a notice state, C would win on the same basis even if B had not recorded.) However, O could not reacquire the land and defeat A's interest as the recording act cannot be used to perpetrate a fraud.

Example 2. [§ 14–67] O conveys to A, who does not record. O dies, leaving B as his sole heir. B conveys to C, a purchaser without notice of the deed to A. C records. B has no priority of his own. Even though B had nothing to transfer, C will win in most jurisdictions as C qualified as a bona fide purchaser without notice in his own right.

G. RECORDING SYSTEM REFORMS. [§ 14–68]

The inefficiencies and uncertainties created by our traditional recording system, which persist even after mechanical improvements such as tract indexes and computerization, have led to several noteworthy attempts at reform. The three most commonly encountered are: 1) curative acts, 2) title standards; and 3) marketable record title acts.

1. Curative Acts. [§ 14–69]

In many states, the legislatures have attempted to streamline title examination through statutes which provide that documents which have been recorded for a specified number of years are "cured" of minor defects. For example, some statutes provide that a deed which has been recorded for ten or more years and is otherwise valid is not detrimentally affected by the fact that the notarial seal on the acknowledgement is missing. In the broadest sense of the curative concept, statutes of limitations are curative acts, but the term "curative act" generally refers to statutes which deal with the form and format, i.e., technical requirements of recorded documents. Not all states have curative acts. In the states that do have curative acts, title examiners still need to perform a full historical search. The curative acts simply allow the examiner greater certainty in the validity of recorded instruments that would otherwise be considered ineffective.

2. Title Standards. [§ 14–70]

In many states, the bar association, in cooperation with the state supreme court, have issued "trade union" type rules of principles to be followed by attorneys who give title opinions. For example if there is no release of dower on the record for documents which have been recorded for more than x number of years, no exception will be made for such technical defect. Title standards do not normally have the force of law but simply establish professional standards.

3. Marketable Record Title Acts [MARTA]. [§ 14–71]

Many states have enacted marketable record title acts which are designed to reduce the period of title search and clear titles from ancient and outmoded encumbrances.

a. Operation of Statute. [§ 14–72]

Such an act declares that any estate or interest reflected by the recorded chain of title for the statutory period is marketable. All conflicting interests which are older than the root of title, subject to designated exceptions, are extinguished.

b. Interests Cut Off. [§ 14–73]

A marketable record title act operates against persons under a disability and it invalidates future as well as present interests, and outstanding interests; it does not simply "cure" formal defects, but requires periodic recording of outstanding interests in order to preserve them.

c. Root of Title Is the Basis of the Statutory Marketable Title. [§ 14–74]

Root of title is any title transaction purporting to create or transfer the estate claimed by any person and which is the most recent title transaction to have been recorded at least a given number of years (commonly 30 or 40 years) prior to the time when marketability is being determined. The date of the root of the title is the date it was recorded. For example, if the marketable record title act specifies 40 years and if the examiner was making a search of the record in 2010, a deed recorded in 1975 could not be the root of title but a deed recorded in 1965 could be the root of title.

d. Statutory Exceptions. [§ 14–75]

A statutory marketable record title is generally subject to certain exceptions, common examples of which are the following:

(1) Interests Disclosed in Document Which Is Root of Title. [§ 14–76]

Interests disclosed by, and defects inherent in, the document upon which the root of title is based are not extinguished by marketable record title acts. Thus, a root of title showing a defeasible title remains a defeasible title; the act does not purport to enlarge it into a fee simple absolute.

(2) Recordings Subsequent to the Root of Title. [§ 14–77]

Marketable record title act have no effect on documents recorded subsequent to the root of title.

(3) Interests Preserved by Filing Notice Within the Statutory Period. [§ 14–78]

Any interest which arose before a root of title may be preserved by filing a notice of this interest within a specified statutory period.

(4) Rights of Any Person in Possession. [§ 14–79]

A party in possession of the property is deemed to have given all other parties notice of their claim to the property under many marketable record title acts.

(5) Rights of Assessed Taxpayers. [§ 4–80]

The rights of persons in whose name the land was assessed for taxes within a specified period of time are not extinguished by some marketable record title acts.

e. The Acts Construed. [§ 14–81]

(1) Competing Chains of Title. [§ 14–82]

The Illinois Supreme Court has held that the state's marketable record title act was inapplicable to a situation where there were two competing chains of title which satisfied the statutory requirements. The court reasoned that the marketable record title act contemplated only one chain of title and that the particular dispute would have to be resolved by traditional doctrines.

(2) Void Deed May Be Adequate. [§ 14–83]

The Supreme Court of Florida has held that its marketable record title act could validate a chain of title which is based on a void deed (the void deed in the instant case being a forged deed which preceded the root of title). (See Case Squib: *Marshall v. Hollywood, Inc.*)

(3) Quitclaim Deed May Be Inadequate. [§ 14–84]

There is some judicial authority to the effect that a pure quitclaim deed cannot be a root of title since it does not purport to convey any particular estate, but this issue has not yet been fully resolved.

REVIEW PROBLEMS—RECORDING ACTS

Recording act based exam questions usually emphasize the operative differences between the three types of recording acts (notice, race, and race-notice) when O conveys Blackacre to A who does not record the deed and then O conveys the same piece of property, Blackacre, to B. Questions are usually reducible to this simple format even though they are complicated by subsequent conveyances, that may or may not be recorded, by A and B to third parties.

> O, owner of Blackacre in fee simple absolute, conveys it to A who does not record. Later, O conveys Blackacre to B, who pays value and has no notice of the earlier conveyance to A. A records A's deed after the conveyance to B but before B records B's deed. Who owns Blackacre in a notice jurisdiction? A race-notice jurisdiction? A race jurisdiction?
>
> > **Answer:** In a notice jurisdiction, B owns Blackacre since B can qualify as a bona fide purchaser without notice. It is irrelevant in a notice jurisdiction that A records before B since the only requirement for B to prevail is that B be a bona fide purchaser without notice at the time the deed is delivered by O to B. In a race-notice jurisdiction, A owns Blackacre because a race-notice recording act requires B to be a bona fide purchaser without notice at the time the deed is delivered and also requires that B record before A records. In a race jurisdiction, A owns Blackacre because A recorded before B. No other requirement is imposed and B would have owned Blackacre if B had recorded first even if B was not a bona fide purchaser without notice.

CHAPTER XV

RIGHT TO USE AND ENJOYMENT OF PROPERTY

A. OVERVIEW. [§ 15–1]

A landowner has the right to use her property without unreasonable interference by neighbors. Additionally, one of the miscellaneous rights of a landowner is to have her land supported in its natural state by neighboring land. Although the principles covered in this section are taken largely from tort law, they are sometimes covered in property courses, in order to give the fullest possible picture of a landowner's rights.

B. NUISANCE. [§ 15–2]

Nuisance law regulates land uses that are considered an unreasonable interference with another person's use and enjoyment of her land. The two basic types of a nuisance are private nuisance and public nuisance.

1. Private Nuisance. [§ 15–3]

A private nuisance is a situation or conduct that creates an unreasonable, substantial interference with the plaintiff's use or enjoyment of her property. The gravity of harm from the defendant's conduct must outweigh the utility of the defendant's conduct for the court to find liability for nuisance. Factors a court will weigh in making this determination include the use being made of the plaintiff's property, the use being made of the defendant's property, the suitability of the conduct to the character of the neighborhood, the social value of the competing land uses, the ability of the parties to avoid or prevent the damages, and the overall extent and nature of the harm. The question of whether conduct is unreasonable or creates a substantial interference with another's use and enjoyment of her property is a question of both fact and law. Courts will often articulate different tests to measure unreasonableness, for instance, so you should be aware of this area as one that is ripe for discussion in class and exam testing.

a. Elements of Liability. [§ 15–4]

According to the Restatement (Second) of Torts, liability for private nuisance can arise based upon conduct that is either: (1) intentional and

269

unreasonable or (2) unintentional and reckless, negligent, or abnormally dangerous. Most of your discussions will likely concern the issue of intentional, as opposed to unintentional, nuisances. The Restatement (Second) of Torts articulates two tests for unreasonableness in the context of intentional nuisances. An invasion is unreasonable if the utility of the activity is outweighed by the severity of the harm. (See Case Squib: *Morgan v. High Penn Oil Co.*) Also, an invasion is unreasonable if the activity creates serious harm and it would still be feasible for the defendant to continue her conduct if the defendant provided financial compensation to the plaintiff for the harm the plaintiff suffered.

b.   Particular Considerations. [§ 15–5]

Certain situations or arguments are routinely addressed in nuisance cases.

(1)   Coming to the Nuisance. [§ 15–6]

A court may look at which of the conflicting uses was the first in time at the location. If the defendant was using her property in the manner the plaintiff is complaining about before the plaintiff even located to the area, the court will be less likely to find a nuisance, because the plaintiff could have avoided the harm by never locating to the area to being with. (See Case Squib: *Spur Industries, Inc. v. Del. E. Webb Development Co.*)

(2)   Use of Zoning Ordinances. [§ 15–7]

Generally, zoning ordinances are admissible to show that the public views the use as reasonable. However, it is not determinative of the issue if the defendant can show her use is consistent with zoning ordinances, because under the particular circumstances this use might still be a nuisance to adjacent property owners.

(3)   Property Value. [§ 15–8]

Merely showing that an adjacent use has lowered a plaintiff's property value will not be sufficient to constitute a nuisance. However, depreciation of property value combined with other interferences may be enough for a court to find a nuisance.

c.   Distinguished From Trespass. [§ 15–9]

Trespass requires a physical invasion onto the plaintiff's property. However, a nuisance only requires an unreasonable interference with the plaintiff's use of her property, which does not require a physical invasion. Certain conduct can create both a nuisance and constitute trespass (e.g., large particle air pollution such as soot).

d. Differences Between Nuisance Per Se and Nuisance in Fact. [§ 15–10]

A nuisance per se is conduct, activity, or a situation that is a nuisance under all circumstances, regardless of its location. Courts will typically only find conduct that is unlawful or unreasonably dangerous to constitute a nuisance per se. A nuisance in fact is conduct, activity, or a situation that constitutes a nuisance only because of its effect under the particular circumstances such as the location or surroundings. Indeed, a nuisance in fact is typically legal in certain locations and has social value.

e. Remedies. [§ 15–11]

There are generally three remedies a court might impose in a nuisance action in which the plaintiff has prevailed. First, the court may issue an injunction prohibiting the defendant from engaging in the nuisance. (See Case Squib: *Morgan v. High Penn Oil Co.*) Second, the court may grant the plaintiff monetary damages only. (See Case Squib: *Boomer v. Atlantic Cement Co.*) This remedy forces the plaintiff to sell her right of property enjoyment to the defendant. Courts will use this remedy when the hardship to the defendant is much greater than the harm to the plaintiff. This remedy is criticized as constituting a taking under the Fifth Amendment for private use, not public use, which is unconstitutional. Third, a court may issue an injunction prohibiting the nuisance and grant the defendant damages. (See Case Squib: *Spur Industries, Inc. v. Del. E. Webb Development Co.*) This remedy gives the right of property enjoyment to the plaintiff, but it requires the plaintiff to pay the defendant for this right.

2. Public Nuisance. [§ 15–12]

A public nuisance is an activity that interferes with the rights of the general public. Courts may consider conduct a public nuisance if it affects the public health, safety, or even certain harms to the public's morals. A public nuisance differs from a private nuisance because the conduct affects the public's rights, not private property rights. Some examples of public nuisances include pollution, gambling, concerts, and creating a traffic hazard. To show a public nuisance, the test of unreasonable interference is the same as for a private nuisance.

a. Private Cause of Action. [§ 15–13]

The state may always bring an action to abate a public nuisance, because it has standing to act in the public interest. However, private parties will only have standing to sue for damages for a public nuisance if they can demonstrate a special harm. The plaintiff must show that he or she is affected by the defendant's conduct in a different way than the general public. To sue for injunctive relief, a private party must be entitled to damages or "have standing to sue as a representative of the general public, as a citizen in a citizen's action or as a member of a class in a class action." (Restatement (Second) of Torts § 821(C)).

C. LAND SUPPORTED IN NATURAL STATE. [§ 15–14]

Any landowner has the right to have his land supported in its natural state (without buildings or improvements) by adjacent land. This right to lateral and subjacent support places a corollary restriction on the owner of the adjacent land; the owner may not excavate on his own land in such a manner as to withdraw the natural support owing his neighbor.

1. Excavations. [§ 15–15]

Cases involving the right to support generally involve excavations on adjacent land which remove side (or lateral) support.

2. Mining Operations. [§ 15–16]

Cases involving removal of subjacent support, typically involving mining operations, are less common. The basic rules are similar. The surface holder is entitled to have his land supported in its natural state.

D. LIABILITY FOR WITHDRAWAL OF SUPPORT. [§ 15–17]

1. Common Law Rules. [§ 15–18]

Assume A owns Blackacre, upon which there is a building. B, owner of adjacent Whiteacre, excavates on his own land adjacent to the common boundary, causing the soil and A's building to fall away. The basic common law rules are as follows:

a. Absolute Duty to Support Land but Not Buildings. [§ 15–19]

Even if B has not been negligent, he will be liable for damage to the land if the soil falls of its own pressure (and not because of added pressure from the building). There is a split of authority as to whether or not he is liable also for injury to the building. (See Restatement (Second) of Torts § 817.) If the weight of the building causes the land to fall, B is not liable for damage to either the soil or the building unless he was negligent.

b. Liability for Negligence. [§ 15–20]

Although less clear, it is likely that B might also be held liable in tort if he excavates negligently and causes the building to fall, even though the soil would not have subsided without the added weight of the building. (See Restatement (Second) of Torts § 819.) In determining whether B was negligent, the following circumstances may be relevant: the nature of the excavation; the type of soil; and whether there was notice to the adjacent owner of the excavation plans.

2. Statutory Rules—Excavations More Than Twelve Feet Deep. [§ 15–21]

In at least one state, liability in connection with excavations at a depth of twelve feet or more is governed by statute. An adjoining landowner excavating at a depth of more than twelve feet is required to provide support not only to adjacent land in its natural state, but in its improved state as well. Hence, the excavating landowner is liable for damages to the building (and for incidental damages as well) even if it is the building's own weight which causes it to fall.

CHAPTER XV

REVIEW PROBLEMS—RIGHT TO USE
AND ENJOYMENT OF PROPERTY

Many fist year property exams will include a question on nuisance. Pay particular attention for fact patterns that you can analyze as a nuisance problem, a violation of a real covenant, and as trespass.

A is owner of Blackacre, which is adjacent to Greenacre owned by B. Both Blackacre and Greenacre are one-acre lots located in a relatively urban area only ten miles from a major city. After living harmoniously as neighbors for several years, B decides to start raising potbellied pigs to be sold later as pets. At any given time B has twenty to thirty pigs on his property. A is not pleased because he can no longer eat outside due to obnoxious odors, and he has trouble sleeping at night as the pigs root loudly twenty-four hours a day. A brings a nuisance suit against B seeking an injunction prohibiting B from raising potbellied pigs. What result?

Answer: A will probably win because the harm to A includes a likely loss in property value, an inability to sleep at night, and an inability to breathe the air on his property without feeling nauseous. In contrast, there is little social utility to having a pig production business located in an urban area. B is earning a living from this enterprise, but his business is much better suited to a rural location. Therefore, it is likely that a court would find the gravity of harm to A outweighs the social utility of B's conduct. Further, the doctrine of coming to the nuisance is not applicable in this situation because A was living on Blackacre before B initiated this business.

Chapter XVI

PUBLIC LAND USE CONTROL

A. OVERVIEW. [§ 16–1]

At the current time, the most severe limitations placed on the use of land come not from the many property law concepts discussed up to this point but from the exercise, by myriad government entities, of their police power based land use regulatory authority and their exercise of their power of eminent domain. These interrelated topics are considered in depth in land use planning and control law courses but many real property casebooks and professors attempt an overview of these subject areas in the basic property course. Consequently, such an overview is included as the final topic in this Quick Review.

B. INTRODUCTION TO LAND USE PLANNING AND CONTROL: ZONING AND SUBDIVISION CONTROL. [§ 16–2]

1. Nature and Source of the Power. [§ 16–3]

The power of states and local governments to plan for and control the use of land within their jurisdictions is grounded in the police power, i.e., the power of a government to protect and promote the public health, safety, morals, and general welfare of the community. (See Case Squib: *Village of Euclid v. Ambler Realty*) The power is inherent for state governments. However, pursuant to state constitutional concepts in regard to the "home rule" power of local governments in some states, local governments must receive special grants of power to exercise land use control. Zoning enabling acts are the traditional method of accomplishing such delegation from the states to their local governments.

2. Interrelationship of Land Use Control Devices. [§ 16–4]

Although zoning was the traditional method whereby local governments exercised land use control power, today, planning, zoning, and subdivision control are usually combined. All three are grounded in the police power and are subject to the same prerequisites and restrictions.

3. Presumption of Validity. [§ 16–5]

Properly enacted zoning and other land use control measures are legitimate exercises of legislative power. Consequently, they are entitled to judicial deference pursuant to the separation of powers doctrine and are presumed to be valid if reasonably related to police power objectives. (See Case Squib: compare *Village of Euclid v. Ambler Realty* and *Nectow v. City of Cambridge*)

a. Legislative Acts: The Fairly Debatable Rule. [§ 16–6]

The courts will consider a land use control measure that is legislative in nature, such as zoning and rezoning, to be reasonable if it meets the fairly debatable test, i.e., it will be held invalid only if no reasonable person could agree that the legislative classification is reasonable. The fairly debatable rule creates a presumption of validity in favor of the government that is difficult to overcome. You should note that the strength of the fairly debatable rule has been eroded in many states in recent times.

b. Administrative and Quasi–Judicial Acts: Less Deferential Standard of Review. [§ 16–7]

Not all acts of land use control and planning are legislative in nature, some are administrative or quasi-judicial. For instance, in many states, actions of zoning boards of adjustment are treated as administrative or quasi-judicial zoning actions. These actions are not treated with the same degree of deference and presumption of validity as are legislative acts. Courts sometimes require substantial evidence to support administrative and quasi-judicial zoning actions meaning the government's decision will be sustained by a court only if the government can show competent, material, or substantial evidence in support of its land use decision. (See Case Squib: *Puritan–Greenfield Improvement Assoc. v. Leo, Fasano v. Board of County Commr's, and Board of County Commissioners of Brevard County v. Snyder*)

4. Limitations on Exercise of the Land Use Control Power. [§ 16–8]

a. Conformity With Comprehensive Plans. [§ 16–9]

At least in theory, comprehensive land use planning is a prerequisite to the valid exercise of the land use control power. In fact, the Standard State Zoning Enabling Act (SZEA) commands that land use regulations be in conformity with a comprehensive plan. The SZEA was released in 1924 and all fifty states adopted enabling acts that were substantially modeled after the SZEA. Presently, a few states have enacted statutes that depart from the SZEA; however, it remains extremely influential as does its mandate that zoning be accomplished within the context of a comprehensive plan. Without comprehensive planning, zoning and other land use regulations are subject to attack as arbitrary, unreasonable, and capricious. Also, the failure to treat similar land comparably situated in the community may result in the declaration that a given zoning designation is spot zoning (an island of more intensive use surrounded by less intensive use) and deprives the landowner of equal protection of the law. Caveat: Many courts accept a mere zoning map as a comprehensive land use plan if it indicates that all land in the jurisdiction is subject to land use control and if there is no statutory requirement for and definition of "comprehensive plan."

Additionally, consistency between the comprehensive plan and the measures that implement the comprehensive plan is an important requirement. Practically speaking, this means that the comprehensive plan and the regulations promulgated under the comprehensive plan must be consistent. (See Case Squib: *Fasano v. Board of County Commr's and Udell v. Haas*). It also means, in many jurisdictions, that there must be consistency between the local plan and any permits or development orders that are issued. Challenges to land use decisions frequently raise questions as to whether the regulation itself, or its application to a specific property is directly related to a legitimate public purpose. One means of establishing such a relationship (and substantiating the legitimacy of an ordinance and its administration) is to show that the regulation, and/or a specific decision made under its authority, implements and is consistent with the goals and policies set forth in the comprehensive plan.

b. Destruction of Economic Value: The Taking Issue. [§ 16–10]

Early on, the United States Supreme Court rejected the idea that excessive or improper use of the police power became a taking. (See Case Squib: *Mugler v. Kansas*). The Court's view was that regulations under the police power were reviewed solely under the substantive due process standard that required a law to be upheld if it promoted a legitimate public end in a rational way. The Court's subsequent expansion of the takings clause to include regulations is generally viewed as occurring in the case of *Pennsylvania Coal v. Mahon.* In that case, The Court articulated that the major restriction of the land use control power is that zoning and other land use regulations must not so severely restrict the use of land as to leave it with no meaningful economic use. If the land use regulation destroys too much of the economic value ("goes too far") then it cannot be validly enforced as police power regulation but must instead be considered an exercise of the power of eminent domain and just compensation must be paid to the landowner. (See Case Squib: *Pennsylvania Coal v. Mahon*) This topic is explored in section [§ 16–68] on inverse condemnation.

C. ZONING PRINCIPLES. [§ 16–11]

Zoning is the most frequently used method by which local governments regulate the use of land. Most zoning restrictions are directed to regulation of permitted uses and the permissible height, area, location of buildings, as well as the density of development. The police power underpinnings of zoning were established in *Village of Euclid v. Ambler Realty*, (see Case Squibs section).

1. Cumulative versus Non–Cumulative Zoning. [§ 16–12]

Under a cumulative zoning ordinance a hierarchy of uses is established. Imagine a pyramid. Residential uses would be at the top of the pyramid, followed by commercial and industrial. Classifications at the top of the pyramid are more restricted by land use controls and regulations. Under cumulative zoning, higher uses are permitted in lower use zones but not vice versa. For example, a residence could be built in commercial or industrial zones but industries could not be located in residential or commercial zones. Zoning ordinances organized in this manner are frequently labeled "Euclidian" ordinances because the zoning scheme upheld in *Euclid v. Ambler* was cumulative. Under non-cumulative zoning ordinances each (or most) zone(s) are exclusive. For example, only residences may be located in residential zones and only industries may be located in industrial zones. Both cumulative and non-cumulative zoning are constitutionally permissible.

2. Non–Conforming Uses. [§ 16–13]

A use which was lawfully in existence when a zoning regulation prohibiting such a use was enacted (e.g., a grocery store located in an area subsequently zoned residential) is called a non-conforming use. If the use did not lawfully pre-date the new zoning regulation, it will not qualify as a non-conforming use and the government will typically enjoin the continuation of the use immediately. The continuation of lawfully pre-existing non-conforming uses must be allowed for at least a sufficient length of time for the owners to recover an appreciable percentage of their investment so as to avoid a successful regulatory takings challenge. However, it is constitutionally permissible for a zoning ordinance to forbid reconstruction or improvement of a non-conforming use. For example, the grocery store cannot be rebuilt if it burns down nor can a fast-food service be added if none was in operation at the time the grocery became a non-conforming use.

Non-conforming uses fall into one of four categories. First, there are non-conforming buildings such as an office building in a multi-family residential zone. Second, there are conforming uses of non-conforming buildings. An example of this second type of non-conformity would be using the building in the first example as residences for multiple families. Third, there are nonconforming uses of conforming buildings such as a single family house, located in a single family residential zone, but used as a hair salon or antique store. Lastly, there are non-conforming uses of land. Using unimproved land located in a residential zone for a fish farm is an example of such a non-conformity. The nature of the classification may impact the decision-making process regarding the termination or continuance of the non-conformity.

3. Exclusionary Zoning Prohibited. [§ 16–14]

Exclusionary zoning is the use of zoning ordinances to exclude certain types of housing and is most frequently practiced by suburban communities. Exclusionary zoning is frequently based upon race, economic status, handicap, or familial status. Zoning ordinances may not be considered reasonable if their effect is to exclude certain groups, such as economic and racial minorities, from the community. The exclusion or severe restriction of low-rent housing is particularly suspect. (See Case Squib: *Southern Burlington County NAACP v. Township of Mt. Laurel*). Discrimination in favor of racial and economic minorities and/or the elderly, may be upheld. Planners often blame exclusionary zoning for the over-representation of minorities and of the poor in urban centers and affordable housing advocates blame the practice for the escalating costs of affordable housing.

The essence of zoning is that it separates incompatible uses; therefore, all zoning results in excluding certain uses from each zoning district. However, not all zoning is exclusionary. Zoning becomes exclusionary when it totally prohibits particular types of residential land uses (such as multi-family or affordable housing) or when the zoning ordinance contains restrictions that limit the amount of land available for certain "vulnerable" groups such as racial minorities, the poor, the handicapped and "non-traditional" families.

Several zoning techniques have been the principal focus of attack as exclusionary zoning practices.

a. The Single–Family Use Exclusive Zone. [§ 16–15]

In *Village of Belle Terre v. Borass* (See Case Squibs section) the United States Supreme Court first addressed the validity of land use ordinances that restricted use based upon family status. At issue was the constitutionality of the definition of "family" in a zoning ordinance that restricted the entire area of a village exclusively to single-family use. The Court applied the standard of review for equal protection social and economic legislation, *rational basis*, after finding that the case did not involve a fundamental right guaranteed by the federal constitution. The ordinance was upheld. But this was just the beginning of cases challenging the validity of land use ordinances that based land use on familial status. Just a few years later in *Moore v. City of East Cleveland* (See Case Squibs section) the court considered another family zoning ordinance according to which the plaintiff and her grandsons, all of whom were related by blood, were prohibited from living together. This time, the court applied strict scrutiny review and found that the ordinance violated the substantive due process protections of the Fourteenth Amendment. The case was distinguished from *Village of Belle Terre* because the ordinance affected the fundamental right of association by prohibiting blood-related individuals from living together.

Students should be aware that under the federal Fair Housing Act (FHA), it is unlawful to make housing unavailable because of an individual's familial status. Thus, the FHA has had important and lasting impacts on local land use regulations and should be considered as local authorities consider family use ordinances.

b. Density Restrictions, Large–Lot Zoning. [§ 16–16]

Zoning has been used to restrict the supply of available housing sites and to increase the cost of residential land by requiring large minimum lot sizes. Relatedly, this zoning technique has been used to reduce the availability of low and moderate cost housing and is a popular device used in suburban communities. (See Case Squib: *Johnson v. Town of Edgartown*). Justifications for minimum lot size requirements are often based upon arguments of environmental protection, health, and aesthetics and typically rational basis review is applied by the courts.

c. Maximum and Minimum House Size Requirements. [§ 16–17]

In addition to minimum lot size requirements, exclusionary zoning can also take the form of minimum building size requirements. As with minimum lot size requirements, minimum building size requirements are often justified based upon health and aesthetic concerns. (See Case Squib: *Lionshead Lake, Inc. v. Township of Wayne*).

Maximum house size regulations are relatively new and are a response to what has become popularly known as "McMansions," "monster homes," or "starter castles." Courts have upheld limitations on the size of houses by local governments that believe that such large houses are inconsistent with the community character and adversely impact the supply of affordable housing. (See Case Squib: *Board of County Commissioners of Teton County v. Crow*).

d. Excessive Regulation of Group Homes for the Handicapped. [§ 16–18]

Most zoning regulations that affect the handicapped involve the regulation of group homes that seek to allow unrelated handicapped individuals to live together in single-family areas. Communities may attempt to zone out group homes under family use ordinances that limit the ability of unrelated individuals to live together. (See Case Squib: *City of Cleburne v. Cleburne Living Center*). As with family use ordinances, the FHA applies to the handicapped and prohibits discrimination in housing against the handicapped and should be considered as one is evaluating the validity of ordinances that regulate the location and operation of group homes.

e. Prohibition of Manufactured Housing. [§ 16–19]

Manufactured housing is an increasingly important component of the affordable housing market, especially in a market of escalating housing prices. Some municipalities have attempted to either completely exclude manufactured housing or to sequester manufactured housing away from residential areas and into mobile home parks. In some states, legislation prohibits the total exclusion of manufactured housing. Some courts have held that the sequestering technique is a violation of the police power while other courts have used aesthetic concerns to justify deferring to the legislative judgment and have upheld ordinances that place limitations on the location of manufactured housing.

f. Race–Based Exclusions. [§ 16–20]

Exclusionary zoning claims have been most successful in federal court when they have been based upon claims that the zoning ordinances indirectly discriminate based upon race by excluding moderate and low income housing from suburban communities. Litigants have found it difficult to prevail on racial discrimination claims in zoning under the equal protection clause of the Fourteenth Amendment of the federal constitution. Though allegations of racial discrimination are reviewed under the strict scrutiny standard, the plaintiff must prove discriminatory intent to prevail on a Fourteenth Amendment claim, which is often difficult to do. (See Case Squib: *Village of Arlington Heights v. Metropolitan Housing Development Corp.*). However, racial discrimination in zoning can be challenged under the FHA where a plaintiff can prove a prima facie case by showing that a zoning regulation has a discriminatory effect.

4. Procedural Relief From Zoning Hardship: Variances and Special Exceptions. [§ 16–21]

The unique nature of land virtually guarantees that certain parcels will suffer hardship not suffered by all land so restricted. Zoning ordinances are required to contain some provision for relief of such situations. Variances are designed to afford relief from technical restrictions such as height, bulk and set-back limitations. Caveat: A use variance, i.e., a provision allowing administrative variance of use restrictions may be held invalid since a legislative act, re-zoning, should be required to change the permissible use. Even in the minority of jurisdictions in which re-zoning may be treated as quasi-judicial, use variances may be problematic because use variances may result in piecemeal re-zoning, conflict with the comprehensive plan, or may be accomplished by the improper authority. Special exceptions provide flexibility and relief from hardship by specifying in the ordinance that otherwise impermissible uses can be made if certain specified conditions are met.

5. Zoning Concepts. [§ 16–22]

The use of zoning has been given greater flexibility by the introduction of new concepts which merit attention.

a. Clustering. [§ 16–23]

Traditional Euclidian zoning presumed one structure per lot. Many modern ordinances allow buildings to be clustered in certain areas so as to leave open spaces and take advantage of construction and design economies without varying the density of development permitted on large tracts of land.

b. Planned Unit Developments ("PUD"). [§ 16–24]

PUDs introduce the previously rejected concept of combining uses in a development. PUDs are both a type of development and a legal process that must be used to approve the development. PUDs frequently combine high density and low density residential uses with appropriate commercial and business-professional uses in order to make housing developments more self-sufficient and more interesting. PUDs differ from traditional zoning ordinances because they allow a development project to be reviewed comprehensively, in an integrated manner, and they also allow for the mixing of different types of residential and nonresidential uses, which most conventional zoning ordinances do not permit. PUDs developed as a means of promoting well-designed and planned mixed use developments, see *infra* § 16–28.

c. Floating Zones. [§ 16–25]

The "mapping" (i.e., location on a map), of all permitted uses was contemplated in traditional zoning. The use of "floating zones" allows greater flexibility by allowing landowners to apply for permission to replace their existing zoning restrictions with uses permitted under specified circumstances (such as PUDs and low rent housing). If the landowner's application is granted, the floating use is said to "sink" and replace the preexisting zoning designation.

d. Conditional versus Contract Zoning. [§ 16–26]

Courts refuse to allow zoning authorities to enter into contracts with landowners making special arrangements for specified parcels. Such "contracts" are said to violate delegation of legislative power concepts. However, many courts do allow zoning authorities to impose conditions which landowners may accept in order to accomplish goals desired by both the landowners and the zoning authorities. There is increasing use via this approach of private land use restrictions (real covenants and servitudes) imposed by landowners on their land at the request of zoning authorities.

Sometimes developers and municipalities seek to enter into development agreements. These agreements can benefit both parties. Developers obtain greater certainty because the development agreement will contain a promise by the municipality freezing the regulations on the site of the development for a period of time which is one solution to the problem of vested rights. Simultaneously, development agreements may increase the opportunities for municipalities to impose exactions and conditions on developers. Development agreements find support in some state statutes but even when statutorily authorized, they have been challenged as illegal contract zoning. Some of the cases addressing contract and conditional zoning have tested the validity of development agreements by considering: [1] the duration of any freezes on zoning pursuant to the development agreement and [2] broad public benefits in addition to the benefits that are unique to the developer.

e. Interrelationship of Zoning and Private Land Use Control Devices. [§ 16–27]

Zoning restrictions are often imposed on land already subject to private land use restrictions such as real covenants or negative easements. If the public and private restrictions conflict, the public will prevail. However, the mere fact that the restrictions differ will not necessarily mean there is a conflict. For example, A's land is subject to a real covenant limiting the land to residential uses. The zoning ordinance in question designates the land for commercial use. If the zoning code in question is cumulative, there is no conflict since residences would be permissible in commercial zones. If the zoning ordinance in question is non-cumulative and only commercial uses are permitted in commercial zones, then the private and the public restrictions conflict and the public will prevail.

f. Mixed–Use Developments. [§ 16–28]

Mixed-use development blends a variety of uses such as cultural, commercial, residential, institutional, and sometimes industrial. Proponents of mixed-use development herald it for (1) promoting environments that are friendly for pedestrians and cyclists, (2) reducing sprawl by incentivizing the creation of more compact development and allowing for a greater variety and density of development, and (3) strengthening the character of neighborhoods. PUDs, as planning tools, can promote the use

283

of mixed-use developments. The implementation of mixed-use developments can also promote smart growth, discussed *infra* § 16–32.

g.   Transit Oriented Development. [§ 16–29]

Transit oriented development is designed to be pedestrian friendly, to encourage people to drive their cars less and to use mass transportation more. It is an important component of the Smart Growth Movement, *infra* § 16–32, and is characterized by mixed-use developments that are compact and intentionally located near existing or new public transportation systems. Common transit oriented development characteristics or goals include: (1) pedestrian walkways and walkable designs; (2) some form of mass-transit as a central feature of the town center; (3) high-quality, high density development that surrounds the town center; and (4) lanes for bicyclers, rollerbladers, and scooter users.

h.   Conservation Subdivisions. [§ 16–30]

Conservation subdivisions are designed to protect natural resources and farmland while simultaneously permitting the maximum amount of residential development allowed under the existing subdivision and zoning regulations. They typically contain clustered lots, compactly developed, along with common open space. Density bonuses for developers may be offered to encourage their development, but not always. If a density bonus is not offered, the conservation subdivision could contain the same density level and number of lots as a typical subdivision. Thus, one should not assume that a conservation subdivision will necessarily have fewer lots allowed to be built than in a typical subdivision. Some of the challenges that are associated with conservation subdivisions are the ownership and management of land within the subdivision that has been dedicated for preservation and decisions regarding the locating and clustering of homes.

i.   The New Urbanism. [§ 16–31]

New urbanism describes an approach to the development of communities that, in contrast to urban sprawl, promotes compact, mixed-use neighbourhood development and integrated land use and transportation strategies. New urbanism emerged in the late 1980's and is characterized by several major principles. Developments should be compact and should have walkable districts or neighbourhoods with an interconnected network of streets that encourage pedestrian traffic and the use of public transportation to connect neighbourhoods to one another. There should be a mix of uses and activities with public spaces and buildings being given priority and sited in locations that are prominent.

j. Smart Growth. [§ 16–32]

Smart growth is anti-sprawl development through the use of comprehensive planning that is designed to promote sustainable developments that increase the quality of life of citizens. Characteristics and principles associated with smart growth include, but are not limited to the following: [1] creating diverse housing options; [2] decreasing traffic congestion through the creation of communities with a range of transportation options such as biking, walking, and mass transportation; [3] urban revitalization; [4] making development decisions cost effective, fair, and predictable (i.e. decreasing the costs of infrastructure and taxes); and [5] promoting attractive communities while protecting prime agricultural lands, open spaces, and wetlands.

k. Urban Growth Boundaries. [§ 16–33]

Unlike the growth management strategies which address the phasing of new development and assuring the provision of adequate facilities to support the development, (see § 16–35), urban growth boundaries (UGBs) are a means of imposing limitations on permissible growth. Once an urban growth boundary is placed around an urbanized area, it establishes the limits of urban growth. Development is allowed to occur within the confines of the boundary but is not allowed outside of it. One of the criticisms of urban growth boundaries is that they can have negative, sometimes unintended, impacts on housing by constraining housing choices and increasing the cost of land and of housing. As you can imagine, these negative impacts would be felt most by households with low, moderate, and middle incomes. Thus, important decisions must be made before the imposition of an urban growth boundary such as: [1] the amount of land to include within the growth area, [2] the shape of the boundary and what the policy will be regarding the future expansion of the boundary, and [3] how to manage growth on the borders of the urban growth boundary in anticipation of its extension.

6. Infrastructure Requirements and Financing. [§ 16–34]

Effective land use planning will coordinate the development of a community and the financing, timing, and location of infrastructure necessary to support the development. Increasingly, communities are paying closer attention to decisions about when and where to place public facilities and how to finance them.

a. Growth Management. [§ 16–35]

Growth management refers to the process of ensuring that public facilities and services keep up with demand as the population grows. Growth management is an essential component of land use regulation. Without the implementation of growth management techniques, rapid population growth can overwhelm communities and sprawl (leap frog, low density growth and land development) can result. The leading case on phased growth programs is *Golden v. Ramapo Planning Board* in which the court held that the state's enabling statute, modeled after the Standard Zoning Enabling Act (SZEA), authorized the municipality to place controls upon the sequencing and timing of development. (See Case Squibs section). In upholding the legitimacy of the town's program, the court noted that efforts to disguise exclusionary zoning as a phased growth program would not be permitted.

A variety of growth management strategies have been developed and adopted throughout the country. Quotas on new development, adequate public facilities programs, and even direct limits on areas of urban growth can all be components of a growth management strategy. Traditional land use control techniques—subdivision and zoning controls—have always had the potential to affect the growth rate of communities. Growth management plans address concerns about when growth should occur and about how much growth should be permitted. Growth management is as much concerned about these growth issues as it is about the traditional Euclidian preoccupation with the separation of uses and the location of development.

b.   Impact Fees. [§ 16–36]

Infrastructure finance is an important component of land use planning and development and impact fees are a means of securing this financing. Impact fees are charges levied against new developments in order to generate revenue to fund the capital improvements that are necessitated by the new development. Increasingly, impact fees are serving an important role in the efforts of local governments to address some of the economic burdens of population growth that saddle burgeoning communities such as the need for new schools, sewer and water treatment facilities, parks, jails and public buildings.

Impact fees are similar to in lieu fee in that both require developers to pay for capital facilities that are necessitated by the new development. (See § 16–43). However, the concept of the impact fee is more flexible and comprehensive as a cost shifting mechanism. In lieu fees are predicated upon dedication requirements and should only be used where dedications of land by the developer could be appropriately used i.e. in regard to site-related or project improvements Impact fees normally are used to finance construction of non site-related or system improvements.

The dual rational nexus test is used in most states, through statutory provisions or court decisions, to determine the validity of impact fees as reasonable exercises of the police power. The first prong of the dual rational nexus test establishes the principle of proportionate share, i.e. that a developer can be charged no more than the cost that the local government will incur in providing the type of infrastructure needed to service the particular development being assessed the fee. The second prong of the test requires the local government collecting impact fees to spend them for the purpose for which they were collected and so as to benefit the development paying them. (See Case Squib: *Jordan v. Village of Menomonee Falls*)

c. **Required Dedications and Exactions. [§ 16–37]**

Required dedications or payments in lieu (see § 16–43) as a condition to subdivision approval were the original approach to developer financing of public infrastructure. It is a means of shifting the cost of capital expenses from the municipality and to the developer. Local governments would condition their approval of the developer's project on the developer's agreement to provide and to dedicate improvements such as drainage ways and streets. Required dedications are now ubiquitous components of subdivision regulations and are typically approved by courts if they are reasonable. (See Case Squib: *Rohn v. City of Visalia*).

Exactions occur when a governmental body conditions approval of a permit on the individual giving property to the government. These cases differ from many other takings cases because, at least hypothetically, the plaintiff has the choice of not relinquishing his or her property to the government. Nevertheless, the Supreme Court has found that exactions can constitute a taking unless there is an essential nexus between the state's interest and the exaction by the government that bears a rough proportionality to the negative impact that the plaintiff's development will cause on the public. (see Case Squib: *Nollan v. California Coastal Commission; Dolan v. City of Tigard*).

d. **Concurrency. [§ 16–38]**

Concurrency policy is a tool implemented by some local governments to address financial difficulties and infrastructure management challenges that accompany growth and development. When concurrency policy is implemented, its effect is to withhold approval for land development until it is determined that identified services and facilities will be provided in a manner that meets the local standard of service levels, by the time those services and facilities are impacted by the land development. It is a component, along with exactions, dedications, and in-lieu fees, of a robust growth management policy. Essentially, concurrency is one of the more recent policies, in a series of such policies, pursuant to which local governments require developers to assume responsibility for the financial costs of infrastructure that are associated with subdivision and other forms of land development.

D. SUBDIVISION CONTROL. [§ 16–39]

Subdivision controls are used to regulate and structure previously undeveloped land. The subdivision control power of governmental units comes from the police power and is subject to the same restrictions and requirements previously discussed in regard to zoning.

1. Platting. [§ 16–40]

The procedure and technique for the exercise of subdivision control power is to require landowners who wish to subdivide their land into two or more lots to file a "plat" with the land use control authority. A "plat" is a map or drawing of the way in which the land will be subdivided. Normally plats show the lot lines, roads and other easements, building setback lines, dimensions, and number of each lot. Usually, a legal description of the development area and private use restrictions are also given on the plat.

a. Prerequisites to Plat Approval. [§ 16–41]

Land use control authorities implement their subdivision control power by refusing to approve plats unless certain conditions are met. These requirements fall into two groups: technical and exactions.

b. Technical Requirements. [§ 16–42]

Most jurisdictions have important but usually non-controversial requirements relating to the physical format and content of the plat.

c. Exactions or Required Dedications. [§ 16–43]

As a precondition to plat approval, many land use control authorities require the subdivider to make capital funding contributions to help pay the cost of providing governmental services for the new development. Usually, such goals are accomplished by requiring the developer to dedicate one or more lots to the governmental unit for use for schools, parks, water treatment plants, police stations, or other governmental services. When the local government needs money rather than land, the subdivider is permitted, or required, to pay the cash value of one or more lots "in lieu of" dedicating the lot(s) to public use. Such payments are labeled "in lieu" payments. See *supra* § 16–37.

(1) Validity of Exactions. [§ 16–44]

The constitutional validity of required dedications and "in lieu" payments is heavily litigated and not yet uniformly recognized. The definite trend, however, is to approve them if they are reasonable as measured against the cost and size of the subdivision, and if the land or money will be used to provide governmental services necessitated by the subdivision in question. If either of these conditions is not met, they will be declared invalid as a taking of property without compensation.

E. EMINENT DOMAIN. [§ 16–45]

1. Nature and Source of the Power. [§ 16–46]

a. Inherent Governmental Power. [§ 16–47]

The power of the federal and state governments to take title to private property for public purposes is an inherent attribute of sovereignty. It need not be expressly granted in constitutions or elsewhere.

b. Power May Be Delegated. [§ 16–48]

The Federal Congress, state legislatures, and state constitutions can, and frequently do, delegate the power of eminent domain to governmental agencies and units, privately owned utilities and transportation companies, educational institutions, urban renewal organizations, historical societies and the like. Such delegations are generally strictly construed and are subject not only to limitations made part of the delegation but also to the limitations to which the delegating government is subject.

2. Limitations on the Exercise of the Power of Eminent Domain. [§ 16–49]

The Fifth Amendment to the United States Constitution limits the power of eminent domain by providing that: "No person shall be . . . deprived of . . . property without due process of law, nor shall private property be taken for public use without just compensation." These limitations are placed on the states through the Due Process Clause of the Fourteenth Amendment. Most state constitutions also contain provisions comparable to the Fifth and Fourteenth Amendments to the United States Constitution.

a. Substantive Due Process. [§ 16–50]

The due process requirements of notice and opportunity to be heard guaranteed by the Fifth and Fourteenth Amendments apply to exercises of the power of eminent domain. For twenty-five years, a regulatory takings test articulated by the United States Supreme Court held that an exercise of eminent domain through government regulation constitutes a regulatory taking if the regulation failed to " 'substantially advance a legitimate state interest.' " (See Case Squib: *Agins v. City of Tiburon*). Later, the Court reconsidered this regulatory takings test in another case, *Lingle v. Chevron U.S.A. Inc.*. The Court held that the "substantially advance" language is a product of due process precedent, not takings precedent. Thus, a regulation that fails to substantially advance a legitimate interest of government may be so irrational and arbitrary that it violates the Due Process Clause.

b. Public Use. [§ 16–51]

Although the Fifth Amendment refers to "public use" as a prerequisite for the exercise of eminent domain, federal and most state courts now define "public use" as the equivalent of "public purpose." In short, the test is not "use" by the public but whether or not legitimate public purposes will be served. (See Case Squib: *Hawaii Housing Authority v. Midkiff* and *Kelo v. City of New London, Conn.*) Though the United States Constitution does not expressly prohibit the taking of private property for private purposes, the Fifth Amendment is interpreted as prohibiting such government conduct as a violation of the due process clause.

(1) Example. [§ 16–52] The Federal Government may use the power of eminent domain to acquire land for flood control projects even though not every member of the public will be benefited.

(2) Resale of the Land. [§ 16–53]

The Federal Government can take land for urban renewal projects even though the land will later be sold to private developers for private use. **Caveat:** Some state courts still interpret "public use" as requiring at least some public access and control.

c. Public Necessity Need Not Be Established. [§ 16–54]

The courts will not determine whether an exercise of the power of eminent domain is necessary, wise, economically sound, or the best course of action to achieve the public purpose involved. Thus, the courts will not consider landowners' objections to the effect that different, more, or less property should be taken.

d. Just Compensation. [§ 16–55]

Due to the limited review available to landowners of governmental decisions to exercise the power of eminent domain, the determination of just compensation is usually the only issue considered by the courts.

(1) Definition. [§ 16–56]

The just compensation to which the landowner is entitled is said to be the fair market value of the property taken measured in money or its economic equivalent.

(2) Fair Market Value. [§ 16–57]

Fair market value is the amount of money a willing buyer, under no compulsion to buy, would pay and a willing seller, under no compulsion to sell, would accept for the property in question with the intention of devoting the property to its highest and best economic use.

(3) Value to Condemnor. [§ 16–58]

The value the property will have or not have, once the condemnor acquires it, is irrelevant and not to be considered in establishing fair market value.

(4) Value to Condemnee. [§ 16–59]

The presence or absence of special value to the condemnee is not to be considered in establishing fair market value. Thus, the fact that the condemnee uses the property for purposes which make it less valuable than if it were devoted to its highest and best economic use do not decrease the just compensation to which the condemnee is entitled. Likewise, the fact that because of special skills or abilities the condemnee is able to make the land more profitable than others does not entitle the condemnee to more than fair market value.

(5) Determination of Fair Market Value: Comparable Sales. [§ 16–60]

Under federal law, the judge, jury, or a special commission determines fair market value. The preferred basis is by evaluating comparable sales, i.e., the selling price of nearby land similar in use, location, and area. Recent sales of the subject property are to be considered but cost to the condemnee is not conclusive because the condemnee may have paid more or less than fair market value or may have over-improved the property.

(6) Determination of Fair Market Value: Influence of Condemnation Project. [§ 16–61]

Any increase or decrease in value to the land resulting from the condemnation project is to be disregarded.

(7) Severance Damages Compensable. [§ 16–62]

When only a portion of a tract of land is taken by eminent domain the landowner is entitled to compensation for any decrease in value suffered by his retained land as well as compensation for the land and improvements taken. For example, in partial takings, just compensation is calculated by taking the fair market value of the entire tract prior to taking and subtracting from it the fair market value of the retained land after its severance from the taken portion of the tract.

(a) **Example.** [§ 16–63] A owns 1,000 acres of land worth $1,000 per acre ($1,000,000). The government takes 800 acres leaving a 200–acre tract now worth only $500 per acre ($100,000) because of the reduced size of the landholding. A's just compensation is $900,000 [i.e., 800 acres at 1,000 or $800,000 for the land taken and $500 times 200 acres ($100,000) severance damages to the retained land].

(8) Offset of Special Benefits. [§ 16–64]

Under federal (but not most state) law if only a portion of a tract of land is taken and the retained portion is increased in value by the taking, such increase is setoff against the fair market value of the taken land in determining just compensation.

(a) **Example.** [§ 16–65] A owns a 1,000 acre tract with a fair market value of $1,000 per acre ($1,000,000) prior to the taking of 900 acres by the government for the construction of a reservoir. After the taking, the retained 100 acres are worth $5,000 per acre ($500,000) as lake front lots. Even though the fair market value of the land taken was $900,000 (900 acres at $1,000 per acre), A's just compensation is only $500,000. [Value of entire tract prior to taking $1,000,000 less $500,000 (value of retained land) equals $500,000. Note, that if the value of the retained land (because of the special benefit it receives) exceeds the fair market value of the taken land, the just compensation is $0; i.e., A has no obligation to pay the government for his economic windfall, but no money need be paid A on the theory that the enhanced fair market value of the retained land constitutes just compensation for the land taken.]

(9) Consequential Damages. [§ 16–66]

Generally, and particularly under federal law, the condemnor need compensate only for what it takes (land, buildings, easements, water rights, etc.) and any decrease in market value (severance damages) to retained land. Loss of business or "good will," moving expenses, and other consequential damages need not be compensated. Caveat: Many states, by statute and/or judicial decisions require compensation for specified consequential damages under certain circumstances.

(10) Valuation of Leaseholds. [§ 16–67]

The value of a leasehold extinguished by the exercise of the power of eminent domain is valued in light of the market expectation of the likelihood of its being renewed at the end of its term. (See Case Squib: *Almota Farmers Elevator v. U.S.*)

F. INVERSE CONDEMNATION. (TAKINGS) [§ 16–68]

Landowners subjected to severe land use restrictions frequently assert that the governmental unit enacting the zoning or other land use measure has exceeded its regulatory power and is instead exercising the power of eminent domain, thereby entitling the landowner to relief from the restriction or, if the restriction is enforced, to payment of just compensation. The use of the "taking issue" in this context is usually referred to as an "inverse condemnation" action. It is "inverse" or "reversed" because the landowner, and not the government, files the action to establish the exercise of the power of eminent domain.

Government actions that can constitute a taking in this context fall into a few general categories.

1. Taking Permanent Possession of Property—Per Se Taking. [§ 16–69]

Any permanent physical invasion by the government is considered a taking. Additionally, a taking occurs when the government allows a third party to permanently invade an individual's property. (See Case Squib: *Loretto v. Teleprompter Manhattan CATV Corp.*) The *Loretto* per se takings test has been narrowly applied by most courts including the United States Supreme Court. (See Case Squib: *Yee v. City of Escondido*)

2. Taking Through Regulations. [§ 16–70]

Even the Supreme Court of the United States has noted that no "clear test" exists to determine when a land use restriction is to be considered a permissible regulation rather than a "taking" of property, which will be invalid without payment of compensation. The ultimate test becomes one of reasonableness (in the eyes of the judge) and a weighing and consequent balancing of public and private interests. Courts frequently quote Justice Holmes' statement in *Pennsylvania Coal v. Mahon*, 260 U.S. 393 (1922) (see case squibs), that regulation versus taking is a "matter of degree." Nonetheless, several concepts have become accepted although their actual use and interpretation varies from court to court and time to time.

a. Deprivation of Highest and Best Use Does Not Constitute a Taking. [§ 16–71]

The fact that a land use restriction prevents a landowner from making the highest and best economic use of his property does not constitute a "taking" as long as an economically meaningful use of the property is still permitted.

    (i) **Example.** [§ 16–72] A's land would be worth $100,000 if he could use it for commercial purposes. The applicable zoning code permits only residential use of the property and its value when put to residential use is $70,000. The zoning restriction, if in pursuit of a valid police power objective, is unlikely to be considered a taking even though A has lost $30,000 of market value.

b. Public Harm versus Public Benefit. [§ 16–73]

A land use restriction designed to prevent a public harm will more likely be labeled a permissible regulation (as opposed to a taking) than a restriction designed to provide a public benefit.

    (i) **Example.** [§ 16–74] If A's water-front lot is subjected to a severe set-back restriction, to protect the lake as a water supply source, it will more likely be labeled a permissible regulation than if the same set-back line were imposed to preserve the view from a nearby state park.

c. The Multifactor Takings Test and the Whole Parcel Rule. [§ 16–75]

The United States Supreme Court first articulated a comprehensive, three-part, regulatory taking balancing test in *Penn Central Transportation v. City of New York* (see Case Squib). The *Penn Central* balancing test is used to determine whether a regulation rises to the level of a taking when the regulation: (1) falls short of a total deprivation of value (the *Lucas v. South Carolina Coastal Commission* per set taking rule, *supra* § 16–69) and (2) does not involve a permanent physical occupation of property (the *Loretto v. Teleprompter Manhattan CATV Corp.* per se taking rule, *supra* § 16–69.

Additionally, the Court in *Penn Central* also addressed the question of segmentation, whether a property owner's interest can be divided in order to define the relevant parcel for purposes of the takings analysis. Thus, *Penn Central* is also an important case because it announced, what has come to be known as the "whole parcel" or "denominator" rule.

(1) The Multifactor Takings Test. [§ 16–76]

The Court identified three factors that should be weighed when considering a regulation that does not constitute a per se taking. First, the amount of economic impact, understood as the amount of the economic loss the landowner will suffer from a land use restriction is important when deciding whether the regulation constitutes a taking. (See Case Squib: *Keystone Bituminous Coal Ass'n v. DeBenedictis*).

Second, courts will attempt to determine whether and to what extent the land use restriction destroys the landowner's "distinct investment backed expectations." However, such expectations must be established as reasonable. (See Case Squib: *Penn. Central Transportation v. City of New York.*) If they are reasonable, the owner's investment backed expectations are probably one of the most important factors in deciding whether a regulation constitutes a taking, but this factor alone is most likely not dispositive of the issue. Third, the character of the government action is important. A regulation is more likely to be found to be a taking if "the interference with property can be characterized as a physical invasion by Govenrment. . . ."

(2) The Whole Parcel or Denominator Rule. [§ 16–77]

Importantly, the *Penn Central* Court addressed the segmentation issue, whether a parcel may be divided or segmented into discrete parcels when applying the multifactor takings test. There are three types of segmentation: (1) temporal as in the case of development moratorium, *infra* § 16–80; (2) geographic whether horizontal (i.e. the subdivision of property) or vertical (i.e. division into subsurface, surface and air rights); or (3) conceptual such as when a stick in the bundle of property rights is taken (i.e. the taking of the right to exclude by condemning an easement). When measuring the amount of the economic impact of a regulation one first must determine the nature and extent of the property interest, before the regulation, this is the denominator. Next, one must determine what has been taken by the regulation, this is the numerator. If the denominator is large relative to the numerator in the takings equation, then the impact of the regulation will appear to be small and the likelihood that a compensable taking will be found under the *Penn Central* multifactor test is decreased. But, if the denominator is small relative to the numerator, then the impact of the regulation on the property interest would appear to be great and the likelihood that a compensable taking will be found is increased. Thus, the segmentation issue is extremely important in evaluating takings claims under the *Penn Central* test.

The Court in *Penn Central* rejected segmentation and announced that in considering takings claims, courts should focus on the parcel as a whole.

d. Rendering Land Valueless—Per Se Taking. [§ 16–78]

A regulation that denies all economically beneficial uses of land is a taking unless the state can prove that the regulation was preventing a common law nuisance. At common law the state could abate a nuisance without paying any compensation because the landowner never had the property right to use his or her property in a manner that constituted a nuisance. (See Case Squib: *Lucas v. South Carolina Coastal Commission*).

e. Landowner May Have No Inherent Right to Develop Land So as to Change Its Natural State. [§ 16–79]

Several state court decisions suggest that a landowner has no inherent right to change the natural condition of his land if such change would cause a public harm. (See Case Squib: *Just v. Marinette*). The decision of the Supreme Court of the United States in *Lucas v. South Carolina Costal Commission*, (see Case Squibs section), may be inconsistent with this development in the state courts because of its re-emphasis that a regulation which renders land valueless is a taking.

f. Temporary Takings. [§ 16–80]

A landowner can recover damages for the period of time before it is finally determined that a land use regulation constituted a taking. Once it is determined that a regulation constitutes a taking, the government has several choices. It can maintain the regulation and compensate the landowner, it could amend the regulation, or it could remove the regulation. Regardless of which choice the government makes, it must compensate the landowner for the period of time while the regulation was in effect. (See Case Squib: *First English Evangelical Lutheran Church v. County of Los Angeles, California*). However, this rule does not mean that a government must compensate a landowner for a reasonable moratorium that prohibits all economic use of the property for a brief period of time. The distinction is based on the fact that a reasonable moratorium does not constitute a taking to begin with. (See Case Squib: *Tahoe–Sierra Preservation Council, Inc. v. Tahoe Regional Planning Agency*).

3. Transferable Development Rights. [§ 16–81]

The United States Supreme Court first considered the concept of transferable development rights in *Penn Central Transportation Co. v. City of New York* (see Case Squib section). The Court held that the value of transferable development rights should be taken into account when considering the "economic impact" of a regulation which is one of three parts of the regulatory takings test articulated by the Court. Nearly twenty years later, in *Suitum v. Tahoe Regional Planning Agency* (see Case Squib section), Justice Scalia argued, in a concurring opinion, that transferable development rights should not be considered as part of the regulatory takings analysis but rather should be considered after a court has decided that a taking has occurred and is considering the compensation side of the takings analysis. Justice Scalia distinguished *Penn Central* and the mitigating role of transferable development rights in the takings analysis because the property owners in *Penn Central* owned some of the lots in the receiving zone to which the development rights would be transferred. He argued that the relevant land in *Penn Central* could be considered all of the owners' parcels that were subject to the regulation or at least the parcels that were contiguous.

Transferable development rights programs can help address the problem of uneven impacts that can exist as a result of Euclidean zoning and related zoning plans. The uneven impacts occur because landowners fortunate enough to own land in areas zoned for high intensity development receive economic benefits while those who own land principally in areas that have been zoned to limit development are economically hurt. The essence of a transferable development rights program is that a market is created where the development potential for parcels of property can be sold; thus, a parcel's development potential is separated from the parcel itself. Sending zones are created that allow only limited development. From these sending zones, transferable development rights are exported to receiving zones. More intense development is then permitted in the receiving zones than would otherwise be allowed under the general zoning regulations. As long as there is a viable market for the transferable development rights, one would expect that the owner of property in a sending zone (Owner A) should be able to identify a landowner in the receiving zone (Owner B) who would be interested in purchasing Owner A's transferable development rights so that Owner B could engage in a more intense development of his property than otherwise allowed. Thus, the negative economic effect on Owner A of owning property in an area zoned to limit development is tempered by Owner A's ability to sell development rights to Owner B.

4. Barriers to Judicial Relief—Ripeness. [§ 16–82]

It is not easy to bring a takings claim. The property owner must overcome the ripeness doctrine if the owner is going to be able to bring a regulatory takings claim against a state entity in federal court. First, the property owner must receive a final decision from the governmental entity that is charged with implementing the challenged land use regulation. According to the ripeness doctrine, a case is not ripe "until the government entity charged with implementing the regulations has reached a final decision regarding the application of the regulations to the property at issue." Second, if the state provides adequate procedures for seeking compensation, the property owner must use the state's inverse condemnation proceedings before initiating suit in federal court. (See Case Squib: *Williamson County Regional Planning Commission v. Hamilton Bank of Johnson City* and *Suitum v. Tahoe Regional Planning Agency*). The purpose of the finality requirement is to allow the court to determine whether a regulation has "gone too far" and therefore resulted in a taking. (See Case Squib: *Pennsylvania Coal v. Mahon*). The implementing entity's decision must be sufficiently definitive so that a court can determine the amount of development that will be permitted. Property owners must use available state inverse condemnation processes because, even if there is a taking, there is no Fifth Amendment violation if the state entity pays just compensation.

Property owners bringing facial takings claims are not subject to the ripeness doctrine because, by definition, the property owner is alleging that the mere enactment of the law, not the law's application to the property owner, results in a taking of the property. Neither are physical invasions subject to the ripeness doctrine because the scope of the taking is established by the physical taking itself. Thus, as-applied, regulatory takings actions require ripeness.

5. Judicial Takings. [§ 16–83]

As suggested by its name, the judicial takings doctrine inquires whether a state court decision that interprets state law can result in an unconstitutional taking or whether such decisions are exempt from takings jurisprudence. In other words, can takings of private property arise only from governmental and administrative acts and not from judicial acts? The United States Supreme Court has not directly answered the question though it did come close in a recent case, *Stop Beach Renourishment, Inc. v. Florida Dept. of Environmental Protection*. (See Case Squib). Several of the justices stated that judicial actions could constitute a taking under the Fifth Amendment; others argued that the issue might better be argued as a deprivation of procedural and substantive due process. None of the justices rejected, categorically, the notion of judicial takings.

REVIEW PROBLEMS—PUBLIC LAND USE CONTROL

Exams in property courses which cover public land use control law often include an issue on takings. Particularly, a student may need to analyze a hypothetical regulation to determine whether or not it constitutes a taking. The key to this type of question is to remember that there is no single test for determining a regulatory taking. Instead, the determination may require the application of factors such as interference with investment-backed expectations, or it might require the application of a categorical rule such as complete loss of all economic value. Keep in mind that a thorough analysis may require application of several tests.

> A wants to add a fourth floor to her existing three story home. A applies to the city for a permit to add this fourth story, and the city informs her that it will grant the permit only if she will dedicate to the city the 150 square feet in the northwest corner of her property. This portion of A's land includes a large oak tree, which is adjacent to the city's sidewalk. The city intends to place a bench under the tree so people walking on the sidewalk can have a seat in the shade and rest. A is not happy with the city's response, so she files suit arguing this permit condition constitutes a taking of her property without just compensation. What result?
>
> > **Answer:** A will probably be successful because there is no essential nexus between the city's interest in regulating house height and the exaction of A's oak tree. An exaction will constitute a taking unless there is an essential nexus between the state's interest and the exaction. Here, the city's interest in regulating house height is to avoid one home disrupting the view and light of another home. However, the city's desire for the oak tree does nothing to further this interest. Enhancing the community's walking experience is not related to the loss of view the community will experience from A's fourth floor. Therefore, this exaction is most likely a taking.

CHAPTER XVII

PRACTICE MULTIPLE CHOICE QUESTIONS

Questions 1–2 are based on the following fact situation.

Oscar, owner of a fee simple absolute in Blackacre, conveyed it to Anne and the male heirs of her body. Anne died leaving a will devising Blackacre to her only son, Bob. Bob conveyed Blackacre to the University of Florida "provided that the land be used as the site of a law school and if not so used it shall revert automatically."

1. In conveying the land to the University of Florida, Bob sought to retain

(A) a reversion.

(B) a right of re-entry.

(C) a possibility of reversion in a springing charitable use.

(D) a possibility of reverter.

2. In most states today, Bob's estate prior to his conveyance is

(A) a fee tail.

(B) a fee simple absolute.

(C) a fee simple conditional.

(D) a use upon a use.

Questions 3–5 are based on the following situation.

Oscar, owner of a fee simple absolute in Blackacre, conveyed it in 1986 to "Dew Drop Inn, Inc. for so long as it is used for tavern purposes, and if such use ever ceases then to Anne if living, and, if deceased, to my heirs."

Anne died in 1998, and Oscar died intestate in 1999 leaving Henry as his heir.

In 2000, the Dew Drop Inn lost its liquor license for selling intoxicating products to minors, and the Inn was padlocked. In 2002, Henry claims title to Blackacre and seeks to use the premises as a small commune for young people, but the Inn claims absolute title and plans to erect an office building.

3. The original conveyance gave Dew Drop Inn a

(A) fee simple subject to an executory interest.

(B) fee simple determinable.

(C) life estate since no words of limitation were used.

(D) fee simple subject to condition subsequent.

4. Under the original conveyance Anne acquired

(A) an executory interest because it is an interest created in a third person following a defeasible fee simple. It is valid under the Rule Against Perpetuities because it is certain to either vest or fail within Anne's lifetime.

(B) a contingent remainder.

(C) an executory interest which is invalid under the Rule Against Perpetuities because the condition of Blackacre not being used for tavern purposes might occur more than 21 years after the deaths of all relevant lives in being.

(D) a present fee simple subject to the rights of the Inn, which has a term of years of indefinite duration.

5. From the original conveyance, Oscar's heirs acquired

(A) a valid executory interest because Oscar's heirs will be determined at his death.

(B) an alternative contingent remainder which is valid under the Rule Against Perpetuities because no later than the deaths of Oscar and Anne they will know whether or not the land will cease to be used for tavern purposes.

(C) nothing since Oscar is alive and a living person has no heirs.

(D) nothing because of the Doctrine of Worthier Title.

Question 6

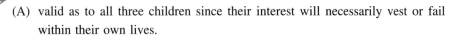

T to children of F who get to 30
F died 4, 7, 9

Testator devised Whiteacre "to the children of my brother Frank who attain the age of 30." Frank died one year before Testator and left three children, aged 4, 7 and 9. Regarding the Rule Against Perpetuities, the devise is

(A) valid as to all three children since their interest will necessarily vest or fail within their own lives.

(B) invalid as to all since the two youngest could take more than 21 years after the deaths of Frank and Testator, the measuring lives.

(C) valid as to the oldest but invalid as to the others.

(D) invalid as to all since there is no absolute certainty of vesting as to any one.

Questions 7–8 are based on the following facts.

Thomas wishes to operate a clothing store. In 2000, Thomas enters into a five-year lease with Laura for the use of a small building. Thomas does very well at first, but in 2003 his business drops off considerably after a new shopping mall is opened directly across the street from his store.

7. Thomas moves out of the premises in 2003. Which of the following would release Thomas from his obligations for the remaining period of the lease?

(A) Laura makes no attempt to find a new tenant although she could easily find a qualified replacement.

(B) Laura moves onto the premises and uses it as an office for the management of her rental properties.

(C) Laura finds a new tenant who agrees to pay the same rent, and Laura tells Thomas that she has relet the premises for his benefit.

(D) Laura finds a new tenant who agrees to pay a higher rent, and Laura tells Thomas that she has relet the premises for his benefit.

303

8. Assume that Thomas does not vacate, but instead attempts to transfer his remaining interest to Sally, a highly reliable businesswoman. If there is a provision in the Thomas–Laura lease prohibiting subleasing, the transfer is

(A) invalid as a sublease because it violates the Thomas–Laura lease.

(B) invalid even if it is not technically a sublease.

(C) valid because Sally is a reliable replacement.

(D) valid because the arrangement was an assignment and restraints on alienation are strictly construed.

Questions 9–10 are based on the following facts.

Landlord and Tenant entered into a lease of certain commercial premises for a period of five years, with Tenant having an option to renew for successive five-year periods for a total of 20 years. The rental was $500 per month plus a percentage of the gross receipts. The lease provided that Tenant would use the premises as a retail hardware store, that Tenant would not operate another hardware store within a radius of five miles of the existing store, and that Landlord would not lease any premises within a radius of five miles to be used for a hardware store. Another clause provided that all covenants would run with the land and would be binding on successors to the original parties. Thereafter, Tenant assigned the lease to Anne, and Landlord sold her reversion to Roberta.

9. Anne fell into arrears in her rent during the original five-year term. Which of the following alternatives best describes the rights and obligations of the parties?

(A) Roberta may sue either Tenant or Anne for the rent.

(B) Roberta may sue only Tenant for the rent.

(C) Roberta may sue only Anne for the rent.

(D) Landlord, but not Roberta, may sue either Tenant or Anne for the rent.

10. After Tenant assigned to Anne and Landlord sold to Roberta, assume that Roberta leased another parcel of land within the five-mile radius to Xavier for the purpose of operating a hardware store. Assume also that this other parcel was owned by Roberta when she purchased the original hardware store from Landlord. Which of the following states the best legally sustainable solution to the Roberta–Anne controversy?

(A) Anne has no right to relief because in a landlord-tenant relationship the covenant runs only with the reversion and leasehold, not with other land.

(B) Anne can recover damages in a suit at law because non-competition covenants are especially favored.

(C) The non-competition agreement between Landlord and Tenant is not illegal, and therefore subsequent parties taking with notice of the lease's provisions may be bound in equity by such provisions.

(D) Non-competition agreements do not touch and concern the land, therefore Anne has no remedy.

Questions 11–14 are based on the following facts.

Anne and Bob were owners of adjacent tracts of 200 acres of farm land. In 1995, in order to preserve as much rural atmosphere as possible, they entered into a written agreement whereby each promised the other that their respective parcels of land would not be used for other than agricultural or recreational purposes for a period of 50 years, and that no more than five families should be permitted to dwell on either parcel during such period. Both parties agreed to not permit their respective parcels to be used for any type of housing development or home subdivision purpose, and that the obligations thereto would be binding on both parties, their heirs, successors, and assigns, and for the benefit of the respective other party, his heirs, successors, and assigns. A copy of the agreement was recorded and indexed under both Anne–Bob and Bob–Anne in the official indexes.

In 1998, Anne sold her land to Cathy. In 2000, Bob sold his land to Don. Cathy is using her land for agricultural purposes. Don, however, plans to convert the former farm into a community of a thousand dwelling units. Cathy alleges that this would spoil the rural tranquility of the neighborhood, and seeks your advice.

11.   If Cathy seeks an injunction against Don, which is the most correct statement?

(A) Cathy would be unsuccessful because there is no privity of estate between Cathy and Don.

(B) Because Cathy seeks an injunction and not money damages, privity of estate is not required.

(C) In equity, it is not necessary to have privity of estate for the benefit to run, but it is necessary for the burden to run. Hence, Cathy could sue Bob if Bob were still the owner and about to breach, but she cannot sue Don.

(D) In equity, it is not necessary to have privity of estate for the burden to run, but it is necessary for the benefit to run. Hence, Anne could have sued Don if Anne had not sold to Bob, but Bob cannot sue Don.

12. If Cathy seeks money damages from Don, which is the most correct statement?

(A) Privity of estate is satisfied since there has been succession to the respective estates of the covenanting parties.

(B) Privity of estate is not satisfied since there was no transfer of an interest between Anne and Bob at the time the covenant was entered into.

(C) Privity of estate is no longer required for a covenant to run at law.

(D) Privity of estate is not required if the covenant touches and concerns the land.

13. Insofar as the requirement that the benefit and burden touch and concern the land

(A) the benefit does not touch and concern the land since if the covenant is allowed to run, subsequent parties are deprived of the increase in value of the land resulting from a change in use.

(B) the burden does not touch and concern the land because the covenant is negative in character.

(C) both the burden and benefit touch and concern the land because each party thereto has a benefit of a right to rural tranquility, and a burden restricting the uses to be made of the land.

(D) touch and concern is not required to enforce the covenant in equity.

14. Regarding the parties' intent that the benefit and burden run

(A) the agreement indicates that the burden is to run, but not the benefit.

(B) the agreement indicates that the benefit is to run, but not the burden.

(C) the agreement indicates that both the benefit and burden are to run.

(D) regardless of intent, neither the benefit nor the burden can run because the law will not sanction any new and unusual property interests and the agreement does not constitute an easement.

Questions 15–19 are based on the following facts.

In 1975, Conrad, owner of Blackacre, bought from Sam a lot and cottage on the ocean which was part of adjacent Whiteacre. The deed contained the following language: "Excepting, however, unto the said grantor, his heirs, and assigns forever, the right to use said land for launching boats."

The distance by road from Conrad's house on Blackacre to the cottage is two miles. By crossing Whiteacre the distance is one-half mile. Consequently, Conrad asked Sam: "Can my family and I cross over Whiteacre to get to our cottage?" Sam answered: "You sure can, anytime." Conrad and his family walked across Whiteacre practically every weekend until 1980 when Conrad sold and transferred Blackacre and the cottage to Barbara.

Barbara and her family walked over Whiteacre almost every weekend since acquiring Blackacre, and at the same place where Conrad's family had worn a path.

In 2001, Sam sold Whiteacre to Harry. Harry recently told Barbara that she and her family must stop crossing over Whiteacre.

15. The initial interest of Sam to launch boats from Whiteacre is best described as

(A) a license.

(B) an easement by implied reservation.

(C) an easement by express reservation.

(D) an easement by express grant.

16. If Sam seeks to use Barbara's land to launch boats, his strongest argument is that

(A) since the cottage lot on the ocean is not adjacent to Whiteacre, the easement cannot be appurtenant.

(B) since the initial easement was created by express reservation, the easement must be in gross.

(C) since the original easement was for recreational purposes, it must be in gross.

(D) since the easement could be beneficial to Sam wherever he lives and since there is no showing of an intent to benefit Whiteacre instead of Sam as an individual, the easement is in gross.

17. If Harry seeks to use Barbara's land to launch boats, Barbara's strongest argument is that

(A) easements are not assignable.

(B) Harry has not acquired an easement unless the easement was mentioned in the deed because an easement must be transferred by a written instrument.

(C) the fact that Sam is still claiming the right to use the easement after he sold Whiteacre indicates that Sam intended an easement in gross when the easement was created.

(D) the transfer of Whiteacre to Harry without including the easement would amount to an attempted severance of an appurtenant easement and would thereby destroy it.

18. Which of the following best describes Conrad's original right to cross Whiteacre?

(A) Although the permission was oral, it can be regarded as ancillary to the sale of the cottage land, and is therefore an easement appurtenant to such land.

(B) Since Whiteacre lies between Blackacre and the cottage land, the use of Whiteacre by the owner of Blackacre to reach the cottage land may be regarded as an easement by implication created in connection with the sale of the cottage land.

(C) The oral permission resulted initially in Conrad obtaining a revocable license.

(D) When Conrad transferred Blackacre to Barbara, Barbara also acquired the license to cross Whiteacre since a license, not being an interest in land, need not be transferred in writing.

19. If Barbara seeks a court order requiring Harry to allow Barbara and her family to cross Whiteacre, which of the following arguments is most likely to aid Barbara

in establishing that she had a prescriptive easement (assuming a 20–year statutory period)?

(A) Even though the use was initially permissive, such use became adverse when the sale occurred and therefore could give rise to a prescriptive easement.

(B) The sale of Blackacre to Barbara had no effect on the permissive character of the use since Barbara's family continued such use.

(C) Tacking of periods of adverse use is permitted in the acquisition of prescriptive easements.

(D) Since the acquisition of a prescriptive easement requires that the use be continuous, without interruption, and with the knowledge of the servient owner, it is clear that such an easement may result from the continuous exercise of a license.

Questions 20–23 are based on the following facts.

Rancher executed a will devising Blackacre, a cattle farm, to his cousin, Mabel, in exchange for her promise to move into his home and care for him for life. Thereafter, Mabel moved into Rancher's home, but finding him mentally incompetent, had him committed to a state institution. Mabel remained in the home from 1958 until Rancher died in 1960.

Harry, Rancher's only child and heir, qualified as administrator of Rancher's intestate estate and paid Mabel $50,000 in satisfaction of her claim to Blackacre. Mabel did not offer the will for probate but nevertheless leased Blackacre to various livestock dealers between 1960 and 1985, refusing to pay any of the rent to Harry. She also remained in the home, moving her furniture in to replace the furniture removed by Harry. Mabel allowed Harry to visit the home at intervals "as a guest." Mabel paid all taxes for both Blackacre and the home.

In 1985, Harry contracts to sell both Blackacre and the home to Erik. After making this contract, Erik comes to you for advice. You determine that the will in favor of Mabel is invalid because it is clear that Rancher was mentally incompetent at the time of execution.

A state statute imposes a 20–year limitation on land recoveries.

20. Mabel's best chance of being deemed the owner of Blackacre and prevailing over Harry is to

309

(A) rely on the doctrine of adverse possession.

(B) claim as a devisee under the will because at the time it was executed Rancher was not an adjudicated incompetent.

(C) seek specific performance of the contract to devise Blackacre based on Mabel's partial performance.

(D) ask the court to impose a constructive trust to prevent unjust enrichment.

21. Insofar as adverse possession of the home is concerned

(A) the statute of limitations began to run in 1958 when Mabel moved in and had Rancher committed.

(B) the statute of limitations never began to run since the possession began in subordination of Rancher's title, and a permissive possession never ripens into title no matter how long it continues.

(C) the inception of the possession could not be regarded as permissive or in subordination of Rancher's title since he was in fact incompetent and could not give permission.

(D) Mabel's continued possession of the home after Rancher's death in 1960 and the satisfaction of her claim against his estate might be regarded as the assertion of an adverse title and may therefore start the running of the statute of limitations.

22. Which of the following would be most damaging to Mabel's claim of adverse possession of Blackacre?

(A) Mabel never used Blackacre for her own benefit since it was leased to others at all times.

(B) Harry never demanded that Mabel turn the leasing fees over to him.

(C) Harry had orally told Mabel that she could use Blackacre for her own purposes for as long as she lived.

(D) Harry and Mabel maintained a close personal relationship throughout the entire period and thus there was no hostile possession of Blackacre.

23. Which of the following best describes Erik's rights with regard to the two parcels?

(A) Since an adverse possessory title is unmarketable, Erik is perfectly safe in buying from Harry even if Mabel has acquired title by adverse possession.

(B) Erik could accept a deed from Harry. Because there is no will or other instrument recorded purporting to give any interest in either parcel to Mabel, Harry has marketable record title.

(C) Harry, as heir, is the owner of both parcels and therefore can convey good title.

(D) Erik may refuse to accept any deeds from Harry unless Harry can provide similar valid deeds from Mabel.

Questions 24–25 are based on the following situation.

Owner and Purchaser entered into a written contract for the sale of Blackacre, a parcel of land improved with a residence. The sale price was $150,000, with $15,000 to be paid upon signing the contract and the balance to be paid upon delivery of the deed within 60 days. Owner remained in possession.

Before the closing, the house was struck by lightning and burned to the ground. The house was worth $100,000; the land $50,000. Owner was covered by insurance to the extent of $70,000; Purchaser had no insurance.

After the fire, Purchaser demanded the return of her deposit and asserted that the transaction was rescinded because the subject matter of the contract was largely destroyed. Owner counterclaimed for specific performance without an abatement of the purchase price.

24. Which of the following arguments will afford Owner the best chance of success?

(A) Purchaser's claim is without merit since the subject matter of the sale is Blackacre, a parcel of realty, and the parcel is still in existence; therefore there was no destruction of the subject matter.

(B) Purchaser had an insurable interest as a result of her purchase contract, and if she neglected to insure against casualty loss, that is her problem.

(C) Since Purchaser could have sued for specific performance of the agreement to sell, Purchaser was in fact the beneficial owner of the real estate and is subject to all fluctuations in value, decreases as well as increases.

311

(D) The doctrine of equitable conversion regards the purchaser as the owner and, therefore, the risk bearer.

25. Assume for the purposes of this question that there is a statute placing the risk of loss on the purchaser, and that the insurance company had paid $70,000 to the vendor for the loss of the building prior to the litigation between Owner and Purchaser. Which of the following alternatives best describes the likely result of the Owner v. Purchaser litigation and all other related disputes?

(A) Purchaser is required to purchase Blackacre without any abatement of the purchase price, and the insurance company cannot recover the $70,000 paid to Owner since Owner had an insurable interest at the time of the loss.

(B) Purchaser is required to purchase Blackacre without an abatement of the purchase price, and the insurance company can recover the $70,000 paid to Owner since Owner will suffer no loss from the fire.

(C) Purchaser is required to purchase Blackacre, but with a $70,000 abatement of the purchase price, the insurance proceeds being regarded as a substitute for the house which was destroyed.

(D) Purchaser is required to purchase Blackacre, but with a $100,000 abatement of the purchase price, since Owner was underinsured.

Questions 26–29 are based on the following facts.

On January 10, 1981, Adam conveyed Blackacre for valuable consideration, to Bob by a quitclaim deed. Record title to the land was in Adam, but at all relevant times Diane was in actual possession of Blackacre under a claim of title adverse to Adam.

On January 11, 1986, Bob, who never attempted to enter into possession of Blackacre, conveyed it for valuable consideration to Charles by a general warranty deed in the usual form.

When Charles attempted to obtain possession of Blackacre, he was met with Diane's claim of title, which a court of competent jurisdiction sustained on an adverse possession theory. Both Bob and Adam had notice of this action, but neither interceded on Charles' behalf.

26. Charles now brings an action against Bob. Which of the following is the most likely result?

(A) Charles will lose because the general warranty deed from Bob contained only those warranties given by Bob's grantor; since Adam gave no covenants to Bob, Bob gave no covenants to Charles.

(B) Charles will lose because Diane's rights existed before Charles obtained the land and thus any breach of a covenant took place before he obtained any rights in Blackacre.

(C) Charles will win because he had notice of Diane's rights and thus took subject to them.

(D) Charles will win because general warranty deeds normally include all of the common law covenants for title.

27. Assuming the Bob-to-Charles deed included the covenant of right to convey and that Diane acquired title by adverse possession in 1985, if Charles sues Bob he will

(A) lose, because the covenant of right to convey does not require that the grantor be in possession.

(B) lose, because Bob did not breach the covenant at the time of his conveyance since Diane's title had not yet been judicially determined.

(C) lose, because the covenant of seisin and the covenant of right to convey are synonymous.

(D) win.

28. Assuming that Diane acquired title by adverse possession in 1985, which of the following is the most likely result if Charles sues Adam?

(A) Charles can recover from Adam because the covenant of seisin runs with the land.

(B) Charles can recover from Adam on the covenant of seisin because Diane's title relates back to her original entry.

(C) Charles cannot recover from Adam because Adam conveyed by quitclaim deed.

(D) Charles cannot recover from Adam because there was no privity of contract between them.

29.   Assume for this question that Adam gave Bob a deed containing a covenant of general warranty and that Diane acquired title by adverse possession in 1980, which of the following states the probable result if Charles sues Adam?

(A) Charles cannot recover because the covenant of general warranty does not run with the land.

(B) Charles cannot recover because Diane's claim is not a claim through Adam.

(C) Charles cannot recover because Diane's title did not exist until after Adam conveyed.

(D) Charles can recover because Adam breached his covenant to Bob.

Question 30

Oscar, owner of Blackacre, prepared a deed which on its face transferred Blackacre to Anne. Oscar handed the deed to Xavier to be given to Anne after Oscar's death. Which of the following instructions to Xavier would most likely result in a determination of a valid delivery?

(A) "Unless you hear from me to the contrary, give this deed to Anne in case I die."

(B) "I am giving Blackacre to Anne. Give her this deed when I die."

(C) "I want Anne to have Blackacre after I am gone. Give her this deed after my death."

(D) "I am about to undertake a dangerous mission. If anything should happen to me, that is, if I should be killed, give this deed to Anne."

Questions 31–32 are based on the following fact situation.

Xavier has good title to Blackacre. Xavier conveys a fee to Anne. Then Xavier deeds the mineral rights to Bob. Finally, Xavier executes a mortgage to Cathy. After the mortgage to Cathy, Anne records her deed, then Bob records his deed and Cathy records her mortgage. Assume that Anne, Bob, and Cathy have no actual notice of each others' interests.

31.   Cathy brings suit to quiet title to Blackacre. Assuming that Blackacre is in a notice jurisdiction, what is the result?

(A) Anne would take because her deed is superior in time.

(B) The court would either partition the fee or make Anne, Bob and Cathy tenants in common.

(C) Cathy would take a fee because the last party to take without notice prevails in a notice jurisdiction regardless of the order of recording.

(D) Cathy's mortgage interest would prevail over the interest of both Anne and Bob. Anne would own the fee, but subject to the mortgage of Cathy and the mineral rights of Bob.

32.   Assume the same facts as in question 31, except that Blackacre is located in a race-notice jurisdiction. What is the result?

(A) Anne would take only the surface fee subject to Cathy's mortgage and Bob's rights to the minerals.

(B) Cathy would take because she is the last to take and had no notice of Anne and Bob.

(C) Anne would take because the other parties had record notice of her interest.

(D) Anne would take because her conveyance is prior in time.

Question 33

Vernon and Paul entered into a written contract for Blackacre. The contract was silent concerning the quality of title to be conveyed and the type of deed to be employed.

In checking the title, Paul's attorney discovered that Xavier had an outstanding right to all minerals that might underlie the land, and an unused but legally created 30–foot easement of ingress and egress through the middle of the parcel.

Paul planned to excavate a large lake in the center of the tract and use the fill for developing roads and homesites. Paul demanded that Vernon obtain releases of all subsurface rights to minerals and of the right of way across the center of the tract, and he stated that unless Vernon obtained the necessary releases within 60 days, he would regard the contract as terminated and demand a return of the down payment. Vernon refused to attempt to obtain such releases.

Which of the following alternatives best describes the rights of the parties?

(A) Paul's demand is unreasonable because the contract contained no warranty as to Vernon's title, and warranties are not implied into the sales of real estate.

(B) Paul is required to consummate the sale, but is entitled to a warranty deed. If he suffers a loss as a result of title defects, he can then sue Vernon for breach of warranty.

(C) Paul is entitled to the relief demanded because every contract for the sale of realty, unless otherwise provided, implies that the vendor will have marketable title, and 60 days is a reasonable time for the vendor to cure such defects.

(D) Paul is entitled to the relief only if he can show that there is a strong possibility that the outstanding interest will be exercised.

Questions 34–36 require you to classify the quoted recording acts as one of the following types:

(A) Race.

(B) Notice.

(C) Race-notice.

(D) Period of grace.

34. "No conveyance, transfer or mortgage of real property shall be good and effectual in law or equity against subsequent purchasers for a valuable consideration and without notice unless the same be recorded according to law."

35. "Every conveyance of real estate which shall not be recorded as hereinafter provided shall be void as against any subsequent purchaser in good faith and for a valuable consideration of the same real estate whose conveyance shall be first duly recorded."

36. "No conveyance of land shall be valid to pass any property as against lien creditors or purchasers for a valuable consideration from the donor or grantor but from the time of registration thereof."

Questions 37–39 are based on the following facts.

Oscar, owner of Blackacre, executes and delivers to Anne a deed conveying Blackacre to Anne. Anne does not record. Oscar then executes and delivers to Bob a deed to the same land, and Bob purchases with knowledge of Anne's prior unrecorded deed. Bob records his deed and then executes and delivers to Cathy a deed to the same land and Cathy purchases without knowledge of Anne's prior unrecorded deed. Anne then records. Cathy then records.

37.   In a jurisdiction having a notice type recording statute, which of the following alternatives states the probable result in a contest between Anne and Cathy?

(A) Anne prevails because Bob had notice of Anne's deed and Cathy can get no better title than Bob had.

(B) Anne prevails because Anne recorded before Cathy.

(C) Cathy prevails because she was a subsequent bona fide purchaser without notice and Anne had not recorded at the time Cathy purchased.

(D) Cathy prevails because since Bob recorded first, Bob prevailed against Anne.

38.   In a jurisdiction having a race-notice recording statute, which of the following states the probable result in a contest between Anne and Cathy?

(A) Anne wins because she was the first grantee.

(B) Anne wins because Bob purchased with notice of Anne's deed.

(C) Cathy prevails because she was a subsequent bona fide purchaser without notice and Anne had not recorded when Cathy purchased.

(D) Cathy prevails because since Bob recorded first, Bob prevailed against Anne.

39.   In a jurisdiction with a race recording statute, which of the following states the probable result in a contest between Anne and Cathy?

(A) Anne wins because she was first in time and she perfected her title by eventually recording.

(B) Anne wins because Bob was not a bona fide purchaser.

(C) Cathy wins because she took from Bob, who had better title than Anne.

317

(D) Since Bob's deed was already recorded, Cathy wins because Anne could not be a bona fide purchaser when Anne recorded.

ANSWERS TO THE MULTIPLE CHOICE QUESTIONS

Note: Remember that on multiple choice exams you are normally asked to choose the "best" answer and not the "absolutely correct" or "only correct" answer.

Answer to Question 1.

(D) is the best choice.

Since Bob used words of limitation in the grant, he expressly granted less than a fee simple absolute to the University, and retained a future interest pursuant to which the property will automatically revert to him should the specified event (use for other than a law school site) occur. Such a future interest is a possibility of reverter. Answers A & B name other future interests. Option C is a non-existent interest.

Answer to Question 2.

(B) is the best choice.

The language used by Oscar would have created a fee tail at common law, but most jurisdictions have abolished the fee tail and such language is construed to create a fee simple absolute. Therefore Anne received a fee simple absolute and devised the same to Bob. In a few states, Anne received a life estate and Bob received a fee simple absolute. Answer A would have been correct at common law but not today. Answer C refers to an interest which has not existed since the 13th Century. Answer D has no relevance.

Answer to Question 3.

(A) is the best choice.

B and D are incorrect because upon the occurrence of the defeasible event (when the land is no longer used as a tavern), the right to possession shifts to a third party rather than returning to the Grantor as is the case with a fee simple determinable or a fee simple upon condition subsequent. C is incorrect because words of limitation **are** used. This leaves A as the best answer because it correctly recognizes that the fee is subject to an executory interest.

Answer to Question 4.

(A) is the best choice.

There can be no remainder after a fee simple of any kind; hence the interest is an executory interest. Since Anne would only take if living, the interest would vest if at all within her own lifetime and is therefore valid under the Rule Against Perpetuities. Answers B and D specify incorrect estates and Answer C misapplies the RAP.

Answer to Question 5.

(D) is the best choice.

A limitation in favor of the heirs of the grantor in an inter vivos conveyance is void under the Doctrine of Worthier Title. Answers A, B and C mislabel the interests created and ignore the doctrine of Worthier Title.

Answer to Question 6.

(A) is the best choice.

The will of Testator takes effect at his death, and at that time Frank was already dead and could have no more children. Therefore, the existing children of Frank are the only relevant lives, and they will take or fail to take within their own lives which satisfies the RAP. Options B, C and D could result only from incorrect applications of the RAP.

Answer to Question 7.

(B) is the best choice.

Use of the premises for the landlord's own benefit constitutes acceptance of a surrender. Option A is incorrect because at common law the landlord has no duty to relet the premises. Although there is such an obligation today, its breach normally affects only damages and not termination of the lease. Options C and D are incorrect as reletting is not a surrender of the landlord's rights if she notifies the tenant that she has relet the premises for his benefit.

Answer to Question 8.

(D) is the best choice.

Because Thomas purported to transfer his entire remaining interest, the transfer was an assignment, not a sublease. As correctly stated in option D, a prohibition of a sublease is not a prohibition of an assignment.

Answer to Question 9.

(A) is the best choice.

Tenant remains liable for rent based on privity of contract, and Anne is liable based on privity of estate. When Landlord transferred the reversion of Roberta, she should be regarded as also assigning the right under the original lease, to sue Tenant for rent. B, C and D misapply the rules relating to assignments and are based upon an incorrect assumption that this is a sublease.

Answer to Question 10.

(C) is the best choice.

While the covenant probably cannot be enforced at law because of the reason given in choice A, the burden of a covenant can be enforced in equity as a servitude against one taking with notice. Options B and D are incorrect statements of law.

Answer to Question 11.

(B) is the best choice.

An action for an injunction is an action in equity and privity of estate is not necessary for either the benefit or burden of a covenant to run in equity. Option A incorrectly applies legal and not equitable principles. Options C and D incorrectly state the rules in equity.

Answer to Question 12.

(B) is the best choice.

An action for money damages is an action at law. A is correct under the minority rule, but B accurately states the majority position that horizontal privity is required at law. Options C and D are incorrect statements of the majority and minority and minority positions.

Answer to Question 13.

(C) is the best choice.

Both the benefit and burden affect the respective parties as owners of the particular land, and hence they touch and concern the land. Option D is an incorrect statement of law and option A does not correspond to the facts given.

Answer to Question 14.

(C) is the best choice.

The use of "heirs, successors, and assigns" as to both the benefit and burden indicates an intent that both should run. Options A and B are factually unsupportable and option D makes no sense.

Answer to Question 15.

(C) is the best choice.

Since the deed specifically reserves in the grantor the right to use the land of the grantee, it is an easement by express reservation. That the deed used the word "excepting" rather than "reserving" is irrelevant. Option A is incorrect because the interest satisfies the requirements for easements not the requirements for a license which is a revocable interest. Option B is incorrect on the facts, i.e. the easement is expressed and therefore cannot be and need not be implied. Option D is incorrect because a "grant" creates an interest in a grantee not a grantor.

Answer to Question 16.

(D) is the best choice.

Option A is wrong on the facts, and options B and C are incorrect statements of law. Option D applies easement principles to the facts in the way most favorable to Sam.

Answer to Question 17.

(C) is the best choice.

This does not guarantee that Barbara will win, but it is her best argument since A, B and D are incorrect statements of law.

Answer to Question 18.

(C) is the best choice.

This is the only possible choice. A license is generally not transferable; there are insufficient facts to demonstrate the required necessity for an easement by implication; and an easement cannot be created by oral permission. Options A, B and D are therefore based on incorrect statements of the law of easements.

Answer to Question 19.

(A) is the best choice.

The sale automatically revoked any preexisting license; hence under this rationale, contrary to the principle in answer B, these would become adverse after the sale. C is wrong because even though tacking is permitted, Conrad's use was permissive, not adverse, (also, tacking is unnecessary since Barbara, alone, used the path for more than 20 years). D is wrong because a prescriptive easement cannot result from the exercise of a license.

Answer to Question 20.

(A) is the best choice.

Adverse possession seems to be her only chance because of Rancher's incompetence when the will was executed and also probably at the time of the contract. Since Mabel had Rancher committed, she hardly carried out her contractual obligations of caring for him for the rest of his life. So option C is not supported by the facts. Option D would require facts to support unjust enrichment of Harry but none are given.

Answer to Question 21.

(D) is the best choice.

The essence of adverseness is that the owner has a cause of action against the possessor. Harry's cause of action against Mabel arose in 1960 after Mabel was paid for services rendered in favor of the deceased Rancher. It was also at this time that she took possession of Blackacre and leased it. Note that choice D says that the statute might start to run, not that it definitely would. The court could conceivably go either way on adverseness, but choice D is the best choice, since option A ignores probable tolling of the statute due to Harry's incompetence and options B and C relate to the less plausible theory that Mabel satisfied adverse possession requirements against Rancher.

Answer to Question 22.

(C) is the best choice.

Oral permission is sufficient to show that there was no adverse possession. Options A, B and D are not supported by the facts.

Answer to Question 23.

(D) is the best choice.

Since there is at least a reasonable possibility that Mabel has acquired title by adverse possession, Harry does not have marketable title. Answers A, B and C are incorrect conclusions of law and facts.

Answer to Question 24.

(D) is the best choice.

Traditionally, the doctrine of equitable conversion regarded the purchaser under an enforceable contract to convey as the equitable owner of the real estate and the risk bearer. Note that answers B and C are also correct, but D is better because of its reference to the doctrine of equitable conversion. A is also a possible argument but not as likely to prevail today as at earlier common law.

Answer to Question 25.

(C) is the best choice.

Under this alternative, the risk of loss is placed on P as the law of the jurisdiction requires, but the insurance company is not let off the hook, nor is the seller enabled to keep a windfall profit. Thus, this solution provides the most equitable results. Option A, B and D result in less fair treatment of the parties.

Answer to Question 26.

(D) is the best choice.

While covenants are not implied, a general warranty deed in the usual form contains the normal warranties of title. Answers A, B and C are based on incorrect statements of law and facts.

Answer to Question 27.

(D) is the best choice.

While the covenant of right to convey does not require the grantor to be in possession, it does require him to have good title. Diane had good title in 1985 regardless of whether there had been a judicial determination of this fact and regardless of whether she had marketable title. Answers A, B and C incorrectly apply the legal principles just explained.

Answer to Question 28.

(C) is the best choice.

Adam conveyed by quitclaim deed which means he gave no title warranties but simply transferred his interest, if any, in Blackacre. Answers A and B are incorrect statements of law. Answer D is incorrect because privity of contract is irrelevant.

Answer to Question 29.

D) is the best choice.

Contrary to the statements in Answers A and B, the general warranty covenant does run with the land and does not require that the displacing party claim through the covenantor. Option C is wrong on the facts.

Answer to Question 30.

(B) is the best choice.

There is no contingency here except the time of death. Thus, the effect of the deed is to immediately vest in the grantee a valid future interest. It could be construed as either a springing executory interest or a vested remainder with Oscar reserving a life estate. The statements in answers A, C and D do not indicate an intent to immediately and irrevocably vest a future interest in Blackacre in Anne at the time of the physical delivery to Xavier.

Answer to Question 31.

(D) is the best choice.

A notice statute provides that an unrecorded instrument is invalid as against a subsequent bona fide purchaser without notice. For the bona fide purchaser to prevail, it is not necessary that she record first. Cathy was the last party to take without notice, and thus has the best claim to title among the parties. Answers A, B and C are contrary to the rules of law in a notice jurisdiction.

Answer to Question 32.

(D) is the best choice.

Under a race-notice statute, a subsequent bona fide purchaser must record first in order to prevail against a prior grantee. Since neither Bob nor Cathy qualify as a BFP who recorded first, the statute does not apply and the common law rule of first in time first in right applies to give Anne an unencumbered fee simple absolute. Answers A, B and C violate the rule just stated.

Answer to Question 33.

(C) is the best choice.

Unless otherwise expressed, there is an implied obligation for the seller to furnish marketable title. Unless excepted from such requirement, the existence of the easement and the mineral rights would render the title unmarketable and interfere with the purchaser's intended use of the land. Answers A, B and D are incorrect statements of the law.

Answer to Question 34.

(B) is the best choice.

The essence of a notice statute is that an unrecorded instrument is invalid as against a subsequent bona fide purchaser without notice. For the bona fide purchaser to prevail, he need not record first. The statute quoted expresses the principles and therefore answers

Answer to Question 35.

(C) is the best choice.

Under this statute, the subsequent bona fide purchaser must also record first in order to prevail against a prior grantee. The key is the phrase "whose conveyance shall be first duly recorded." This is the essence of a race notice statute and therefore answers A, B and D cannot be correct.

Answer to Question 36.

(A) is the best choice.

This statute says that a conveyance shall not be valid to pass title as against creditors and purchasers unless it is recorded. Hence, as to those persons, recording is essential for the conveyance to become operative. Note that it is not necessary for the purchaser for value to be either bona fide or without notice in order to prevail against an unrecorded instrument. This is the essence of a race statute and therefore answers B, C and D cannot be correct.

Answer to Question 37.

(C) is the best choice.

Although Anne would have prevailed over Bob since Bob had notice, Cathy became a subsequent bona fide purchaser relying on the recorded chain of title and without notice of Anne's claim. Hence, Cathy prevails over Anne. Answers A, B and D incorrectly apply notice jurisdiction rules.

·Answer to Question 38.

(C) is the best choice.

Although Bob would not have prevailed over Anne because Bob had notice, Cathy does qualify as a subsequent bona fide purchaser as in question 37. The problem is whether Cathy can satisfy the requirement of first recording when in fact Anne deposited her deed with the recorder before Cathy did. Giving due regard to the mechanics of tracing title through grantor-grantee indices, "who first records" should be construed as meaning the first chain of title to be recorded. Anne's deed should be subordinated to Cathy's claim because it was recorded out of the chain of title. A, B, and D are either incorrect or ignore the requirements of "bona fide purchaser" and "first to record."

Answer to Question 39.

(C) is the best choice.

In a race jurisdiction, although Bob had notice, he perfected title when he recorded; thus, he could pass title to Cathy. Answers A, B and D all incorrectly state the law in a race jurisdiction.

CHAPTER XVIII

PRACTICE ESSAY QUESTIONS AND SUGGESTED ANSWERS

Question 1

Shortly after a recent tornado in Atlanta, Mr. DuBois was walking across a vacant lot owned by Mr. Ricard. Having traversed the lot about half way Mr. DuBois' attention was caught by something shiny in the rubble, doubtlessly strewn there by the tornado. The shiny object turned out to be a very nice and only slightly damaged silver tray. DuBois took the tray that same day to the nearby Lion d'Or Jewelry Store to have the tray repaired and his initials placed thereon. The personnel of the jewelry store repaired the tray but not having operative engraving equipment took it to the O'Hara Engraving Co. to have the initials placed thereon. While the tray was at the O'Hara establishment, a jeweler from the nearby Lion d'Argent Jewelry Store, a tornado damaged establishment in the same area, saw the tray and identified it as one kept at his shop for the past five years for a customer who had not yet returned to claim it. The Lion d'Argent demanded its return. Before any action was taken in respect to the tray the O'Hara establishment burned down and the tray perished.

Write a memorandum of law discussing the rights and liabilities of the parties involved. [Incidentally, you learn as part of your investigation of the matter that when DuBois left the tray at the Lion d'Or he was given a claim check which had printed on it "Not responsible for loss caused by fire or theft."]

Question 2

A, owner of Blackacre and B, owner of Whiteacre, entered into a contract whereby each promised that all development on their respective parcels would be residential. This contract was recorded.

A conveyed a fee simple absolute interest in Blackacre to C, who leased the eastern half of Blackacre to D for 30 years and the western half to E for 30 years. D immediately transferred all of his interest to F, and E immediately transferred all of her interest to G for 20 years.

B conveyed a life estate in Whiteacre to X.

F and G are now in the process of installing a cattle feedlot on Blackacre. X consults you as his attorney and asks what rights and remedies are available to him. Advise X.

Question 3

O, owner of Blackacre, conveys Blackacre to A, who does not record the deed. O subsequently conveys Blackacre to B for valuable consideration. B has no knowledge of A's deed. A records, then B records. Thereafter, B sells the western half of Blackacre to C, and the eastern half back to O. Who owns Blackacre and why?

Question 4

O owned a building in State of Paradise, USA. The building contained an impressive law office suite on the ground floor and a residential dwelling unit on the second floor. In 1970, O leased the premises for a total rental payment of $20,000, payable on execution of the lease, "to my daughters L and M as joint tenants, for a period of thirty years from the date hereof provided that the building continue to be devoted to its current use." From 1970 to 1980, L and M, who were sisters, occupied the premises jointly—practicing law downstairs and living upstairs. In 1980, L and M had a terrible disagreement and M moved to Hawaii. Until 1985, L continued to occupy the building as before.

In 1985, L leased the building to S, another lawyer, for a monthly rental of $5,000. The lease specified that the lease would be automatically renewed each month S tendered and L accepted the rental payment. In 1990, a hurricane damaged the roof of the building. S requested that L and O repair the roof, but both refused on the ground that both leases were silent regarding the landlord's repair obligations. S moved out of the upstairs rooms because of the leaking roof, but continued to occupy and use the law office. S reduced his monthly rent payments to $1,000.

Three months ago, S moved out completely and informed L and O that he was terminating the lease because of the roof. Last month, L sued S for unpaid and future rent. L died last week, leaving X as her sole heir and devisee. M has consulted you regarding her rights and liabilities in relation to O, X, and S. Please advise her.

Question 5

Professor V. Feudal, a famous future interests professor, died last week. In her validly drafted and executed will, she left all of her property "to my children A and B and the heirs of their bodies provided that they continue to reside in the State of Paradise. If they ever cease to do so, then title to my property shall go to Kumquat University Foundation." Professor Feudal was survived by her children A and B, A's son X, and B's daughter Y. Professor Feudal owned the following items of property, all of which were specifically mentioned in the will which was executed just a few hours prior to her death:

1) Georgia O'Keefe's painting "Seaweed."

2) $100,000 in cash.

3) Blackswamp (100 acres of real estate that I purchased from Farmer Jones).

4) Greenswamp (a 1000 acre tract of land "which I have been adversely possessing 100 acres in the southwest corner for the past 22 years.)

5) A railcar full of fresh strawberries.

Professor Feudal's children and grandchildren and the Kumquat University Foundation have come to you for your opinion as to what interests, if any, they have inherited. Please advise them. In making your analysis, please remember that Paradise has a statute providing:

> No property, real or personal, shall be entailed in this state. Any instrument purporting to create an estate tail, express or implied, shall be deemed to create an estate for life in the first taker with remainder per stirpes to the lineal descendants of the first taker in being at the time of his death. If the remainder fails for want of such remainderman, then it shall vest in any other remaindermen designated in such instrument, or, if there is no such designation, then it shall revert to the original donor or to his heirs.

Question 6

Andre and Barbara owned adjoining farms, Blackacre and Whiteacre. Andre's farm was unimproved, and in 1960, Andre, by parol, granted Barbara an easement to lay a 6″ drainage tile at a depth of four feet across Blackacre for the purpose of draining a low spot on Whiteacre. Barbara constructed the drain.

In 1970, Andre retired from farming and conveyed Blackacre to Charles, one of his two sons. The deed was duly executed and recorded and conveyed Blackacre "to Charles for life, and at my death the farm to be divided among my heirs." Charles farmed Blackacre until his death in 1986. He was survived by Andre and his brother, Davis.

Thereafter Andre constructed a house and outbuildings on Blackacre and executed and delivered a warranty deed of the premises to Everett, who took possession in January 1987. In February the furnace developed serious faults and the sewer pipe appeared not to drain properly. Andre and Davis were notified of these complaints but refused to help. The furnace replacement eventually cost Everett $2,000. The sewer line was dug up and had to be lowered at a cost of $1,500. Barbara's drainage tile was discovered during this process, and it had to be severed and capped. Barbara has threatened to sue Everett if the tile is not restored and reconnected.

Everett has asked your advice as to his remedies and defenses. Advise him.

Question 7

In 1980 Chuck, owner of Greenacre, conveyed Greenacre by an unrecorded written deed in fee to himself and to his sons, Howard and Ian, as "joint tenants and not as tenants in common." Chuck died in 1984, and Howard and Ian thereupon agreed by an unrecorded written contract that each should take an undivided one-half interest in Greenacre as tenants in common. While Howard was in Mexico on a singing tour, Ian planted a crop on Greenacre, sold it, and kept the proceeds.

Greenacre bordered on a navigable stream. During a sudden storm in 1985, the stream changed course and ten acres were added to Greenacre. The land remained vacant from 1985 to 1986 when Ian conveyed all of it in fee to Leigh. Leigh knew that Howard owned a half interest, but she recorded the deed and took open possession of all of Greenacre including the additional ten acres. Both Leigh's deed and Chuck's deed described Greenacre as "bounded by the stream." Howard died one year later leaving Sharon, age 16, as his only heir.

Sharon now consults you as to her rights. Advise her.

Question 8

In 1970 Frank conveyed Blackacre to Mildred "for so long as it shall be used as a forest preserve; and if it ceases to be so used Blackacre shall thereupon become mine again." Mildred immediately recorded the deed.

Frank was committed to a State mental institution in 1975, and remained there until his death in 1991. In 1975, following Frank's commitment, Mildred sold all of the timber on Blackacre and subdivided the land into 40 separate lots which she conveyed by grant deed to various individuals, including Arthur and Bernard who are still in possession of their respective lots. All such deeds restricted the grantees' use of their lots to residential purposes, and all have been duly recorded. Frank died intestate, and his entire estate was distributed to Stan, his son and sole heir.

Last week Bernard converted his house into a sports bar.

Arthur and Stan request your advice as to their respective rights against Bernard. Discuss.

Question 9

Jill deeded Whiteacre to Laura in 1978. Whiteacre was a vacant and undeveloped 160–acre tract owned by Natalia. In 1980, Laura leased Whiteacre to Mark for 20 years, with Mark covenanting to develop Whiteacre for agricultural purposes. Mark immediately went on the land and cleared and farmed 80 acres. He remained in possession until the latter part of 1982, and then assigned all his interests to Peter. During the six months period prior to this assignment, Mark did not further develop Whiteacre.

Peter, upon taking possession, farmed some of the cleared land, cut and sold timber, and sold gravel from a 30–acre deposit on Whiteacre. In 1987, Natalia notified Peter that she owned Whiteacre. Natalia leased Whiteacre to Peter, and Peter covenanted to construct buildings for the gravel business and to pay Natalia twenty per cent of the gross receipts. Peter immediately transferred his interests to Ryan at the same rental, but retained a right of re-entry if monthly gross income did not exceed $10,000 within six months.

An eight-year statute of limitations applies to actions for possession of realty. All agreements satisfied the Statute of Frauds. Discuss the rights of all parties.

Question 10

Ewa entered into a written contract to purchase a large tract of land from Joan for the purpose of building a suburban shopping center. Ewa's intention was known to Joan, but was not stated in the contract.

The contract provided for a lapse of several months before closing in order to permit Ewa to arrange mortgage financing. Ten percent of the purchase price was paid upon signing the contract, the balance to be paid at closing.

Between the signing of the contract and the closing, a zoning ordinance was passed by the proper municipal authority placing the tract in a residential zone from which businesses of the type contemplated in Ewa's proposed shopping center were excluded. Ewa was unsuccessful in her attempt to secure a variance from the Board of Zoning Appeals. During the same period, an assessment was made for municipal improvements which had been substantially completed before the contract was signed.

Based on these events, Ewa notified Joan that she refused to proceed and demanded the return of her deposit. Will Ewa succeed in an action against Joan to recover the deposit? Discuss.

Question 11

In 1980 Chris owned Blackacre—a rectangular city lot, 200 feet by 200 feet, bounded by University Avenue on the south and Second Street on the west. Blackacre was situated in a jurisdiction with a notice type recording act. Chris built a store on the east half, and an office building on the west half. Chris conveyed Blackacre to Al by a deed executed and recorded on June 11, 1984. Al conveyed Blackacre to Owens by a deed executed and recorded September 10, 1991. Al and Owens each gave adequate consideration.

Brown, a motion picture producer, is negotiating to purchase the west half of Blackacre from Owens. In addition to using Blackacre as the headquarters for his film company, Brown plans to edit films (e.g., cutting and splicing film and sound tracks) on the premises. The film processing and the making of prints for distribution will be done elsewhere.

A title insurance company has agreed to insure Brown's title to the west half of Blackacre except as to any limitations on the use of or claims of interest which might arise out of the following matters:

(1) A buried sewer pipe running from the building on the east half of Blackacre under the west half to a city sewer under Second Street.

(2) A deed from Al to Leak Oil Company granting "all my right, title and interest in the SW 1/4 of Blackacre" executed May 15, 1984 and recorded May 26, 1984. (Owens denies any knowledge of this deed.)

(3) A city zoning ordinance which permits business and commercial uses in the area, but prohibits manufacturing.

Brown has consulted you. Advise him of the extent, if any, to which each of the foregoing matters may affect his interest in, title to, or use of the west half of Blackacre. Discuss.

Question 12

The concept of adverse possession and the Rule Against Perpetuities may appear to have little in common. However, the two doctrines arguably have similar underlying policies. Explain.

Question 13

Ira and Fran Boris owned an empty lot adjacent to their home. They conveyed that lot "*to Dell Ryan and his heirs for the conditional purposes of building a residence only*." When Dell finally decided to develop the property, he began to construct a dental office on the lot. Upon seeing the office construction, Ira and Fran claim that ownership of the land reverts to them. Dell disagrees. Discuss the arguments for each party. Who should prevail? Why?

Question 14

Eric and Emily Thompson own a one acre parcel of land on which they have built their primary residence. Their home is situated on the lot so that it abuts the ninth hole of golf course that is part of an exclusive private golf club. Golfers frequently misdirect their balls into the Thompson's backyard and then enter the Thompson's backyard to retrieve their golf balls. Some of these golfers are golf pros and are employed by the private golf club that owns and operates the golf course. Part of the job of the golf pros is to accompany golfers and play golf with them providing companionship and golf tips. The frequency of traffic has steadily increased and is now bothersome to the Thompsons. The Thompsons contacted the golf club and asked the club to take steps to keep the golfers and their misdirected balls on the golf course and out of their backyard. The Thompsons also posted no trespassing signs. The golf club was sympathetic but did not believe it could take any remedial measures and the no trespassing signs have been totally ineffective.

The Thompsons come to you for advice. They want to know: (1) what are the possible legal consequences should they fail to remedy the situation; (2) what actions you recommend they take. The Thompsons are not inherently adversarial and are interested in "working with the golf club" if possible; but, if an amicable solution cannot be reached, they are willing to pursue all of their options.

Question 15

On October 20, 1955, the Executor of the Estate of John Sherman Hoyt conveyed certain property known as 94 Maywood Road, Norwalk, Connecticut and consisting of 2.186 acres more or less, to Howard W. Carr and Mabel C. Carr, husband and wife, as joint tenants. The property was conveyed by an executor's deed recorded in Volume 443 at Page 584 of the Norwalk Land Records.

The executor's deed stated that the grantor, for himself and his heirs and assigns, conveyed the property subject to certain restrictions including a restriction that: "no building shall be erected on the premises . . . except one single family dwelling house and the premises hereinabove conveyed shall not be subdivided for the purposes of sale . . ."

The Carrs did not have children though Mabel C. Carr had a disabled nephew, Edmund Dell, the son of her sole brother. In her will, Mabel C. Carr devised certain real property, including all of her interest in the 94 Maywood Road property to Edmund Dell. Thereafter, Mabel C. Carr died and Howard W. Carr remained in sole possession of the property, under a claim of ownership. After several years, Howard W. Carr married the defendant, Angela Rosser, now Angela Rosser Carr, who has always asserted that she became the sole owner of the premises upon the death of Howard C. Carr as the sole devisee in his will.

Janice Kosinski, the plaintiff, and her husband Robert Kosinski occupied the property for approximately two and one-half years as the tenants of the defendant prior to the plaintiff purchasing the premises from the defendant. According to the lease, the lease term commenced on April 1, 1995 and ended on March 31, 1999. The lease contained a purchase option exercisable at any time during the lease term.

The plaintiff purchased the property from the defendant on April 1, 1998 for $260,000. In connection with the April 1, 1998 sale, each party was represented by her own separate lawyer. Prior to the April 1, 1998 closing, the plaintiff's attorney did not perform or obtain a title search of the property nor did the plaintiff obtain a title search or title insurance.

At the April 1, 1998 closing, the defendant delivered to the plaintiff a warranty deed to the property, prepared by the defendant-seller's attorney and stating that the grantor, for herself and her heirs and assigns, was conveying "a good indefeasible estate in FEE SIMPLE free from all encumbrances whatsoever except as herein stated." The deed made no reference to the restrictions contained in the executor's deed of October 22, 1955 and the plaintiff had no actual knowledge of them.

The plaintiff purchased the property with the intent to subdivide it into two parcels. The property was legally capable of being subdivided into two parcels under the Norwalk planning, zoning, and subdivision regulations. The plaintiff submitted a subdivision application. The Norwalk Conservation Commission and the Norwalk Zoning Commission approved the application but before the final subdivision map was filed, certain neighbors of the property told the plaintiff about the restrictions contained in the 1955 executor's deed. The neighbors' properties were similarly restricted and the restrictions on the neighbors' properties and on the plaintiff's property were put in place by their common developer at the time of conveyance.

The plaintiff obtained a copy of the 1955 executor's deed, reviewed the restrictions, and thereafter ceased all efforts to subdivide the property based on a threat of a lawsuit from neighboring property owners. The plaintiff would not have purchased the property for $260,000 had she known about the restrictions in the 1955 executor's deed.

A licensed appraiser testified that the value of the premises as of April 1, 1998 as a single lot with a single house encumbered by the restriction against subdivision to be $280,000. The appraiser also found that if the property were not encumbered by the restrictions against subdivision, a second one-acre lot could have been split off having a resale value of $140,000, but the value of the remaining land, then smaller in acreage, would have been reduced to $240,000.

(1) Classify the "no subdivision" restriction. Is it enforceable by the neighboring property owners against the plaintiff? Explain

(2) Angela Rosser Carr believes that she was the owner of the property prior to selling it to the plaintiff.

(A) Explain her argument.

(B) If she did own the property prior to conveying it to the plaintiff, is she liable to the plaintiff in any way? Explain.

(3) The Executor of the Estate of John Sherman Hoyt conveyed the property to Howard W. Carr and Mabel C. Carr by deed.

(A) What type of deed did the executor use to convey the property? Explain.

(B) If Angela Rosser Carr is liable to the plaintiff, can she successfully seek indemnification from the Hoyt estate? Explain.

(4) As between the plaintiff and the defendant, who has the better position? Explain the policy considerations behind your answer.

(5) If defendant wins, then plaintiff's damage award is $0. What would be the measure of plaintiff's damage award if she is successful? Explain.

Question 16

Lot 65, as recorded on the Plat of Woodmere Subdivision is located in the State of Property, County of Wentworth. It is a lakefront lot and consists of 25 acres. Below is a diagram showing the location of Lot 65 in relation to the lake and the main road servicing the subdivision.

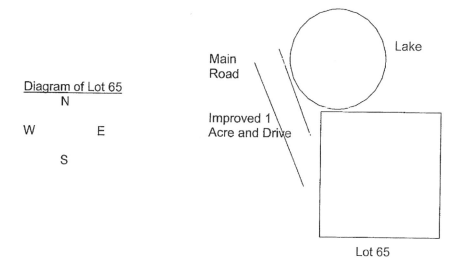

Prior to 1970, Lot 65 belonged to Alma Adams, a prominent attorney. In 1970, Alma Adams conveyed Lot 65 to "the heirs and devisees of Brenda Bullock, who died April 1, 1960 as joint tenants." Brenda Bullock had two sisters, Carolina Carter and Deborah Daniels. Carolina Carter submitted an affidavit to Alma Adams stating that she and Ms. Daniels were Ms. Bullock's only heirs. Based upon this affidavit, Alma Adams wrote to Carolina Carter and Deborah Daniels on May 1, 1972 advising that they were the owners of Lot 65 in fee simple absolute.

On September 1, 1972, Carolina Carter and Deborah Daniels entered into a purchase and sale agreement regarding Lot 65 pursuant to which Carter and

Daniels sold Lot 65 for $120,000 to Mr. and Mrs. Edgeworth (collectively, the Edgeworths). Pursuant to the purchase and sale agreement, a title insurance company was retained to insure Carter and Daniels's title to Lot 65. The company disclosed that its investigation revealed that Brenda Bullock had a brother, Franklyn Finger, who predeceased her and who had a sole heir, his nineteen year old son, Gregory Givens. Despite this revelation, the Edgeworths purchased Lot 65 and immediately moved onto the property, constructed a driveway extending out to the main road abutting Lot 65, and spent nearly $65,000 in additional funds to improve the property by constructing, among other things, a two bedroom lake house with a red-tin roof. Carolina Carter conveyed title to her interest in Lot 65 to the Edgeworths by quitclaim deed and Deborah Daniels conveyed title to her interest by general warranty deed. The deeds were properly and promptly recorded on the afternoon of the closing. The legal descriptions contained in the two deeds were identical and described the entirety of Lot 65.

In an effort to resolve the matter regarding the nature and extent of Brenda Bullock's heirs, Alma Adams filed a complaint in December, 1972 and all of the known potential heirs (Carter, Daniels, and Givens) were made parties. At the conclusion of the matter, the court entered an order providing that each of the three owned an undivided equal share of Lot 65. After the judgment was entered, Givens told Carter and Daniels that he wanted his fair share of Lot 65. Carolina Carter and Deborah Daniels rebuffed Givens. They told him that, no matter what the court said, he was undeserving of any part of Lot 65, that they had no intention of sharing Lot 65 with him and that besides, they had already sold all of Lot 65 to a very nice couple, the Edgeworths. Carolina Carter and Deborah Daniels contacted the Edgeworths after the decision was entered and advised them of both the decision and of the request made by Gregory Givens. The Edgeworths wrote Givens a stern letter, also in December, 1972 and warned him that they were the "exclusive" owners of Lot 65 and that if he ever attempted to enter their property, he would be treated as a trespasser.

Meanwhile, the Edgeworths continued to openly enjoy their lakefront property. They spent every other weekend and virtually all of their holiday and vacation time at Lot 65, except for the summer of 1978 when Mr. Edgeworth was hospitalized. During this summer, they only used the lake house during the first weekend in June and did not return until the following year. Over the ensuing years, they continued to improve the property. They cut 50 trees so as to allow the lake and their lovely home to be visible to passersby on the road. They expanded and paved the driveway in black asphalt and they added a second story to their lake house while maintaining the bright red color of the roof. All of the improvements made by the Edgeworths to Lot 65 are located on one acre in the far North West portion of Lot 65. In 1980, the Edgeworths sold Lot 65, by quitclaim deed to Harold Hopkins which deed was promptly recorded.

During the summer of 1993 Givens returned to the State of Property. Recalling Lot 65, he drove by the property to see what had become of the place. Upon noticing all of the improvements, particularly the lovely lake house, Givens contacted an old lawyer friend, Irvin Islay, advised him of the above facts and asked how he might claim his rightful interest in Lot 65. Islay, who was always fond of Givens, offered to file a quiet title action on behalf of Givens.

After being served with the complaint, Harold Hopkins contacted you and asked for advice. Discuss the following:

1. The nature of the fee simple estate interest held by Carter, Daniels and Givens.

2. Who is entitled to possession of Lot 65?

3. Any claims Hopkins may have against any of the other parties, at law or in equity.

Assume, when and if applicable, that the following statutes are in effect.

Section 1–15   Twenty years adverse possession. No action for recovery or possession of real property shall be maintained when the person in possession thereof, or defendant in the action, or those under whom he claims, has possessed the property adversely to all other persons for twenty years; and such possession, so held, gives a title in fee to the possessor, in such property, against all persons not under disability.

Section 1–20   Disabilities. A person entitled to commence an action . . . who is, at the time the cause of action accrued, either under the age of 21 or of unsound mind, may bring his action within the time herein limited, or in an action for the recovery of real property, within three years next after the removal of the disability, and at no time thereafter.

Question 17

First time home buyers contacted a listing broker to buy a home. They were interested in buying the house located at 4361 Bayou Drive. The broker showed home buyers 4361 Bayou Drive which he erroneously believed was listed with the brokerage office by the Veteran's Administration (VA), which two years ago obtained title after a foreclosure of a mortgage.

Part of the confusion stemmed from the fact that the VA, in dealing with the house, consistently used the address "4369 Bayou Drive." The actual house address of the VA-owned home was 4360 Bayou Drive, and the house across the street, the one actually shown to the home buyers, was 4361 Bayou Drive. Everyone was aware that the actual address of the house at 4361 Bayou Drive was not 4369 Bayou Drive, but they assumed that this was a VA error in the designation of the house located at 4361 Bayou Drive and that the red tape would grow waist high if they tried to change things. The house at 4361 Bayou Drive was actually owned by a builder, who apparently was paying very little attention to it. The 4369 Bayou Drive address was actually for a vacant lot further down the street.

The home buyers decided to buy the house at 4361 Bayou Drive and they signed a purchase and sale agreement identifying the property being purchased as "4369 Bayou Drive." They took a mortgage from the VA. They received a general warranty deed at the closing. The deed's legal description contained a subdivision lot designation for 4360 Bayou Drive, the VA-owned home, but no one noticed it. The deed did not contain a street address.

Home buyers moved into 4361 Bayou Drive and lived there relatively uneventfully for six years, making some improvements. The tax bills for 4360 Bayou Drive, the only tax bills they received, came to the 4361 Bayou Drive address. The tax bills they received identified the property being taxed in the same manner as the deed the couple had received and the tax collector credited the payments on 4360 Bayou Drive. The tax bills for 4361 Bayou Drive were being mailed to the builder's business address and paid by him.

Six years after home buyers moved into their little nest, the builder, who was the record owner of 4361 Bayou Drive, showed up and demanded possession. The house at 4360 Bayou Drive has been empty all this time, deteriorating, and suffering some damage as the result of a fire set by vandals three months ago. It is a real eyesore and parents are concerned that their children might run into the yard of 4360 Bayou Drive, chasing an errant ball, and injure themselves on the piles of debris and construction materials that have fallen off of the house and now litter the yard.

You have been asked for your legal opinion on the various issues implicated by these facts. Consider the following matters. Be certain to provide rationales for your answers.

1. Home buyers vs. Builder: The home buyers are now claiming title by adverse possession. Will the home buyers be successful in their claim of title by adverse possession? Explain. (You may assume that the statutes of limitations period is five years. You may also assume that the jurisdiction follows the common law and that, as to common law rules in which jurisdictions are split, these are <u>questions of first impression</u> in this jurisdiction.)

2. Home buyers v. Broker: The home buyers sue the broker for breach of fiduciary duty. Are they likely to prevail, why or why not?

3. Home buyers v. VA: The home buyers want to sue the VA for damages. What are their likely causes of action? Explain your answers.

4.   Neighbors v. City: The neighbors allege that the conditions at the house at 4360 Bayou Drive are a nuisance. They sue the city seeking demolition of the house and clean-up of the lot. Are the neighbors likely to win this suit against the city? Be certain to provide clear rationales for your answers.

Suggested Analysis to the Essay Questions

Answer to Question No. 1

This question is designed to require discussion and analysis of the law of "found" goods or chattels and the law of bailments. It is a good fact situation for the student to demonstrate her understanding of the concept of relativity of title. It is probably best to divide the answer into two parts: (1) Acquisition of rights by "find" and the relativity of title that they indicate and (2) the law of bailments. It is also probably best to do the analysis in each part by analyzing the rights and responsibilities of each party mentioned in the fact situation.

A.   Acquisition of Rights by "Find"

1.   Rights of DuBois

DuBois is the finder of the tray. If no other parties were involved he would have superior right to the tray to everyone except the (unknown) true (original) owner (TO). Unless the tray was abandoned (which is unlikely under the circumstances), DuBois as finder will be considered a bailee of the goods and must make some reasonable effort to find the true owner. It is possible that a state statute or local government ordinance in the jurisdiction in question will establish rules that finders must follow such as filing a report with the local police. If the true owner never claims the tray DuBois will become its "owner."

2.   Rights of DuBois v. Ricard

Ricard owned the land on which DuBois found the tray. Whether or not he has superior rights to DuBois likely will be determined by how a court will classify the tray—i.e. whether it is lost, mislaid, or abandoned property. Lost and abandoned property usually is awarded to the finder unless the find occurred in the course of employment which is not indicated in this fact situation. Mislaid property, on the other hand is more frequently awarded to the owner of the land where the find occurs particularly if the finder is a trespasser—which is likely in this case. Without the true owner to tell us the circumstances under which he parted with the property—in which case the issue would be moot since the tray would be returned to the true owner—it is impossible to be sure of the proper classification but the tornado is such a likely explanation that "lost property" is the most likely label to be used by the court. Another possible—but unlikely— label that might be considered is treasure trove. Usually treasure trove is considered only in regard to buried items and even though DuBois found the tray "in the rubble" there seems to be no basis for thinking that it was buried there. If a court chooses to consider this category, DuBois' rights would likely be held to be superior to Ricard but a governmental entity might also claim some rights to the "treasure."

B. Bailment

3. DuBois' bailment to Lion d'Or Jewelry Store

Even though as between himself and Ricard, DuBois probably has superior rights, he still is obliged to hold the tray for the true owner (TO) and to make a reasonable effort to find her. Taking the tray for repair is probably permissible and the TO, if she ever comes to claim the tray might be obligated to reimburse DuBois for reasonable repairs but DuBois' order to have his initials put on the tray could at this point of time be held violative of TO's rights and be held a conversion of the property.

4. Lion d'Or and O'Hara Engraving

When DuBois took the tray to Lion d'Or, he became a bailor and Lion d'Or a bailee. The bailee had the duty to treat the bailed good with reasonable care. At common law, duties of a bailee were divided according to whether the bailment was for the benefit of the bailor, or the bailee or for both. Today most courts impose a duty of reasonable care under the circumstances. Since under the old analysis, this would be a bailment for mutual benefit, the standard of care under the old and new approach would be the same—reasonable care under the circumstances. Whether or not Lion d'Or acted reasonable by sending the tray to O'Hara for engraving would be the issue. Its resolution would probably depend on trade practice in regard to such situations.

The destruction of the ill-fated tray in the fire at O'Hara raises further issue of liability for the bailee. O'Hara status was that of a bailee of Lion d'Or which itself was a bailee. The general standard of care of a bailee has just been discussed. The attempt of Lion d'Or to limit its liability by the "Not responsible . . ." notation on the claim check will be a factor for the court to consider but generally bailees are not allowed to contract out of liability for negligence. Whether any parties were negligent in the tray's destruction is not indicated in the fact situation.

5. Lion d'Argent

If Lion d'Argent can establish that it is the bailee of the true owner, then it probably had the right (as well as the responsibility) to claim the tray on behalf of the TO. Bailees have the right and duty to protect bailed property items vis à vis third parties. Lion d'Argent should be entitled to the tray vis à vis all other parties. Since the tray has been destroyed, Lion d'Argent can probably seek recovery from DuBois for conversion by his bailment for getting his initials put on the tray and for negligence if any can be established against Lion d'Or or O'Hara.

Answer to Question No. 2

X's rights and remedies depend on the nature of the contract. If the contract is enforceable as a real covenant, X can bring an action at law against F and G. If the contract is not a real covenant, its enforceability will depend on whether it is an equitable servitude or a reciprocal negative easement. It is not an affirmative easement, a license, nor a profit.

The agreement is not a real covenant because there was no horizontal privity between A and B, and the majority of courts require horizontal privity for a covenant to be enforceable at law. (The Restatement does not require horizontal privity for the benefit to run.) Otherwise, the agreement would be an enforceable covenant because it satisfies the Statute of Frauds, it touches and concerns the lands, the parties intended for the agreement to be binding, and some amount of vertical privity exists. Vertical privity is an issue because X has a lesser estate than B.

X could not enforce the contract against F or G because neither has the same estate as C had to convey. Therefore, the agreement is not enforceable at law as a covenant.

Answer to Question No. 3

The answer depends on the jurisdiction's recording statute. In a race jurisdiction, the first to record wins. Since A was the first to record, A wins. Some jurisdictions require the person to be a bona fide purchaser (for value and without notice of the prior conveyance).

In a notice jurisdiction, the goal is to protect the subsequent bona fide purchaser. Under the shelter rule, which gives C the same rights her grantor has under the applicable statute, C may prevail despite the fact that A recorded first. Since B is a bona fide purchaser without notice, B is entitled to convey his title to C. The shelter rule allows C to circumvent any problems with A's recorded deed. However, O may lose because the shelter rule will not protect an original grantor due to the potential for fraud.

In a race-notice jurisdiction, a bona fide purchaser must also record first to prevail. In this case, A can argue that he was the first to record. The shelter rule will not help O, so A may be able to get a lien on the property if the conveyance to C is upheld, if the court finds that the balance weighs in A's favor. C has a strong argument that she was the first to properly record since A's deed was recorded outside the chain of title. If C is successful, O may avoid the shelter rule's bar on grants back to the original grantor because all of the statutory criteria will be met. However, this is unlikely because, unless O was incompetent, he had actual notice of the conveyance and will not qualify as a bona fide purchaser.

Answer to Question No. 4

The original lease created a term of years determinable. Therefore, if the building's use changes, the lease will automatically terminate. The first question is whether L and M were joint tenants or tenants in common. At common law, the courts presumed a joint tenancy, but the modern rule is to presume O intended a tenancy in common. Therefore, the court will look to O's intent. Although the conveyance did not mention a right of survivorship, it did specify that the lease was a joint tenancy. Also, because O, L, and M were family members, the court may be more likely to find that O intended to create a joint tenancy.

The next issue is whether the agreement between L and S was a sublease or an assignment. Because the original lease was silent on the issue and due to the policy favoring free alienability, the court would allow either. Because L conveyed only a month-to-month periodic tenancy to S, which was less than she had, the court will likely find the agreement to be a sublease. Therefore, L and O remain in privity of estate and contract and can sue each other. At common law, O and S could not sue each other because they are not in privity of estate. L and S can definitely sue each other because they are in privity of estate and contract.

Another issue is what effect the sublease had on the joint tenancy, if it was a joint tenancy, between L and M. At common law, a lease was often considered to have broken the four unities and converted a joint tenancy into a tenancy in common. The modern view is that a lease merely conveys the joint tenant's rights to the lessee for the lease period. Because the joint tenant's interest is extinguished at death, so is the lessee's. Therefore, M may argue that the joint tenancy was not destroyed, and upon L's death, she took the entire estate with no share passing to X and is now entitled to exclusive possession of the premises. Since M was not a party to the lease between L and S, she had no privity of contract or estate with S and is therefore not liable to S.

Because S was in rightful possession of the premises prior to L's death, the court may find either: 1) that the joint tenancy between L and M was destroyed by the sublease from L to S, in which case L and M would be tenants in common with X's interest being subject to S's lease and M being entitled to concurrent possession with S; or, 2) that the joint tenancy was not severed by the sublease, but that even though M took the whole interest via the right of survivorship, she took subject to S's interest. This raises the issues of the duties among O, L (as succeeded by either X and M or only M), and S.

Under the common law doctrine of waste, the tenant had the duty to repair unless the lease provided otherwise. The modern view, at least with respect to residential leases, is that the duty to repair falls on the landlord pursuant to an implied warranty of habitability.

A covenant of quiet enjoyment is implied into all leases and requires the landlord to refrain from doing anything that will interfere with the tenant's use and enjoyment of the property. Under this theory, S must claim constructive eviction which requires him to actually vacate the premises. The fact that S vacated only part of the premises is problematic. For this reason, S may argue that the warranty of habitability has been breached and that he was justified in vacating the apartment and reducing his rental payments. However, because the warranty of habitability is implied only into residential leases, the mixed character of the lease may work against S if the court views the lease as primarily of a commercial nature. It will also be difficult for S to justify such a substantial reduction in rental payments and the two-year delay in vacating the premises. Even if the court finds a breach of the implied warranty of habitability in 1990, S would still owe rent equal to the fair market value of the property.

As the representative of L's estate, X may be liable to M for an accounting during the period that M was in Hawaii. Because M left voluntarily, she could not prevail on an ouster theory. In most jurisdictions, M would not be entitled to half of the fair market rental value of the period that L remained in possession. However, once L subleased the premises to S, she was required to account to M for her share of the net profits.

Answer to Question No. 5

At common law, one could not create a fee tail estate in personal property. Despite the statute converting a fee tail into a life estate with a fee simple in the remaindermen, the court will likely find that the legislature did not intend to simultaneously create and destroy a new type of property interest. Therefore, the court will probably allow the personal property to descend as it would have in absence of the statute.

The title to the items of personal property will likely pass to A and B subject to an executory interest in the Kumquat University Foundation. If Feudal intended this condition to apply to descendants of A and B, this will not violate the common law Rule Against Perpetuities because the Rule is inapplicable to personal property. If the court applies the statute, A and B will get life estates. They can hang the O'Keeffe painting, but they probably cannot sell it because this would constitute waste of the remaindermen's interest. They can invest the $100,000 and spend the income, but they cannot invade the principal. They can eat the strawberries, but if they sell them they must invest the proceeds and can only reach the income, not the principal. Employing the modern presumption in favor of a tenancy in common rather than a joint tenancy, at the death of A and B, X and Y will succeed to their interests subject to the restriction that they remain in Paradise.

As to Blackswamp and Greenswamp, the statute will convert the conveyance to a life estate in A and B and a fee simple in the remaindermen. However, A and B may only get 100 acres of Greenswamp—the portion adversely possessed by Feudal—unless Feudal was holding the entire 1000 acres under color of title or it can be established that Feudal's occupation of the 100 acres was the normal and customary use for the entire 1000 acres (e.g., if the balance was under water). A and B can get no more interest than Feudal had in Greenswamp. It is unclear under the statute whether when A and B die, X and Y will take a fee simple subject to condition subsequent or a fee simple absolute.

Answer to Question No. 6

Everett will sue Andre and Davis for the replacement cost of the furnace ($2,000); for the lowering of the sewer line ($1,500); for the existence of the easement despite the warranty deed; and for indemnity for any liability he may have to Barbara.

The conveyance from Andre was "to Charles for life, and at my death the farm to be divided among my heirs." This raises the issue of what are the property interests if Charles dies before Andre. The most likely construction of "and at my death" is that the grantor was granting a life estate back to himself after Charles's death with a remainder to his heirs. The grant to the heirs would violate the Doctrine of Worthier Title and would likely be stricken by construction—the heirs of the grantor take by descent rather than by purchase. Since the grant to the heirs will be stricken, Andre owns the property in fee, and Davis has no interest against which Everett could make any claims.

Everett's only claims will be against Andre. There will be no claim against Andre for the faults of the furnace. Unless there is an express warranty, the sale of a constructed house generally carries with it no warranties of fitness or use. The deed given was a warranty deed, and therefore only warrants that there are no outstanding superior titles; it does not protect against the failure of the sewer pipe to drain properly. However, Everett does have a claim against Andre if Barbara holds a valid easement for drainage. The existence of the easement would violate the deed's covenants of warranty and quiet enjoyment. If Barbara's easement is established (either by a prior grant of a legal interest or by necessity, implication, or prescription), then Everett purchased subject to the easement. There is, however, no easement. There is no easement by grant because it was by parol and violates the Statute of Frauds. There is no easement by prescription because, even though the 27–year continuous use was actual and exclusive and would most likely satisfy the prescriptive period, the original use was permissive, not adverse or hostile. Also, since the tile was buried, it is questionable whether it was open and notorious. There is no easement by necessity because there is no strict necessity nor prior common ownership shown. There is no easement by implication because there is no showing of prior ownership (and even if there was, the grantor had never used the tile for the benefit of the conveyed land since Barbara installed the tile), nor any apparent prior use since the tile was underground.

Answer to Question No. 7

Sharon will seek a cotenancy interest in half of Greenacre through Howard and a right of partition of the co-tenancy. Leigh will claim the entire property based on the conveyance from Ian and on her adverse possession of the other half.

Whether Sharon can recover depends upon the jurisdiction's period of limitations. The first issue is whether Sharon should sue immediately through a guardian or whether the period of limitation will be tolled because of her disability. Because Sharon is a minor, the limitations period might be tolled for five years—until she reaches age 21; or two years in states that have lowered the legal age of majority to 18. However, because the disability arose after the cause of action arose, their limitation period would not be tolled. The cause of action arose when Ian conveyed to Leigh (Howard was still alive). A subsequent intervening disability does not toll the limitations period.

Sharon will argue that Howard and Ian held the property as tenants in common and that she inherited her one-half interest in the property at Howard's death. In 1980, Chuck had the capacity to change the ownership interest by granting to himself, Howard, and Ian as joint tenants and not as tenants in common. Therefore, Chuck's interest passed equally to the survivors (Howard and Ian) upon his death. Howard and Ian could change the joint tenancy to a tenancy in common, destroying the right of survivorship. Thus, when Howard died, his interest passed to his heir, Sharon, and not to Ian.

The next issue concerns the effect of Ian planting a crop and keeping the proceeds. Each of the tenants in common is entitled to full and undivided possession. This includes the right to plant crops and to keep the proceeds. Such an action by one tenant in common does not amount to an ouster. However, when Ian conveyed the entire interest to Leigh in 1986, that was an act against the interest of the other tenant in common. When Leigh took open possession, and, more importantly recorded her deed, she both ousted and gave constructive notice of the ouster to Howard. Leigh was then the rightful possessor of an undivided one-half interest, and claimed the rest by adverse possession. If Leigh satisfied the limitations period in the year between the recording of the deed and Howard's death, Sharon has no rights at all. Although the limitations period is unknown, it may only be five years. If so, and the age of majority is 21, and if Sharon waits until she is 21, she would be barred by the statute of limitations. If, however, Sharon sues immediately through a guardian, she will have a claim to a one-half undivided interest as a tenant in common with Leigh.

Another issue concerns the acreage added by the stream's abrupt change of course. Absent the change in course, because the deed described Greenacre as "bounded by the stream" the owners of the fee of Greenacre owned one-half of the stream bed because it was a boundary marker having width. Whether the additional ten acres is added to Greenacre depends on the doctrine of accretion. Generally, in order to add land to a fee by accretion, the addition must result from a gradual change in course. Here, the change resulted from a sudden storm, and thus the extra acreage was added by avulsion, and not by accretion. Thus, the boundary remains the same, without the extra acreage.

Answer to Question No. 8

Stan obtains his rights directly as an heir from Frank, but what are those rights? The conveyance from Frank to Mildred "for so long as it shall be used as a forest preserve; and if it ceases to be so used, Blackacre shall thereupon become mine again," created a fee simple determinable. Mildred's cutting and selling the timber violated the limitation. Since Frank's interest was a possibility of reverter, the land will automatically revert back to him upon violation of the limitation. Mildred would then be occupying the land as an adverse possessor. However, because of Frank's disability, the statute of limitations for adverse possession would have been tolled, and the fee will have passed to Stan. Stan can now sue to recover the entire property.

The 40 purchasers from Mildred all took subject to the limitation since the restriction was contained in a deed recorded within their own chain of title. Since courts generally try to avoid a forfeiture, the purchasers may argue that Frank's grant created a fee on condition subsequent and that the failure to exercise the right of re-entry for 21 years coupled with the severe changes to the land constitute a waiver of Frank's rights. Frank's disability weakens this argument, but his rights could have been protected by his guardian.

The next issue is whether Arthur, if he does have title, can enjoin Bernard from building the sports bar. Arthur may claim the restriction in Mildred's deed to Bernard is a covenant that runs with the land. The first question is whether the burden of the covenant ran with the land that Mildred conveyed to Bernard, and then whether Arthur can enforce that covenant (i.e., whether the benefit ran to Arthur). There is no issue of whether the burden runs with the land since the defendant, Bernard, was the original covenantor. Privity between the covenantor and the person seeking to enforce the covenant is not required for the benefit to run as long as there was privity between the person enforcing the covenant (Arthur) and the original covenantee (Mildred). Even if privity was required between the original covenanting parties, most states hold that grantor-grantee privity is sufficient. Such privity existed when Mildred transferred the property to Bernard. The restriction on Bernard's land touches and concerns Arthur's land, since Arthur's land is made more valuable to Arthur due to the restriction. Because the restriction on Bernard's land was part of a comprehensive plan to subdivide Mildred's land, it is logical to assume that the parties intended the benefit to run to their successors.

Similarly, we could argue that the restriction against Bernard could be enforced as an equitable servitude. The restriction touches and concerns Arthur's land and Bernard's land and was intended to benefit and does benefit land in the neighborhood; and Bernard has notice of the restriction because it is in his own deed.

Answer to Question No. 9

Peter will claim title based on adverse possession. If he can tack onto his period of possession the periods of possession of Mark and Laura (if Laura went into possession in 1978, when he received the deed from Jill), then Peter will have obtained title by adverse possession. Generally, unrelated strangers who succeed each other may not tack their periods of adverse possession. Yet here there was a transfer of the possessory interest in writing from Laura to Mark, and a similar transfer from Mark to Peter. Therefore, Peter can tack all the periods, claim a nine-year period of possession from 1978 to 1987, and thus perfect adverse possession under the eight-year statute of limitations.

However, we do not know whether Laura went into possession in 1978. We only know that Whiteacre was vacant and undeveloped, and that Laura leased Whiteacre to Mark for 20 years. Adverse possession requires possession. If there were no possessions until 1980, then the period did not begin until that point, and Peter could not establish adverse possession. Though as a lessee from Natalia, Peter may be estopped to deny Natalia if third parties make a claim, Peter would not be estopped from asserting his own title if he had perfected title by adverse possession. However, if possession did not begin until 1980, then the lease from Natalia to Peter would break the period of the running of limitations because at that point Peter's possession was permissive, not hostile. In addition, Peter would be liable for the damage he did as a trespasser to Whiteacre prior to 1987, including damage from farming, cutting timber, and selling the gravel. The lease between Natalia and Peter is valid despite the rental provision of 20 percent of the gross receipts. A percentage lease is valid, even though the exact amount of the rental is unknown.

The transfer of interest from Peter to Ryan at the same rental was an assignment because, as far as we know, Peter transferred his total interest in time. The fact that he retained the right of reentry if the monthly gross income did not exceed a minimum does not make it a sublease. Since the transfer from Peter to Ryan was an assignment, Ryan is a substituted lessee and Natalia would have all remedies against him from those covenants that ran with the land. The rental covenant runs with the land and Ryan would be liable under it to Natalia. However, the covenant to construct buildings for the gravel business did not run with the land because there is no intention shown that it run with the land, and Ryan would not be liable under it. Ryan and Natalia are in privity of estate, and the promise to construct the building touches and concerns the land. However, since the building did not exist when the promise to construct it was made, under the rule of construction of Spencer's case there must be a specific intention shown in order for the burden of covenant to run. There is no use of the word "assigns" here, as is required to indicate that intention.

Natalia has an action in damages against Mark for the damage caused while he was in possession. Mark has an action against Laura for a breach of the implied covenant of quiet enjoyment in the lease from Laura to Mark. As with all leases, that lease contains an implied covenant of quiet enjoyment under which the landlord guarantees against superior outstanding title. Laura has no such action against Jill, because all she obtained from Jill was a deed, which so far as we know contained no covenant of title. Peter has no interest against Mark because he received an assignment in which there were no implied covenants of title. However, Peter would have an action against Laura, since the benefit of the implied covenant of quiet enjoyment runs with the land to Peter. Peter can also assert his rights under the assignment against Ryan.

Answer to Question No. 10

Ewa will claim that she no longer has any obligation because the purpose of the land sale contract has been frustrated; that because of the assessment for municipal improvement, Joan cannot deliver marketable title upon closing; and that even if Ewa breaches, she is entitled to her deposit unless Joan can show a drop in market price or other damages.

The purpose of building a suburban shopping center was not mentioned in the contract. Nevertheless, it can form the basis for a claim of frustration of purpose since it was known and understood by Joan. Ewa will claim that the purpose of building a suburban shopping center has been frustrated by a subsequent supervening event that was not foreseeable when the contract was signed. It is arguable that the risk of zoning decisions ought to be known to both parties to the contract. Nevertheless, when the risk of zoning changes is not allocated by the contract, and there is a subsequent zoning change which frustrates the purpose of the contract, Ewa can claim that she is entitled to rescission of the contract.

Furthermore, the vendor's obligation under the land sale contract is to deliver marketable title. Marketable title is title which is reasonably free of all claims or liens on the property. A property delivered with an assessment on it is not free of liens, taxes or other claims, and is therefore not marketable. The fact that the municipal improvements had been substantially completed before the contract was signed does not alter Ewa's claim because she has a right to receive marketable title. If, under either theory, Ewa is able to back out of the contract, she is entitled to her deposit. Even if she breaches, she may still get her deposit.

The vendor, Joan, is entitled to damages for breach. Such damages are generally measured by the drop in market value. Here, a drop in market value resulted from zoning changes, and thus Joan would have a claim for damages. If Ewa is found to have breached the contract, she can only recover her deposit to the extent it exceeds the damages. If Joan's damages were greater than the deposit, Ewa would also be liable for additional sums.

Answer to Question No. 11

The first issue concerns the sewer pipe. If the sewer pipe is found to be either an easement by implication or necessity, it will not be destroyed by the recording statute. An easement by implication would be an easement by implied reservation because the servient tenement (the west half) is being transferred, and the dominant tenement is being retained. All of the requirements for an easement by implication are met, with the possible exception of one: there was common ownership; there is contiguous land; and there was a prior use which seems to be strictly necessary, if there is no other feasible sewer hook-up; but the prior use may not have been apparent. Though the sewer is underground and cannot be seen, the fact that it is operable should be apparent. Therefore, the easement by implied reservation may be present and thus may be on the west half of Blackacre.

There is also an easement by necessity. There was common ownership, and from the facts, it seems the sewer is strictly necessary. Easements by necessity for sewer purposes may arise.

The next issue concerns the deed from Al to Leak, which predates the date on which Al acquired the property. Absent recording considerations, this would be a clear case of estoppel by deed. Al transferred his interest before he actually owned it, so the moment he acquired the interest, it would pass through him to Leak. However, the notice recording statute alters the analysis. It is the responsibility of the title searcher to look in the grantor index for other deeds from Al only after the date he acquired title, on June 11, 1984. The deed to Leak was executed before that, on May 15, 1984, and therefore, the recording would not have given a subsequent grantee constructive notice. Since Owens did not have actual notice, he will take as a bona fide purchaser for value and will be protected under the notice statute. Brown, as a purchaser from a bona fide purchaser for value, will be similarly protected under the shelter rule.

The last issue concerns the zoning ordinance, which although it would not affect Brown's legal title, it could affect his use of the property. The ordinance would not prevent Brown from using the property as an office building, but depending on what constitutes "manufacturing," it may prevent him from cutting and splicing film and soundtracks. Editing probably does constitute manufacturing, and therefore the ordinance would limit Brown's use of the property. However, the ordinance would not cloud his title or prevent him from obtaining title insurance subject to (1) and (2).

Answer to Question 12

1.   Policies underlying adverse possession and the Rule Against Perpetuities: They are the function of similar normative approaches used to determine how to construct property law.

A.   Utilitarian approach. The focus is on comparing the costs and benefits of different definitions and allocations of property entitlements. Social utility, wealth maximization, human preference can all be used to justify a property allocation under the utilitarian approach.

1.   If you value utility maximization expressed under any of the above, you might prefer an application of the adverse possession and Rule Against Perpetuities doctrines so as to facilitate acquisition of property by those who are productive and by those who are present, as opposed to allowing the dead hand to rule.

a.   Adverse possession—Hostility: you would prefer the majority Connecticut test (objective standard) over the Main (knowing wrongdoer) or the good-faith view, both of which are minority views. Tacking: You would also prefer a liberal tacking policy where an adverse possessor transfers by deed so you would like an approach which allowed tacking where the property in dispute was not included in the deed but was intended to be included as opposed to the view that tacking is not permitted unless the disputed parcel is actually described by the deed.

b.   Rule Against Perpetuities—Wait and see: you would reject the wait and see approach and apply the Rule as it traditionally has been applied. Exemptions: You might argue that future interests in transferors should not be exempt under the Rule.

2.   Utility approaches are tailored to promote the general welfare of the society in which the rule is operating.

B.   Social relations and justified expectations approach. If you find that property rules should reflect justified expectations and should promote human flourishing and social relations, you may or may not take a different approach to the Rule and to adverse possession. You might argue that the future is uncertain for everyone and the dead have an interest in managing wealth long past their death. Also, folks expect to own what they have paid for and possessed. Rewarding labor by allowing a trespasser to eventually acquire good title by adverse possession promotes labor and development over social relations and arguably creates instability.

C.   Distributive justice approach. Both systems promote and facilitate the distribution, re-distribution, and de-consolidation of property.

Answer to Question 13

"To Dell Ryan and his heirs for the conditional purposes of building a residence only." Ira and Fran should win unless the state they are in has modified the Rule in favor of Ryan as set forth below and if this is interpreted as an estate. If this is argued as a covenant, then there are arguments Ryan can make in his favor.

A.   Arguments in favor of Ira and Fran. Their best argument is that this is a defeasible fee and that it is a fee simple determinable. Their second best argument is that it is a fee simple subject to condition subsequent and they have a right of re-entry.

1.   The grant conveys the land subject to a condition of defeasance. Although the grant does not fit either the fee simple determinable nor the fee simple on condition subsequent perfectly, it does not matter for purposes of the Rule. It does matter in terms of when the estate ends upon breach of the condition because fee simple determinables automatically terminate upon breach and a fee simple on condition subsequent requires the grantor to assert a property right to get the property from the grantee. In either case, the future interest is in the grantor; thus, the future interest is exempt from the Rule Against Perpetuities. The condition was breached and if the present estate was a fee simple determinable, the present estate in Dell automatically terminated upon breach and the possibility of reverter became a present interest of a fee simple absolute. If the grant created a present estate of a fee simple on condition subsequent, Ira and Fran have asserted their right of entry/ power of termination and thus hold the present estate.

2.   As long as there is no RAP issue, then there is likely no statute of limitations issue either because Ira and Fran's cause of action ripened once the condition was broken and they promptly took action; thus, they are likely not barred by laches, etc.

B.   Arguments in favor of Ryan.

1.   Best Argument: The language creates a covenant and violation only entitles Ira and Fran to damages or an injunction. Ryan is going to first argue that this is a covenant therefore if it is violated, the only relief is damages and injunctive relief under equity. If it is an estate, Dell would argue that it violates the RAP as set forth above. He will argue the language is ambiguous and therefore courts are free to construe it as a covenant. Also, because courts favor

the current possessor in the sense of interpreting ambiguous language so as to allow a current possessor to retain possession of the property and that would be a covenant interpretation.

2. Next Best Argument: Common Law: Ryan will need to argue that the conveyance violates the common law rule against unreasonable restraints on alienation. Thus, it should be modified by striking the impermissible restraint which is the conditional language. Striking this language leaves Ryan with a fee simple absolute. The common-law rule evaluates the reasonableness of the restraint based upon its duration, purpose. If it is an unreasonable restraint, it is unreasonable regardless of whether it is a covenant or an estate!

3. Least Best Argument: If it is a defeasible fee, Ryan should argue it is a fee simple on condition subsequent and Ira and Fran have not asserted their rights.

Answer to Question 14

The golf scenario.

A. Possible legal consequences of failing to stop the trespass:

1. Easement by prescription held by golfers and by the private golf club: The Thompsons might be in jeopardy of a court finding that the golfers have acquired prescriptive easements to hit their balls onto the Thompsons' property as well as prescriptive easements to access the Thompsons' property for the limited purpose of retrieving the errant golf balls. Likewise, a court may also find that the golf club, via its agents in the form of the golf pros, also has acquired prescriptive easements as set forth above.

2. Elements of easement by prescription: The use must be [1] open; [2] uninterrupted by the true owner; [3] peaceable; [4] notorious; [5] adverse; [6] under claim of right; [7] continuous for the required period. Exclusivity is not an element for an easement by prescription but if you are in a jurisdiction that includes it as an element, it is not the type of exclusivity that is necessary to acquire title by adverse possession. Exclusivity in this sense means that the claimant made use of the way based upon a right that does not depend upon a light right in others.

B. Options:

1. If the Thompsons want the trespass to stop and nothing less will do, they will need to sue the individual golfers and the golf club seeking injunctive relief for trespass. The lawsuit interrupts the continuity necessary to establish an easement by prescription.

2. If the Thompsons are willing to allow some access by golfers and their balls in exchange for monetary compensation, the Thompsons could negotiate an express easement agreement with the golf club allowing the golf club, via

its employees, the right to limited access for purposes of playing golf and retrieving balls. The easement could be drafted to last for a limited duration so that the terms and a fee could be renegotiated over time. Also, the easement could require the golf course to perhaps erect some type of fence or netting to at least limit, if not totally eliminate, the number of balls encroaching onto the Thompsons' property.

3. The Thompsons could reach the individual golfers by an arrangement with the golf club that, as a condition of membership in the golf club, the golfers agree that any access they have to retrieve the balls is as a result of the easement agreement and is therefore permissive, not hostile. This would eliminate the taking of an access easement by prescription.

Answer to Question 15

(1) Classify the "no subdivision" restriction. Is it enforceable by the neighboring property owners against the plaintiff? Explain

Answer: Restrictive Covenant. Neighbors must prove that the benefit runs to them and that the burden runs to the plaintiff.

A. Elements for the benefit to run: intent, relaxed vertical privity of estate, touch and concern.

B. Elements for the burden to run: intent, strict vertical privity of estate, horizontal privity of estate, touch and concern, notice.

C. All the elements are met thus, the covenant is enforceable.

(2) Angela Rosser Carr believes that she was the owner of the property prior to selling it to the plaintiff.

(A) Explain her argument.

Howard and Mabel likely held as joint tenants with a right of survivorship or as tenants in the entirety. In some states, the lack of survivorship language would prohibit them from holding as joint tenants with a right of survivorship but the next strongest argument is that they held as tenants in the entirety. As the unities of time, title, interest, possession (for joint tenants with right of survivorship) and marriage at the time the interest was created (for tenants in the entirety) were not broken prior to the death of Mabel, upon Mabel's death, Howard became the sole, fee simple owner of the property.

Howard had the right to dispose of the property upon his death which he did by will when he conveyed all his property to Angela.

(B) If she did own the property prior to conveying it to the plaintiff, is she liable to the plaintiff in any way? Explain.

Defendant Angela Carr is liable to the plaintiff for damages for breach of the present covenant against encumbrances as contained in the April 1, 1998 warranty deed. The 1955 recorded restrictions are an "encumbrance" upon the property, not carved out of the covenant of the 1998 warranty deed. Plaintiff had record notice because the 1955 deed was in the chain of title. An encumbrance is defined as "every right to or interest in land which may subsist in third persons, to the diminution of the value of the land, but consistent with the passing of the fee by the conveyance."

The covenant against encumbrances is a present covenant and was breached when Carr conveyed to the plaintiff.

(3) The Executor of the Estate of John Sherman Hoyt conveyed the property to Howard W. Carr and Mabel C. Carr by deed.

(A) What type of deed did the executor use to convey the property? Explain.

General warranty deed. He is warranting not only against the actions of the Hoyts but also the actions of predecessors in title.

(B) If Angela Rosser Carr is liable to the plaintiff, can she successfully seek indemnification from the Hoyt estate? Explain.

No. The Hoyts did not violate the warranty against encumbrances covenant when they conveyed by general warranty deed because they expressly excepted out the subdivision restriction from the warranty.

(4) As between the plaintiff and the defendant, who has the better position? Explain the policy considerations behind your answer.

The plaintiff has the better position based upon clear breach of a deed warranty. In this case the right of neighboring property owners having the same restrictions in their chains of title would be the third parties having a claim, right, or interest to block subdivision of the property and would cause a diminution of its value as compared to subdividable property. So, plaintiff can demonstrate breach of a deed warranty and damages.

Defendant claims that the plaintiff cannot prevail because she had constructive knowledge of the 1955 restrictive covenants because the 1955 deed was recorded in the chain of title to the property. It is true that the plaintiff was bound by the restrictive covenants of the 1955 deed even though she was unaware of them, and those covenants could have been enforced against her by neighboring property owners under the doctrine that when a deed is recorded on the land records, the law presumes that every interested party has knowledge of the deed and its contents. But the doctrine of constructive notice cannot relieve the defendant of her responsibility voluntarily and expressly undertaken by the covenant against encumbrances in the 1998 warranty deed. Indeed it has been held that ordinarily, a breach of the covenant against encumbrances is established because of the existence of some outstanding interest of record which is not disclosed in the deed and expressly excepted from the operation of the covenant. The recording of the 1955 deed does not bar the plaintiff from her damage claim.

(5) If defendant wins, then plaintiff's damage award is $0. What would be the measure of plaintiff's damage award if she is successful? Explain.

Answer: $100,000

The rule of damages for breach of the covenant against encumbrances is the loss actually sustained by the grantee because of the breach of covenant as measured by the difference in value of the property unencumbered by the encumbrance in question as compared to the value of the property as so encumbered.

In this case the Court has found the value of the premises as of April 1, 1998 as a single lot with a single house encumbered by the restriction against subdivision to be $280,000. The Court has also found that if the property were not encumbered by the restrictions against subdivision, a second one-acre lot could have been split off having a resale value of $140,000, but the value of the remaining land, then smaller in acreage, would have been reduced by $40,000. Without the restrictions, then, the combined two parcels would have had a net value of $380,000 ($280,000 minus $40,000 plus $140,000). The difference in value is therefore $100,000.

Answer to Question 16

I.   Concurrent estates:

    A.   Elements, method of creation, method of termination

    B.   Right to transfer, interest conveyed

    C.   Statute and presumption

II. Adverse possession

    A.   Elements

    B.   Party

    C.   Constructive adverse possession (not an issue because of the tenancy)

    D.   Has there been ouster of a co-tenant

    E.   Tacking

    F.   Disability

III. Liability created by methods of conveyancing

    A. Quitclaim deed—Caroline Carter

        1. *Warranties (none)

        2. *Remedies for breach (none because no warranties)

    B. General Warranty deed—Deborah Daniels

        1. *Warranties (list the six)

        2. *To whom do they run

        3. *Was there a breach in this case

    C. Quitclaim deed—Edgeworths

IV. How does Hopkins take title: 2/3 by deed transfer and 1/3 by adverse possession

Concurrent Estates:

The conveyance by Alma Adams to "the heirs and devisees of Brenda Bullock . . . as joint tenants" creates a tenancy between the heirs and devisees. You should identify the type of tenancy created between Carter, Daniels and Givens and based upon this assessment, discuss what, if any, interest in Lot 65 Carter and Daniels could and /or did convey to the Edgeworths in 1972. Most courts hold that the words "as joint tenants" alone are not sufficient to create a joint tenancy with right of survivorship and that the addition of the words "with rights of survivorship" is necessary to create a joint tenancy with rights of survivorship.

Once you identify that Carter, Daniels and Givens are tenants in common, you should discuss the impact of the grant by Carter and Daniels. The interest of a tenant in common is freely alienable inter vivos. The result of the initial conveyance by Carter and Daniels to the Edgeworths is that at the moment the conveyance was completed, the Edgeworths became owners of an _undivided_ 2/3 interest in Lot 65. Givens still owned a 1/3 _undivided_ interest in Lot 65 and held this interest as a _tenant in common_ with the Edgeworths. Thus, Givens's interest in Lot 65 was not transferred or destroyed as a result of the Carter/Daniels conveyance, the identity of the tenants in common just changed. Givens still had the right to possess _all_ of Lot

65 as his interest is undivided; however, he does not have the right to possess it exclusively and neither do the Edgeworths or their successor (Hopkins) unless Givens loses his interest through adverse possession, a topic that should be addressed based upon the facts.

The nature of the interest that the Edgeworths transferred to Hopkins is an absolute, indefeasible undivided interest in 2/3 of Lot 65 and perhaps the ability to tack on to their possession of the 1/3 undivided interest belonging to Givens. Thus, this conveyance creates a tenancy in common between Hopkins and Givens. Hopkins has the opportunity to adversely possess Givens but until he does so, Givens is entitled to concurrent possession of Lot 65.

A good essay will correctly identify the estate created and as a result, the interest transferred by Carter and Daniels. It will also identify the nature of the relationship between the Edgeworths and Givens as concurrent estate holders and will move into a discussion of the nature of the relationship between Hopkins and Givens prior to the point of adverse possession, if such in fact occurs.

Adverse Possession:

Elements:

To be adverse, possession must be actual, open and notorious, hostile, exclusive and continuous. Following is a discussion of the various elements as covered by the cases.

Possession is likely to be deemed ***actual*** if the acts of ownership are of such a character as to openly indicate an assumed control or use of the property which is consistent with the character of the property

Open and notorious possession is possession that is not secret or clandestine. The adverse possessor must occupy as an owner would occupy for all the world to see.

Possession is ***hostile and under claim of right*** if it is possession that is held against the whole world including the true owner. The adverse possessor need not believe the land is his in order for the possession to be hostile and under claim of right. To understand the reason why, one must look to the purpose of the statute of limitations: [1] to suppress long dormant claims and quiet men's estates, and [2] require diligence on the part of the owner. The minority view is that a bona fide belief that one has title to land is required before title by adverse possession can be obtained.

In summary, hostile possession is simply an assertion of ownership adverse to that of the true owner and all others. The claimant must occupy the land with the intent to possess it as his own and not in subservience to a recognized, superior claim of another.

Exclusive possession means sole physical occupancy by the adverse possessor or (occupancy by another with the permission of the person claiming a title by adverse possession). In order to deprive an owner of his title, the adverse claimant's actions must be such as to evidence a purpose to exercise exclusive dominion over the property. In determining exclusivity, the character and locality of the property and the uses and purposes for which it is naturally adopted are considered. Mere casual and occasional trespasses upon the land by a stranger are not generally considered as interrupting the continuity of adverse possession of land.

To be *continuous*, possession must be peaceable and without abatement, abandonment or suspension in occupancy by the claimant and also without interruption by either physical eviction or action in court. In other words, there must be an unbroken continuity of possession for the statutory period. (The use must be such as one would expect typically of this type of property). Query, what is the impact of the failure of the Edgeworths to use the property during the summer of 1998 on the issue of continuity?

A good essay will articulate the elements of adverse possession and then, based upon the facts, highlight, discuss and focus upon those elements that are most implicated by the facts.

Ouster:

The facts indicate that the conveyance by Adams created a tenancy in common between Carter, Daniels and Givens regarding Lot 65. (See discussion regarding concurrent estates) Ouster is a subset of the element of hostility; it is a specialized aggravated form of hostility that is required in certain kinds of adverse possession cases. Generally, as part of the better view, there is no requirement that hostility means anything more than nonpermissive.

There are several important ouster issues implicated. First, did the sale of Lot 65 by Carter and Daniels constitute sufficient acts to oust Givens for purposes of adverse possession? If not, did the sale by Carter and Daniels coupled with their statement, after the court decision was rendered, that they had no intention of sharing Lot 65 with Givens constitute sufficient acts and notice to Givens so as to rise to the level of ouster? If Givens was not ousted by the initial sale of Lot 65, did the letter the Edgeworths wrote warning him that they were the exclusive owners of Lot 65 constitute an ouster? Establishing the point at which ouster occurs is critical as the statute of limitations for adverse possession will not run until Givens has been ousted.

The general category of cases in which hostility must involve an ouster are those in which the adverse claimant has a present legal right of possession and the disseisee(s) (person wrongfully dispossessed) also has or have a present or future legal right of possession. In practice, this means cases in which claimant and disseisee(s) are, respectively: (1) co-tenant and fellow co-tenants(s); (2) tenant and landlord; (3) owner of a life estate and owners(s) of future estates; or (4) owner of a fee tail and owner(s) of the reversion. Cases 1 and 2 are the only ones that occur with any frequency. The difficulty is that the adverse claimant's possession is not wrongful, at least not initially; he or she had every right to possession. Thus, how can the possession become wrongful? How can it become hostile as to one's co-owners, landlord or owner of a future interest.

The adverse possessor must have a subjective intent to claim against the party being dispossessed and it is likely that the person being dispossessed must have actual knowledge of the acts or words that constitute the ouster; certainly the acts or words must be so obvious that they should know.

A good essay will spot the ouster issue and identify the various arguments that the parties can make regarding when the ouster occurred.

Constructive Possession:

Not a real issue in this case because of the tenancy. Because every tenant is entitled to possession of the whole, every tenant is in constructive possession of the whole.

Constructive possession relates to the element of actual possession and arises when the facts, indicate that the actual possession may not be sufficient to adversely possess part or all of the estate in question. In this hypothetical, you were told that Lot 25 consists of 25 acres but that all of the improvement and actual physical possession has occurred only on 1 of the 25 acres. You should question whether Hopkins can show actual possession of all of Lot 25. If he cannot, then has he constructively possessed that part of Lot 25 which he did not actually possess?

One may constructively possess land if one holds part of the land in actual possession and the remainder under color of title. Color of title usually means some writing which evidences an attempt to convey the subject land. The deeds from C and D constitute sufficient color of title. There are some limitations on the amount of land that can be constructively possessed. Most courts find that the area constructively possessed must be reasonable in relation to the area actually possessed. Nothing in this question indicates that the area potentially constructively possessed is unreasonable in relation to the portion of Lot 65 actually possessed. Note, the doctrine of constructive possession arguably flies in the face of the usual policies and requirements of adverse possession, that the law favors one who actually uses land and that the record owner should be put on notice of an adverse claim.

A good essay will identify that Hopkins, as a tenant, is entitled to possession of the whole and therefore is in constructive possession of the whole. Thus color of title really would not be important in the context of constructive possession. Hopkins may defend against the quiet title action by alleging that through adverse possession he became the fee simple owner of Givens's share of Lot 65. Givens may counter by alleging that Hopkins failed to meet one or more of the adverse possession elements and therefore did not adversely possess any of his interest. Givens would likely be unsuccessful in arguing that Hopkins was only in actual possession of the 1 acre of Lot 65 that was improved and that, as to the remaining 24 acres, Hopkins was not in adverse possession. Hopkins may then respond by alleging actual adverse possession of the 1 improved acre and constructive adverse possession of the remaining 24 acres.

Tacking:

Tacking implicates the element of continuous, uninterrupted use. Under certain circumstances, an adverse possessor is allowed to tack his possession to that of his predecessor in title for purposes of satisfying the time requirement for adverse possession under the relevant statute or under the common law if the jurisdiction in question does not have a statute of limitations. For purposes of this question, you are given a adverse possession statute. The question is whether Hopkins can tack on to the period of possession by the Edgeworths for purposes of satisfying the time period requirements of the statute of limitations.

Why should an adverse possessor be allowed to tack his possession to that of his predecessor? Generally, the thought is that the adverse possessor has a right to the land in question that is good against all the world except the true owner or one with a better right. And, because we believe in the free alienability of property of any kind, tacking does not present policy or ideological problems

In this case, the Edgeworths have purported to convey, by quitclaim deed, all of Lot 65 and the legal description in the deed to Lot 65 contains all of the adversely possessed land. You should assume this because you are told that the deeds into the Edgeworths from Carter and Daniels both purport to convey all of Lot 65. Thus, we do not have a statute of frauds issue or an issue of intent regarding whether the Edgeworths intended to convey to Hopkins both the estate they took from Carter and Daniels by right as well as Givens's interest in Lot 65 that they are adversely possessing.

In order to tack successive periods of possession, courts say that there must be "privity of estate" between the parties and there must be mutual consent to the transfer. Thus, if one adverse possessor is ousted by another adverse possessor prior to the running of the statute of limitations, the second adverse possessor ***cannot*** tack the period of the first adverse possessor onto his own. (Privity of estate is the existence of a relationship in the same land between two different persons at the same time). There are two kinds of privity of estate: [1] mutual, continuing privity such as in the landlord-tenant relationship and [2] there is successive, instantaneous privity which occurs when there is a transfer of all of the grantor's interest in land. In this case, the type of privity present between the Edgeworths and Hopkins is of the successive/instantaneous kind. So there should be no problem applying the tacking doctrine.

Disability

The existence of a disability can result in a tolling of the statute of limitations. In this case, the disability is that Givens is a minor when the adverse possession occurs. His disability ends in 1974 when he turns 21 years old. You should identify that the issues of disability and tolling are raised and should discuss what if any impact they have on the point at which Hopkins may have adversely possessed Givens. In this case, the statute of limitations for adverse possession of real property is 20 years. The disability statute says that a person disabled under the statute must commence an action within the statutory period or within 3 years after the removal of the disability and at no time thereafter. If the disability statute would result in a shorter period of time to bring the cause of action than the applicable statute of limitations, then you apply the statute of limitations and not the disability statute. In this case, the 20 years runs by December, 1992 if you assume at the latest that Givens was completely ousted in December, 1972 when Carter, Daniels and the Edgeworths communicated with him. If the disability statute applied, he would have to bring the action within 3 years of turning age 21. He turned age 21 in 1974 (the facts say that he is 19 years old in September of 1972) and so he would have to bring the action no later than 1977 if the disability statute applied. Thus, as written, it appears that Givens can maintain a cause of action up until the 20 years run pursuant to the adverse possession statute.

Liability Created by Methods of Conveyancing

If Givens is found to have retained his 1/3 undivided interest in Lot 65, Hopkins will be interested in which party or parties he may look to for compensation for his damages. He should consider any possible claims against Carter, Daniels and /or the Edgeworths.

Carolina Carter:

Carter conveyed her interest in Lot 65 to the Edgeworths by quitclaim deed. A quitclaim deed releases **whatever interest** the grantor has. No covenants of title are included or implied. It is a deed in which the grantor does not claim to have any interest in the estate, but to the extent she does have an interest, she conveys it all to the grantee. Thus, Carter made no warranties whatsoever regarding Lot 65 and/or the nature, extent, characteristics of her interest, if in fact she had any interest at all in Lot 65 and would not be liable to Hopkins.

Deborah Daniels:

Daniels conveyed by general warranty deed and, as a result, she made certain covenants to both the Edgeworths as well as to the successors to the Edgeworths. There are three covenants contained in her deed. The first three are usually termed present covenants since they can be breached only at the moment the deed is delivered. The present covenants are personal to the grantee and do not run with the land. ***Present covenants:***

[1] ***Covenant of seisin***. This is a promise by the grantor that she owns the land, although not necessarily free of encumbrances. (It represents a promise of the seller that the seller has title and possession and can validly convey both). A few states treat it as a covenant that the grantor possesses the land, whether or not by legal right, but this is a minority view. The distinction is important if the land is transferred while an adverse possessor or holdover tenant is in possession. Daniels breached this covenant but, as it is a present covenant, only the Edgeworths would have cause of action for breach of the covenant of seisin.

[2] ***Right to convey***. This covenant usually overlaps the covenant of seisin but not always. A grantor who is attorney in fact for the owner of the land under a valid power of attorney would have the right to convey, but would not have seisin. In this case, clearly Daniels did not have the right to convey away the interest Givens held in Lot 65 which is exactly what she did by purporting to convey a fee simple absolute interest in all of Lot 65. Thus, Daniels breached this covenant, but as with the covenant of seisin, it is a present covenant and only the Edgeworths would have a cause of action for its breach.

[3] ***Against encumbrances***. This is a promise that title is passing free of mortgages, liens, easements, future interests in others, covenants running with the land, etc. Since in many cases the grantee is aware of and intends to take subject to some encumbrances, the careful lawyer who prepares a deed for a grantor containing this covenant will list on the face of the deed, as exceptions to the covenant, the encumbrances which the grantee has agreed to accept. The facts do not indicate that any exceptions were listed in the Daniels deed. Thus, it is likely that the covenant against encumbrances has not been breached. Givens certainly has a present interest in the land but it does not constitute the "future interest in others" that is anticipated in the definition of the warranty. Again, only the Edgeworths, as the grantees would have a cause of action for its breach.

The next three types of covenants are usually termed future covenants since they are by definition breached only when an eviction of the grantee occurs and this may be some time after the delivery of the deed itself. Because a future covenant is breached only in the future, it runs with the land and can be enforced by ***ALL*** subsequent purchasers.

[4] and [5] ***Warranty and Quiet enjoyment***. These two covenants are in substance identical. They amount to a promise by the grantor to compensate the

grantee for the loss if the title turns out to be defective or subject to an encumbrance, and the grantee thereby suffers an eviction. Thus, these warranties represent the promise of the seller that the seller will protect the buyer against anyone who later shows up and claims title. Clearly these warranties may be breached as Givens is claiming title as a tenant in common with Hopkins. If Givens is successful, Hopkins will be evicted in the sense that he is no longer entitled to exclusive possession of the whole; rather he would only be entitled to an undivided interest in 2/3 of the estate so he is in jeopardy of a partial eviction. As this covenant is a future covenant and runs with the land, Hopkins has a cause of action against Daniels for damages in the event Givens is successful. Additionally, he may be able to recover attorneys fees for defending against Givens even if he is ultimately successful and is not evicted.

[6] ***Further assurances***. This is a promise by the grantor to execute such further documents as may be necessary to perfect the grantee's title. For example, if the grantor did not have title at the time he made the original deed to the grantee, but later obtained title, he could be compelled to execute a further deed to the grantee. The covenant is enforceable in equity by a decree of specific performance. This covenant is not implicated because greater title is never vested in Daniels.

The Edgeworths:

The discussion for the Edgeworths is analogous to that of Carter as they also conveyed their interest in Lot 65 by quitclaim deed.

Answer to Question 17

Home buyers vs. Builder: Adverse possession of 4361 Bayou Drive

A. Elements of adverse possession.

1. Actual entry.

2. Exclusive of true owner

3. Open and notorious

Use is open and notorious. You can distinguish from cases where there were several surveys and only the last revealed that everyone was on the wrong lot. Here, everyone knew there was a problem with the designation of the house numbers but they just did not want to investigate and spend the time and money to fix things—wanted to avoid the "red tape."

4. Adverse/hostile and under claim of right

5. Continuous for the statutory period (5 years in this case)

B.   What is the best theory of adverse possession in your opinion, answering this will determine the position you take on questions of first impression and where there are multiple options or points of view—rewarding diligent trespassers, penalizing dormant owners, quieting titles and correcting errors in conveyancing, etc.)

C.   Equitable considerations. The facts say "Everyone was aware that the actual address of the house at 4361 was not 4369 but they assumed that this was a VA error . . . and that the red tape would grow waist high if they tried to change things." Should this information held by the home buyers in any way impact their ability to adversely possess the true owner? You might consider this issue.

D.   What is not implicated: tacking, disability, color of title (b/c the 5 year statute of limitations is met, period and the deed does not purport to transfer title to the property in which the home buyers reside.)

Home buyers v. Broker: Breach of fiduciary duty question.

Broker likely did not breach duty owed to home buyers

A.   Broker is a listing broker, fiduciary duties are owed solely to the VA under the traditional listing broker relationship. Broker owed the VA the fiduciary duties of loyalty and good faith. What of duties owed to home buyers though? Clearly broker owed duty to deal fairly

B.   Alternatives to traditional brokers' relationships. Theories that might give rise to greater duties owed by broker to home buyers.

1.   Dual agency. If you can show facts that give rise to a dual agency, then broker would owe the same duty of loyalty and good faith to home buyers.

2.   Buyer's broker. If you can show the broker was in fact the home buyer's broker then the broker would owe fiduciary duties to the home buyers. No facts indicate that the broker is the buyer's broker.

Home buyers v. VA: default under purchase and sale agreement, breach of deed warranties (general warranty deed)

1.   Courses of thought

   a.   breach of contract of sale—fails because of merger doctrine

   b.   breach of general warranty deed—fails because deed describes property actually owned by VA

   c.   fraud or misrepresentation or negligence by VA or its agent or breach of a duty of disclosure

A. Contract of sale: no viable claim—Merger Doctrine. VA breached the contract of sale. 1. Marketable title: An implied condition of a contract of sale is that the seller must convey marketable title. The VA did not have title to 4361 and so could not convey marketable title. Unless stated otherwise, VA would have had until closing to make title marketable but this would only be an issue if the home buyers had noticed the defect before closing and sought to terminate the agreement prior to closing. 2. Buyer friendly restrictions on buyer beware: Where seller knows of facts materially affecting the value of the property which are not readily observable and are not known to the buyer, seller is under a duty to disclose them to the buyer. (Not applicable, defect was observable to buyer and buyers actually knew of the error in addresses).

Where a condition which has been created by the seller materially impairs the value of the contract and is peculiarly within the knowledge of the seller or unlikely to be discovered by a prudent purchaser exercising due care with respect to the subject transaction, nondisclosure constitutes a basis for rescission as a matter of equity. (Not applicable for same reasons above).

Merger doctrine: But, there is no cause of action because of the merger doctrine. When the buyer accepts the deed, the buyer can no longer sue the seller on promises in the contract of sale not contained in the deed but must sue the seller on the warranties, if any, contained in the deed. Recognized exceptions to the doctrine are fraud, and contractual promises deemed collateral to the deed.

B. Deed warranties—general warranty deed: no viable claim because the warranties all pertain to the correct piece of property, 4360, which the VA actually owned.

You may have been tempted to go down this road of analysis. Present warranties: [1] seisin (grantor warrants he owns the estate); [2] right to convey (grantor warrants he has the right to convey the property); [3] encumbrances (no encumbrances on the property). Future warranties: [4] general warranty (grantor warrants he will defend against lawful (meaning grantor is not liable for fees if grantee is successful in defending claim) claims and will compensate grantee for any loss that the grantee may sustain by assertion of superior title); [5] covenant of quiet enjoyment (grantor warrants grantee will not be disturbed in possession and enjoyment by one with superior title); [6] covenant of further assurances (grantor warrants to execute other documents. Necessary to perfect title).

Correct answer: VA did not breach a deed warranty. The deed warranty was for the property designated in the deed, 4360, which the VA owned (no evidence of breach of the present warranties of seisin and right to convey. No evidence of an encumbrance). Also, 4360 has always been empty so there is no cause for breach of a future warranty.

1. Present covenants: At the time of the conveyance, the VA breached the present warranties of seisin and right to convey. No evidence of breach of covenant against encumbrances. Part of the definition is an estate or interest in the property *less than the fee*, like leases, life estates or dower rights. . . . Here there is no indication of the above nor of any other interest in the property like liens, mortgages, leases, life estates, easements, servitudes, etc.

2. Future covenants: They are breached, if at all, at the time the grantee or a successor is evicted from the property, buys up the paramount title, or is otherwise damaged. Covenant of general warranty may be breached if the home buyers are not successful in defending title because this would mean that the builder's claim is lawful. Covenant of quiet enjoyment same as covenant of general warranty. If you find the facts are substantial enough to constitute a constructive eviction, then warranty has been breached.

C. Fraud or misrepresentation or negligence or breach of some duty of disclosure. Seller's duty to disclose defects. Exception to caveat emptor where seller creates material impairment unknown and likely undiscoverable by prudent purchase. Nondisclosure can be a basis for rescission.

Neighbors v. City: nuisance claim.

Unlikely that the interference is substantial and unreasonable enough to give rise to nuisance claim. Also, the city is not the property owner so it is likely the property owner is the first, best defendant in a nuisance action. For the city to be liable, one would have to essentially assert that the city had an affirmative obligation to condemn the property, no discretion or at least very little. It will be hard to prove the nature of the city's "invasion" of the neighbors' private use and enjoyment or right common to the public. Having said this, the likely best chance of the neighbors to win is under public nuisance.

A. Private nuisance results from a non-trespassory invasion of another's interest in the private use and enjoyment of land. To be liable for private nuisance, the offender's conduct must be the legal cause of the invasion of another's right. Also, the interference must be substantial. De minimis interferences are not sufficient to result in liability.

The invasion can be *intentional*—and a person is subject to liability under this test when his conduct involves a substantial interference with use and enjoyment and the conduct must be intentional *and* unreasonable under the circumstances of the particular case.

1. Courts *define intentional* (invasion is intentional in the law of private nuisance when the person whose conduct is in question as a basis for liability [a] acts for the purpose of causing it, or [b] knows that it is resulting from his conduct, or [c] knows that it is substantially certain to result from his conduct. Most modern day nuisance fall into this category 2. What is the definition of unreasonable? Is the relevant inquiry:

366

a.   Economic/Social Importance Argument: Some type of cost benefit analysis, whether the social benefits of the defendant's conduct outweigh its expected costs? If so, we must be carefully to properly define our plaintiff group and our defendant group so that the costs and benefits are properly measured.

b.   Is the relevant inquiry whether the interference crosses some threshold that marks the point of liability? So that economic and social cost are not to be considered?

The invasion can be *unintentional*—and a person is subject to liability for an unintentional invasion when his conduct involves a substantial interference with use and enjoyment and the conduct must be is negligent, reckless or ultra-hazardous. All of these have a component of unreasonableness in them.

B.   Public nuisance is an unreasonable interference with a right common to the public that impairs the health, safety, morals or comfort of the community. Public nuisances usually are continuing in nature or have long-term or permanent effects and the offender has reason to know of such effect on the common right.

C.   Which one are the neighbors most likely to pursue? Note the distinctions between the two: private nuisance arises from interference with the use and enjoyment of land so only owners of interests in land can bring suit. Second, public nuisance arises from interference with public rights so any member of the affected pubic can sue, but usually only if the person bringing suit can show special injury. Remedies for public nuisance are civil injunction and criminal prosecution and for private nuisance remedies are injunction and monetary damages.

Chapter XIX

CASE SQUIBS

Agins v. City of Tiburon, 447 U.S. 255 (1980). The Agins challenged the zoning classification that the City of Tiburon placed upon their property as part of its implementation of its comprehensive plan. The Agins never sought development approval even though the zoning classification permitted open-space use, single-family dwellings and accessory buildings; rather, they challenged the regulation on its face. They argued that because their property had the greatest market value of all of the property in the City, the rezoning totally destroyed their property's value for any purpose or use. The Court dismissed the Agins' facial takings claim and held that an ordinance will result in a taking if it does not substantially advance legitimate state interests . . . or denies an owner economically viable use of his land. . . . Twenty-five years later, in *Lingle v. Chevron U.S.A. Inc.*, *infra*, the Court overturned the substantially advances prong of the *Agins* takings test.

Albert M. Greenfield & Co. v. Kolea, 475 Pa. 351, 380 A.2d 758 (1977). L and T entered into two two-year leases, one for a garage and one for the adjoining land. After one year, the garage burned down and the fire department barricaded both of the properties. T stopped paying rent and L sued. The court rejected the common law presumption which provided that the total destruction of the leased premises did not relieve a tenant's rent obligation because the lease was for the land, not the building. Instead, the court held that the court must look to the facts in each case to determine whether the parties bargained for the existence of a building. If so, the parties should be relieved of their obligations when the building ceases to exist. Case remanded.

Allen v. Hyatt Regency, 668 S.W.2d 286 (1984). The plaintiff parked his car in a garage owned by the defendant; he locked the car and kept the keys. The vehicle was stolen and the plaintiff sued the defendant alleging negligence. The garage was an enclosed, indoor commercial garage with an attendant who controlled the exit and regular security personnel who patrolled the garage for safety. The court found that under these facts, a bailment for hire was created when the plaintiff parked his car in the garage and that upon proof of nondelivery, the plaintiff was entitled to the statutory presumption of negligence as set forth in the applicable state statute. The court acknowledged that there was a question of whether there had been sufficient delivery of possession and control to create a bailment since the plaintiff parked and locked the car and retained the keys. Nevertheless, the court found that the defendant was required to provide attendants and protection.

Almota Farmers Elevator & Warehouse Co. v. United States, 409 U.S. 470 (1973). Pursuant to its eminent domain power, the government condemned property in which the Elevator had a leasehold interest. The Court held that because of the Elevator's legitimate expectations that the lease would be continually renewed, "just compensation" required payment of the fair market value of the constructed improvements and not merely the salvage value.

Arlington Heights, Village of v. Metropolitan Housing Development Corp., 429 U.S. 252 (1977). Metropolitan Housing Development Corp. applied to the Village of Arlington Heights for a rezoning of 15 acres of land from single-family to multi-family so that it could build a federally subsidized housing project for moderate and low income housing. The Village refused the request based upon a buffer policy that allowed multi-family zoning only if it would serve as a buffer between single-family use and industrial use. Metropolitan Housing Development Corp. sued on equal protection grounds and the Court upheld the Village's refusal to rezone the land. The Court held that the developer failed to prove discriminatory intent, as required by the equal protection clause, rather than discriminatory effect. The Court held that evidence of the disparate impact of the ordinance on racial minorities could only be used as evidence of intent by showing a "clear pattern" of discriminatory effect.

Armory v. Delamirie, 93 ER 664 (K.B. 1722). A chimney sweeper's boy found a jewel and took it to a goldsmith to have it identified and appraised. The goldsmith refused to return the jewel, claiming that the boy didn't own it. The court held that the claim of the boy, as a prior possessor, prevailed over the claim of the goldsmith, a subsequent possessor. Although the boy did not acquire ownership of the jewel against the true owner, by merely possessing the jewel the boy held a property interest good against all subsequent possessors, including the goldsmith.

Armory Park Neighborhood Ass'n v. Episcopal Community Services in Arizona, 148 Ariz. 1, 712 P.2d 914 (1985). APNA sued on public nuisance grounds to enjoin ECS' operation of a food distribution center for the homeless. Evidence showed that the center resulted in an influx of transients and caused a variety of associated problems such as increased crime. The court held that public and private nuisance theories are not mutually exclusive; that based on the special harms suffered by the neighboring property owners, APNA did have standing to bring a public nuisance action; that to constitute a public nuisance the act must be unreasonable under the circumstances (balancing benefits and harms); that compliance with zoning laws does not establish per se reasonableness; and that a criminal violation is not a prerequisite for maintaining a public nuisance action.

Beal v. Beal, 282 Or. 115, 577 P.2d 507 (1978). R and B purchased a home together while cohabitating. The court rejected the traditional doctrine that courts should not become involved in settling property disputes arising from "meretricious" relationships, and also refused to apply ordinary cotenancy rules due to evidentiary problems. Instead, the court held that courts may consider the express or implied intent of the parties. Since R and B intended to pool their resources, they should be considered equal co-tenants until separation, and as traditional co-tenants after separation.

Bean v. Walker, 95 A.D.2d 70, 464 N.Y.S.2d 895 (1983). The defendants and plaintiffs entered into an installment land sales contract pursuant to which the defendants contracted to purchase the plaintiffs' house for fifteen thousand dollars, at five percent interest, over fifteen years. The defendants took possession and paid installments for eight years and then they defaulted. The plaintiffs sued in ejectment to enforce the terms of the contract which allowed them, upon default by the defendants, to retake possession and retain all of the money paid under the contract as liquidated damages. The court ruled against the plaintiffs and held that equitable conversion applied. The defendants held equitable title while the plaintiffs held legal title in trust for the defendants with an equitable lien for the purchase price. The court treated the defendants as though they were mortgagors and the plaintiffs as though they were mortgagees. Therefore, the plaintiffs had to foreclose in order to retake possession and any excess proceeds at the foreclosure sale over the amount of the remaining debt would belong to the defendants.

Belle Terre, Village of v. Borass, 416 U.S. 1 (1974). Belle Terre enacted a land use ordinance that restricted land use to one-family dwellings which the ordinance defined as related persons or not more than two unrelated persons. A landowner who rented his house to six unrelated persons sued and challenged the ordinance on several grounds. The Court upheld the ordinance under the rationale basis standard of review as an ordinary zoning measure. The Court did not regard the ordinance as involving any fundamental rights that required strict scrutiny review.

Berg v. Wiley, 264N.W.2d 145 (1978). Landlord and tenant had a five year lease which reserved the right to the landlord to retake possession of the leased premises if the tenant failed to meet the conditions of the lease. The landlord was displeased with the tenant's remodeling of the leased premises without his permission and with the manner in which the tenant operated her business on the leased premises. After heated arguments between the two and upon the advice of the landlord's attorney, the landlord, with the assistance of a police officer and of a locksmith, entered the leased premises while the tenant was away, changed the locks and locked the tenant out. The tenant sued the landlord on several grounds, including wrongful eviction. The landlord counterclaimed for damages to the leased premises. The court held that the landlord's self-help repossession was wrongful as a matter of law and found in favor of the tenant. The court stated that the landlord's entry was not peaceable and therefore could not be justified under the common law rule which allowed landlords to use self help if they were legally entitled to possession and exercised the right to enter in a peaceable manner. The record showed a history of animosity and vigorous dispute between the landlord and tenant and the landlord's acts of repossession could have easily resulted in an altercation between the landlord and tenant. The legislature had enacted forcible entry and unlawful detainer statutes to discourage self-help and had also provided summary proceedings allowing landlords to recover possession through the judicial process in a speedy manner.

Board of County Commissioners of Brevard County v. Snyder, 627 So. 2d 469 (Fla. 1993). The Snyders filed an application to rezone their one-half acre parcel from general use, which permitted the construction of a single-family residence, to a zoning classification that permitted the construction of fifteen units per acre. The planning and zoning board voted to approve the rezoning request after finding that the proposed multi-family use was consistent with the comprehensive plan and with the applicable flood plain restrictions. When the matter went before the board of county commissioners, the commission denied the rezoning request without stating a reason for the denial. The Snyders challenged the decision and the county alleged that its decision was legislative in nature and was therefore subject to the deferential, fairly debatable standard of review. The court disagreed and held that the decision on the Snyders' application was quasi-judicial in nature and therefore subject to review by strict scrutiny. The court held that a landowner seeking to rezone property must prove that the rezoning is consistent with the comprehensive plan. If the landowner is successful, the burden then shifts to the governmental body to prove that maintaining the zoning classification achieves a legitimate public purpose. Thus, the governmental body must prove that its decision not to rezone is not arbitrary, unreasonable, or discriminatory. If the governmental body meets its burden, the landowner's application should be denied.

Board of County Commissioners of Teton County v. Crow, 65 P.3d 720 (Wyo. 2003). Homeowners wanted to expand an existing home to 11,000 square feet. They challenged an ordinance that imposed a 8,000 square foot maximum on housing size and alleged, in part, that the ordinance violated their due process rights. The county articulated two goals for limiting house size. First, the county wanted to preserve its small-town, rural character. Second, it wanted to promote economic and social diversity by maintaining housing affordability as part of its effort to promote the general welfare. The court ruled in favor of the county and found that the ordinance did not violate the homeowners' due process rights, either facially or as applied.

Board of Educ. of Minneapolis v. Hughes, 118 Minn. 404, 136 N.W. 1095 (1912). Hoerger executed a blank deed and delivered it to Hughes. Later, Hoerger executed and delivered a deed to D & W. D & W then executed and delivered a deed to the Board of Education. Hughes then filled his name in on the blank deed from Hoerger. The deeds were subsequently recorded in the following order: 1) D & W to Board; Hoerger to Hughes (after Hughes filled his name in as grantee); then Hoerger to D & W. This was a race-notice jurisdiction. The court held for Hughes because the Board's deed was "wild"—the deed from Hoerger to D & W was missing from the chain of title and could not be found with a reasonable search. The court held that Hughes became a "purchaser" when he filled his name in, not when he received the blank deed.

Boomer v. Atlantic Cement Co., 26 N.Y.2d 219, 309 N.Y.S.2d 312, 257 N.E.2d 870 (1970). Atlantic Cement created a nuisance by emanating dirt, smoke and vibration from its plant. The court departed from the traditional rule that a nuisance will be enjoined even though there is a large disparity in economic consequences between the effect of the injunction and the effect of the nuisance. Atlantic Cement had an investment of over $45,000,000 in the plant and employed over 300 employees. The court decided to avoid the devastating effect that an immediate injunction would have on Atlantic Cement and the community by requiring Atlantic Cement to pay plaintiffs permanent damages. Permanent damages would impose a servitude on plaintiffs' land, which would preclude any future nuisance suits by plaintiffs. Nevertheless, Atlantic Cement still had an incentive to clean up its plant because the possibility remained that the government might bring an action for public nuisance where court might order a permanent injunction.

Bridges v. Hawkesworth, 21 LJNS 75 (1851). The plaintiff found a bag of money on the floor in the defendant's shop. The plaintiff gave the bag of money to the defendant to keep until the true owner appeared to claim it. After three years, the true owner never appeared and the plaintiff asked the defendant to turn the money over to him; the defendant refused. Citing Armorie v. Delamirie, the court held that the finder of lost property has a superior claim to everyone except for the true owner. The characterization of the locus in quo, the place where the lost item is found, as private or public is of no legal significance.

Brown v. Lober, 75 Ill.2d 547, 27 Ill.Dec. 780, 389 N.E.2d 1188 (1979). The Bosts purchased property, with the seller reserving 2/3 of the mineral rights. The Bosts then conveyed to the Browns by general warranty deed (the Browns failed to do a title check). The Browns then contracted to sell the mineral rights to a coal company. After the coal company checked title and discovered that the Browns only owned 1/3 of the minerals, the purchase price was revised accordingly. The Browns sued the Bosts' executor, claiming a breach of the covenant of quiet enjoyment and constructive eviction. The court rejected this claim, finding that the mere existence of a paramount title did not constitute a breach of the covenant of quiet enjoyment. For a breach to occur, the holder of paramount title must actually interfere with the right of possession, or a constructive eviction must occur.

Brown v. Southall Realty Co., 237 A.2d 834 (D.C. App. 1968). L rented an apartment with knowledge that conditions in the apartment violated several housing codes and made the premises unsuitable for use as a residence. T abandoned the premises and L sued for possession based on T's failure to pay rent. T claimed the lease was void because the housing code violations made it an illegal contract. The court found for T and held that the lease was illegal and therefore unenforceable.

Brown v. Voss, 105 Wash.2d 366, 715 P.2d 514 (1986). The issue here was whether the owner of the dominant tenement could extend the easement for the benefit of another piece of land. The Vosses owned the servient tenement which was subject to an easement (driveway) for the benefit of the adjacent lot. Subsequently, the Browns purchased the adjacent lot and an additional adjacent parcel and wanted to extend the drive to the additional parcel. The Vosses obstructed the easement and sued for an injunction. Because the Browns had spent $11,000 developing the additional parcel, the court denied the injunction as inequitable and held that the Vosses could instead be awarded damages.

Caullett v. Stanley Stilwell & Sons, Inc., 67 N.J.Super. 111, 170 A.2d 52 (1961). Stillwell, a developer, conveyed a lot to Caullett, with a provision in the deed reserving in Stillwell the right to build or construct the original dwelling on the lot. Shortly thereafter, Caullett sued to quiet title claiming the deed gave Stillwell no rights. The court ruled for Caullett, holding that where the benefit is in gross, the burden will not run with the land.

City of Cleburne v. Cleburne Living Center, Inc., 473 U.S. 432 (1985). The United States Supreme Court considered an equal protection challenge to a municipal zoning ordinance that subjected group homes for the mentally handicapped to a special use permit requirement. The Court refused to treat the mentally handicapped as a quasi-suspect class entitled to intermediate level review and instead applied rational basis scrutiny. The Court held that the ordinance was based upon irrational prejudice against the handicapped and invalidated the ordinance as it was applied to the particular group home that was the subject of the case. Importantly, the Court did not decide the broader question of whether the ordinance was invalid on its face. Also, the case is often critiqued as an example of the Court going beyond traditional rational basis review even though not expressly so.

Crechale & Polles, Inc. v. Smith, 295 So.2d 275 (1974). The landlord and tenant entered into a five year term of years lease. Near the end of the term, the tenant met with the landlord to try to negotiate a month-to-month extension of the lease because the new building he was going to move into after the termination of the lease was not completed. The parties sharply disagree about the outcome of the meeting. The landlord maintained that he told the tenant he did not want to enter into a month-to-month lease. The tenant alleged that the landlord orally agreed to extend the lease to allow him to stay until the landlord either sold the building or until the tenant's new building was completed. The landlord wrote to the tenant denying the existence of an oral agreement to extend the lease and requested that the tenant vacate at the end of the lease or be subject to double rent for any holdover. After the term of years lease ended, the landlord accepted a check from the tenant for one additional month and then rejected a second check for an additional month because it was market "final payment." The landlord's attorney then wrote to the tenant advising the tenant that the landlord was electing to treat the tenant's holding over as a renewal of the term of years lease for an additional five year term. The tenant refused to treat the lease as renewed for an additional five year term and vacated the premises. The landlord sued for past due rent.

The court held that when a tenant holds over after the end of a lease, the landlord can either [1] evict the tenant for trespass or [2] hold him as a tenant. The court held that the landlord initially elected to treat the tenant as a trespasser but, the landlord refused to pursue his remedy of eviction against the tenant and instead accepted a monthly check for rent. Having done so, the court held that the landlord, in effect, agreed to an extension of the lease on a month-to-month basis. The court found that because the landlord initially elected not to accept the tenant as a tenant under a new lease, the landlord could not subsequently change his election and hold the tenant as a tenant for a new term.

Daniels v. Anderson, 162 Ill.2d 47, 204 Ill.Dec. 666, 642 N.E.2d 128 (1994). Daniels contracted to purchase two lots from Jacula. The contract also contained a right of first refusal to purchase an adjacent lot. The contract of sale containing the right of first refusal was not recorded. The deed from Jacula to Daniels was recorded but it did not mention the right of first refusal. Later, Jacula contracted with Zografos to sell the adjacent lot that was the subject of the earlier right of first refusal. Zografos did not know about the Daniels option and Daniels did not know of the offer by Zografos and the subsequent sale. After Zografos had paid forty thousand dollars of the sixty thousand dollar purchase price, Zografos received actual notice from Daniels' wife of Daniels' right of first refusal. Zografos paid the remaining twenty thousand dollars of the purchase price, received a deed and recorded the deed. Daniels sued seeking specific performance of the option. Zografos defended that he was a bona fide purchaser for value. The court held that Zografos was not a bona fide purchaser because he received actual notice of the option before he paid the full purchase price. The court ordered Zografos to convey the adjacent parcel to Daniels and ordered Daniels to pay Zografos the sixty thousand dollar purchase price and eleven thousand dollars in taxes that Zografos had paid.

Dolan v. City of Tigard, 512 U.S. 374 (1994). Dolan applied to the city for a permit to redevelop her plumbing and electric supply store, which would double the size of her store and pave a 39–space parking lot. The city granted her permit subject to the condition that Dolan dedicate the portion of her property lying within the 100–year floodplain for improvement of the storm drainage system, and an additional 15 foot strip adjacent to the floodplain as a bicycle path. Dolan claimed the city's permit conditions constituted a taking. The court found the Nollan "essential nexus" test was met in this situation because it was obvious that a nexus existed between the city's desires to prevent flooding and provide alternative means of transportation and the exactions on Dolan. However, the court also held that these exactions must bear a "rough proportionality" to the projected impact of Dolan's proposed development, and the exactions did not.

Edwards v. Habib, 397 F.2d 687 (D.C. Cir. 1968), cert. denied, 393 U.S. 1016 (1969). L and T entered into a month-to-month lease. Shortly after T filed a complaint with the authorities alleging housing code violations, L gave T 30 days notice to terminate the lease and sued for possession. T claimed that the lease was terminated in retaliation for her complaint. The court implied a prohibition on retaliatory eviction into the statute and remanded for a determination of whether the eviction was retaliatory.

Ernst v. Conditt, 54 Tenn.App. 328, 390 S.W.2d 703 (1964). The Ernsts (Es) leased property to Rogers (R) for one year. The lease prohibited subletting or assignment without the Es' prior approval. In the event of sublease or assignment, R was to remain liable on all of the lease covenants. With Es' permission, the lease term was extended and R "sublet" to Conditt (C) for the remaining lease period. C defaulted on the rent payments, but stayed in possession for the remainder of the term. The issue was whether the arrangement was an assignment or a sublease. The court held that under either of two tests (the parties' intent test, and the transfer of entire interest test), the transfer from R to C was an assignment. The fact that the parties called it a sublease was immaterial. R would have remained liable to the Es under either scenario because they were in privity of contract.

Euclid, Village of v. Ambler Realty Co., 272 U.S. 365 (1926). This was a landmark case which upheld constitutionality of zoning. The Village enacted a zoning ordinance designating allowable uses in various property zones. The effect of this zoning reduced the value of Ambler Realty's property to 25% of its former value. Ambler Realty challenged the ordinance, in its entirety, as a denial of equal protection and a deprivation of property without due process. The Court upheld the ordinance as a reasonable exercise of police power. Such exercises of the police power are given a presumption of constitutional validity.

Fasano v. Board of County Commr's of Washington County, 507 P.2d 23 (1973). In this landmark case, the county commissioners created a floating zoning for mobile home parks in order to meet the local needs for a diverse housing stock. Later, the county commissioners rezoned a tract of land from single-family use to mobile home use, consistent with the floating zone. When the neighbors challenged the rezoning, the developer and the county asserted the presumption of validity for legislative acts and argued that the neighbors had to prove that the rezoning was arbitrary. The court ruled in favor of the neighbors and held that site-specific rezoning was quasi-judicial in nature and therefore, was not entitled to the presumption of validity. According to the court, the rezoning reflected the application of policy and not the creation of policy and therefore was not entitled to the presumption of validity reserved for legislative decision-making. Additionally, the case is important because the court held that any zoning change had to be consistent with the comprehensive plan.

Favorite v. Miller, 176 Conn. 310, 407 A.2d 974 (1978). X knowingly entered the private property of Y for the purpose of discovering fragments of the equestrian statue of King George III. The fragments were known to have been scattered there by the King's loyalists in 1776. Successfully recovering some of the historic fragments, X sold them to the Museum of the City of New York for $5500. Y, having learned of the discovery and that it occurred on his property, asserted that, as the owner of the land, his claim to the statue fragments was superior to X's. The court held that since X was a trespasser on the land, the claim of Y, the landowner, prevailed. This policy was intended to discourage unlawful entry or trespass onto real property.

First English Evangelical Lutheran Church v. County of Los Angeles, California, 482 U.S. 304 (1987). This case involved the issue of whether a landowner can recover damages for the period of time before it is finally determined that a land-use regulation constituted a taking. The court held that the constitution required compensation for this period of time. The decision was based on the reasoning that where a government regulation creates a taking, the government is free to amend or remove the regulation, but there is no action that can relieve the government from its duty to compensate the landowner for the period of time during which the taking occurred.

Frimberger v. Anzellotti, 25 Conn.App. 401, 594 A.2d 1029 (1991). The defendant's predecessor in title built a bulkhead and filled in a portion of a tract of land that was adjacent to a wetlands and also built a house on the tract. The defendant's predecessor in title conveyed the tract to the defendant by quitclaim deed. Later, the defendant conveyed the tract to the plaintiff by general warranty deed. Several years later, the plaintiff learned that the bulkhead and filled portion of the tract and possibly a portion of the house violated a state statute by encroaching on tidal wetlands. The plaintiff sued the defendant for breach of the present warranty against encumbrances and for innocent misrepresentation. The court held that a latent violation of a land use regulation or statute, existing when the general warranty deed is made, is not a breach of the covenant against encumbrances. The court was concerned about enlarging the covenant against encumbrances in a manner that would increase uncertainty attending land conveyancing and title insurance and noted that parties could protect themselves from similar situations by including express provisions in the deed and in the contract of sale. The court also held that the claim of innocent misrepresentation had not been proven because no representation had been made regarding the wetlands area.

Ganter v. Kapiloff, 69 Md. App. 97, 516 A.2d 611 (1986). Ganter found the Kapiloffs' stamp collection, worth approximately $150,000, in the drawer of a dresser Ganter purchased at a used furniture store. The Kapiloffs demanded the stamps' return. When Ganter refused to return the collection, the Kapiloffs sought a declaratory judgment that they were the "true owners" of the collection. Although the court recognized that Ganter's finder's rights were "tantamount to ownership" and good against the whole world, these rights were not good against the true owners once they were identified. The court held that Ganter essentially held the stamp collection as a bailee for the Kapiloffs, the true owners.

Garner v. Gerrish, 63 N.Y.2d 575, 483 N.Y.S.2d 973, 473 N.E.2d 223 (1984). Tenant (T) and Landlord (L) entered into a lease for a house for a stated rent, but no stated term. The lease provided that T "has the privilege of termination . . . at a date of his own choice." The question was what type of interest this created. The court held that the lease created a determinable life estate in T (determinable upon T's death or surrender of possession). In order to create a tenancy at will, both parties must have the power to terminate the lease.

Ginsberg v. Yeshiva of Far Rockaway, 45 A.D.2d 334, 358 N.Y.S.2d 477 (1974), aff'd mem., 36 N.Y.2d 706, 366 N.Y.S.2d 418, 325 N.E.2d 876 (1975). A religious group purchased two lots in a residential neighborhood that were restricted to residential use by a private covenant. The group built and operated a religious school despite enforcement threats from neighboring property owners. The court enforced the covenant, distinguishing private restrictive covenants from zoning laws and rejecting arguments that such enforcement constituted state action and violated the free exercise clause of the first amendment.

Golden v. Planning Board of Town of Ramapo, 30 N.Y.S. 2d 359 (1972). The Town of Ramapo adopted a comprehensive zoning ordinance and phased growth development plan that intended to eliminate urban sprawl, premature subdivision, and development without adequate municipal facilities and services. Under the plan, any person desiring to engage in residential development had to obtain a special permit. The standards for issuing the permits were framed in terms of the availability of certain enumerated essential facilities or services. The plan did not rezone or reclassify any land into different use or residential districts. Property owners and a builders' association attacked the ordinance on its face. The court upheld the ordinance and stated that when a community's existing financial and physical resources are inadequate to provide the essential facilities and services that are necessitated by an increase in population, a rational basis exists for phased growth programs.

Gruen v. Gruen, 104 A.D.2d 171, 488 N.Y.S.2d 401 (1984). The plaintiff's father, Victor Gruen, wrote the plaintiff and stated that he was giving the plaintiff a Klimt painting for his twenty-first birthday but that he wished to retain possession of the painting for his lifetime. When Victor died, his wife, the plaintiff's stepmother, refused to give the painting to the plaintiff. The plaintiff sued for damages. The defendant contended that the alleged gift was testamentary in nature and therefore invalid as the requirements of the Statute of Wills were not met. Alternatively, the defendant argued that a donor cannot make a valid inter vivos gift of chattel and retain a life estate with a complete right of possession. The court ruled in favor of the plaintiff and found that Victor had made a valid inter vivos gift of a remainder interest in the painting to the plaintiff and had retained a life estate. To have a valid inter vivos gift: [1] the donor must intend to make a present irrevocable transfer of ownership; [2] the gift must be delivered to the donee, either actually or constructively; and [3] the donee must accept. The court found that the letters written by Victor to the plaintiff evidenced an intention to make a present irrevocable transfer of a remainder interest. The court found that the letter delivering the remainder interest to the plaintiff constituted symbolic delivery and that the plaintiff accepted the gift by acknowledging it in various ways.

Guillette v. Daly Dry Wall, 367 Mass. 355, 325 N.E.2d 572 (1975). The court held that a subsequent purchaser is charged with constructive notice of restrictions in all deeds out from a common grantor and subdivider to other purchasers in a subdivision (i.e. all deeds from the common grantor are in the chain of title).

Hadacheck v. Sebastian, 239 U.S. 394 (1915). The Court upheld a zoning ordinance prohibiting a property owner from operating a brickyard in a residential area based on a public nuisance theory. The fact that the brickyard had existed for several years before housing development encroached was immaterial.

Hannah v. Peel, 1 K.B. 509 (1945). Hannah found a brooch on the top of a window frame in a house that was owned by Peel. Hannah was stationed at the house while serving in the battery of the Royal Artillery. Peel was the owner of the house though he had never personally occupied it. Hannah turned the brooch over to the police. Two years later, the true owner having never been found, the police handed the brooch over to Peel who sold it. Hannah sued Peel claiming that as the finder of the brooch, his claim to it was superior to everyone except for the true owner. Peel defended claiming that as the owner of the house, he was in prior constructive possession of everything attached to or in the house, including the brooch, and therefore had a better claim to the brooch than Hannah. The court ruled in favor of Hannah. It characterized the brooch was lost property and held that because Peel never had physical possession of the house he never had prior possession of the brooch.

Hannan v. Dusch, 154 Va. 356, 153 S.E. 824 (1930). Tenant (T) and Landlord (L) entered into a lease wherein T was to take possession on a certain date. On that date, the former tenant was still in possession and L refused to take action to evict. T sued, claiming L had a duty to deliver actual possession. L claimed he merely had a duty to give T the **legal right** of possession. Following the American rule, which does not imply a covenant by the landlord to deliver physical possession, the court held for L.

Hardy v. Burroughs, 251 Mich. 578, 232 N.W. 200 (1930). Hardy mistakenly constructed a home on Burrough's lot, and Burrough's thereafter occupied the house and property. It was not alleged that Burroughs, the owner of the land, was guilty of fraud or of conduct to constitute estoppel, such as knowingly allowing Hardy to complete construction of a house on the wrong property. However, the court held that since Burrough's had not the "slightest title" to the house, Burroughs was required to pay fair market value for the house or, in the alternative to sell the land to Hardy, an innocent wrongdoer, for the value of the unimproved land.

Harms v. Sprague, 105 Ill.2d 215, 85 Ill.Dec. 331, 473 N.E.2d 930 (1984). Two brothers were joint tenants in a piece of property. One brother, John, cosigned a note for a friend and gave the creditor a mortgage on his undivided interest in the property. The other brother, William, knew nothing about the mortgage. John died and left all of his property to the friend. The first issue was whether the mortgage severed the joint tenancy and destroyed the right of survivorship. The court held that the mortgage did not sever the joint tenancy, therefore William took title to the entire estate at John's death. The second issue was whether the mortgage was still operative against the property. The court held that because the mortgage accompanied the mortgaging tenant's interest, it was extinguished when his interest in the property ceased to exist—at his death.

Hawaii Housing Authority v. Midkiff, 467 U.S. 229 (1984). This case involved the definition of "public use" under the Fifth Amendment. The Court held that a Hawaii statute transferring ownership of land from lessors to lessees for the purpose of reducing land ownership concentration constituted a "public use."

Hilder v. St. Peter, 144 Vt. 150, 478 A.2d 202 (1984). The tenant rented an apartment from landlord for herself, three children and one grandchild under an oral lease. The tenant always paid her rent. There were several defects in the premises which the landlord refused to correct or repair such as broken fixtures, leaking water, a broken sewage pipe in the basement of the building which resulted in odor in the tenant's apartment, improperly connected electrical service for the tenant's furnace, inoperable bathroom lights and outlets and dangling plaster. The tenant sued the landlord and the court adopted the implied warranty of habitability for residential leases. In order to bring a claim for breach of the implied warranty of habitability, the tenant must show that the landlord had notice of a defect or deficiency in the leased premises that impacts habitability and that the landlord failed to remedy the defect or deficiency within a reasonable time. The implied warranty of habitability cannot be waived nor can a tenant lose the protections of the warranty by entering the premises with knowledge of the defect, thereby assuming the risk.

Hill v. Community of Damien, 121 N.M. 353, 911 P.2d 861 (1996). Plaintiffs argued that defendant's use of its property as a group home for individuals with AIDS violated a restrictive covenant. The covenant restricted the property to single family residential uses. The court held that the group home constituted a residential use because the purpose of a group home is to provide individuals with a traditional family structure and support. Further, the court relied on the public policy embodied in the Federal Fair Housing Act and the New Mexico Developmental Disabilities Act in rejecting plaintiffs' argument that the term "family" only includes individuals related by blood or law. Defendant was allowed to continue to use its property as a group home because this use did not violate the terms of the restrictive covenant.

Hocks v. Jeremiah, 92 Or.App. 549, 759 P.2d 312 (1988). Hocks placed a number of bonds and a diamond in a safety deposit box rented in both his and his sister, Jeremiah's name. Both kept a key to the box. Oral promises and two hand-written notes found in the box indicated that Hocks intended for ownership of the box's contents to vest in Jeremiah upon his death. The court held that since the donor retained the power to enter the safety deposit box, and at one point identified its contents as collateral for a loan, he still had dominion and control over the property throughout his lifetime, and no inter vivos gift was made. There was not sufficient evidence of Hocks' intent to part with control and possession of the property at the time it was placed in the safety deposit box.

Holbrook v. Taylor, 532 S.W.2d 763 (Ky. 1976). In this case, T purchased property from H which adjoined H's land. With H's permission, T used a road over H's land to access the property. After T built a $25,000 home on the property, H demanded that T pay for the use of the road. T refused, and H obstructed the roadway. There was no other reasonable alternative for a roadway. The court held that H was estopped from revoking the license because T had spent substantial funds in reliance and revocation would be unfair.

Horn v. Lawyers Title Insurance, 89 N.M. 709, 557 P.2d 206 (1976). The court took the minority view and held that a title insurance company has no duty to disclose discovered title defects to the insured.

Howard v. Kunto, 3 Wash.App. 393, 477 P.2d 210 (1970). This case involved a conflict between the deed descriptions and actual land occupancy for a group of summer homes—everyone was off by one lot. The court held that the claimants, who had occupied the property for less than one year, could meet the timing requirement by "tacking" onto the time period of adverse possession of the prior possessors from whom they purchased the property (i.e. were in privity). The court also held that seasonal use of a summer home met the requirement of continuous use.

In re Cohn, 187 A.D. 392, 176 N.Y.S. 225 (1919). Cohn, in the presence of his family and on his wife's birthday, handed her a note which read: "I give this day to my wife, Sara K. Cohn, as a present for her (46th) forty-sixth birthday (500) five hundred shares of American Sumatra Tobacco Company common stock." Cohn died six days later. At the time of the writing, the stock certificates were still in the name of Cohn's dissolved firm and were kept in a safety deposit box in another city. Taking these factors, as well as Cohn's poor health into consideration, the court held that the writing accomplished constructive delivery of the stock certificates. Where actual delivery is made impracticable or impossible, constructive delivery by a writing is sufficient.

In re **Estate of Thompson,** 66 Ohio St.2d 433, 423 N.E.2d 90 (1981). Thompson opened several bank accounts and was the primary contributor to them. Intending to retain control over the accounts during his lifetime. Thompson prohibited his wife from making withdrawals, claiming that the funds were to be used by her only in the event of his death or serious illness. The court found that Thompson's statement that the accounts belonged to both him and his wife indicated his intention to create a survivorship interest and to merely authorize his wife to use the funds at his death or disablement. The court held that Thompson lacked the intent to make his wife a co-owner of the accounts.

In re Nols' Estate, 251 Wis. 90, 28 N.W.2d 360 (1947). Decedent delivered a parcel to a store owner, saying, "Here is a parcel and you keep it, and if I don't come back, you can have it." Decedent's heirs challenged the validity of the transaction, claiming it failed as a gift. The court held that the act constituted a valid gift causa mortis since it was made by physical delivery of the property, with the intent that the gift be effective at decedent's death. The court further found that the words "if I don't come back" were spoken with a view to decedent's present illness and were sufficient evidence that the gift was made in apprehension of death from that illness.

Ink v. City of Canton, 4 Ohio St.2d 51, 212 N.E.2d 574 (1965). The Inks conveyed 33.5 acres to the City "for the use and purpose of a public park, but for no other use or purpose whatsoever." The state condemned 27 acres of the park to build a highway and paid the city compensation for the 27 acres taken and for damages to the remaining 6.5 acres. The Inks claimed that their future interest entitled them to get part of this money. The court held that the City and the Inks should split the money for the 27 acres taken, with the City receiving an amount representing the value of structures built by the City on the property plus the portion representing the value of the land when used as a park, and the Inks receiving the portion representing the value of the land when used for non-park purposes. The City received the money representing damages to the remaining 6.5 acres, but was required to use it for park purposes.

Jacque v. Steenberg Homes, Inc., 209 Wis.2d 605, 563 N.W.2d 154 (1997). Defendant delivered a mobile home across plaintiffs' land without permission. Plaintiffs brought suit for trespass and were awarded $1 in nominal damages and

$100,000 in punitive damages. Defendant argued that a court cannot award punitive damages unless the award is supported by an award of compensatory damages. The court upheld the jury's verdict for punitive damages reasoning that in an action for trespass the real harm is not done to the land, but to the owner's right to exclude others, and an invasion of this right may be punished by punitive damages. Moreover, the court found that punitive damages are necessary to deter people from intentionally trespassing.

Javins v. First National Realty Corp., 428 F.2d 1071 (D.C. Cir.), cert. denied, 400 U.S. 925 (1970). In this case, the court took a contract approach and implied a warranty of habitability into a residential lease, stating that the housing code mandated such an implication. The court rejected the traditional property view that T's promise to pay rent and L's (implied) promise to provide habitable premises were independent promises. L not only has a duty to deliver habitable premises, but has a continuing duty to keep them habitable.

Jee v. Audley, 1 Cox 324, 29 Eng.Rep. 1186 (1787). A will bequeathed a sum of money "unto my niece Mary Hall and the issue of her body . . . , and in default of such issue . . . to the daughters then living of John and Elizabeth Jee." When the testator died, Mary was forty and unmarried. The Jees were 70 and had four daughters. The Jee daughters sued to force Mary to put up security for the money. The court held that the conveyance to the Jee daughters violated the Rule Against Perpetuities and was therefore void. For example, Mary could have children, and the failure of her issue might not occur until long after her death. The gift to the Jee daughters was not certain to vest within the required period because the Jees could have another daughter. Therefore, the gift could vest in this unborn daughter more than 21 years after the death of all lives in being.

Johnson v. Davis, 480 So.2d 625 (Fla. 1985). Davis contracted to buy a home from Johnson. During an inspection, Davis noticed stains and peeling plaster. Johnson stated that there had been a minor problem with the roof, but that it had been corrected. Davis then put down a substantial deposit. Shortly thereafter, a major rainstorm occurred and water gushed into the home in several spots. Roofers determined that a new roof was required—at a cost of $15,000. Davis sued to rescind the contract and to recover the deposit. The court found for Davis, holding that a seller has a duty to disclose a material fact which is not readily observable and of which the buyer has no knowledge.

Johnson v. M'Intosh, 21 U.S. 543 (1823). Plaintiffs claimed ownership of lands allegedly conveyed to them by the Illinois and Piankeshaw Indian nations. The issue before the court was whether the Indians ever held legal title that could be transferred for consideration to the plaintiffs, or any other buyer. The court held that upon the arrival of the white man, the Indians were merely occupants of the land, and were therefore incapable of holding or transferring absolute title to another party. The court characterized the Indians as savages, whose barbarous nature deemed them unfit for integration into civilized society, including the ability to own and convey lands.

Johnson v. Town of Edgartown, 425 Mass. 117 (1997). The plaintiffs challenged a three-acre minimum area requirement for residential lots in the Town of Edgartown, located on Martha's Vineyard. They alleged the three-acre minimum was arbitrary and unreasonable because it did not advance a valid zoning objective. The court held that the ordinance served permissible public purposes and was therefore valid. In part, the court found that the ordinance was justified by the 'unique natural, historical, ecological, scientific, cultural, and other values' of the island on which the town is located. The Town provided evidence of the need to protect the local ecology as well as the character of its local resorts and amenities. The court noted that as minimum residential lot sizes increased, it would become increasingly more difficult to justify the requirements.

Jordan v. Village of Menomonee Falls, 28 Wis.2d 608, 137 N.W.2d 442 (1965). The plaintiff challenged an ordinance which imposed exactions for school, park, or recreational sites as a condition for approval of a subdivision plat. The ordinance also allowed the village to require a per lot fee in lieu of a dedication of land where not feasible. The court held that the ordinance was authorized by statute relating to local subdivision regulation and was a proper exercise of the police power. The court formulated a test for the reasonableness of required dedications and other exactions which is now called the dual rational nexus test. Prong 1 of the test states that a development cannot be required to pay more than its proportionate share of the need for new infrastructure. Prong 2 requires that the land or money obtained from the new development must be used to benefit it.

Just v. Marinette, 56 Wis.2d 7, 201 N.W.2d 761 (1972). Here, the court upheld the constitutionality of the state's wetlands regulations. Because the purpose of the regulation was to prevent harm to others which would arise from a change in the natural character of the plaintiff's property and was not to gain a public benefit, there was no taking.

Kaiser Aetna v. United States, 444 U.S. 164 (1979). At considerable expense, Kaiser converted a pond on its property into a marina by dredging a channel from the pond to a nearby bay which was a navigable U.S. waterway. The federal government claimed this action caused the pond to become a navigable U.S. waterway and that Kaiser must therefore grant the public access (i.e., a navigational servitude). The court found a taking because the government action went "too far" in taking away Kaiser's fundamental property right to exclude others and resulted in a physical invasion.

Keeble v. Hickeringill, 11 East 574, 103 Eng.Rep. 1127 (Q.B. 1707). P owned a meadow and built a duck decoy pond to attract ducks to his property for hunting purposes. D, another duck hunter, repeatedly fired a gun to scare the ducks from P's property. The court held that D unlawfully interfered with P's lawful use of his property. Of particular importance was the fact that D was interfering with P's employment.

Kelo v. City of New London, Conn., 545 U.S. 469 (2005). The United States Supreme Court considered whether the decision of the City of New London to exercise its power of eminent domain to take Kelo's property for purposes of economic development constituted a 'public use' as required by the Fifth Amendment. The Court relied upon some of its earlier eminent domain jurisprudence, including *Hawaii Housing Authority v. Midkiff, supra,* and held that the redevelopment constituted a public use. The decision reaffirms two principles: first, the judiciary will defer to legislative determinations regarding what constitutes a public purpose and second, public use is to be broadly interpreted to include public purposes.

Kendall v. Ernest Pestana, Inc., 40 Cal.3d 488, 220 Cal.Rptr. 818, 709 P.2d 837 (1985). This case dealt with a commercial lease that prohibited the tenant from assigning or subletting without the landlord's written consent. The issue was whether the landlord could withhold consent for no reason. Because of the policy against restraints on alienation and the implied contractual duty of good faith and fair dealing, the court held that in commercial leases the landlord may withhold consent only for commercially reasonable objections to the proposed use or assignee.

Keystone Bituminous Coal Ass'n v. DeBenedictis, 480 U.S. 470 (1987). A coal mining law prohibited the mining of coal that would cause subsidence and was interpreted as requiring that fifty percent of the coal beneath certain structures be left in place. The Court applied the whole parcel rule that had been announced in *Penn Central Transportation v. City of New York, infra,* and upheld the act. The plaintiffs could not reduce the denominator in the takings equation by segmenting the coal that had to be left in place and then claiming a taking of all of this interest.

Kline v. 1500 Massachusetts Ave. Apartment Corp., 141 U.S.App.D.C. 370, 439 F.2d 477 (D.C.Cir. 1970). Plaintiff (Tenant) was injured when criminally assaulted and robbed in the hallway of her apartment building. Using tort, contract, and landlord and tenant (implied warranty of habitability) concepts, the court held that a landlord has a duty to take steps to protect tenants from foreseeable criminal acts committed by third parties.

Knell v. Price, 77 Md.App. 331, 550 A.2d 413 (1988). H & W were unofficially separated after 22 years of marriage. W remained in the home they owned as tenants by the entirety, and H began living with another woman (A). Eighteen years after the separation, H purchased a second home. H then conveyed the home to a trustee, the trustee reconveyed the home to H in a deed that purported to convey an entire fee simple. However, a clause in the deed provided that H had only a life estate, with full power in H to sell or otherwise dispose of the property, and that any property remaining at his death should go to A. W claimed this clause worked a fraud on rights in marital property. The court held that H's purpose was not **solely** to defraud W of her marital property rights, but rather intended to make a gift to A.

Lindh v. Surman, 560 Pa. 1, 742 A.2d 643 (1999). This case involved the issue of whether a donee of an engagement ring must return the ring when the donor breaks the engagement. The court answered the question in the affirmative, reasoning the fault of the parties is irrelevant to the decision because it would be extremely difficult for a court to determine who was right and who was wrong in the context of today's complex relationships. Instead, the benefits from a bright-line rule requiring the return of an engagement ring regardless of who broke off the engagement outweighs any inequitable results that might occur.

Lingle v. Chevron, U.S.A. Inc., 544 U.S. 528 (2005). The lower courts applied the substantially advances test of *Agins v. City of Tiburon, supra,* and struck down a Hawaii state statute that limited the amount of rent that oil companies could charge to dealers leasing services stations owned by the oil companies. The courts held that the statute was an uncompensated taking of private property in violation of the Fifth and Fourteenth Amendments because it did not substantially advance the interest Hawaii asserted in controlling the prices of certain gasoline. The United States Supreme Court held that the substantially advances prong of the *Agins* regulatory takings test was an invalid takings test though it was still a relevant test for a due process challenge.

Lionshead Lake, Inc. v. Township of Wayne, 10 N.J. 165 (1952). Wayne Township imposed minimum building requirements of 768 square feet for single story houses, 1,000 square feet for two story houses that had an attached garage, and 1,200 square feet for two story houses that did not have an attached garage. A builder challenged the ordinance and the court ruled in favor of Wayne Township. The court noted that small houses could create health problems and also stated that the ordinance preserved property values by prohibiting the construction of homes that could adversely affect the character of the community and the aesthetics of the community. Two decades later, the New Jersey Supreme Court implicitly overruled the case in *Home Builders League of South Jersey v. Township of Berlin.*

Lohmeyer v. Bower, 170 Kan. 442, 227 P.2d 102 (1951). Lohmeyer contracted to purchase a lot from Bower. The contract provided that Bower would convey a deed with "good merchantable title," but subject "to all restrictions and easements of record". Lohmeyer sued to rescind the contract when the title abstract showed that the house on the property violated a private covenant and a zoning ordinance. The court held that the contract waived the existence but not the violation of private covenants. Similarly, the existence of zoning restrictions does not make title unmarketable, but a violation of such restrictions does. Therefore, Lohmeyer could rescind the contract.

Loretto v. Teleprompter Manhattan CATV, 458 U.S. 419 (1982). A New York statute authorized cable television companies to install cable and other transmission equipment (wires, boxes, bolts, plates and screws) on private rental properties, even over the objection of the property owner. The court held that "any permanent physical occupation" of property, no matter how minor, is a taking. The right to exclude was held to be absolute; not subject to the balancing test often used to limit other rights associated with the ownership of property. By way of the Taking Clause, this ruling fortified the property owner's right to exclude others from his property, no matter how minor the intrusion.

Lucas v. South Carolina Coastal Commission, 505 U.S. 1003, 112 S.Ct. 2886 (1992). Lucas paid $975,000 for two coastal lots on which he planned to build homes. Two years later, the state enacted a statute which in effect prohibited Lucas from building any permanent habitable structures on the lots; a situation that the state supreme court found to render Lucas' lots "valueless." Rejecting what appeared to be a valid "ripeness" challenge, the Court held that the Act resulted in a taking of Lucas' property without payment of just compensation because it denied Lucas "all economically viable or productive use" of his property. The court rejected the state's argument that no compensation was required when the purpose of the regulation was to prevent a harmful use. The court stated that the owner's reasonable investment-backed expectations were to be determined in light of the "relevant background principles" of state property and nuisance law.

MacDonald, Sommer & Frates v. Yolo County, 477 U.S. 340 (1986). The developer submitted plans to subdivide land zoned for residential use into 159 lots for single-family and multi-family housing. The planning commission determined that there were inadequacies in sewer and water services, police protection and access and rejected the developer's plans. The developer sued in state court and asserted that its property had been condemned in order to open space. The Court held that the action was not ripe because the developer had not received a final decision regarding the type of development that would be permitted. According to the Court, if the available procedures are unfair or futile, they need not be pursued to ripen a case; however, if the development plans that are rejected are exceedingly grandiose the Court will not imply that more modest plans will also be rejected.

Mahrenholz v. County Board of School Trustees, 93 Ill.App.3d 366, 48 Ill.Dec. 736, 417 N.E.2d 138 (1981). The grantor conveyed land to a school district "to be used for school purposes only; otherwise to revert to Grantors herein." The issue was whether these words created a fee simple determinable or a fee simple subject to condition subsequent. After several years, the school district consolidated and stopped holding classes on the property. The grantor's heir, Hutton, conveyed his reversionary interest in the land to Mahrenholz without reentering the property. However, before this conveyance was recorded, Hutton disclaimed his interest to the school district. The trial court found that the deed created a fee subject to condition subsequent and therefore Hutton had nothing to convey to Mahrenholz because he had not exercised his right of entry. The appellate court reversed, holding that the deed created a determinable fee in the school district and a possibility of reverter in the grantor. Therefore, Hutton automatically received a fee simple absolute and the conveyance to Mahrenholz was valid **if** the condition was breached. The case was remanded for determination of whether the condition was breached.

Mannillo v. Gorski, 54 N.J. 378, 255 A.2d 258 (1969). The defendant and the plaintiffs owned adjacent, residential lots. The defendant built a walk and steps that encroached by fifteen inches onto the plaintiffs' lot. The defendant later claimed possession of the contested strip of the plaintiffs' lot by adverse possession. The plaintiffs alleged that the defendant's possession was not hostile because the defendant mistakenly encroached on their lot which did not constitute a knowing wrongful taking as required by the Maine doctrine. The court rejected the Maine doctrine in favor of the modern view, known as the Connecticut doctrine. According to the modern view, the subjective state of mind of the trespasser is irrelevant for purposes of adverse possession. Any entry that is exclusive, continuous, visible, notorious and uninterrupted can support a claim of title by adverse possession. The court also analyzed whether the defendant's encroachment was open and notorious and held that it was not because the encroachment was of a small area that would require an on-site survey for certain disclosure. The court held that in the case of minor border encroachments, the possession will only be deemed to be open and notorious if the true owner had actual knowledge of the encroachment. The court remanded the case to determine whether the plaintiffs had actual knowledge of the defendant's encroachment.

Marable v. H. Walker & Assoc., 644 F.2d 390 (5th Cir. 1981). Prospective T sued L for racial and sex discrimination under federal civil rights laws after L refused to rent an apartment to him. The court held that L's unequal application of rental criteria (marital status, employment history, credit history) based on race resulted in disparate treatment and violated federal civil rights laws.

Marshall v. Hollywood, Inc., 236 So.2d 114 (Fla. 1970), cert. denied, 400 U.S. 964. This case involved a forged deed. The court held that the state's marketable record title statute established marketable record title in persons whose title is in a chain of title based on a root of title more than 30 years old, even if that root title was forged.

Matter of Totten, 179 N.Y. 112, 71 N.E. 748 (1904). Decedent created several bank accounts as trustee for various named individuals, contributing and withdrawing funds freely from these accounts during her lifetime. Parting with traditional trust theory, the court recognized this sort of deposit to be a trust revocable at will, until the depositor died or otherwise completed the gift.

Commonly known as "Totten trusts," these valid trusts are created when A deposits money into the account of "A in trust for B." During his lifetime, A may withdraw money from the trust and even revoke the trust by closing the account or depleting it of all funds. When A dies, B's ownership is complete and she may claim whatever amount remains in the account, with no claim on funds withdrawn prior to A's death.

Messersmith v. Smith, 60 N.W.2d 276 (N.D. 1953). In this case in a race-notice jurisdiction, the court held that an instrument with a defective acknowledgement is not properly recorded and cannot defeat a prior unrecorded claim. Further, no later instruments in the chain of title are properly recorded. Here, Caroline conveyed her 1/2 interest to her cotenant Fred, who did not record. Caroline later conveyed an undivided, 1/2 interest in the minerals to Smith in a defectively acknowledged deed which was recorded. Smith conveyed his 1/2 interest in the minerals to Seale (who had no notice of Fred's claim) in a deed which was recorded. Fred subsequently recorded his claim. Fred brought an action to quiet title and won.

Miller v. Lutheran Conference and Camp Association, 331 Pa. 241, 200 A. 646 (1938). Frank Miller was granted the exclusive right to fish and boat in Lake Naomi. Frank then conveyed to his brother, Rufus, a one-fourth interest in the fishing, boating rights. Moreover, he also purported to convey a one-fourth interest in bathing rights but since Frank had no bathing rights, this conveyance was ineffective. Frank and Rufus formed a partnership and exploited Lake Naomi for fishing, boating and bathing. Over time, Frank and Rufus acquired a right to bathe by prescription. Rufus died and his executors granted a one-year license to the Lutheran Conference and Camp Association to fish, boat, and bathe in Lake Naomi. Frank and his wife Katherine, who owned an interest in the lake that was subject to the easement rights of Frank and Rufus, sued to enjoin the Lutherans from fishing, boating and bathing in the lake. The court held that that the easement granted to Frank to fish and boat in Lake Naomi was an easement in gross and that the parties intended it to be assignable. Having determined that the easement to fish and boat was assignable, the court held that once Frank divided the easement by assigning a one-fourth interest to Rufus, the easement had to be used as "one stock," meaning with the unanimous consent of all. Therefore, Frank had the right to veto the actions of Rufus' executors in permitting the Lutheran Church to use the lake for fishing and boating.

Moore v. City of East Cleveland, 431 U.S. 494 (1977). Three years after applying rationale basis review and upholding a family use ordinance in *Village of Belle Terre v. Borass, supra*, the Court considered another challenge to a family use ordinance. This time, the ordinance, which was aimed at only permitting single families within single homes, contained a complex definition of what constituted a family. As applied to the plaintiff, the ordinance precluded the plaintiff from living in the same house with her son and her two grandsons, who were also first cousins. The Court distinguished the case from *Village of Belle Terre v. Borass*, applied strict scrutiny review, and struck the ordinance down. According to the Court, the city could not establish a compelling justification for such an intrusive regulation of the family.

Morgan v. High Penn Oil Co., 238 N.C. 185, 77 S.E.2d 682 (1953). A house, restaurant, and trailer park are located on plaintiff's land. Defendant operates a refinery about one thousand feet away. Plaintiff sues for damages and injunctive relief alleging that the defendant's operation of the refinery interferes with their use and enjoyment of their property and is a nuisance. A nuisance can arise from either negligent operations or from intentional and unreasonable activities. For purposes of nuisance claims, "intentional" means acting for the purpose of causing the invasion or knowing that the invasion is substantially certain to result from the conduct. The court found that there was evidence to support a finding of nuisance based both on negligence and on intentional acts.

Morse v. Curtis, 140 Mass. 112, 2 N.E. 929 (1885). This case took the opposite view of *Woods v. Garnett*, holding that it is too burdensome to require a purchaser to search for late recorded deeds. The purchaser need only search up to the date when the grantor recorded the deed transferring title.

Mugler v. Kansas, 123 U.S. 623 (1887). This is one of the earliest Supreme Court cases to consider whether regulatory impacts resulting from the exercise of the police power can result in compensatory takings. A brewery owner argued that a state alcohol prohibition law left his brewery business practically worthless and that therefore his property had been taken and he should receive compensation. The Court rejected the brewery owner's argument and held that police power regulations were not subject to the compensation requirement of the Fifth Amendment. Such regulations were subject to review solely under the substantive due process standard. Thus, the Court held that a regulation should be upheld as long as it promoted a legitimate public end in a rational manner. The Court would later expand the reach of the takings clause to include regulations in *Pennsylvania Coal v. Mahon, infra.*

Mullett v. Bradley, 24 Misc. 695, 53 N.Y.S. 781 (1898). Plaintiff delivered a sea lion, which he owned, to New York, where the animal escaped from the plaintiff's possession. Plaintiff assumed the animal was gone with no prospect of its return. However, two weeks after its escape, a fisherman in New Jersey found the sea lion and in a fish pond and kept it as his own. When plaintiff asserted ownership over the sea lion, the court held that an owner looses his property interest in a wild animal once that animal regains its natural liberty and shows no intention of returning to its place of captivity.

Nectow v. City of Cambridge, 277 U.S. 183 (1928). In this case, the Court held a zoning ordinance invalid "as applied" to a particular piece of property. Although zoning laws are given a presumption of validity, particular applications of such laws may be arbitrary and unreasonable. The zoning ordinance at issue placed a 100 foot strip of the plaintiff's land into a residential district, making it virtually unusable, for no apparent purpose relating to the promotion of health, safety, or welfare.

Neponsit Property Owners' Ass'n v. Emigrant Indus. Savings Bank, 278 N.Y. 248, 15 N.E.2d 793 (1938). The lots in a subdivision were conveyed with covenants that the owners would pay annual charges for maintenance of roads, parks, etc. The charges were to be a lien on the land. The Bank foreclosed on the lot in question and refused to pay the charges. The property owner's association sued to foreclose the lien. First, the court held that based on the facts of the case, the covenant to pay money did touch and concern the land, and therefore was binding on assigns. Second, the court held that the traditional privity of estate requirement for enforcing an equitable servitude did not prevent the homeowner's association from suing to enforce the covenant because the association was an agent for the property owners.

Newman v. Bost, 122 N.C. 524, 29 S.E. 848 (1898). While on his death bed, intestate called his housekeeper into his room and handed her the keys to a number of household furnishings, explaining that these things were to be hers when he died. A bureau, which was located in his room, and which could be unlocked by the keys, held a life insurance policy on intestate's life. The court held that since the policy was in the presence of the intestate and was capable of manual, or actual, delivery, constructive delivery of the insurance policy was not accomplished.

Nollan v. California Coastal Commission, 483 U.S. 825 (1987). Nollans decided to replace the dilapidated bungalow on their beachfront property with a larger home. Based on the Commission's finding that the new home would block the public's view of the beach and create a psychological barrier to coastal access, it conditioned the required coastal development permit upon Nollans granting the public an easement across their property. The Court held that a "taking" had occurred—the easement constituted a permanent physical occupation which did not substantially advance a legitimate state interest due to the insufficient nexus between the end sought (view access) and the means chosen (lateral access).

O'Keeffe v. Snyder, 83 N.J. 478, 416 A.2d 862 (1980). O'Keefe alleged that she was the owner of three paintings that had been stolen from a gallery more than thirty years ago. Snyder purchased the paintings sometime between when they were allegedly stolen and when O'Keefe learned of their location. O'Keeffe sued for return of the paintings and Snyder moved for summary judgment on the theory that O'Keefe's action was barred by the statute of limitations. For purposes of the summary judgment motion, Snyder conceded that the paintings had been stolen. The Supreme Court of New Jersey held that, assuming the paintings had been stolen, the cause of action accrued at the time of the theft, absent concealment or fraud, unless O'Keefe was entitled to the benefit of the discovery rule. If the discovery rule applied, the cause of action would not accrue until O'Keefe discovered, or by the exercise of reasonable diligence and intelligence, should have discovered facts which would form the basis of a cause of action. Thus, the owner's conduct was controlling under the discovery rule, not the possessor's. If O'Keefe could not show due diligence, then the statute of limitations would begin to run from the time of the theft of the paintings. The case was remanded to the trial court for consideration but the parties settled.

Othen v. Rosier, 148 Tex. 485, 226 S.W.2d 622 (1950). This case involved a landlocked parcel. The court held that there was no easement by necessity because the party seeking the easement did not prove that the necessity existed when the tract was severed by the common grantor. An easement by necessity is only implied when land is divided. Nor was there an easement by prescription, because the use was permissive rather than adverse.

Palazzolo v. Rhode Island, 533 U.S. 606 (2001). Palazzolo invested in beachfront property by creating a corporation, which purchased the property. While the corporation owned the property, Rhode Island enacted environmental regulations that affected the property. After these regulations were in effect, the property was transferred from the corporation to Palazzolo. Over the years, Palazzolo and the corporation attempted, to no avail, on multiple occasions to gain governmental approval for a fill permit on the property. The State argued that the regulations did not constitute a taking because Palazzolo's claim was not ripe, and he had no right to challenge regulations placed on the land before he obtained title. The Supreme Court disagreed holding that the claim was ripe because the agency did not have discretion to permit any development, and therefore, the permissible uses of the property were known to a reasonable degree of certainty. Further, the court found that Palazzolo did have the right to challenge the regulations because "a regulation that otherwise would be unconstitutional absent compensation is not transformed into a background principle of the State's law by mere virtue of the passage of title." The court would not allow a windfall for the State if the property owner at the time of the regulation's enactment was unable to bring an inverse condemnation action due to ripeness.

Peet v. Roth Hotel Co., 191 Minn. 151, 253 N.W. 546 (1934). Plaintiff left her engagement ring with defendant's cashier for delivery to one of defendant's guests. The ring was lost, probably stolen by an outsider. The plaintiff sued to recover from the defendant, as bailee, the value of the ring. The defendant claimed that there was no bailment because the plaintiff failed to disclose the unusual value of the ring when she left it with defendant's cashier. The court found that the mutual assent necessary to create a bailment was created when the plaintiff delivered and the defendant's cashier accepted the ring with its identity and outward characteristics being obvious. Having found that a bailment was created, the court stated that the defendant bore the burden of proving that the loss did not result from the defendant's negligence. The care required was that of ordinary care and the court found that the defendant failed to meet its burden and ruled in favor of the plaintiff.

Penn Central Transportation Co. v. City of New York, 438 U.S. 104 (1978). New York City had designated Grand Central Terminal as an historic landmark and, pursuant to its historic landmarks preservations law, rejected Penn Central's plans to construct an office building on top of the terminal. The law provided that owners could get "transfer development rights" (TDRs) if the law prevented them from developing the property to the fullest extent of the applicable zoning laws. The Court rejected Penn Central's taking claim, reasoning that mere diminution in value does not constitute a taking; that Penn Central's reasonable investment-backed expectations were not unduly interfered with; that Penn Central received a reciprocal benefit from the preservation law; and that the availability of TDRs mitigated the economic impact. An important point is that the Court looked at the entire property interest, not merely the air rights, in determining economic impact.

Pennell v. City of San Jose, 485 U.S. 1 (1988). The City enacted a rent control ordinance that allowed Ls to raise rents by a certain percentage each year. If an L requested a greater percentage increase, a hearing was held to determine the reasonableness of the request. One factor to be considered by the rent control board was hardship to the specific T. In this facial challenge, the court found that the taking claim was unripe; that there was no violation of due process because protecting consumer welfare was a legitimate goal of price regulation; and that treating Ls differently based on their T's hardship was reasonable and did not violate equal protection.

Pennsylvania Coal Co. v. Mahon, 260 U.S. 393 (1922). The coal company owned property and sold the surface estate to Mahon, reserving for itself the right to remove the subsurface coal. Subsequently, Pennsylvania enacted a statute prohibiting coal mining that caused the subsidence of any dwelling. The Court held the regulation to be a taking and an invalid exercise of the police power. The Court reasoned that by making it commercially impracticable to mine the coal, the regulation deprived the company of all its value in the property (defined narrowly as the coal rights) and therefore went "too far."

Pierson v. Post, 3 Cai. R. 175 (N.Y. 1805). Post and his dogs were pursuing a fox. Right in front of Post and with full knowledge that Post was in pursuit, Pierson shot the fox and kept it. The court held that no property rights attach in wild animals until the animal is actually captured. This establishes a bright line rule and fosters the public policy of encouraging the capturing and killing of wild animals.

Prah v. Maretti, 108 Wis.2d 223, 321 N.W.2d 182 (1982). Prah installed a solar heating system on his property. Subsequently, Maretti purchased the adjacent lot and began constructing a home despite Prah's protests that this would block the sunlight to his solar system. Prah sued for an injunction, alleging that he had an unrestricted right to the sun. The court granted Prah's injunction on nuisance grounds.

Preseault v. United States, 100 F.3d 1525 (1996). The Preseaults owned several parcels of land over which a railroad company had earlier acquired a right-of-way, laid rails, and operated a railroad. The railroad eventually ceased operating and removed the railroad tracks. The Interstate Commerce Commission (ICC) authorized conversion of the former railroad right-of-way to use as a public trail. The Preseaults sued alleging that the conversion with the permission of the ICC constituted a compensable taking under the Fifth Amendment of the United States Constitution. The court considered four issues. First, the court held that the railroad acquired an easement in the right-of-way and not fee simple title to the land over which is operated. It found that there was an implied limitation upon the power of designated public bodies to acquire private property that the company will only take as much as is necessary. Even when the power of eminent domain is not exercised, the proceedings often retain their compulsory/eminent domain flavor. Second, the court held that conversion of the easement to a public trail exceeded the scope of the original easement and was not reasonably foreseeable at the time the easement was established. Third, the court considered whether the easement had been abandoned. Abandonment of an easement requires, in addition to nonuse, unequivocal acts by the owner of the dominant estate that evidences either a present intent to relinquish the easement or a purpose that is inconsistent with the continuation of the easement. Removal of the tracks combined with cessation of service on the line was sufficient evidence for the court to find that the easement had been abandoned. Fourth, the court found the Preseaults were entitled to damages for a taking. If the easement had not been abandoned at the time the ICC authorized conversion to a public trail, there was a taking because the conversion was outside the scope of the easement. If the easement had been abandoned at the time the ICC authorized conversion to a public trail, there was a taking because private property had been converted by the government to public use.

Puritan-Greenfield Improvement Ass'n v. Leo, 153 N.W.2d 162 (Mich. Ct. App. 1967). John Leo owned a one-story, single-family dwelling on a lot along a major road. The lot was zoned single-family residential. Leo applied for a variance from the Board of Zoning Appeals in order to sell the property for use as a dental and medical clinic. The variance was granted on the basis that the landowner demonstrated a showing of practical difficulty and undue hardship. This determination was due to the heavy traffic on the road fronting the property and the closeness of "the business section" immediately to the west. The Circuit Court reversed the Board's grant of a variance. The Court of Appeals affirmed the Circuit Court's decision. It held that a use variance should not be granted unless the Board of Zoning Appeals can find on the basis of substantial evidence that the property cannot reasonably be used in a manner consistent with existing zoning and there was no evidence upon which the Board could have found that the property could not reasonably be used for single family residential.

Redarowicz v. Ohlendorf, 92 Ill.2d 171, 65 Ill.Dec. 411, 441 N.E.2d 324 (1982). The issue in this case was whether a builder could be held liable to a subsequent purchaser for damages due to construction defects. The traditional barrier to such a suit is the lack of privity of contract. The court extended the implied warranty of habitability (or marketability) to subsequent purchasers in situations where latent defects manifest themselves within a reasonable time after purchase.

Reste Realty v. Cooper, 53 N.J. 444, 251 A.2d 268 (1969). L and T entered into a 5–year commercial lease of a basement. Whenever it rained, the basement flooded and T would complain to L's agent. Attempts to fix the problem were futile. After three years, a major rainstorm caused severe flooding and L refused to fix the problem. T vacated. L's successor sued T for unpaid rent, and T claimed constructive eviction for breach of the implied covenant of quiet enjoyment. Holding for T, the court broadly interpreted the covenant of quiet enjoyment as "any act or omission . . . which renders the premises substantially unsuitable for the purpose for which they were leased," found that the flooding was a permanent interference, and that T left within a reasonable time under the circumstances.

Riddle v. Harmon, 102 Cal.App.3d 524, 162 Cal.Rptr. 530 (1980). This case involved the issue of whether a joint tenant could unilaterally sever a joint tenancy by reconveying her interest to herself as a tenant in common. The court answered the question in the affirmative, disregarding the archaic common law rule necessitating conveyance through a "straw person."

Rockafellor v. Gray, 194 Iowa 1280, 191 N.W. 107 (1922). The issue was whether a covenant for title could be enforced against the covenantor by a transferee of the covenantee (i.e., did the covenant "run with the land"). The court held that the original grantee impliedly assigned the chose in action (i.e., right to sue) to the subsequent grantee. The fact that neither the covenantor nor the covenantee had taken possession was irrelevant.

Rohn v. City of Visalia, 214 Cal. App. 3d 1463 (1989). The Rohns owned land in the City of Visalia on which a single-family house was located. The land was zoned for either single-family or multi-family residences. They applied for an amendment to the general plan to change the land use designation from residential to professional administrative offices because they intended to convert the house to an office building. The planning commission approved the amendment to the general plan. Both the planning commission and the city council noted that the conversion would not create any greater traffic than the multi-family developments for which the land was already zoned. When the Rohns applied for a rezoning amendment, the city council approved the rezoning of their land on the condition that the Rohns dedicate fourteen percent of their land for a street realignment. The Rohns challenged the dedication condition. The court held that there was no reasonable relationship between the dedication requirement and the proposed use of the property. It found that the street realignment was necessitated by poor planning that predated the Rohns' development plans and that there was no nexus between the alleged traffic burden created by the Rohns' conversion and the dedication condition. The court ruled for the Rohns and, citing *Nollan v. California Coastal Commission, supra*, stated that if the City of Visalia wanted to acquire the subject property, it would have to pay the Rohns.

Rosengrant v. Rosengrant, 629 P.2d 800 (1981). Harold and Mildred Rosengrant wanted to give their farm to their nephew Jay Rosengrant upon their death. Harold and Mildred had their banker prepare a deed conveying the farm to Jay. They told Jay that they were going to give him the farm but that they wanted Jay to leave the deed with the banker until they died, at which time Jay should get the deed from the banker and record it. The banker put the deed in an envelope and typed "J.W. or Harold H. Rosengrant" on the outside of the envelope. Jay recorded the deed after Harold and Mildred died and the other nieces and nephews sued to cancel the deed on the grounds that it was never legally delivered during life and was ineffective as a will because it did not comply with the formalities of the Statute of Wills. The court treated the transaction as a revocable escrow; therefore, the delivery failed and the transaction was void. The court concluded that it was a revocable escrow in part because the banker typed both Harold's and Jay's names on the envelope and a bank teller testified that, under such circumstances, the bank's custom was that Harold could have gotten the deed back during his life. Had the escrow been irrevocable, it would have been a valid delivery and a valid escrow.

Sabo v. Horvath, 559 P.2d 1038 (Alaska 1976). Lowery occupied land and had applied for a patent from the federal government. However, before he received the patent, he quitclaimed to Horvath and Horvath recorded. Horvath knew Lowery had not yet received a patent. Subsequently, Lowery received his patent and conveyed the property to Sabo. The issue was whether Horvath's recordation gave Sabo constructive notice. This was a race-notice jurisdiction. The court held for Sabo, finding it too burdensome to require a subsequent purchaser to search under the grantor's name **prior** to when the grantor actually received title.

Sanborn v. McLean, 233 Mich. 227, 206 N.W. 496 (1925). The McLaughlins subdivided property into 91 lots and conveyed approximately half of the lots with covenants expressly restricting use of the property to residential purposes, and the other half with no express restrictions. Several years later, McLean purchased lot 86, a lot for which the deed contained no express restrictions, and started to build a gas station. The neighbors sued for an injunction. The court held that reciprocal negative easements (i.e. equitable servitudes) were implied on the McLaughlins' (common grantor) retained lots because the common grantor had a **scheme** to develop a residential area.

Sawada v. Endo, 57 Haw. 608, 561 P.2d 1291 (1977). Mr. Endo and his wife owned property as tenants by the entirety. The Sawadas were injured by Mr. Endo in an auto accident and sued Mr. Endo. The issue was whether the Sawadas (creditors) could reach this property. The court held that because of the nature of the tenancy by the entirety (one spouse cannot unilaterally destroy the right of survivorship or alienate his interest), the estate was not subject to the claims of creditors of one of the spouses during their joint lives.

Skelly Oil v. Ashmore, 365 S.W.2d 582 (Mo. 1963). Skelly Oil contracted with the Ashmores to purchase for $20,000 a lot on which there was a building. Prior to the closing date, a fire destroyed the building and the Ashmores collected $10,000 under an insurance policy. Skelly sued to enforce the contract and to reduce the purchase price by the amount of the insurance proceeds, and the court granted this relief. The court adopted the Massachusetts rule which puts the risk of loss on the seller while a contract is executory.

Sommer v. Kridel, 74 N.J. 446, 378 A.2d 767 (1977). The issue in this case was whether L must mitigate damages when T vacates the premises and stops paying rent before the lease term expires. The court took the contract approach and held that L has a duty to mitigate damages by making reasonable efforts to re-rent the premises.

South Staffordshire Water Co. v. Sharman, L.R. 2 QB 44 (1896). A landowner hired a number of workers to come onto his property for the limited purpose of cleaning a pool. While doing so, one of the workers found two gold rings and, after the police failed to find the owner, asserted ownership over the rings. The court held that since the worker found the rings while acting within the scope of his employment, the landowner's claim on the rings prevailed, even if the landowner did not know the rings were there.

Southern Burlington County N.A.A.C.P. v. Township of Mount Laurel (Mount Laurel II), 92 N.J. 158, 456 A.2d 390 (1983). This case was a follow-up to *Mount Laurel I* where the court held that exclusionary zoning practices preventing a locality from providing its fair share of low and moderate income housing for the region violated the state constitutional rights of substantive due process and equal protection. Here, the court stated that the locality had not met its affirmative duty of ensuring that such housing needs were met and that it must take realistic rather than theoretical steps to remedy the problem (e.g., subsidies, exactions).

Spiller v. Mackereth, 334 So.2d 859 (1976). Spiller and Mackereth owned a commercial building as tenants in common. Spiller began using the entire building as a warehouse. Mackereth demanded that Spiller either vacate one-half of the building or pay one-half of the rental value; Spiller refused and Mackereth sued. The court held that since Spiller and Mackereth did not have an agreement to pay rent, Mackereth would have to prove that Spiller ousted her before Spiller would be obligated to pay Mackereth rent. The court adopted the majority view on ouster of a co-tenant. According to the majority view, the occupying co-tenant (Spiller) is liable for rent to the out of possession co-tenant (Mackereth) if the out of possession co-tenant demands or attempts to enter and is denied by the occupying co-tenant. The court found that Mackereth never demanded to enter and enjoy the premises; rather, she only demanded that Spiller vacate one-half of the building or pay rent. Thus, Mackereth failed to prove that she had been ousted. The court noted that according to the minority view, liability for rent arises if the occupying co-tenant continues in possession after a demand to vacate or pay rent but again, the court refused to follow the minority approach.

Spur Industries, Inc. v. Del E. Webb Development Co., 108 Ariz. 178, 494 P.2d 700 (1972). Spur's predecessors developed feedlots in an area that was primarily agricultural. Just a few years later, Del Webb began developing a retirement community in the same general area. Spur then purchased its feedlot and began expanding to the north and south. Del Webb expanded in a southerly direction toward Spur's feedlot. Over time, Del Webb's operations and Spur's development grew closer together; eventually they were separated by only five hundred feet. Del Webb began to encounter sales resistance and sued for an injunction claiming that Spur's operations constituted a public nuisance because of flies and odors. The court found that the feedlots were a public and a private nuisance because of the annoying and perhaps unhealthy affect on the residents in the area. The court, sitting in equity, was concerned about issues of justice as Spur's feedlot was a lawful business and only became a nuisance because of the encroachment of Del Webb's development into an agricultural area. The court found that Del Webb was guilty of coming to the nuisance. Thus, the court enjoined Spur's operations but held that Del Webb had to indemnify Spur for the reasonable cost of moving or shutting down its operations.

St. Louis County National Bank v. Fielder, 364 Mo. 207, 260 S.W.2d 483 (1953). Kessler executed and delivered a deed to his residence to Fielder. In the deed, Kessler reserved for himself a life estate and retained the power to sell or otherwise dispose of the property. Kessler died without exercising this power. The issue was whether the deed was void as an invalid testamentary disposition. The court held that there was effective delivery. Kessler's reservation of the power to revoke, in itself, did not make the deed testamentary.

State v. Schingen, 20 Wis. 74 (1865). S, an employee of M, was instructed to deliver several kegs of beer to another town using M's horses and wagons. Without completing the delivery, S went to another town and unsuccessfully attempted to sell M's horses. The court found that while acting within the scope of his employment, S had lawful custody of the horses and wagons, while, legal possession was with M, his employer. However, at the point where S took M's property to places beyond the scope of his employment with the intent to convert the property to his own use, he committed larceny, regardless of the fact that he failed to actually sell the horses.

State ex rel. Stoyanoff v. Berkeley, 458 S.W.2d 305 (Mo. 1970). A city zoning ordinance which gave an architectural board power to deny a building permit based on aesthetic non-conformity was challenged as unconstitutional. P wanted to build an ultra-modern home in an architecturally traditional neighborhood. The court upheld the ordinance, finding it neither arbitrary nor unreasonable. It is important to note that the court characterized the ordinance as one promoting the general welfare by protecting property values, not one solely aimed at aesthetics.

Stop the Beach Renourishment, Inc. v. Florida Dept. of Environmental Protection, 130 S. Ct. 2592 (2010). Affected littoral property owners sued, challenging the validity of the Florida Beach and Shore Preservation Act (the Act). Under the Act, beaches that had been critically eroded by hurricanes could be renourished by placing large amounts of sand on these beaches. The sand would be placed seaward and landward of the dividing line separating publicly-owned beaches from privately-owned property. Owners of littoral property argued that the Act authorized the government to physically occupy their private property by the sand placement and that the Act also granted to the state of Florida title to the new strip of beach created by the renourishment. The United States Supreme Court affirmed the lower court's decision that the Act did not, on its face, take the littoral rights of upland property owners without just compensation. The Court cited background principles of Florida's state property law that: (1) permitted the state to fill state-owned submerged land under specified circumstances and (2) provided that the State owns previously submerged land seaward of littoral property if that land is exposed by avulsion. Regarding judicial takings, the Court refused to categorically reject the concept of judicial takings and several justices asserted that judicial action could constitute a taking under the Fifth Amendment.

Suitum v. Tahoe Regional Planning Agency, 520 U.S. 725 (1997). The United States Supreme Court clarified the finality requirement for a takings case to be brought in federal court. Suitum's application to build a home on her lot was denied. She appealed the decision administratively and the denial was affirmed. Suitum was eligible to receive transferable development rights that she could sell to other landowners after receiving the appropriate approvals. Instead of applying to use her transferable development rights, Suitum sued claiming a regulatory taking of her property without just compensation. The Court determined that Suitum had satisfied the finality requirement and that her claim was ripe. The Court said that the finality requirement was satisfied because there was no question about how the regulations would apply to Suitum's land. The agency had finally determined that no additional development would be permitted on her land. Because the agency did not have any discretion to exercise over Suitum's right to build on her land, the Court said it need not apply the requirements set-forth in *Williamson County Regional Planning Commission v. Hamilton Bank of Johnson City, infra,* that landowners seek a final decision about the permissible uses of the land.

CHAPTER XIX

Swartzbaugh v. Sampson, 11 Cal.App.2d 451, 54 P.2d 73 (1936). Husband and wife owned 60 acres as joint tenants. Despite Wife's repeated protests, Husband leased part of the land for a boxing pavilion. Wife sued to have the leases canceled. The court denied her request because, as joint tenants, each had an equal right to possess the property. Neither had a right to possess the whole to the exclusion of the other. The leases did not sever the joint tenancy. Wife's remedies include the following: sue for partition (physical partition, or partition sale); sue the lessee for half of the reasonable rental value of the property if the lessee ousted her; or sue Husband for half of the rents received from the lessee.

Sweeney v. Sweeney, 126 Conn. 391, 11 A.2d 806 (1940). Maurice Sweeney wanted to cut his estranged wife out of her elective forced share of a tract of land he owned. Maurice wanted the land to go to his brother John if he died before John. Maurice and John had the town clerk prepare two deeds, one from Maurice to John and the other from John to Maurice. The first deed from Maurice to John was recorded but the second deed was taken away by Maurice and never recorded. Later, Maurice delivered both deeds to John. Maurice died and his widow sued alleging that the second deed from John to Maurice was delivered unconditionally to Maurice thereby moving title back to Maurice. John claimed that there was no delivery and that even if there was a delivery, it was conditional on Maurice surviving John. The court held that there was manual delivery of the John to Maurice deed with intent to pass title. Next, the court held that oral conditions cannot be attached to a deed delivered to a grantee. In such cases, the delivery is good and the conditions are void. An enforceable conditional delivery can only be made by placing the deed with a third person to be kept by the third person until the happening of the event that is the subject of the condition at which time the deed is to be delivered over by the third person to the grantee.

Symphony Space, Inc. v. Pergola, 88 N.Y.2d 466, 646 N.Y.S.2d 641, 669 N.E.2d 799 (1996). Broadwest transferred a commercial building to Symphony, but Broadwest retained a lease and an option giving it the exclusive right to repurchase the property from Symphony. Later, Broadwest assigned these interests to Pergola. After several years, Pergola notified Symphony that it was exercising the option. Symphony filed a declaratory judgment action arguing the option was invalid as it violated the Rule against Perpetuities. Pergola argued that the rule does not apply to commercial options because the pressures that lead to the creation of the rule, limiting control of the dead hand, are not present in arms-length business transactions. The court found the rule applicable to commercial option contracts because the option holder's ability to repurchase the property at a stipulated price discourages the property owner from investing in improvements and renders the property unalienable to a third party until the option has expired. Applying the rule to the option, the court found that the option holder could potentially exercise it more than 24 years after its creation. Since the parties were corporations and no measuring lives were stated in their contract, the perpetuities period was 21 years. Therefore, the option was invalid.

Tahoe–Sierra Preservation Council, Inc. v. Tahoe Regional Planning Agency, 535 U.S. 302 (2002). The Tahoe Regional Planning Agency (TRPA) imposed two moratoria on property located in the Lake Tahoe Basin. The moratoria, which lased 32 months, were imposed to allow time for TRPA to create a land use plan for the basin. Property owners affected by the moratoria brought suit asserting the moratoria constituted a taking. The property owners argued that a regulation imposing a temporary deprivation of all economically viable use is a *per se* taking regardless of how long the deprivation lasts. This would have required the court to sever the 32–month segment from the remainder of each property owner's fee simple estate and then determine if a total deprivation of all economic viable use occurred during this particular time period. Instead, the Court looked at the property as a whole. In rejecting the property owners' suggested *per se* taking rule, the Court reasoned the duration of a restriction is an important factor in deciding whether a taking has occurred. However, the Court held that other factors such as the economic effect on the landowner, the interference with reasonable investment-backed expectations, and the character of the government action must also be relied on when deciding a regulatory takings case. The Court observed that moratoria are an essential tool for successful land use planning, and moratoria would be rendered completely unusable by the suggested *per se* taking rule even if the moratoria were necessary, in good faith, and reasonable.

Tulk v. Moxhay, 2 Phillips 774, 41 Eng.Rep. 1143 (1848). This case created the equitable servitude. Tulk sold a town square to Elms. Elms promised that neither he, his heirs, nor his assigns would build on the square. Elms conveyed the square to Moxhay. Moxhay proposed to build on the Square, even though he was aware of the covenant between Tulk and Elms. Tulk sued for an injunction, and the court granted it based on an unjust enrichment theory and notice.

Udell v. Haas, 21 N.Y.2d 463, 288 N.Y.S.2d 888, 235 N.E.2d 897 (1968). The plaintiff challenged the validity of a municipality's rezoning of two parcels of property from business to residential use resulting in a substantial reduction in property value. The plaintiff had assembled the property in a heavily trafficked area anticipating commercial use. The court held that the zoning ordinance changing the zoning of plaintiff's parcels was invalid as it was discriminatory and not done in accordance with the comprehensive plan. The court emphasized consistency with the comprehensive plan and the broad purpose of zoning.

United States v. Maryland Bank & Trust Co., 632 F.Supp. 573 (D.Md. 1986). The Bank foreclosed on a mortgage and later purchased the property in a foreclosure sale. The issues were whether the Bank was liable as an "owner and operator" for hazardous waste cleanup costs under the Comprehensive Environmental Response,

Compensation, and Liability Act (CERCLA); and if so, whether the Bank was entitled to the secured creditor defense. Noting that Congress intended CERCLA's liability provisions to be very broad, the court held that "owner and operator" means owner **or** operator, and that the Bank met this description; and that the secured creditor exemption did not apply once the Bank purchased the property to protect its investment (versus merely protecting its security interest).

Van Sandt v. Royster, 148 Kan. 495, 83 P.2d 698 (1938). B owned property over which she constructed a private sewer drain. B subsequently divided the property into three lots and conveyed the two lots closest to the public sewer hookup. No mention was made of any easement. The court held that a quasi-easement existed before the property was divided and implied the reservation of an easement on this basis. Also important were the facts that the easement was reasonably necessary and apparent.

Van Valkenburgh v. Lutz, 304 N.Y. 95, 106 N.E.2d 28 (1952). In New York, if an adverse possession claimant does not enter with color of title, she can only prevail if she substantially encloses the land or improves or cultivates the land in the usual manner. Here, the Lutzes failed to prove they sufficiently cultivated or improved the land, and their occupation of the land was not hostile enough to constitute a claim of title.

Western Land Co. v. Truskolaski, 88 Nev. 200, 495 P.2d 624 (1972). Western Land Company subdivided forty acres and restricted all of the acres to single-family dwellings. Western Land Company still owned 3.5 acres in the subdivision. A few years later, Western Land Company filed a map with the county recorded abandoning the subdivision map as it applied to the 3.5 acres and the city council adopted a resolution of intent to reclassify the 3.5 acres from residential to commercial but the zoning change never occurred. The homeowners in the subdivision sued Western Land Company to enjoin it from constructing a shopping center on the 3.5 acres. Western Land Company responded that the single-family residential covenant should not be enforced because the subdivision had radically changed since the covenants were imposed so as to nullify their purpose. The court held that there was no evidence that the subdivision had become undesirable for residential purposes; therefore, the court enjoined Western Land Company. The change must affect the entire subdivision, not merely border lots, in order for the court to refuse equitable relief.

Wetherbee v. Green, 22 Mich. 311 (1871). Wetherbee converted Green's timber into barrel hoops, under an agreement made with a former tenant in common with Green. Although the former tenant in common held no interest in Green's land when he made the agreement, Wetherbee was unaware of this and entered into the agreement in good faith, without intention to commit a wrong. The issue was whether Green, as owner of the land, could reclaim the hoops into which his trees had been wrongfully transformed. The court recognized the general rule that the true owner of property has a right to reclaim that property taken from him, so long as it has not been transformed in such a way to make identification of it impracticable. However, the court noted the substantial increase in the timber's value once Wetherbee had converted it into hoops, and held that where timber, valued at twenty-five dollars, had been, in good faith, converted into hoops, valued at $700, the title to the property, in its converted form, remained with the party by whose labor the change had been made.

Wiggins v. Parson, 446 So.2d 169 (Fla. App. 1984). A opened a joint account with right of survivorship in her name and the names of her three siblings. Several years later A removed her name from the account. One sibling then withdrew all funds and divided them among herself, another joint owner of the account and a sister whose name was not on the account. One joint owner was excluded entirely from the distribution. When the excluded joint owner sought recovery of her one-third share, the court held, first, that a present inter vivos gift is presumed to arise when a joint bank account is established. As such, the gift is essentially revocable since the donor-depositor may withdraw all funds from the account during his lifetime. Second, when the jointly owned funds were withdrawn, the joint tenancy was destroyed, leaving the withdrawing party liable to the other joint owners for that person's share.

Willard v. First Church of Christ, Scientist, 7 Cal.3d 473, 102 Cal.Rptr. 739, 498 P.2d 987 (1972). M owned a vacant lot which she let her church use for parking. M conveyed this lot to P, but reserved an easement in her church for parking purposes. P conveyed the lot to W by deed which did not mention the easement. W sued to quiet title. The court rejected the old rule that forbid creating an easement in favor of a third party, and upheld the validity of the church's easement.

Williamson County Regional Planning Commission v. Hamilton Bank of Johnson City, 473 U.S. 172 (1985). A residential developer received preliminary plat approval from the planning commission for a cluster home development. Several years later, the planning commission rejected revised plats that were submitted. The reasons for rejecting the revised plats varied, some were based upon old law and some were based upon new law. The developer sued in federal court and the Court found that the action was not ripe. The developer had not applied for variances that would have allowed the developer to develop in accordance with its proposed plat, if granted. Together, the board of zoning appeals and the planning commission had the authority to grant variances for all of the planning commission's objections to the developer's plans. Additionally, the developer had not used the state inverse condemnation process. The Court held that even if the restrictions constituted a taking under the Constitution, there is no Fifth Amendment violation unless compensation is not paid. As long as the state had an adequate inverse condemnation remedy, the developer had to utilize the state procedure first.

CHAPTER XIX

Woods v. Garnett, 72 Miss. 78, 16 So. 390 (1894). This case held that a purchaser has constructive notice of deeds from the grantor recorded **after** the record shows the grantor parted with title. In other words, for each former owner, a purchaser must search up until the current date to uncover any late recorded deeds.

Yee v. City of Escondido, 503 U.S. 519 (1992). The plaintiffs owned mobile home parks and rented land to mobile home owners. State law generally required park owners to accept purchasers of mobile homes as new tenants if the purchasers could pay the rent and limited the circumstances under which park owners could require a mobile home to be removed when it was sold. Escondido adopted a rent control ordinance that set rents back to an earlier level and prohibited rent increases without city council approval. The Yees alleged that the rent control ordinance amounted to a taking of their property by permanent physical occupation, *supra Loretto v. Teleprompter Manhattan CATV Corp.*. The Court rejected an argument that together the state law and the rent control ordinance authorized a physical taking by giving the mobile home owners and their successors in interest the right to permanently occupy and use the Yees' land. The Court held that the state and local laws involved in the case merely regulated the use of the Yees' land by regulating the landlord and tenant relationship. The Court also stated that the Yees voluntarily rented their land and the regulatory scheme did not compel the Yees to continue doing so. Park owners who wished to change the use of their land could do so and evict their tenants with the appropriate amount of notice. Thus, the Court seemed to limit the application of the *Loretto* per se category of takings to actual physical occupations of land.

XX

TABLE OF CASES

References are to section numbers.

INDEX

References are to section numbers.

†

QUICK REVIEW OF PROPERTY	BERNHARDT American Casebook Series	BRUCE & ELY 6th Ed.	CASNER, LEACH, FRENCH, KORNGOLD, VANDERVELDE 5th Ed.	CRIBBET, FINDLEY, SMITH & DZIENKOWSKI 9th Ed.	DUKEMINIER, KRIER, ALEXANDER & SCHILL 7th Ed.	HILTON, CALLIES, MANDELKER & FRANZESE 3rd Ed.	RABIN, KWALL & ARNOLD 6th Ed.	SINGER 4th Ed.	JOHNSON, SALSICH, SHAFTER, BRADSTEIN & WEIDBERGER 3rd Ed.	KURTZ & HOVENKAMP 5th Ed.	NELSON, STOEBUCK & WHITMAN 3rd Ed.	FREYERMUTH, ORGAN & NOBLE-ALLGIRE 3rd Ed.
IV. THE LAW OF PERSONAL PROPERTY [CHATTELS] §§3-1 – 3-100	1-30	143-211	34-114; 191-284	63-78; 101-168; 193 235	18-96; 151-181	3-15;32-73		32-63; 75-97; 101; 102; 1087- 1171	1-22; 38-70	8-70; 86-163	31-90	56-156; 205-236
V. FRAGMENTATION OF OWNERSHIP; THE DEVELOPMENT OF TENURE §§4-1 – 4-18	76-77	212-215	299-318	238-250	183-190	407-409		493-505	115-118	251-265	245-249	237-240
VI. ESTATES IN LAND [FREEHOLDS] §§5 1 – 5 95	77 78	215 227	319 361	251 306	191 252	410 419	179 200; 239-276	505 526	118 141; 147-152	268 298	250 272	240 290
VII. FUTURE INTERESTS §§6-1 – 6-218	78-104	228-242	361-401	307-370	253-317	419-437; 551-566	179-256	505-567	141-147; 152-196	294-355	273-338	290-333S
VIII. CONCUR RENT ESTATES AND MULTIPLE OWNERSHIP §§7-1 – 7-62	104-184	242-288	553-623	371-448	319-418	381-407	277-343	569-635	197-279	356-469	339-427	3334-392
IX. LANDLORD AND TENANT [NONFREEHOLD ESTATES] §§8-1 – 8-159	185-343	21-141	403-551	449-558	419-515	445-500; 675-703	39-178	639-742	280-447	470-622	428-627	393-519
X. EASEMENTS, PROFITS, AND LICENSES §§9-1 – 9-112	344-374; 398-416; 432-517	294-359	889-954	559-617	763-847	501-547; 567-577	345-460	317-365	711-774	623-686; 726-728	770-870	520-582
XI. COVENANTS RUNNING WITH THE LAND EQUITABLE SERVITUDES §§10-1 -10-102	374-398; 416-522	359-410	889-893; 954-1063	617-672	847-924	578-671	461-562	365-490	774-848	686-757	628-769	582-665

QUICK REVIEW OF PROPERTY	BERNHARDT American Casebook Series	BROCE & ELY 6th Ed.	CASNER, LEACH, KORNGOLD, VANDERVELDE 5th Ed.	CRIBBET, FINDLEY, SMITH & DZIENKOWSKI 9th Ed.	DUKEMINIER, KRIER, ALEXANDER & SCHILL 7th Ed.	HYLTON, CALLIES, HANDELMAN & FRANZESE 3rd Ed.	RABIN, KWALL, KWALL & ARNOLD 6th Ed.	SINGER 4th Ed.	JOHNSON, SALSICH, SHAFFER, BRAUNSTEIN & WEINBERGER 3rd Ed.	KURTZ & HOVENKAMP 5th Ed.	NELSON, STOEBUCK & WHITMAN 3rd Ed.	FREYERMUTH, ORGAN & NOBLE-ALLGIRE 3rd Ed.
XII. ADVERSE POSSESSION §§11-1 - 11-67	30-63	496-518	125-190	153-193	116-164	221-237	859-903	179-226	71-98	191-250; 735-742	90-142	162-204
XIII. LAND SALES CONTRACTS §§12-1 - 12-27	751-857; 909-941	427-459	680-714; 734-744	915-1068	541-584	305-334	995-1046	748-779	477-489; 591-601	1078-1080; 1096-1150	872-995	671-715
XIV. DEEDS §§13-1 - 13-116	835-908	538-563;	714-733	1069-1128	585-615	335-357; 370-374	905-972; 1081-1101	779-783	490-510; 517-523	1151-1191	996-1140	715-725; 766-778
XV. RECORDING ACTS §§14-1 - 14-84	857-909	463-495; 519-537	744-784	1129-1188	645-727	357-370	1103-1141	783-799	523-530	1205-1229	1070-1108	725-757
XVI. RIGHT USE AND ENJOYMENT OF PROPERTY §§15-1 - 15-21	500-522	625-636	841-888	673-750	729-761	102-114	563-590	227-316	848-879	758-805	143-229	822-840
XVII. PUBLIC LAND USE CONTROL §§16-1 - 16-83	523-702	678-816	1065-1324	751-914	925-1195	75-102; 133-204; 243-302; 705-819	591-824	911-1067	887-1036	806-1019	1142-1344	841-970